Henry Hart Milman

History of Latin Christianity

Henry Hart Milman

History of Latin Christianity

ISBN/EAN: 9783741171628

Manufactured in Europe, USA, Canada, Australia, Japa

Cover: Foto ©Lupo / pixelio.de

Manufactured and distributed by brebook publishing software (www.brebook.com)

Henry Hart Milman

History of Latin Christianity

HISTORY

OF

LATIN CHRISTIANITY;

INCLUDING THAT OF

THE POPES TO THE PONTIFICATE OF NICOLAS V.

BY HENRY HART MILMAN, D.D.,
DEAN OF ST. PAUL'S.

IN NINE VOLUMES.—Vol. VI.

FOURTH AND REVISED EDITION.

LONDON:
JOHN MURRAY, ALBEMARLE STREET.
1867.

The right of Translation is reserved.

CONTENTS

OF

THE SIXTH VOLUME.

BOOK IX.—*continued.*

CHAPTER IX.

NEW ORDERS.—ST. DOMINIC.

A.D.		PAGE
	Preaching rare	1
	The Ritual	2
	Monasticism	3
	Intellectual movement	5
	Heresy	*ib.*
	St. Dominic and St. Francis	8
1170	Birth of Dominic—Education	11
1203–1205	In Languedoc	12
	Dominic in the war	14
	In the tribunals	15
1217	Foundation of Order of Friar Preachers	17
1220	First Chapter	19
1221	Second Chapter	*ib.*
	Death of Dominic	22

CHAPTER X.

ST. FRANCIS.

1182	Birth and youth	25
1206	Embraces mendicancy	27
	His followers	29
	Before Innocent III.	30

A.D.		PAGE
	Foundation of the Order	30
	Foreign missions	32
	St. Francis in the East	ib.
	Martyrs	33
	Poetry of St. Francis	35
	Tertiaries	37
1224	The Stigmata	38
	Rule of St. Francis	42
	Close of Innocent III.'s Pontificate	45

BOOK X.

CHAPTER I.

HONORIUS III.— FREDERICK II.

1216	Election of Honorius	54
	His mildness	55
	Crusade of Andrew of Hungary	57
	Death of Otho	58
1219	Correspondence with the Pope	60
1220	Diet of Frankfort—Election of Henry King of the Romans	62
	Frederick's laws in favour of ecclesiastics; against heretics	66
	Loss of Damietta	69
1222	Meeting at Veroli—at Ferentino	60
1225	Meeting at San Germano	71
	Frederick's marriage with the Princess Iolante	72
1226	Angry correspondence	75
1227	Death of Honorius	77

CHAPTER II.

HONORIUS III. AND ENGLAND.

Pope protects Henry III.	80
Peter's Pence	83
Benefices held by Italians	84
Tenths	86

CHAPTER III.

FREDERICK II. AND GREGORY IX.

A.D.		PAGE
1227	Gregory IX.	89
	Frederick II.	90
	The Court	91
	The Crusade urged on Frederick	92
	Preparations	103
	Return of Frederick	104
	Excommunication of Frederick	ib.
	Second excommunication	111
	Gregory driven from Rome	112
1228	Frederick sets sail for the Holy Land	115
	In Palestine	122
	Sultan Kameel of Egypt	123
	Treaty	124
	Frederick at Jerusalem	126
	Anger of Mohammedans at the Treaty	130
	Condemned by the Pope	133
	Frederick leaves Palestine	136
	Election to Archbishopric of Canterbury	138
1229	Return of Frederick	139
	Christendom against the Pope	141
1230	Peace	144
	Frederick as Legislator	147
	Laws relating to religion	150
	Civil Constitution	152
	Cities, Peasants, &c.	153
	Intellectual progress	158
	Gregory IX. and the Decretals	163

CHAPTER IV.

RENEWAL OF HOSTILITIES BETWEEN GREGORY IX. AND FREDERICK II.

		PAGE
	Persecution of heretics	167
1230-1330	Gregory and the Lombards	170
1236	Lombards leagued with Princes	176
1237	Battle of Corte Nuova	179

CONTENTS OF VOL. VI.

A.D.		PAGE
1238	Gregory against Frederick	182
	Excommunication	ib.
	Frederick's reply	184
	Appeal to Christendom	187
	Gregory's reply	192
	Public opinion in Christendom—England	195
	Empire offered to Robert of France	201
	Germany	203
	Albert von Beham	204
	The Friars	207
	John of Vicenza	208
1239	War	211
1240	Advance of Frederick on Rome	214
	Council summoned	217
	Battle of Meloria	219
1241	Fall of Faenza	220
	Death of Gregory IX.	221
	Coelestine IV.	223

CHAPTER V.

FREDERICK AND INNOCENT IV.

1243	Accession of Innocent IV.	225
	Defection of Viterbo	227
	Negotiations	228
	Flight of Innocent to France	230
	Innocent excommunicates the Emperor	233
	Martin Pope's Collector in England	235
1245	Council of Lyons	237
	Thaddeus of Suessa	240
	Frederick deposed	243
	Frederick appeals to Christendom	244
	Innocent claims both spiritual and temporal power	247
1246	Mutual accusations	251
	Innocent attempts to raise Germany	254
	Albert von Beham—Otho of Bavaria	255
1247	Election and death of Henry of Thuringia	257
1248	Siege of Parma	259
	King Enzio	260
	Peter de Vineâ	263

CONTENTS OF VOL. VI.

A.D.		PAGE
1250	Death of Frederick II.	264
	Character	265
	Papal Legates	270
1251	Innocent's return to Italy	273
	Kingdom of Naples	ib.
	Brancaleone	276
1253	Death of Prince Henry	279
	Manfred	281
	In revolt	284
1254	Death of Innocent	285
	Robert Grostête, Bishop of Lincoln	288
	Vision to Innocent	293

BOOK XI.

CHAPTER I.

St. Louis.

	Character of St. Louis	295
1226	Blanche of Castile—Youth of St. Louis	297
	His virtues	300
1246	Preparations for Crusade	302
1249	Crusade	305
1250	Defeat and Captivity	306
	Ransom and Release	308
1252	Return to Europe	310
	Contrast between St. Louis and Frederick II.	311
1232–44	Code of Inquisition	312
	Insurrection against Inquisition	314
1239	Persecution in France	316
1260	Pragmatic Sanction	319

CHAPTER II.

Pope Alexander IV.

1254	Election	320
	Manfred	ib.
	Edmund of England King of Sicily	321

CONTENTS OF VOL. VI.

A.D.		PAGE
1250	Boniface Archbishop of Canterbury	324
1252	The Senator Brancaleone	326
	Manfred King of Sicily	329
1259	Ecelin da Romano	331
	Alberic da Romano	332
	The Flagellants	333
1251	The Pastonreaux	336
	The Mendicant Friars	341
1231-52	University of Paris	343
	William of St. Amour	347
	The Everlasting Gospel	349
	The Perils of the Last Times	351

CHAPTER III.

URBAN IV. — CLEMENT IV. — CHARLES OF ANJOU.

1261	Death of Alexander IV.	357
	Election of Urban IV.	ib.
	Manfred	360
	State of Italy	ib.
	Charles of Anjou	362
	Ugo Falcodi Legate in England	363
1264	Death of Urban IV.	368
	Pope Clement IV.	ib.
1265	Charles of Anjou at Rome	370
	Battle of Benevento	372
	Tyranny of the French	375
	England	ib.
	Simon de Montfort	377
	Reaction	380
	Council of London	381
	James of Arragon	382
1267	Conradin	383
	Henry of Castile	386
1268	Conradin in Italy	388
	Defeat and death	390
	Battle of Tagliacozzo	ib.
	Death of Clement IV.	392

CHAPTER IV.

GREGORY X. AND HIS SUCCESSORS.

A.D.		PAGE
	More than Two Years' Vacancy in the Popedom	394
1268	Pragmatic Sanction	395
1270	Death of St. Louis	398
1271–2	Gregory X.	399
1273	Rodolph of Hapsburg Emperor	403
1274	Council of Lyons	405
	Law of Papal Election	407
1276	Death of Gregory X.	408
	Rapid Succession of Popes — Innocent V.— Hadrian V.	409
	John XXI.	410
1277	Nicolas III.	411
	Greeks return to Independence	413
1280	Schemes and Death of Nicolas III.	417
	Martin IV.	419

CHAPTER V.

SICILIAN VESPERS.

		PAGE
	Discontent of Sicily	421
	Tyranny of Charles of Anjou	422
	John of Procida	426
1282	Sicilian Vespers	429
	Revolt of Sicily	430
	Conduct of Charles of Anjou	433
	Siege of Messina	435
	Peter of Arragon King of Sicily	436
	Martin condemns the King of Arragon	440
1283	Challenge—Scene at Bordeaux	442
1285	Death of Charles of Anjou, of Philip of France, and Martin IV.	445
1286	James crowned	446
	Honorius IV.	ib.
1288	Nicolas IV.	447
	Nicolas and the Colonnas	451
1292	Death of Nicolas IV.	458

VOL. VI.   b

CONTENTS OF VOL. VI.

CHAPTER VI.
Cœlestine V.

A.D.		PAGE
	Conclave	454
1293	Peter Morrone—Cœlestine V. Pope	456
	Inauguration in Naples	461
	Abdication	466
	Jacopone da Todi	468

HISTORY
OF
LATIN CHRISTIANITY.

BOOK IX.—*continued.*

CHAPTER IX.

New Orders. St. Dominic.

THE progress of the new opinions in all quarters, their obstinate resistance in Languedoc, opinions, if not yet rooted out, lopped by the sword, and seared by the fire, had revealed the secret of the fatal weakness of Latin Christianity. Sacerdotal Christianity, by ascending a throne higher than all thrones of earthly sovereigns, by the power, the wealth, the magnificence of the higher ecclesiastics, had withdrawn the influence of the clergy from its natural and peculiar office. Even with the lower orders of the priesthood, that which in a certain degree separated them from the people, set them apart from the sympathies of the people. The Church might still seem to preach to all, but it preached in a tone of lofty condescension; it dictated rather than persuaded; but, in general, actual preaching had fallen into disuse; it was in theory the special privilege of the bishops, and the bishops were but few who had either the gift, the inclination, or the leisure from their secular, judicial, or warlike occupations to preach even in their cathedral cities; in the

Preaching rare.

rest of their dioceses their presence was but occasional;
a progress or visitation of pomp and form, rather than
of popular instruction. The only general teaching of
the people was the Ritual.

But the splendid Ritual, admirably as it was constituted to impress by its words or symbolic
forms the leading truths of Christianity upon
the more intelligent, or in a vaguer way upon the more
rude and uneducated, could be administered, and was
administered, by a priesthood almost entirely ignorant,
but which had just learned mechanically, not without
decency, perhaps not without devotion, to go through
the stated observances. Everywhere the bell summoned to the frequent service, the service was performed, and the obedient flock gathered to the chapel
or the church, knelt, and either performed their orisons,
or heard the customary chant and prayer. This, the
only instruction which the mass of the priesthood could
convey, might for a time be sufficient to maintain in
the minds of the people a quiescent and submissive
faith, nevertheless, in itself could not but awaken in
some a desire of knowledge, which it could not satisfy.
Auricular confession, now by Innocent III. raised to
a necessary duty, and to be heard not only by the
lofty bishop, but by the parochial priest, might have
more effect in repressing the uneasy or daring doubts
of those who began to reason; doubts which would
startle and alarm the uneducated priest, and which he
would endeavour to silence at once by all the terrors of
his authority. Though the lower priesthood were from
the people, they were not of the people; nor did they
fully interpenetrate the whole mass of the people. The
parochial divisions, where they existed, were arbitrary,
accidental, often not clearly defined; they followed in

The Ritual.

general the bounds of royal or aristocratical domains. A church was founded by a pious king, noble, or knight, with a certain district around it; but in few countries was there any approach to a systematic organisation of the clergy in relation to the spiritual wants and care of the whole Christian community.

The fatal question of the celibacy of the clergy worked in both ways to the prejudice of their autho- Celibacy of clergy. rity. The married clergy, on the whole no doubt the more moral, were acting in violation of the rules of the Church, and were subject to the opprobrious accusation of living in concubinage. The validity of their ministrations was denied by the more austere; the doctrines of men charged with such grievous error lost their proper weight. The unmarried obeyed the outward rule, but by every account, not the bitter satire of enemies alone but the reluctant and melancholy admission of the most gentle and devout, in general so flagrantly violated the severer principles of the Church, that their teaching, if they attempted actual teaching, must have fallen dead on the minds of the people.

The earlier monastic orders were still more deficient as instructors in Christianity. Their chief, if Monasticism. not their sole exclusive and avowed object, was the salvation, or, at the highest, the religious perfection of themselves and of their own votaries. Solitude, seclusion, the lonely cell, their own unapproached, or hardly approached, chapel, was their sphere; their communication with others was sternly cut off. The dominant, the absorbing thought of each hermit, of each cœnobite, was his own isolation or that of his brethren from the dangerous world. But to teach the world they must enter the world. Their influence, therefore, beyond their convent walls was but subordinate and accessory. The halo of their sanctity might awe, attract others; the zeal of love might, as to their more immediate neighbours, struggle with the coercive and emprisoning discipline. But the admiration of their sanctity would act chiefly in alluring emulous votaries within, rather than in extending faith and holiness beyond their walls. Even their charities were to relieve their own souls, to lay up for themselves treasures of good works, rather than from any real sympathy for the people. The loftier notion of combining their own humiliation with the good of mankind first dawned upon the founders of the Mendicant orders. In the older monasteries beneficence was but a subsidiary and ancillary virtue. The cultivation of the soil was not to increase its fertility for the general advantage; it was to employ their own dangerous energies, to subdue their own bodies by the hard discipline of labour. At all events, the limit of their influence was that of their retainers, tenants, peasants, or serfs, bounded by their own near neighbourhood. No sooner indeed had any one of the older Orders, or any single monastery attained to numbers, rank or influence, than it became more and more estranged from the humbler classes; the vows of poverty had been eluded, the severer rule gradually relaxed; the individual might remain poor, but the order or the convent became rich; narrow cells grew into stately cloisters, deserts into parks, hermits into princely abbots. It became a great religious aristocracy; it became worldly, without impregnating the world with its religious spirit; it was hardly less secluded from popular intercourse than before; even where learning was cultivated it was the high scholastic theology: theology which, in its pride, stood as much aloof from the popular mind as the feudal bishop or the mitred abbot.

But just at this time that popular mind throughout Christendom seemed to demand instruction. There was a wide and vague awakening and yearning of the human intellect. It is impossible to suppose that the lower orders were not to a certain extent generally stirred by that movement which thronged the streets of the universities of Paris, Auxerre, Oxford, with countless hosts of indigent scholars, which led thousands to the feet of Abélard, and had raised logical disputations on the most barren metaphysical subjects to an interest like that of a tournament. An insatiate thirst of curiosity, of inquiry, at least for mental spiritual excitement, seemed almost suddenly to have pervaded society. Intellectual movement.

Here that which was heresy, or accounted to be heresy, stepped in and seized upon the vacant mind. Preaching in public and in private was the strength of all the heresiarchs, of all the sects. Eloquence, popular eloquence became a new power which the Church had comparatively neglected or disdained since the time of the Crusades; or had gone on wasting upon that worn-out and now almost unstirring topic. The Petrobussians, the Henricians, the followers of Peter Waldo, and the wilder teachers at least tinged with the old Manichean tenets of the East, met on this common ground. They were poor and popular; they felt with the people, whether the lower burghers of the cities, the lower vassals, or even the peasants and serfs; they spoke the language of the people, they were of the people. If here and there one of the higher clergy, a priest or a canon, adopted their opinions and mode of teaching, he became an object of reverence and notoriety; and this profound religious influence so obtained was a strong temptation to religious minds. But all Heresy.

these sects were bound together by their common revolutionary aversion to the clergy, not only the wealthy, worldly, immoral, tyrannical, but the decent but inert priesthood, who left the uninstructed souls of men to perish. In their turn, they were viewed with the most jealous hatred by the clergy, not merely on account of their heterodox and daring tenets, but as usurping their office, which themselves had almost let fall from their hands. We have seen the extent to which they prevailed; nothing less might be apprehended (unless coerced by the obedient temporal power, and no other measure seemed likely to succeed) than a general revolt of the lower orders from the doctrines and rule of the hierarchy.

At this time, too, the rude dialects which had been slowly forming by the breaking up of the Roman Latin and its fusion with the Teutonic, were growing into regular and distinct languages. Latin, the language of the Church, became less and less the language of the people. In proportion as the Roman or foreign element predominated, the services of the Church, the speech in which all priests were supposed to be instructed, remained more or less clear and intelligible. It was more so where the Latin maintained its ascendancy; but in the Teutonic or Sclavonian regions, even the priesthood had learned Latin imperfectly, if at all; and Latin had ceased to be the means of ordinary communication; it was a strange, obsolete, if still venerable language. Even in Italy, in Northern and Southern France, in England where the Norman French kept down to a certain extent the old free Anglo-Saxon (we must wait more than a century for Wyclyffe and Chaucer), in Spain, Latin was a kindred, indistinctly significant tongue, but not that of common

New languages.

use, not that of the field, the street, the market, or the fair. But vernacular teaching was in all quarters coetaneous with the new opinions; versions of the sacred writings, or parts of the sacred writings, into the young languages were at once the sign of their birth, and the instrument of their propagation. These languages had begun to speak, at least in poetry, and not only to the knightly aristocracy. The first sounds of Italian poetry were already heard in the Sicilian court of the young Frederick II.: Dante was ere long to come. The Provençal had made the nearest approach perhaps to a regular language; and Provence, as has been seen, lent her Romaunt to the great anti-hierarchical movement. In France the Trouvères had in the last century begun their inexhaustible, immeasurable epopées; but these were as yet the luxuries of the court and the castle, heard no doubt by the people, but not what is fairly called popular poetry,* though here and there might even now be heard the tale or the fable. Germany, less poetical, was at once borrowing the knightly poems on Charlemagne, and King Arthur, and the Crusades; emulating France, reviving the old classical fables, among them the story of Alexander; while in Walter the Falconer[b] are heard tones more menacing, more ominous of religious revolution, more daringly expressive of Teutonic independence.

But this gradual encroachment of the vernacular

---

* See in the 22nd vol. of the Hist. Littéraire de la France the description and analysis of the innumerable Chansons de Geste, Poëmes d'Aventure. With all these were mingled up, both in Germany and France, as interminable hagiological romances, legends, and lives of saints, even the more modern Saints. See, e.g., the French poem on Thomas à Becket, edited in the Berlin Transactions by M. Bekker.

[b] Lachmann has edited the original Walter der Vogelweide with his usual industry; Simrock modernised him to the understanding of the less learned reader.

poetry on the Latin, the vain struggle of the Latin to maintain its mastery, the growth and influence of modern languages must be reserved for a later, more full, and consecutive inquiry.

Just at this juncture arose almost simultaneously, without concert, in different countries, two men wonderfully adapted to arrest and avert the danger which threatened the whole hierarchical system. One seized and, if he did not wrest from the hands of the enemy, turned against him with indefatigable force his own fatal arms, St. Dominic, the founder of the Friar Preachers. By him Christendom was at once overspread with a host of zealous, active, devoted men, whose function was popular instruction. They were gathered from every country, and spoke, therefore, every language and dialect. In a few years, from the sierras of Spain to the steppes of Russia; from the Tiber to the Thames, the Trent, the Baltic Sea; the old faith, in its fullest mediæval, imaginative, inflexible rigour, was preached in almost every town and hamlet. The Dominicans did not confine themselves to popular teaching: the more dangerous, if as yet not absolutely disloyal seats of the new learning, of inquiry, of intellectual movement, the universities, Bologna, Paris, Oxford are invaded, and compelled to admit these stern apostles of unswerving orthodoxy. Their zeal soon overleaped the pale of Christendom: they plunge fearlessly into the remote darkness of heathen and Mohammedan lands, from whence come back rumours, which are constantly stirring the minds of their votaries, of wonderful conversions and not less wonderful martyrdoms.

The other, St. Francis of Assisi, was endowed with that fervour of mystic devotion, which spread like an epidemic with irresistible contagion among the lower orders throughout Christendom. It was a superstition, but a superstition which had such an earnestness, warmth, tenderness, as to raise the religious feeling to an intense but gentle passion; it supplied a never-failing counter excitement to rebellious reasoning, which gladly fell asleep again on its bosom. After the death of its author and example, it raised a new object of adoration, more near, more familiar, and second only, if second, to the Redeemer himself. Jesus was supposed to have lived again in St. Francis with at least as bright a halo of miracle around him, in absolute, almost surpassing perfection.

In one important respect the founders of these new orders fully agreed, in their entire identification with the lowest of mankind. At first amicable, afterwards emulous, eventually hostile, they, or rather their Orders, rivalled each other in sinking below poverty into beggary. They were to live upon alms; the coarsest imaginable dress, the hardest fare, the narrowest cell, were to keep them down to the level of the humblest. Though Dominic himself was of high birth, and many of his followers of noble blood, St. Francis of decent even wealthy parentage, according to the irrepealable constitution of both Orders they were still to be the poorest of mankind, instructing or consorting in religious fellowship with the very meanest outcasts of society. Both the new Orders differed in the same manner, and greatly to the advantage of the hierarchical faith, from the old monkish institutions. Their primary object was not the salvation of the individual monk, but the salvation of others through him. Though, therefore, their rules within their monasteries were strictly and severely monastic, bound by the common vows of chastity, poverty, and obedience, seclusion was no part of their discipline. Their business was abroad rather than at home; their dwelling was not like that of the old Benedictines or others, in the uncultivated swamps and forests of the North, on the dreary Apennine, or the exhausted soil of Italy, in order to subdue their bodies, and occupy their dangerously unoccupied time; merely as a secondary consequence to compel the desert into fertile land. Their work was among their fellow men; in the village, in the town, in the city, in the market, even in the camp. In every Dominican convent the Superior had the power to dispense even with the ordinary internal discipline, if he thought the brother might be more usefully employed in his special avocation of a Preacher. It might seem the ambition of these men, instead of cooping up a chosen few in high-walled and secure monasteries, to subdue the whole world into one vast cloister; monastic Christianity would no longer flee the world, it would subjugate it, or win it by gentle violence.

In Dominic Spain began to exercise that remarkable influence over Latin Christianity, to display that peculiar character which culminated as it were in Ignatius Loyola, in Philip II., and in Torquemada, of which the code of the Inquisition was the statutory law; of which Calderon was the poet. The life of every devout Spaniard was a perpetual crusade. By temperament and by position he was in constant adventurous warfare against the enemies of the Cross: hatred of the Jew, of the Mohammedan, was the herrban under which he served; it was the oath of his chivalry: that hatred, in all its intensity, was soon and easily extended to the heretic. Hereafter it was to comprehend the heathen Mexican, the Peruvian. St. Dominic was, as it were, a Cortez, bound by his sense of duty,

Dominic a Spaniard.

urged by an inward voice, to invade older Christendom. And Dominic was a man of as profound sagacity as of adventurous enthusiasm. He intuitively perceived, or the circumstances of his early career forced upon him, the necessities of the age, and showed him the arms in which himself and his forces must be arrayed to achieve their conquest.

St. Dominic was born in 1170, in the village of Calaroga, between Aranda and Osma, in Old Castile. His parents were of noble name, that of Guzman, if not of noble race.* Prophecies (we must not disdain legend, though manifest legend) proclaimed his birth. It was a tenet of his disciples that he was born without original sin, sanctified in his mother's womb. His mother dreamed that she bore a dog with a torch in his mouth, which set the world on fire. His votaries borrowed too the old classical fable; the bees settled on his lips, foreshowing his exquisite eloquence. Even in his infancy, his severe nature, among other wonders, began to betray itself. He crept from his soft couch to lie on the hard cold ground. The first part of his education Dominic received from his uncle, a churchman at Gamiel d'Izan. At fifteen years old he was sent to the university of Palencia; he studied, chiefly theology, for ten years. He was laborious, devout, abstemious. Two stories are recorded which show the dawn of religious strength in his character. During a famine, he sold his clothes to feed the poor: he offered in compassion to a woman who deplored the slavery of her brother to the Moors, to be sold for his redemption. He had not what may be strictly called a

Birth.

---

* This point is contested. The Father Bremond wrote to confute the Bollandists, who had cast a profane doubt on the noble descent of Dominic.

monastic training.⁴ The Bishop of Osma had changed his chapter into regular canons, those who lived in common, and under a rule approaching to a monastic institute. Dominic became a canon in this rigorous house: there he soon excelled the others in austerity. This was in his twenty-fifth year: he remained in Osma, not much known, for nine years longer. Diego de Azevedo had succeeded to the Bishopric of Osma. He was a prelate of great ability, and of strong religious enthusiasm. He was sent to Denmark to negotiate the marriage of Alfonso VIII. of Castile with a princess of that kingdom. He chose the congenial Dominic as his companion. No sooner had they crossed the Pyrenees than they found themselves in the midst of the Albigensian heresy; they could not close their eyes on the contempt into which the clergy had fallen, or on the prosperity of the sectarians; their very host at Toulouse was an Albigensian; Dominic is said to have converted him before the morning.

In Langue-doc.

A.D. 1203.

The mission of the Bishop in Denmark was frustrated by the unexpected death of the Princess. Before he returned to Spain, Azevedo, with his companion, resolved upon a pilgrimage to Rome. The character of the Bishop of Osma appears from his proposal to Pope Innocent. He wished to abandon his tranquil bishopric, and to devote himself to the perilous life of a missionary, among the Cumans and fierce people which occupied part of Hungary, or in some other infidel country. That

---

⁴ The Chapter of his order was shocked by, and carefully erased from the authorised Legend of the Saint, a passage, "Ubi semetipsum asserit licet in integritate carnis divinâ gratiâ conservatum, nondum illam imperfectionem eradere potuisse, quia magis afficietatur juvencularum colloquiis quam affatibus vetularum."—Apud Bolland. c. 1.

Dominic would have been his companion in this adventurous spiritual enterprise none can doubt. Innocent commanded the Bishop to return to his diocese. On their way the Bishop and Dominic stopped at Montpellier. There, as has been said, they encountered in all their pomp the three Legates of the Pope, Abbot Arnold, the Brother Raoul, and Peter of Castelnau. The Legates were returning discomfited, and almost desperate, from their progress in Languedoc. Then it was that Dominic uttered his bold and memorable rebuke: "It is not by the display of power and pomp, cavalcades of retainers, and richly houseled palfreys, or by gorgeous apparel, that the heretics win proselytes; it is by zealous preaching, by apostolic humility, by austerity, by seeming, it is true, but yet seeming holiness. Zeal must be met by zeal, humility by humility, false sanctity by real sanctity; preaching falsehood by preaching truth." From that day Dominic devoted himself to preaching the religion which he believed. Even the Legates were for a time put to shame by his precept and example, dismissed their splendid equipages, and set forth with bare feet; yet if with some humility of dress and demeanour, with none of language or of heart. As the preacher of orthodoxy, Dominic is said in the pulpit, at the conference, to have argued with irresistible force: but his mission at last seems to have made no profound impression on the obstinate unbelievers. Ere long the Bishop Azevedo retired to Osma and died. Dominic remained alone.

But now the murder of Peter of Castelnau roused other powers and other passions. That more irresistible preacher, the sword of the Crusader, was sent forth: it becomes impossible to discriminate between the successes of one and of the other. The voice of the Apostle is drowned in the din of war; even the conduct of Dominic himself, the manner in which he bore himself amidst these unevangelic allies, is clouded with doubt and uncertainty. His career is darkened too by the splendour of miracle, with which it is invested. These miracles must not be passed by: they are largely borrowed from the life of the Saviour and those of the Saints; they sometimes sink into the ludicrous. A schedule, which he had written during one conference, of scriptural proofs, leaped out of the fire, while the discriminating flames consumed the writings of his adversaries. He exorcised the devil who possessed three noble matrons in the shape of a great black cat with large black eyes, who at last ran up the bell-rope and disappeared. A lady of extreme beauty wished to leave her monastery, and resisted all the preacher's arguments. She blew her nose, it remained in the handkerchief. Horror-stricken, she implored the prayers of Dominic: at his intercession the nose resumed its place; the lady remained in the convent. Dominic raised the dead, frequently fed his disciples in a manner even more wonderful than the Lord in the desert.* His miracles equal, if not transcend those in the Gospel. It must indeed have been a stubborn generation, to need besides these wonders the sword of Simon de Montfort.

Throughout the Crusade Dominic is lost to the sight: he is hardly, if at all, noticed by historian or poet. It is not till the century after his death that his sterner followers boast of his presence, if not of his activity, in exciting the savage soldiery in the day

---

* All these and much more may be found in the lives of St. Dominic, in the Bollandists and elsewhere.

of battle. He marches unarmed in the van of the army with the cross in his hands, and escapes unhurt. The cross was shown pierced everywhere with arrows or javelins, only the form of the Saviour himself uninjured. In modern times there comes another change over the history of St. Dominic; that, of which his contemporaries were silent, which the next generation blazoned forth as a boast, is now become a grave imputation. In later writings, his more prudent admirers assert, that he never appeared in the field of battle; he was but once with the armies, during the great victory of Simon de Montfort, at Muret; and then he remained within the city in fervent and uninterrupted prayer. All, perhaps, that is certainly known is that he showed no disapprobation of the character or of the deeds of Simon de Montfort. He obeyed his call to bless the marriage of his son, and the baptism of his daughter.

So, too, the presence of St. Dominic on the tribunals, where the unhappy heretics were tried for their lives, and the part which he took in delivering them over to the secular arm to be burned by hundreds, is in the same manner, according to the date of the biographer, a cause of pride or shame, is boldly vaunted, or tenderly disguised and gently doubted. The more charitable silence at least of the earlier writers is sternly repudiated by the Bollandists, who will not allow the milder sense to be given to the title "Persecutor of Heretics," assigned to him by the Inquisition of Toulouse. They quote St. Thomas of Aquino as an irrefragable authority on the duty of burning heretics. They refute the more tolerant argument by a long line of glorious bishops who have urged or assisted at holocausts of victims. "What glory, splendour, and dignity (bursts forth Malvendia) belong to the Order of

Preachers, words cannot express! for the Holy Inquisition owes its origin to St. Dominic, and was propagated by his faithful followers. By them heretics of all kinds, the innovators and corrupters of sound doctrine, were destroyed, unless they would recant, by fire and sword, or at least awed, banished, put to the rout." The title of Dominic, in its fiercer sense, even rests on Papal authority, that of Sixtus V. in his bull for the canonisation of Peter Martyr.[f] That indeed which in modern days is alleged in proof of his mercy, rather implies his habitual attendance on such scenes without showing the same mercy. Once he interfered to save a victim, in whom he saw some hopes of reconciliation, from the flames.[g] Calmer inquiry must rob him of, or release him from, these questionable glories. His heroic acts, as moving in the van of bloody battles; his title of Founder of the Inquisition, belong to legend not to history. It is his Order which has thrown back its aggrandising splendour on St. Dominic. So far was the Church from bowing down before the transcendant powers and holiness of the future saints, or discerning with instantaneous sagacity the value of these new allies, both the Father of the Friar Preachers and the Father of the Minorites were at first received with cold suspicion or neglect at Rome; the foundation of the two new Orders was extorted from the reluctant Innocent. The Third Lateran Council had prohibited the establishment of new orders. Well-timed and irresistible visions (the counsels of wiser and more far-sighted men) enlightened

---

[f] "Jam vero ne recrudescerret in posteris malum, aut impia haeresis repullularet ex cineribus suis saluberrimo consilio Romani Pontifices Sanctae Inquisitionis officium austeri S. Dominici instituerant, eidemque B. viro et Fratribus Praedicatoribus praecipue detulerunt."—Reichinius (a Dominican); Praef. in Monetam. p. xxxi.

[g] La Cordaire, S. Dominique.

the Pope, and gently impelled him to open his eyes, and to yield to the revocation of his unwise judgement. Dominic returned from Rome, before the battle of Muret, armed with the Papal permission to enrol the Order of Friar Preachers.

The earliest foundation of Dominic had been a convent of females. He had observed that the noble ladies of Languedoc listened, especially in early life, with too eager ears to the preachers of heretical doctrines. At Prouille, at the foot of the Pyrenees, between Fanjaux and Monreal, he opened this retreat, where their virgin minds might be safe from the dangerous contagion. The first monastery of the Order of Preachers was that of St. Romain, near Toulouse. The brotherhood consisted but of sixteen, most of them natives of Languedoc, some Spaniards, one Englishman. It is remarkable, however, that the Order, founded for the suppression of heresy by preaching in Languedoc, was hardly organised before it left the chosen scene of its labours. Instead of fixing on Toulouse or any of the cities of Provence as the centre of his operations, Dominic was seized with the ambition of converting the world. Rome, Bologna, Paris, were to be the seats of his power. Exactly four years after the battle of Muret he abandoned Languedoc for ever. His sagacious mind might perhaps anticipate the unfavourable change, the fall if not the death of De Montfort, the return of Count Raymond as the deliverer to his patrimonial city. But even the stern Spanish mind might be revolted by the horrors of the Albigensian war; he may have been struck by the common grief for the fall of the noble Spanish King of Arragon. At all events, the preacher of the word in Languedoc could play but a secondary part to the preacher by the sword;

and now that the aim was manifestly not conversion, but conquest, not the re-establishment of the Church, but the destruction of the liberties of the land, not the subjugation of the heretical Count of Toulouse, but the expulsion from their ancestral throne of the old princely house and the substitution of a foreign usurper, the Castilian might feel shame and compunction, even tho Christian might be reluctant to connect the Catholic faith which he would preach with all the deeds of a savage soldiery. The parting address ascribed to St. Dominic is not quite consistent with this more generous and charitable view of his conduct. It is a terrible menace rather than gentle regret or mild reproof. At the convent of Prouille, after high mass, he thus spake: "For many years I have spoken to you with tenderness, with prayers, and tears; but according to the proverb of my country, where the benediction has no effect, the rod may have much. Behold, now, we rouse up against you princes and prelates, nations and kingdoms! Many shall perish by the sword. The land shall be ravaged, walls thrown down; and you, alas! reduced to slavery. So shall the chastisement do that which the blessing and which mildness could not do."[b]

Sept. 13, 1217.

Dominic himself took up his residence in Rome.[l] His success as a preacher was unrivalled. His followers began to spread rumours of the miracles which he wrought. The Pope Honorius III. appointed him to the high office, since perpetuated among his spiritual descendants, Master of the Sacred Palace. He was held in the highest honour by the aged Cardinal Ugo-

[b] MS. de Prouille, published by Père Perrin: quoted by La Cordaire, Vie de S. Dominique, p. 404.

[l] He first established the monastery of San Sisto on the Cœlian Hill, afterward that of Santa Sabina.

lino, the future Pope Gregory IX. For the propagation of his Order this residence in Rome was a master-stroke of policy. Of the devout pilgrims to Rome, men of all countries in Christendom, the most devout were most enraptured by the eloquence of Dominic. Few but must feel that it was a preaching Order which was wanted in every part of the Christian world. Dominic was gifted with that rare power, even in those times, of infusing a profound and enduring devotion to one object. Once within the magic circle, the enthralled disciple either lost all desire to leave it, or, if he struggled, Dominic seized him and dragged him back, now an unreluctant captive, by awe, by persuasion, by conviction, by what was believed to be miracle which might be holy art, or the bold and ready use of casual but natural circumstances. "God has never," as he revealed in secret (a secret not likely to be religiously kept) to the Abbot of Casamare, "refused me anything that I have prayed for." When he prayed for the conversion of Conrad the Teutonic, was Conrad left ignorant that he had to resist the prayers of one whom God had thus endowed with irresistible efficacy of prayer?[k] Thus were preachers rapidly enlisted and dispersed throughout the world, speaking every language in Christendom. Two Poles, Hyacinth and Ceslas, carried the rules of the order to their own country. Dominican convents were founded at Cracow, even as far as Kiow.

Dominic had judged wisely and not too daringly in embracing the world as the scene of his labours. In the year 1220, seven years after he had left Languedoc, he stood, as the Master-General of his order, at the head of an assembly at Bologna. Italy, *Rapid progress of the Order. A.D. 1220.*

---

[k] La Cordaire, p. 539.

Spain, Provence, France, Germany, Poland, had now their Dominican convents; the voices of Dominican preachers had penetrated into every land. But the great question of holding property or dependence on the casual support of mendicancy was still undecided. Dominic had accepted landed endowments: in Languedoc he held a grant of tithes from Fulk Bishop of Toulouse. But the Order of St. Francis, of which absolute poverty was the vital rule, was now rising with simultaneous rapidity. Though both the founders of the new Orders and the brethren of the Orders had professed and displayed the most perfect mutual respect, and even amity (twice, it was said, they had met, with great marks of reverence and esteem), yet both true policy and devout ambition might reveal to the prudent as well as ardent Dominic that the vow of absolute poverty would give the Franciscans an immeasurable superiority in popular estimation. His followers must not be trammelled with worldly wealth, or be outdone in any point of austerity by those of St. Francis. The universal suffrage was for the vow of poverty in the strongest sense, the renunciation of all property by the Order as well as by the individual Brother. How long, how steadfastly, that vow was kept by either Order will appear in the course of our history.

The second great assembly of the Order was held shortly before the death of Dominic. The Order was now distributed into eight provinces, Spain, the first in rank, Provence, France, Lombardy, Rome, Germany, Hungary, and England. In England the Prior Gilbert had landed with fourteen friars. Gilbert preached before the Archbishop of Canterbury. The Primate, Stephen Langton, was so edified by his eloquence, that he at once gave full licence to

A.D. 1221.

preach throughout the land. Monasteries rose at Canterbury, London, Oxford.

But the great strength of these two new Orders was, besides the communities of friars and nuns (each associated with itself a kindred female Order), the establishment of a third, a wider and more secular community, who were bound to the two former by bonds of close association, by reverence and implicit obedience, and were thus always ready to maintain the interests, to admire and to propagate the wonders, to subserve in every way the advancement of the higher disciples of St. Dominic or St. Francis. They were men or women, old or young, married or unmarried, bound by none of the monastic vows, but deeply imbued with the monastic, with the corporate spirit; taught to observe all holy days, fasts, vigils with the utmost rigour, inured to constant prayer and attendance on divine worship. They were organised, each under his own prior; they crowded as a duty, as a privilege, into the church wherever a Dominican ascended the pulpit, predisposed, almost compelled, if compulsion were necessary, to admire, to applaud at least by rapt attention. Thus the Order spread not merely by its own perpetual influence and unwearied activity; it had everywhere a vast host of votaries wedded to its interests, full to fanaticism of its corporate spirit, bound to receive hospitably or ostentatiously their wandering preachers, to announce, to trumpet abroad, to propagate the fame of their eloquence, to spread belief in their miracles, to lavish alms upon them, to fight in their cause. This lay coadjutory, these Tertiaries, as they were called, or among the Dominicans, the Soldiers of Jesus Christ as not altogether secluded from the world, acted more widely and more subtly upon the world. Their rules were not rigidly

Tertiaries

laid down till by the seventh Master of the Order, Munion de Zamora; it was then approved by Popes.*

Death. Dominic died August 6th, 1221. He was taken ill at Venice, removed with difficulty to Bologna, where he expired with saintly resignation.

His canonisation followed rapidly on his death. Gregory IX., who in his internecine war with the Emperor Frederick II. had found the advantage of these faithful, restless, unscrupulous allies in the realm, in the camp, almost in the palace of his adversary, was not the man to pause or to hesitate in his grateful acknowledgements or prodigal reward. "I no more doubt," said the Pope, "the sanctity of Dominic than that of St. Peter or St. Paul." In the bull of canonisation, Dominic is elaborately described as riding in the four-horsed chariot of the Gospel, as it were seated behind the four Evangelists (or rather in the four chariots of Zechariah, long interpreted as signifying the four Evangelists), holding in his hand the irresistible bow of the Divine Word.

Canonisation.

The admiration of their founder, if it rose not with the Dominicans so absolutely into divine adoration as with the Franciscans, yet bordered close upon it. He, too, was so closely approximated to the Saviour as to be placed nearly on an equality. The Virgin Mother herself, the special protectress of the sons of Dominic,*

---

* Among the special privileges of the Order (in the bull of Honorius) was that in the time of interdict (so common were interdicts now become) the Order might still celebrate mass with low voices, without bells. Conceive the influence thus obtained in a religious land, everywhere else deprived of all its holy services.

* There is a strange story of the especial protection extended over the Order by the Virgin. It might seem singularly ill-adapted for painting, but painting has nevertheless ventured, at least partially, to represent it. To this the modesty of more modern manners, perhaps not less real though more scrupulous respect (respect which

might almost seem to sanction their bold raptures of spiritual adulation, from which our most fervent piety might shrink as wild profanation. Dominic was the adopted Son of the Blessed Virgin.°

And this was part of the creed maintained by an Order which under its fourth general, John of Wildeshausen (in Westphalia), in their Chapter-General at Bordeaux, reckoned its monasteries at the number of four hundred and seventy. In Spain thirty-five, in France fifty-two, in Germany fifty-two, in Tuscany thirty-two, in Lombardy forty-six, in Hungary thirty, in Poland thirty-six, in Denmark twenty-eight, in England forty. They were spreading into Asia, into heathen or Saracen lands, into Palestine, Greece, Crete, Abys-

---

falls far short of worship), prescribes more than an allusion: The Virgin is represented with the whole countless host of Dominicans crowded under her dress. In the vision of St. Brigitta, the Virgin herself is made to sanction this awful confusion. Though is the vision there is an interpretation which softens away that which in the painting (which I have seen) becomes actual fact.

°. More than this, of the Father himself. " Ego, dulcissima filia, istos duos filios genui, unum naturaliter generando, alium amabiliter et dulciter adoptando .... Sicut hic Filius a me naturaliter et *æternaliter* genitus, assumptâ naturâ humanâ, in omnibus fuit perfectissime obediens mihi, usque ad mortem, sic filius meus adoptivus Dominicus. Omnia, quæ operatus est ab infantiâ suâ usque ad terminum vitæ suæ, fuerunt angulata secundum obedientiam præceptorum meorum,

me unquam semel fuit transgressus quodcunque præceptum meum, quia virginitatem corporis et animi illibatam servavit, et gratiam baptismi quo spiritualiter renatus est, semper conservavit." The parallel goes on between the apostles of the Lord and the brethren of S. Dominic.—Apud Bolland. xlv. p. 844. See also a passage about the Virgin in La Cordaire, p. 234. In another Vita S. Dominici, apud Bolland. Aug. 4, is this:—There was a prophetic picture at Venice, in which appear St. Paul and S. Dominic. Under the latter, " Facilius Itur per istum." The comment of the biographer is: " Doctrina Pauli sicut et cæterorum apostolorum erat doctrina inducens ad fidem et observationem præceptorum, doctrina Dominici ad observantiam consiliorum, et ideo facilius per ipsum itur ad Christum."—c. vii.

sinin. Nor is it their number alone which grows with such wonderful fertility. They are not content with the popular mind. They invade the high places of human intellect: they are disputing the mastery in the Universities of Italy and Germany, in Cologne, Paris, and in Oxford. Before long they are to claim two of the greatest luminaries of the scholastic philosophy, Albert the Great and Thomas of Aquino.

CHAPTER X.

St. Francis.[a]

ST. FRANCIS was born in the romantic town of Assisi, of a family, the Bernardini, engaged in trade. His birth took place while his father was on a mercantile journey in France; on his return his newborn son was baptised by the name of Francis.[b] His mother, Picca, loved him with all a mother's tenderness for her first-born. He received the earliest rudiments of instruction from the clergy of the parish of St. George: he was soon taken to assist his father in his trade. The father, a hard, money-making man, was shocked at first by the vanity and prodigality of his son. The young Francis gave banquets to his juvenile friends, dressed splendidly, and the streets of Assisi rang with the songs and revels of the joyous crew; but even then his bounty

---

[a] The vast annals of the Franciscan Order, by Lucas Wadding, in seventeen folio volumes, are the great authority: for S. Francis himself the life by S. Bonaventura. I have much used the Chronique de l'Ordre du Père S. François, in quaint old French (the original is in Portuguese, by Marco di Lisbona), Paris, 1623. I have an epic poem, in twenty-five cantos, a kind of religious plagiary of Tasso, San Francisco, ó Gierusalemme Celeste Acquistata, by Agostino Gallucci (1617). The author makes S. Francis subdue the Wickliffites. There is a modern life by M. Malan.

[b] When the disciples of S. Francis were fully possessed with the conformity of their founder with the Saviour, the legend grew up, assimilating his birth to that of the Lord. A prophetess foreshowed it; he was born by divine suggestion in a stable; angels rejoiced; even peace and good will were announced, though by a human voice. An angel, like old Simeon, bore him at the font. And all this is gravely related by a biographer of the 19th century, M. Malan.

to the poor formed a large part of his generous wastefulness. He was taken captive in one of the petty wars which had broken out between Perugia and Assisi, and remained a year in prison. He was then seized with a violent illness: when he rose from his bed nature looked cold and dreary; he began to feel disgust to the world. The stirrings of some great but yet undefined purpose were already awake within him. He began to see visions, but as yet they were of war and glory: the soldier was not dead in his heart. He determined to follow the fortunes of a youthful poor knight who was setting out to fight under the banner of the "Gentle Count," Walter of Brienne, against the hated Germans. At Spoleto he again fell ill; his feverish visions took another turn. Francis now felt upon him that profound religious thraldom which he was never to break, never to desire to break. His whole soul became deliberately, calmly, extatic faith. He began to talk mysteriously of his future bride—that bride was Poverty. He resolved never to refuse alms to a poor person. He found his way to Rome, threw down all he possessed, no costly offering, on the altar of St. Peter. On his return he joined a troop of beggars, and exchanged his dress for the rags of the filthiest among them. His mother heard and beheld all his strange acts with a tender and prophetic admiration. To a steady trader like the father it was folly if not madness. He was sent with a valuable bale of goods to sell at Foligno. On his return he threw all the money down at the feet of the priest of St. Damian to rebuild his church, as well as the price of his horse, which he likewise sold. The priest refused the gift. In the eyes of the father this was dishonesty as well as folly. Francis concealed himself in a cave, where he lay hid for a month in solitary prayer. He returned to Assisi, looking so wild and haggard that the rabble hooted him as he passed and pelted him with mire and stones. The gentle Francis appeared to rejoice in every persecution. The indignant father shut him up in a dark chamber, from which, after a time, he was released by the tender solicitude of his mother. Bernardini now despaired of his unprofitable and intractable son, whom he suspected of alienating other sums besides that which he had received for the cloth and the horse. He cited him before the magistrates to compel him to abandon all rights on his patrimony, which he was disposed to squander in this thriftless manner. Francis declared that he was a servant of God, and declined the jurisdiction of the civil magistrate. The cause came before the Bishop. The Bishop earnestly exhorted Francis to yield up to his father any money which he might possess, or to which he was entitled. "It might be ungodly gain, and so unfit to be applied to holy uses." "I will give up the very clothes I wear," replied the enthusiast, encouraged by the gentle demeanour of the Bishop. He stripped himself entirely naked.* "Peter Bernardini was my father; I have now but one father, he that is in heaven." The audience burst into tears; the Bishop threw his mantle over him and ordered an old coarse dress of an artisan to be brought: he then received Francis into his service.

<small>Gives up his inheritance. A.D. 1206. Ætat 25.</small>

Francis was now wedded to Poverty; but poverty he would only love in its basest form—mendicancy. He wandered abroad, was ill used by robbers; on his escape he received from an old friend at Gubbio a hermit's attire, a short tunic, a leathern girdle, a staff and slippers. He begged at the gates of

<small>Embraces mendicancy.</small>

---

* According to S. Bonaventura, he had haircloth under his dress.

monasteries; he discharged the most menial offices. With even more profound devotion he dedicated himself for some time in the hospital at Gubbio to that unhappy race of beings whom even Christianity was constrained to banish from the social pale—the lepers.[d] He tended them with more than necessary affectionateness, washed their feet, dressed their sores, and is said to have wrought miraculous cures among them. The moral miracle of his charity toward them is a more certain and more affecting proof of his true Christianity of heart. It was an especial charge to the brethren of St. Francis of Assisi to choose these outcasts of humanity as the objects of their peculiar care.[e]

On his return to Assisi he employed himself in the restoration of the church of St. Damian. "Whoever will give me one stone shall have one prayer; whoever two, two; three, three." The people mocked, but Francis went on carrying the stones in his own hands, and the church began to rise. He refused all food which he did not obtain by begging. His father reproached him and uttered his malediction. He took a beggar of the basest class: "Be thou my father and give me thy blessing." But so successful was he in awakening the charity of the inhabitants of Assisi, that

---

[d] There is something singularly affecting in the service of the Church for the seclusion of the lepers, whose number is as sure a proof of the wretchedness of those times, as the care of them of the charity. The stern duty of looking to the public welfare is tempered with exquisite compassion for the victims of this loathsome disease. The service may be found—it is worth seeking for—in Martene de Antiquis Ecclesiæ Ritibus.

It is quoted by M. Malan. Compare on S. Francis and the Lepers, Mr. Brewer's Preface to the Monumenta Franciscana, p. xxiii., et seqq.; and Translation of the Testament of S. Francis, p. 592.

[e] S. Bonaventura says that he healed one leper with a kiss: "Nescio quisnam horum magis sit admirandum, an humilitatis profunditas in osculo tam benigno, an virtutis præclaritas in miraculo tam stupendo."—Vit. S. Francisci.

not only the church of St. Damian, but two others, St. Peter and St. Maria dei Angeli (called the Portiuncula), through his means arose out of their ruins to decency and even splendour. One day, in the church of St. Maria dei Angeli, he heard the text, " Provide neither gold, nor silver, nor brass in your purses. Neither scrip for your journey, neither two coats, neither shoes nor yet staves." He threw away his wallet, his staff, and his shoes, put on the coarsest dark grey tunic, bound himself with a cord, and set out through the city calling all to repentance.

This strange but fervent piety of Francis could not but, in that age, kindle the zeal of others. Wonder grew into admiration, admiration into emulation, emulation into a blind following of his footsteps. Disciples, one by one (the first are carefully recorded), began to gather round him. He retired with them to a lonely spot in the bend of the river, called Rivo Torto. A rule was wanting for the young brotherhood. Thrice upon the altar he opened the Gospels, which perhaps were accustomed to be opened on these passages.[f] He read three texts in reverence for the Holy Trinity. The first was, "If thou wilt be perfect, sell all thou hast and give to the poor;"[a] the second, "Take nothing for your journey;"[b] the third, "If any one would come after me, let him take up his cross and follow me."[1] Francis made the sign of the cross and sent forth his followers into the neighbouring cities, as if to divide the world, to the east and west, the north and south. They reassembled at Rivo Torto and determined to go to Rome to obtain the authority of the Pope for the foundation of their order. On the way they met a knight

---
[f] The poet gives the date, St. Luke's day, Oct. 18, 1212.
[a] Matt. xix. 21.   [b] Mark vi. 8.   [1] Matt. xvi. 24.

in arms. "Angelo," said St. Francis, "instead of that baldrick thou shalt gird thee with a cord; for thy sword thou shalt take the cross of Christ; for the spurs, the dirt and mire." Angelo made up the mystic number of twelve, which the profound piety of his followers alleged as a new similitude to the Lord.[h]

Innocent III. was walking on the terrace of the Lateran when a mendicant of the meanest appearance presented himself, proposing to convert the world by poverty and humility. The haughty Pontiff dismissed him with contempt. But a vision, says the legend, doubtless more grave deliberation and inquiry, suggested that such an Order might meet the heretics on their own ground; the Poor Men of the Church might out-labour and out-suffer the Poor Men of Lyons. He sent for Francis, received him in the midst of the cardinals, and listened to his proposal for his new Order. Some of the cardinals objected the difficulty, the impossibility of the vows. "To suppose that anything is difficult or impossible with God," said the Cardinal Bishop of Sabina, "is to blaspheme Christ and his Gospel."

The Order was now founded; the Benedictines of Monte Subiaco gave them a church, called, like that near Assisi, St. Maria dei Angeli, or de la Portiuncula. In the difficulty, the seeming impossibility of the vows was their strength. The three vital principles of the Order were chastity, poverty, obedience. For chastity, no one was to speak with a woman alone, except the few who might safely do so (from age or severity of character), and that was to urge penitence

_{Foundation of the Order.}

---

[h] It was at this period that he was asked, or said himself that he was transported to heaven, into the actual presence of the Lord, who, according to the poem, gave him a plenary indulgence for himself and his followers:—
"E plenaria indulgenza oggi al dava."
c. vi. 41.

or give spiritual counsel. Poverty was not only the renunciation of all possessions, but of all property, even in the clothes they wore, in the cord which girt them—even in their breviaries.* Money was, as it were, infected; they might on no account receive it in alms except (the solo exception) to aid a sick brother; no brother might ride if he had power to walk. They were literally to fulfil the precept, if stricken on one cheek, to offer the other; if spoiled of part of their dress, to yield up the rest. Obedience was urged not merely as obligatory and coercive: the deepest mutual love was to be the bond of the brotherhood.

The passionate fervour of the preaching, the mystic tenderness, the austere demeanour of Francis and his disciples, could not but work rapidly and profoundly among his female hearers. Clara, a noble virgin of Assisi, under the direction of St. Francis, had in the same manner to strive against the tender and affectionate worldliness, as she deemed it, of her family. But she tore herself from their love as from a sin, entered into a convent attached to the church of St. Damian, and became the mother of the poor sisterhood of St. Clare. Of Clara it is said that she never but once (and that to receive the blessing of the Pope) so lifted her eyelids that the colour of her eyes might be discerned. Clara practised mortifications more severe than any of her sex before. The life of the sisters was one long dreary penance; even their services were all sadness. The sisters who could read were to read the Hours, but without chanting. Those who could not read were not to learn to read. To the prayers of St. Clara it was

---

* At first, says S. Bonaventura, they had no books; their only book was the cross.

attributed that, in later times, her own convent and the city of Assisi were preserved from the fierce Mohammedans which belonged to the army of Frederick II. The Order was confirmed by a bull of Innocent IV.

Francis, in the mean time, with his whole soul vowed to the service of God, set forth to subdue the world. He had hesitated between the contemplative and active life—prayer in the secluded monastery, or preaching the cross of Christ to mankind. The mission of love prevailed; his success and that of his ardent followers might seem to justify their resolution. They had divided the world, and some had already set forth into France and into Spain with the special design of converting the Miramamolin and his Mohammedan subjects. Everywhere they were heard with fanatic rapture. At their first Chapter, held in the church of the Portiuncula, only three years after the scene at Rivo Torto, it was necessary to ordain provincial masters in Spain, Provence, France and Germany: at a second Chapter of the Order in 1219 met five thousand brethren.

Foreign missions.

A.D. 1216.

The holy ambition of St. Francis grew with his success. He determined to confront the great enemy of Christianity in his strength. He set off to preach to the Mohammedans of the East. The Christian army was encamped before Damietta. The sagacity of Francis anticipated from their discord, which he in vain endeavoured to reconcile, their defeat. His prophecy was too fully accomplished; but he determined not the less to proceed on his mission. On his way to the Saracen camp he met some sheep. It occurred to him, "I send you forth as sheep among the wolves." He was taken and carried before the Sultan. To the Sultan he boldly offered the way of salvation.

St. Francis in the East.
A.D. 1219.

He preached (in what language we are not told) the Holy Trinity and the Divine Saviour before these stern Unitarians. The Mohammedans reverence what they deem insanity as partaking of Divine inspiration. The Sultan is said to have listened with respect; his grave face no doubt concealed his compassion. St. Francis offered to enter a great fire with the priests of Islam, and to set the truth of either faith on the issue. The Sultan replied that his priests would not willingly submit to this perilous trial. "I will enter alone," said Francis, "if, should I be burned, you will impute it to my sins; should I come forth alive, you will embrace the Gospel." The Sultan naturally declined these terms, as not quite fair towards his creed. But he offered rich presents to Francis (which the preacher of poverty rejected with utter disdain), and then sent him back in honour to the camp at Damietta. Francis passed through the Holy Land and the kingdom of Antioch, preaching and winning disciples, and then returned to Italy. His fame was now at its height, and wherever he went his wondering disciples saw perpetual miracle. In this respect the life of the Saviour is far surpassed by that of St. Francis.

The Order soon had its martyrs. The Mohammedan Moors of Africa were fiercer than those of Egypt. Five monks, after preaching without success to the Saracens of Seville, crossed into Africa. After many adventures (in one of which during an expedition against the Moorish tribes of the interior, Friar Berard struck water from the desert rock, like Moses) they were offered wealth, beautiful wives, and honours, if they would embrace Mohammedanism. They spat on the ground in contempt of the miscreant offer. The King himself clove the head of one of them with a sword; the rest were despatched in horrible torments.[a] St. Francis received the sad intelligence with triumph, and broke forth in gratulations to the convent of Alonquir, which had thus produced the first purple flowers of martyrdom.

<small>Character of St. Francis.</small> This was no hardness, or want of compassion, but the counterworking of a stronger, more passionate emotion. Of all saints, St. Francis was the most blameless and gentle. In Dominic and in his disciples all was still rigorous, cold, argumentative; something remained of the crusader's fierceness, the Spaniard's haughty humility, the inquisitor's stern suppression of all gentler feelings, the polemic sternness. Whether Francis would have burned heretics, happily we know not, but he would willingly have been burned for them: himself excessive in austerities, he would at times mitigate the austerity of others. Francis was emphatically the Saint of the people—of a poetic people like the Italians. Those who were hereafter to chant the Paradise of Dante, or the softer stanzas of Tasso, might well be enamoured of the ruder devotional strains in the poetry of the whole life of St. Francis. The lowest of the low might find consolation, a kind of pride, in the self-abasement of St. Francis even beneath the meanest. The very name of his disciples, the Friar Minors, implied their humility. In his own eyes (says his most pious successor) he was but a sinner, while in truth he was the mirror and splendour of holiness. It was revealed, says the same Bonaventura, to a Brother, that the throne of one of the angels, who fell from pride,

---

[a] See on these martyrs Southey's ballad:—
"What news, O Queen Orraca,
Of the martyrs five what news?
Does the bloody Miramamolin
Their burial yet refuse?"

was reserved for Francis, who was glorified by humility. If the heart of the poorest was touched by the brotherhood in poverty and lowliness of such a saint, how was his imagination kindled by his mystic strains? St. Francis is among the oldest vernacular poets of Italy.* His poetry, indeed, is but a long passionate ejaculation of love to the Redeemer in rude metre; it has not even the order and completeness of a hymn: it is a sort of plaintive variation on one simple melody—an echo of the same tender words, multiplied again and again, it might be fancied, by the voices in the cloister walls. But his ordinary speech is more poetical than his poetry. In his peculiar language he addresses all animate, even inanimate, creatures as his brothers; not merely the birds and beasts; he had an especial fondness for lambs and larks, as the images of the Lamb of God and of the cherubim in heaven.[p] I know not if it be among the Conformities, but the only malediction I find him to have uttered was against a fierce swine which had killed a young lamb. Of his intercourse with these mute animals, we are told many pretty particularities, some of them miraculous. But his poetic impersonation went beyond this. When the surgeon was about to cauterise him, he said, "Fire, my brother, be thou discreet and gentle to me."[q] In one of his Italian hymns he speaks of his brother the sun, his sister the moon, his brother the wind, his sister the water.[r] No wonder that in this almost perpetual extatic state, unearthly music played

---

* M. de Montalembert is eloquent, as usual, on his poetry.—Preface to "La Vie d'Elizabeth d'Hongrie."

[p] Bonaventura, c. viii.

[q] The words were, "Fratel fuoco, da Dio creato più bello, più attivo, e più giovevole d'ogni altro elemento, noi te mostra or nel cimento discret e mite."—Vita (Faligno), p. 15.

[r] "Laudato sia el Dio, mio Signore con tute le Crenture; specialmente Messer lo frate Sole. . . . Laudato sia il mio Signore per suor Luna, per frate vento, per suor acqua."

around him, unearthly light shone round his path. When he died, he said, with exquisite simplicity, "Welcome, sister Death."[a] St. Francis himself, no doubt, was but unconsciously presumptuous, when he acted as under divine inspiration, even when he laid the ground-work for that assimilation of his own life to that of the Saviour, which was wrought up by his disciples, as it were, into a new Gospel, and superseded the old. His was the studious imitation of humility, not the emulous approximation of pride, even of pride disguised from himself; such profaneness entered not into his thought. His life might seem a religious trance. The mysticism so absolutely absorbed him as to make him unconscious, as it were, of the presence of his body. Incessantly active as was his life, it was a kind of paroxysmal activity, constantly collapsing into what might seem a kind of suspended animation of the corporeal functions.[b] It was even said that he underwent a kind of visible and glorious transfiguration.[c] But with what wonderful force must all this have worked upon the world, the popular world around him! About three years before his death, with the permission of the Pope, he celebrated the Nativity of the Lord in a new way. A manger was prepared, the whole scene of the miraculous birth represented. The mass was interpolated before the prayers. St.

---

[a] "Ben venga la sorella morte."

[b] "E tanto in lei (in Gesu) sovente profondasi, tanto s' immerge, s' abissa, e concentra, che assorto non vide, non ascolta, non sente, e se opera carnalmente, nol conosca, non sel rammenta." This state is thus illustrated: he was riding on an ass; he was almost torn in pieces by devout men and women shouting around him; he was utterly unconscious, like a dead man.—From a modern Vita di S. Francesco. Foligno, 1824.

[c] "Ad conspectum sublimis Seraph et humilis Crucifixi, fuit in viva formæ effigiem, vi quâdam deiformi et ignea transformatus; quemadmodum testati sunt, tactis sacrosanctis jurantes, qui palpaverunt, osculati sunt, et viderunt."—S. Bonaventura, in Vit. Minor. L.

Francis preached on the Nativity. The angelic choirs were heard; a wondering disciple declared that he saw a beautiful child reposing in the manger.

The order of St. Francis had, and of necessity, its Tertiaries, like that of St. Dominic.[a] At his preaching, and that of his disciples, such multitudes would have crowded into the Order as to become dangerous and unmanageable. The whole population of one town, Canari in Umbria, offered themselves as disciples. The Tertiaries were called the Brethren of Penitence; they were to retain their social position in the world: but, first enjoined to discharge all their debts, and to make restitution of all unfair gains. They were then admitted to make a vow to keep the commandments of God, and to give satisfaction for any breach of which they might have been guilty. They could not leave the order, except to embrace a religious life. Women were not admitted without the consent of their husbands. The form and colour of their dress were prescribed, silk rigidly prohibited. They were to keep aloof from all public spectacles, dances, especially the theatre; to give nothing to actors, jugglers, or such profane persons. Their fasts were severe, but tempered with some lenity; their attendance at church constant. They were not to bear arms except in the cause of the Church of Rome, the Christian faith, or their country, and that at the licence of their ministers. On entering the Order, they were immediately to make their wills to prevent future litigation; they were to abstain from unnecessary oaths; they were to submit to penance, when imposed by their ministers.

But St. Francis had not yet attained his height even

---

[a] Chapter of Tertiaries, A.D. 1222; Chroniques, L. ii. c. xxxii.

of worldly fame; he was yet to receive the last marks of his similitude to the Redeemer, to bear on his body actually and really the five wounds of the Redeemer.

A.D. 1224.

That which was so gravely believed must be gravely related. In the solitude of Monte Alverno (a mountain which had been bestowed on the Order by a rich and pious votary, and where a magnificent church afterwards arose) Francis had retired to hold a solemn fast in honour of the Archangel Michael. He had again consulted the holy oracle. Thrice the Scriptures had been opened; thrice they opened on the Passion of the Lord. This was interpreted, that even in this life Francis was to be brought into some mysterious conformity with the death of the Saviour. One morning, while he was praying in an access of the most passionate devotion, he saw in a vision, or, as he supposed, in real being, a seraph with six wings. Amidst these wings appeared the likeness of the Crucified. Two wings arched over his head, two were stretched for flight, two veiled the body. As the apparition disappeared, it left upon his mind an indescribable mixture of delight and awe. On his body instantaneously appeared marks of the crucifixion, like those which he had beheld. Two black excrescences, in the form of nails, with the heads on one side, the points bent back on the other, had grown out of his hands and feet. There was a wound on his side, which frequently flowed with blood, and stained his garment. Francis endeavoured, in his extreme humility, notwithstanding the remonstrances of his disciples, to conceal this wonderful sight; but the wounds were seen, it is declared, at one time by fifty brethren. Countless miracles were ascribed to their power. The wound on his side Francis hid with peculiar care. But it was seen during his life, as it is asserted; the pious curiosity of his disciples pierced through every concealment. Pope Alexander IV. publicly declared that his own eyes had beheld the stigmata on the body of St. Francis. Two years after St. Francis died. He determined literally to realise the words of the Scripture, to leave the world naked as he entered it. His disciples might then, and did then, it is said, actually satisfy themselves as to these signs: to complete the parallel an incredulous Thomas was found to investigate the fact with suspicious scrutiny. It became an article of the Franciscan creed; though the now rival Order, the Dominicans, hinted rationalistic doubts, they were authoritatively rebuked. It became almost the creed of Christendom.[y]

Oct. 4, 1298

Up to a certain period this studious conformity of the life of St. Francis with that of Christ, heightened, adorned, expanded, till it received its perfect form in the work of Bartholomew of Pisa, was promulgated by the emulous zeal of a host of disciples throughout the world. Those whose more reverential piety might take offence were few and silent; the declaration of Pope Alexander, the ardent protector of the Mendicant Friars, imposed it almost as an article of the Belief. With the Franciscans, and all under the

Character of Franciscanism.

---

[y] The Dominican Jacob de Voragine assigns five causes for the stigmata; they in fact resolve themselves into the first, imagination. His illustrations, however, are chiefly from pregnant women, whose children resemble something which had violently impressed the mother's mind. He does not deny the fact. "Summus ergo Franciscus, in visione sibi factâ imaginabatur Seraphim Crucifixum, et tam fortis imaginatione artifit, quod vulnera passionis in carne suâ impressit."—Sermo lii. de S. Francisco. Compare Gieseler, ii. 2, 349. Nicolas IV., too, asserted the stigmata of St. Francis (he was himself a Franciscan); he silenced a Dominican, who dared to assert that in Peter Martyr (Peter was a Dominican) were signa Dei vivi, in St. Francis only Dei mortui.—Raynald, A.D. 1291.

dominion of the Franciscans, the lower orders throughout Christendom, there was thus almost a second Gospel, a second Redeemer, who could not but throw back the one Saviour into more awful obscurity. The worship of St. Francis in prayer, in picture, vied with that of Christ: if it led, perhaps, a few up to Christ, it kept the multitude fixed upon itself. But as soon as indignant religion dared lift up its protest (after several centuries!) it did so; and, as might be expected, revenged its long compulsory silence by the bitterest satire and the rudest burlesque.[a]

Franciscanism was the democracy of Christianity; but with St. Francis it was an humble, meek, quiescent democracy. In his own short fragmentary writings he ever enforces the most submissive obedience to the clergy;[b] those, at least, who lived according to the rule of the Roman Church. This rule would no doubt except the simoniac and the married clergy; but the whole character of his teaching was the farthest removed from that of a spiritual demagogue. His was a pacific passive mysticism, which consoled the poor for the inequalities of this life by the hopes of heaven. But ere long his more vehement disciple, Antony of Padua, sounded a dif-

---

[a] See the Alcoran des Cordeliers. Yet this book could hardly transcend the grave blasphemies of the Liber Conformitatum, *e.g.*, Christ was transfigured once, S. Francis twenty times; Christ changed water into wine once, S. Francis three times; Christ endured his wounds a short time, S. Francis two years; and so with all the Gospel miracles.

[b] In his Testament he writes: "Postea dedit mihi Dominus, et dat tantam fidem in sacerdotibus, qui vivunt secundum Ordinem Sanctæ Romanæ ecclesiæ propter ordinem ipsorum, quod si facerent mihi persecutionem volo recurrere ad ipsos."— Op. S. Francisc. p. 20. "Il disoit que s'il rencontroit un Sainct qui fust descendu du ciel en terre et un Prestre, qu'il baiseroit premièrement la main au Prestre, puis il feroit la reverence au Sainct, recevant de celui-là le corps de nostre Seigneur Jesus Christ, pourquoi il méritoit plus d'honneur."— Chroniques, L. c. lxxiv.

ferent note: he scrupled not to denounce the worldly
clergy. Antony of Padua was a Portuguese, born at
Lisbon. He showed early a strong religious temperament. The reliques of the five Franciscan martyrs,
sent over from Morocco, had kindled the most ardent
enthusiasm. The young Fernand (such was his bap-
tismal name) joined himself to some Franciscan friars,
utterly illiterate, but of burning zeal, and under their
guidance set forth deliberately to win the crown of martyrdom among the Moors. He was cast by a storm on
the coast of Sicily. He found his way to Romagna,
united himself to the Franciscans, retired into a hermitage, studied deeply, and at length was authorised by
the General of the Order to go forth and preach. For
many years his eloquence excited that rapture of faith
which during these times is almost periodically breaking
forth, especially in the north of Italy. Every class, both
sexes, all ages were equally entranced. Old enmities
were reconciled, old debts paid, forgotten wrong atoned
for; prostitutes forsook their sins, robbers forswore their
calling; such is said tô have been the magic of his words
that infants ceased to cry. His voice was clear and
piercing like a trumpet; his Italian purer than that of
most natives. At Rimini, at Milan, in other cities, he
held disputations against the heretics, who yielded to
his irresistible arguments. But the triumph of his
courage and of his eloquence was his daring to stand
before Eccelin of Verona to rebuke him for his bloody
atrocities. Eccelin is said to have bowed in awe before
the intrepid preacher; he threw himself at the feet of
Antony, and promised to amend his life. The clergy
dared not but admire Antony of Padua, whom miracle
began to environ. But they saw not without terror that
the meek Franciscan might soon become a formidable

demagogue, formidable to themselves as to the enemies of the faith,

But what is more extraordinary, already in the time of St. Bonaventura the Franciscans had begun to be faithless to their hard bride, Poverty. Bonaventura himself might have found it difficult to adduce authority for his laborious learning in the rule of his Master. Franciscanism is in both respects more or less repudiating St. Francis. The first General of the Order, Brother Elias (General during the lifetime of the Saint), refused the dignity, because his infirmities compelled him to violate one of its rules, to ride on horseback. He was compelled to assume the honour, degraded, resumed his office, was again degraded; for Elias manifestly despised, and endeavoured to throw off, and not alone, the very vital principle of the Order, mendicancy; he persecuted the true disciples of St. Francis.[b] At length the successor of St. Francis became a counsellor of Frederick II., the mortal enemy of the Pope, especially of the Franciscan Popes, above all of the first patron of Franciscanism, Gregory IX.

The Rule.
The Rule had required the peremptory renunciation of all worldly goods by every disciple of the Order, and those who received the proselytes were carefully to abstain from mingling in worldly business. Not till he was absolutely destitute did the disciple become a Franciscan. They might receive food, clothes, or other necessaries, on no account money; even if they found it they were to trample it under foot. They might labour for their support, but were to be paid

---

[b] Compare Les Chroniques, part li. c. v. p. 4. "Aussi étoit cause de grand mal, le grand nombre des frères qui lui adhéroient, lesquels comme les partisans le suivoient et l'imitoient, l'incitant à poursuivre les frères qui étoient zélés observateurs de la règle." —Regul., cap. II. p. 23.

in kind. They were to have two tunics, one with a hood, one without, a girdle and breeches. The fatal feud, the controversy on the interpretation of this stern rule of poverty, will find its place hereafter.

St. Francis rejected alike the pomp of ritual and the pride of learning. The Franciscan services were to be conducted with the utmost simplicity of devotion, with no wantonness of music. There was to be only one daily mass. It was not long before the magnificent church of Assisi began to rise; and the Franciscan services, if faithful to the form, began soon by their gorgeousness to mock the spirit of their master.

No Franciscan was to preach without permission of the Provincial of the Order, or if forbidden by the bishop of the diocese; their sermons were to be on the great religious and moral truths of the Gospel, and especially short. He despised and prohibited human learning, even human eloquence displayed for vanity and ostentation.[e] Bonaventura himself in his profoundest writings maintained the mystic fervour of his master; but everywhere the Franciscans are with the Dominicans vieing for the mastery in the universities of Christendom; Duns Scotus the most arid dialectician, and William of Ockham the demagogue of scholasticism, balance the fame of Albert the Great and Thomas of Aquino. A century has not passed before, besides the clergy, the older Orders are heaping invectives on the disciples of St. Francis, not only as disturbers of their religious

---

[e] "Je ne voudrais point de plus grands Docteurs de Théologie, que ceux qui enseignent leur prochain avec les œuvres, la douceur, la pauvreté, et l'humilité." He goes on to rebuke preachers who are filled with vain glory by the concourse of hearers, and the success of their preaching.—Chroniques, li. c. xxiv. I find the Saint goaded to one other malediction,—against a provincial, who encouraged profound study at the University of Bologna.—c. xviii. See above his contempt and aversion for books.

peace, as alienating the affections and reverence of their flocks or their retainers, but as their more successful rivals for the alms of dying penitents, as the more universal legatees of lands, treasures, houses, immunities.

The Benedictine of St. Alban's,[d] Matthew Paris, who at first wrote, or rather adopted language, highly commending the new-born zeal, and yet-admired holiness of the mendicants,[e] in all the bitter jealousy of a rival Order, writes thus:—"It is terrible, it is an awful presage, that in three hundred years, in four hundred years, even in more, the old monastic Orders have not so entirely degenerated as these Fraternities. The friars who have been founded hardly forty years have built, even in the present day in England, residences as lofty as the palaces of our kings. These are they, who enlarging day by day their sumptuous edifices, encircling them with lofty walls, lay up within them incalculable treasures, imprudently transgressing the bounds of poverty, and violating, according

Change in the Order.

---

[d] The first Franciscan foundation in England was at Abingdon.—Malan, p. 204. This statement in Paris is singularly illustrated by the documents in the Monumenta Franciscana. Mr. Brewer, in his remarkable Preface, enlarges on the self-devoting usage of the early Franciscans to fix their domicile in the mean, fœtid, unwholesome suburbs of the cities. This seems to have been peculiarly the case in England. In London their first residence is in "Styubinge Lane," in the parish of St. Nicholas in Macello. But ere long grant after grant is recited of houses, lands, and messuages in the same quarter. Till in the reign of Edward I. rises their Church, 300 feet long, 95 wide, 64 high to the roof; the pillars all marble. To this the Queen contributes 200l. sterling. There is a long list of donors, who glazed their windows. At length rises their Library, which cost 556l. 16s. 8d. Richard Whyttyngton, Mayor, gave of this 400l. Multiply this sum by 15, in modern money it amounts to above 8000l. Mr. Brewer, in his fervent admiration of the saintly rise, closes his eyes on the rapid degeneracy of the Order, and their departure from their first principles.

[e] Wendover, ii. p. 210, sub ann. 1207.

to the prophecy of the German Hildegard, the very fundamental rules of their profession. These are they who impelled by the love of gain, force themselves upon the last hours of the Lords, and of the rich whom they know to be overflowing with wealth; and these, despising all rights, supplanting the ordinary pastors, extort confessions and secret testaments, boasting of themselves and of their Order, and asserting their vast superiority over all others. So that no one of the faithful now believes that he can be saved, unless guided and directed by the Preachers or Friar Minors. Eager to obtain privileges, they serve in the courts of kings and nobles, as counsellors, chamberlains, treasurers, bridesmen, or notaries of marriages; they are the executioners of the Papal extortions. In their preaching they sometimes take the tone of flattery, sometimes of biting censure: they scruple not to reveal confessions, or to bring forward the most rash accusations. They despise the legitimate Orders, those founded by holy fathers, by St. Benedict or St. Augustine, with all their professors. They place their own Order high above all; they look on the Cistercians as rude and simple, half laic or rather peasants; they treat the Black Monks as haughty Epicureans."†

Our history reverts to the close of Innocent III.'s eventful pontificate.

In the full vigour of his manhood died Innocent III. He, of all the Popes, had advanced the most exorbitant pretensions, and those pretensions had been received by an age most disposed to accept them with humble deference. The high and blameless, in some respects wise and gentle character of Innocent, might seem to approach more nearly than

<small>A.D. 1216. Death of Pope Innocent III.</small>

---

† Paris reckons the forty years to his own time, sub ann. 1249.

any one of the whole succession of Roman bishops, to the ideal height of a supreme Pontiff: in him, if ever, might appear to be realised the churchman's highest conception of the Vicar of Christ. Gregory VII. and Boniface VIII., the first and the last of the aggressive Popes, and the aged Gregory IX., had no doubt more rugged warfare to encounter, fiercer and more unscrupulous enemies to subdue. But in all these there was a personal sternness, a contemptuous haughtiness; theirs was a worldly majesty. Hildebrand and Benedetto Gaetani are men in whom secular policy obscures, and throws back, as it were, the spiritual greatness; and though the firmness with which they endure reverses may be more lofty, yet there is a kind of desecration of the unapproachable sanctity of their office in their personal calamities. The pride of Innocent was calmer, more self-possessed; his dignity was less disturbed by degrading collisions with rude adversaries; he died on his unshaken throne, in the plenitude of his seemingly unquestioned power. Yet if we pause and contemplate, as we cannot but pause and contemplate, the issue of this highest, in a certain sense noblest and most religious contest for the Papal ascendancy over the world of man, there is an inevitable conviction of the unreality of that Papal power. With all the grandeur of his views, with all the persevering energy of his measures, throughout Innocent's reign, everywhere we behold failure, everywhere immediate discomfiture, or transitory success which paved the way for future disaster. The higher the throne of the Pope the more manifestly were its foundations undermined, unsound, unenduring.

{Results of his Pontificate.}

Even Rome does not always maintain her peaceful subservience. Her obedience is interrupted, precarious;

that of transient awe, not of deep attachment, or rooted reverence. In Italy, the tutelage of the young Frederick, suspicious, ungenerous, imperious, yet negligent, could not but plant deep in the heart of the young sovereign mistrust, want of veneration, still more of affection for his ecclesiastical guardian. What was there to attach Frederick to the Church? how much to estrange! As King of Sicily he was held under strict tributary control; his step-mother the Church watches every movement with jealous supervision; exacts the most rigid discharge of all the extorted signs of vassalage. It is not as heir of the Empire that he is reluctantly permitted or coldly encouraged to cross the Alps, and to win back, if he can, the crown of his ancestors, but as the enemy of the Pope's enemy. Otho had been so ungrateful, was so dangerous, that against him the Pope would support even a Hohenstaufen. The seeds of evil were sown in Frederick's mind, in Frederick's heart, to spring up with fearful fertility. In the Empire it is impossible not to burthen the memory of Innocent with the miseries of the long civil war. Otho without the aid of the Pope could not have maintained the contest for a year; with all the Pope's aid he had sunk into contempt, almost insignificance; he was about to be abandoned, if not actually abandoned, by the Pope himself. The casual blow of the assassin alone prevented the complete triumph of Philip, already he had extorted his absolution; Innocent was compelled to yield, and could not yield without loss of dignity.[s] The

---

[s] Read the very curious Latin poem published by Leibnitz, R. Brunsw. S. ii. p. 525, on the Disputatio between Rome and Pope Innocent on the destitution of Otho. Rome begins:—

"Tibi soli supplicat orbis,
Et genus humanum, te disperente movetur."

Innocent, after some flattery of the greatness of Rome, urges:—

triumph of Otho leads to as fierce, and more perilous resistance to the Papal power, than could have been expected from the haughtiness of the Hohenstaufen. The Pope has an irresistible enemy in Italy itself. Innocent is compelled to abandon the great object of the Papal policy, the breaking the line of succession in the house of Swabia, and to assist in the elevation of a Swabian Emperor. He must yield to the union of the crown of Sicily with that of Germany; and so bequeath to his successors the obstinate and perilous strife with Frederick II.

In France, Philip Augustus is forced to seem, yet only seem, to submit; the miseries of his unhappy wife are but aggravated by the Papal protection. The death of Agnes of Meran, rather than Innocent's authority, heals the strife. The sons of the proscribed concubine succeed to the throne of France.

In England the Barons refuse to desert John when under the interdict of the Pope; when the Pope becomes the King's ally, resenting the cession of the realm, they withdraw their allegiance. Even in Stephen Langton, who owes his promotion to the Pope, the Englishman prevails over the ecclesiastic; the Great Charter is extorted from the King when under the express protection of the Holy See, and maintained resolutely against

---

"Quæ vos stimulavit Krypnis?
Ut sic unanimes relevare velitis Othonem,
Volitis ut Ecclesia Romanæ prædo resurgat,
Hostis Catholicæ fidei, dominando superbus
Non solum factus, sed et ipsa superbia."

Then follow several pages of dispute, kindling into fierce altercation. The Pope winds up:—

"Si tu
Non moverunt super hoc assignatæ rationes
Per quas Ottoni Fredericus substituatur,
Sic volo, sic fiat, sit pro ratione voluntas."

Rome bursts into invective:—

"Qualis
Servorum Christi Servus!
. . . .
Non es apostolicus, sed apostaticus; neque Pastor
Immo lupus, voraciter ipso grege."

Rome appeals to a General Council. Rome, supposing the Council present, addresses it. The Council replies:—

"Roma parens, non est nostrum deponere Papam."

But the Council declares its right to depose Frederick and to restore Otho.

the Papal sentence of abrogation; and in the Great Charter is laid the first stone of the religious as well as the civil liberties of the land.

Venice, in the Crusade, deludes, defies, baffles the Pope. The Crusaders become her army, besiege, fight, conquer for her interests. In vain the Pope protests, threatens, anathematises: Venice calmly proceeds in the subjugation of Zara. To the astonishment, the indignation of the Pope, the Crusaders' banners wave not over Jerusalem, but over Constantinople. But for her own wisdom, Venice might have given an Emperor to the capital of the East, she secures the patriarchate almost in defiance of the Pope; only when she has entirely gained her ends does she submit to the petty and unregarded vengeance of the Pope.

Even in the Albigensian war the success was indeed complete; heresy was crushed, but by means of which Innocent disapproved in his heart. He had let loose a terrible force, which he could neither arrest nor control. The Pope can do everything but show mercy or moderation. He could not shake off, the Papacy has never shaken off, the burthen of its complicity in the remorseless carnage perpetrated by the Crusaders in Languedoc, in the crimes and cruelties of Simon de Montfort. A dark and ineffaceable stain of fraud and dissimulation too has gathered around the fame of Innocent himself.[h] Heresy was quenched in blood; but the earth sooner or later gives out the terrible cry of blood for vengeance against murderers and oppressors.

[h] It is remarkable that Innocent III. was never canonised. There were popular rumours that the soul of Innocent, escaping from the fires of purgatory, appeared on earth, scourged by pursuing devils, taking refuge at the foot of the cross, and imploring the prayers of the faithful.—Chronic. Erfurt. p. 249. Thom. Cantipra., Vit. S. Luitgardæ, ap. Surium, Jan. 10.

The great religious event of this Pontificate, the foundation of the Mendicant Orders, that which perhaps perpetuated, or at least immeasurably strengthened, the Papal power for two centuries was extorted from the reluctant Pope. Both St. Dominic and St. Francis were coldly received, almost contemptuously repelled. It was not till either his own more mature deliberation, or wiser counsel which took the form of divine admonition, prevented this fatal error, and prophetically revealed the secret of their strength and of their irresistible influence throughout Christendom, that Innocent awoke to wisdom. He then bequeathed these two great standing armies to the Papacy; armies maintained without cost, sworn, more than sworn, bound by the unbroken chains of their own zeal and devotion to unquestioning, unhesitating service throughout Christendom, speaking all languages. They were colonies of religious militia, natives of every land, yet under foreign control and guidance. Their whole power, importance, perhaps possessions, rested on their fidelity to the See of Rome, that fidelity guaranteed by the charter of their existence. Well might they appear so great as they are seen by the eye of Dante, like the Cherubin and Seraphin in Paradise.[1]

---

[1] Paradiso, xi. 34, &c.

BOOK X.

CONTEMPORARY CHRONOLOGY.

POPES.	EMPERORS OF GERMANY.	KINGS OF FRANCE.	KING OF ENGLAND.
A.D. A.D.	A.D. A.D. 1215 Frederick II. 1250	A.D. A.D.	A.D. A.D.
1216 Honorius III. 1227			1216 Henry III. 1272
		Philip Augustus 1223 1223 Louis VIII. 1226	
		1226 Louis IX. (Saint) 1270	ARCHBISHOPS OF CANTERBURY.
1227 Gregory IX. 1241			Stephen Langton 1228
1241 Cœlestine IV. 1241			1229 Richard Wethershed 1234
1243 Innocent IV. 1254	1246 Henry Raspe (anti-emperor) 1949		1234 Edmund Rich 1944
1254 Alexander IV. 1261	1250 William of Holland 1256		1944 Boniface of Savoy 1270
	1257 Vacant. Richard of Cornwall (?) Alfonso of Castile (?)		
	ARCHBISHOPS OF MENTZ.		
	Conrad of Wittelsbach 1230		
	1230 Siegfried I. of Epstein 1249		
	1249 Siegfried II. of Epstein 1251		
	1251 Christian II. 1259		
	1259 Gerhard I.		

CONTEMPORARY CHRONOLOGY.

KINGS OF SCOTLAND.	KINGS OF SPAIN.	KINGS OF NAPLES.	EMPERORS OF THE EAST.
A.D. A.D.	A.D. A.D.	A.D. A.D.	A.D. A.D.
	Castile.		*Latin.*
1214 Alexander II. 1249	1217 Alfonso X. 1252		1217 Peter de Courtenay 1220
	1252 Ferdinand III. 1282		1220 Robert 1228
	1252 Alfonso XI., the Wise 1278		1228 Baldwin II. 1261
	Arragon.	Frederick II. 1250	*Greek.*
			Theodore Lascaris 1222
	1213 James.		
1249 Alexander III. 1285		1250 Conrad 1254	1222 John Ducas 1255
	KINGS OF PORTUGAL.	1254 Manfred 1266	1255 Theodorus 1259
			1259 John IV.
	A.D. A.D.		1260 Michael Palæologus
	1212 Alfonso the Fat 1223		
	1223 Sancho II. 1248	1266 Conrad II.	1262 Reunion.
	1248 Alfonso III. 1279	Charles of Anjou.	

BOOK X.

CHAPTER I.

Honorius III. Frederick II.

THE Pontificate of Honorius III. is a kind of oasis of
<small>Honorius III. July 18, 1216. Consecrated July 24.</small> repose, between the more eventful rule of Innocent III. and that of Gregory IX. Honorius
was a Roman of the noble house of Savelli,
Cardinal of St. John and St. Paul. The Papacy having
attained its consummate height under Innocent III.,
might appear resting upon its arms, and gathering up
its might for its last internecine conflict, under Gregory
IX. and Innocent IV. with the most powerful, the ablest,
and when driven to desperation, most reckless antagonist, who had as yet come into collision with the
<small>A.D. 1216 to 1227.</small> spiritual supremacy. During nearly eleven
years the combatants seem girding themselves
for the contest. At first mutual respect or common
interests maintain even more than the outward appearance of amity; then arise jealousy, estrangement,
doubtful peace, but not declared war. On one side
neither the power nor the ambition of the Emperor
Frederick II. are mature: his more modest views of
aggrandisement gradually expand; his own character
is developing itself into that of premature enlightenment and lingering superstition; of chivalrous adventure and courtly elegance, of stern cruelty and generous

liberality, of restless and all-stirring, all-embracing activity, which keeps Germany, Italy, even the East, in one uninterrupted war with his implacable enemies the Popes, and with the Lombard Republics, while he is constantly betraying his natural disposition to bask away an easy and luxurious life on the shores of his beloved Sicily. All this is yet in its dawn, in its yet unfulfilled promise, in its menace. Frederick has won the Empire; he has united, though he had agreed to make over Sicily to his son, the Imperial crown to that of Sicily. Even if rumours are already abroad of his dangerous freedom of opinion, this may pass for youthful levity, he is still the spiritual subject of the Pope.

Honorius III. stands between Innocent III. and Gregory IX., not as a Pontiff of superior wisdom and more true Christian dignity, adopting a gentler and more conciliating policy from the sense of its more perfect compatibility with his office of Vicar of Christ, but rather from natural gentleness of character bordering on timidity. He has neither energy of mind to take the loftier line, nor to resist the high churchmen, who are urging him towards it; his was a temporising policy, which could only avert for a time the inevitable conflict.

<small>Mildness of Honorius.</small>

And yet a Pope who could assume as his maxim to act with gentleness rather than by compulsion, by influence rather than anathema, nevertheless, to make no surrender of the overweening pretensions of his function; must have had a mind of force and vigour of its own, not unworthy of admiration: a moderate Pope is so rare in these times, that he may demand some homage for his moderation. His age and infirmities may have tended to this less enterprising or turbulent

administration.* Honorius accepted the tradition of all
the rights and duties asserted by, and generally ascribed
to the successor of St. Peter, as part of his high office.
The Holy War was now become so established an article
in the Christian creed, that no Pope, however beyond
his age, could have ventured even to be remiss in urging
this solemn obligation on all true Christians. No cardinal not in heart a Crusader would have been raised to
the Papal See. The assurance of the final triumph of
the Christian arms became a point of honour, more than
that, an essential part of Christian piety; to deny it
was an impeachment on the valour of true Christians, a
want of sufficient reliance on God himself. Christ
could not, however he might try the patience of the
Christian, eventually abandon to the infidel his holy
sepulchre. All admonitions of disaster and defeat were
but the just chastisements of the sins of the crusaders;
the triumph, however postponed, was certain, as certain
as that Christ was the Son of God, Mohammed a false
prophet.

Honorius was as earnest, as zealous in the good cause,
as had been his more inflexible predecessor; this was
Honorius the primary object of his ten years' Pontificate;
urges the this, which however it had to encounter the
Crusade. coldness, the torpor, the worn-out sympathies of Christendom, clashed with no jealous or hostile feeling. However severe the rebuke, it was rebuke of which Christendom acknowledged the justice; all men honoured the
Pope for his zeal in sounding the trumpet with the
fiercest energy, even though they did not answer to the
call. The more the enthusiasm of Christendom cooled

---

* "Cum esset corpore infirmus, et ultra modum debilis."—Raynald. sub
ann.

down into indifference, the more ardent and pressing the exhortation of the Popes. The first act of Honorius was a circular address to Christendom, full of reproof, expostulation, entreaty to contribute either in person or in money to the new campaign. The only King who obeyed the summons was Andrew of Hungary. Some German princes and prelates met the Hungarian at Spalatro, the Dukes of Austria and Meran, the Archbishop of Saltzburg, the Bishops of Bamberg, Zeitz, Munster, and Utrecht. But notwithstanding the interdict of the Patriarch of Jerusalem, Andrew returned in the next year, though not without some fame for valour and conduct, on the plea of enfeebled health, and of important affairs of Hungary.[b] His trophies were reliques, the heads of St. Stephen and St. Margaret, the hands of St. Bartholomew and St. Thomas, a slip of the rod of Aaron, one of the water-pots of the Marriage of Cana. The expedition from the Holy Land against Damietta, the flight of Sultan Kameel from that city, its occupation by the Christians, raised the most exulting hopes. The proposal of the Sultan to yield up Jerusalem was rejected with scorn. But the fatal reverses, which showed the danger of accepting a Legate (the Cardinal Pelagius) as a general, too soon threw men's minds back into their former prostration. But even before this discomfiture, King Frederick II. had centred on himself the thoughts and hopes of all who were still Crusaders in their hearts, as the one monarch in Christendom who could restore the fallen fortunes of the Cross in the East. In his first access of youthful pride, as having at eighteen

---

[b] This was the Crusade joined by S. Francis.—See Ch. X.

years of age won, by his own gallant daring, the Transalpine throne of his ancestors; and in his grateful devotion to the Pope, who, in hatred to Otho, had maintained his cause, Frederick II. had taken the Cross. Nor for some years does there appear any reason to mistrust, if not his religious, at least his adventurous and ambitious ardour. But till the death of his rival Otho, he could command no powerful force which would follow him to the Holy Land, nor could he leave his yet unsettled realm. The princes and churchmen, his partisans, were to be rewarded and so confirmed in their loyalty; the doubtful and wavering to be won; the refractory or resistant to be reduced to allegiance.

The death of Otho, in the castle of Wurtzburg, near Goslar, had been a signal example of the power of religious awe. The battle of Bouvines and the desertion of his friends had broken his proud spirit; his health failed, violent remedies brought him to the brink of the grave. Hell yawned before the outcast from the Church; nothing less than a public expiation of his sins could soothe his shuddering conscience. No bishop would approach the excommunicated, the fallen Sovereign; the Prior of Halberstadt, on his solemn oath upon the reliques of St. Simon and St. Jude brought for that purpose from Brunswick, that if he lived he would give full satisfaction to the Church, obtained him absolution and the Last Sacrament. The next day, the last of his life, in the presence of the Empress and his family, the nobles, and the Abbot of Hildesheim, he knelt almost naked on a carpet, made the fullest confession of his sins; he showed a cross, which he had received at Rome, as a pledge that he would embark on a Crusade: "the devil had still thwarted his holy vow." The cross was restored to him. He then crouched down, exposed his naked shoulders, and entreated all present to inflict the merited chastisement. All hands were armed with rods; the very scullions assisted in the pious work of flagellation, or at least of humiliation. In the pauses of the Miserere the Emperor's voice was heard: "Strike harder, spare not the hardened sinner." So died the rival of Philip of Swabia, the foe of Innocent III., in the forty-third year of his age.[a]

With the death of Otho rose new schemes of aggrandisement before the eyes of Frederick II.; he must secure the Imperial crown for himself; for his son Henry the succession to the German kingdom. The Imperial crown must be obtained from the hands of the Pope; the election of his son at least be ratified by that power. A friendly correspondence began with Honorius III. The price set on the coronation of Frederick as Emperor was his undertaking a Crusade to the Holy Land. At the High Diet at Fulda, Frederick himself (so he writes to the Pope) had already summoned the princes of Germany to his great design: at the Diet proclaimed to be held at Magdeburg, he urged the Pope to excommunicate all who should not appear in arms on the next St. John's day. His chief counsellor seemed to be Herman of Salza, the Master of the Teutonic Order, as deeply devoted to the service of the Holy Land, as the Templars and Knights of St. John. On that Order he heaped privileges and possessions. But already in Rome, no doubt among the old austere anti-German party, were dark suspicions, solemn admonitions, secret warnings to the mild Pope, that no son of the house of Swabia could be

Promises to lead the Crusade.

Jan. 12, 1219.

---

[a] Otho died 19th May, 1218.—See Narratio de Morte Ottonis IV. apud Martene et Durand Thes. Hist. Anecdot. iii. p. 1373. "Præcepit coquinariis ut in collum suum conculcarent."— Albert. Stadens. Chron. p. 204.

otherwise than an enemy to the Church: the Imperial crown and the kingdom of Naples could not be in the possession of one Sovereign without endangering the independence of the Papacy. Frederick repelled these accusations of hostility to the Church with passionate vehemence. "I well know that those who dare to rise up against the Church of Rome have drunk of the cup of Babylon; and hope that during my whole life I shall never be justly charged with ingratitude to my Holy Mother. I design not, against my own declaration, to obtain the election of my son Henry to the throne of Germany in order to unite the two kingdoms of Germany and Sicily; but that in my absence (no doubt he implies in the Holy Land), the two realms may be more firmly governed; and that in case of my death, my son may be more certain of inheriting the throne of his fathers. That son remains under subjection to the Roman See, which, having protected me, so ought to protect him in his undoubted rights."[4] He then condescends to exculpate himself from all the special charges brought against him by Rome.

May 16, 1219.

The correspondence continued on both sides in terms of amicable courtesy. Each had his object, of which he never lost sight. The Pope would even hazard the aggrandisement of the house of Swabia if he could send forth an overpowering armament to the East. Frederick, secure of the aggrandisement of his house, was fully prepared to head the Crusade. Honorius consented that, in case of the death of Henry the son of Frederick without heir or brother, Frederick should hold both the Empire and the king-

Sept. 8, 1219. Correspondence with the Pope.

---

[4] Regest. Hon., quoted from the Vatican archives by Von Raumer, iii. p. 324.

dom of Naples during his lifetime. Frederick desired
to retain unconditionally the investiture of both kingdoms; but on this point the Pope showed so much
reluctance that Frederick broke off the treaty by letter,
reserving it for a personal interview with the Pope.
"For who could be more obedient to the Church than
he who was nursed at her breast and had rested in her
lap? Who more loyal? Who would be so mindful of
benefits already received, or so prepared to acknowledge
his obligations according to the will and pleasure of his
benefactors?" Such were the smooth nor yet deceptive
words of Frederick.* Frederick had already consented,
even proposed, that the Pope should place all the German Princes who refused to take up the Cross under the
interdict of the Church, and thus, as the Pope reminds
him, had still more inextricably bound himself, who had
already vowed to take up that Cross. Frederick urged
Honorius to write individually to all the princes among
whom there was no ardour for the Crusade, to threaten
them with the ban if at least they did not maintain the
truce of God; he promised, protesting that he acted
without deceit or subtlety, to send forward his forces,
and follow himself as speedily as he might. The Pope
expressed his profound satisfaction at finding his beloved
son so devoted to God and to the Church. He urged
him to delay no longer the holy design: "Youth,
power, fame, your vow, the example of your ancestors,
summon you to fulfil your glorious enterprise. That
which your illustrious grandfather Frederick I. _{March, 1220.}
undertook with all his puissance, it is your
mission to bring to a glorious end. Three times have I

---

* All this I am not surprised to find by such writers as Höfler represented
as the most deliberate hypocrisy. I am sorry to see the same partial view in
Koehmer's Regesta.

consented to delay; I will even prolong the term to the 1st of May. Whose offer is this?—Not mine; but that of Christ! Whose advantage?—That of all his disciples! Whose honour?—That of all Christians! Are you not invited by unspeakable rewards? summoned by miracles? admonished by examples?"

But, in the mean time, Frederick, without waiting the assent of the Pope, had carried his great design, the election of his son Henry to the crown of Germany. His unbounded popularity, his power now that his rival Otho was dead, the fortunate falling in of some great fiefs (especially the vast possessions of Berthold of Zahringen, which enabled him to reward some, to win others of the nobler houses), his affability, his liberality, his justice, gave him command over the suffrages of the temporal princes. By a great measure of wisdom and justice, the charter of the liberties of the German Church, on which some looked with jealousy as investing him with dangerous power, he gained the support of the high ecclesiastics.¹ The King surrendered the unkingly right or usage of seizing to his own use the personalities of bishops on their decease. These effects, if not bequeathed by will, went to the bishop's successor. The King consented to renounce the right of coining money and levying tolls within the territory of the bishops without their consent; and to punish all forgeries of their coin. The vassals and serfs of the prelates were to be received in no imperial city or fief of the Empire to their damage. The advocates, under pretence of protection, were not to injure the estates of the Church: no one was to occupy by force an ecclesiastical fief. He who did not submit

Diet of Frankfort. April, 1220. Election of Henry as his successor. Apr. 26, 1220.

---

¹ Monument. Germ. iv. 235.

within six weeks to the authority of the Church fell under the ban of the Empire, and could neither act as judge, plaintiff, nor witness in any court. The Bishops, on their side, promised to prosecute and to punish all who opposed the will of the King. The King further stipulated that no one might erect castles or fortresses in the lands of a spiritual prince. No officer of the King had jurisdiction, could coin money, or levy tolls in the episcopal cities, except eight days before and eight days after a diet to be held in such city. Only when the King was actually within the city was the jurisdiction of the prince suspended, and only so long as he should remain.

The election of Henry to the throne of Germany without the consent of the Pope struck Rome with dismay. Frederick made haste to allay, if possible, the jealous apprehension. He declared that it was the spontaneous act of the Princes of the Empire during his absence, without his instigation. They had seen, from a quarrel which had broken out between the Archbishop of Mentz and the Landgrave of Thuringia, the absolute necessity of a King to maintain in Frederick's absence the peace of the Empire. He had even delayed his own consent. The act of election would be laid before the Pope with the seals of all who had been concerned in the affair.[f] He declared that this election was by no means designed to perpetuate the union of the kingdom of Naples with the Empire. "Even if the Church had no right over the kingdom of Apulia and Sicily, I would freely grant that kingdom to the Pope rather than attach it to the Empire, should I die without lawful heirs."[h] He significantly adds, that it

---

[f] Regest., quoted by Von Raumer, p. 335. Pertz, Monumenta.
[h] "Prius ipso regno Romanam Ecclesiam quam Imperium deturemus."—Ibid.

is constantly suggested to him that the love professed to him by the Church is not sincere and will not be lasting; but he had constantly refused to entertain such ungrounded and dishonourable suspicions.

The Abbot of Fulda had, in the mean time, been despatched to Rome to demand the coronation of Frederick as Emperor. This embassage had been usually the office of one of the great prelates of Germany, but the mild Honorius took no offence, or disguised it. At the end of August Frederick descended the Alps into the plain of Lombardy. Eight years before, a boy of eighteen, he had crossed those Alps, almost alone, on his desperate adventure of wresting the crown of his fathers from the brow of Otho. He came back, in the prime of life, one of the mightiest kings who had ever occupied that throne; stronger in the attachment of all orders, perhaps, than any former Swabian king; having secured, it might seem, in his house, at least the Empire, if not the Empire with all its rights in Italy; and with the kingdom of Sicily, instead of a hostile power at the command of the Popes, his own, if not in possession, in attachment. During these eight years Italy had been one great feud of city with city, of the cities within themselves. Milan, released from fears of the Emperor, had now begun a quarrel with the Church. The Podestà expelled the Archbishop. Parma and many other cities had followed this example; the bishops were driven out their palaces destroyed, their property plundered: the great ability of the Cardinal Ugolino, afterwards Gregory IX., had restored something like order, but the fire was still smouldering in its ashes.

Frederick passed on without involving himself in these implacable quarrels: it was time to assert the Imperial rights when invested in the Imperial crown. He had crossed the Brenner, and moving by Verona and Mantua, so avoided Milan. The absence of the Archbishop from Milan was a full excuse for his postponing his coronation with the iron crown of Lombardy. He granted rights and privileges to Venice, Genoa, Pisa; overawed or conciliated some cities. On the thirtieth of September he was in Verona, on the fourth of October in Bologna. His Chancellor, Conrad of Metz, had arranged the terms on which he was to receive the Imperial crown. Frederick advanced with a great array of churchmen in his retinue—the Archbishops of Mentz, of Ravenna, the Patriarch of Aquileia, the Bishops of Metz, Passau, Trent, Brixen, Augsburg, Duke Louis of Bavaria, and Henry Count Palatine. Ambassadors appeared from almost all the cities of Italy: from Apulia, from the Counts of Celano, St. Severino, and Aquila; deputies from the city of Naples. The people of Rome were quiet and well pleased. The only untoward incident which disturbed the peace was a quarrel about a dog between the Ambassadors of Florence and Pisa, which led to a bloody war. On the twenty-second of November Frederick and his Queen were crowned in St. Peter's amid universal acclamations. Frederick disputed not the covenanted price to be paid for the Imperial crown. He received the Cross once more from the hand of Cardinal Ugolino. He swore that part of his forces should set forth for the Holy Land in the March of the following year, himself in August. He released his vassals from their fealty in all the territories of the Countess Matilda, and made over the appointment of all the podestàs to the Pope; some who refused to submit were placed by the Chancellor Conrad under the ban of the Empire. He put the Pope in possession of the whole region from Radicofani to

Frederick in Italy. Aug. 17, 1220.

Ceperano, with the March of Ancona and the Duchy o
Spoleto.

His liberality was not limited to these grants. Two
laws concerning the immunities of ecclesiastics and
the suppression of heretics might satisfy the
severest churchman. The first absolutely an
nulled all laws or usages of cities, communities, o
ruling powers which might be or were employed agains
the liberties of the churches or of spiritual persons, o
against the laws of the Church and of the Empire
Outlawry and heavy fines were enacted not only agains
those who enforced, but who counselled or aided in th
anforcement of such usages: the offenders forfeited, i
contumacious for a whole year, all their goods.[1] N
tax or burthen could be set upon ecclesiastics, churches
or spiritual foundations. Whoever arraigned a spiritua
person before a civil tribunal forfeited his right to im
plead; the tribunal which admitted such arraignmen
lost its jurisdiction; the judge who refused justice thre
times to a spiritual person in any matter forfeited hi
judicial authority.

Laws in favour of ecclesiastics.

The law against heretics vied in sternness with tha
of Innocent III., confirmed by Otho IV.[2] Al
Cathari, Paterines, Leonists, Speronists, Ar
noldists, and dissidents of all other descriptions, wer
incapable of holding places of honour, and under ba;
Their goods were confiscated, and not restored to thei
children; "for outrages against the Lord of Heave:
were more heinous than against a temporal lord.
Whoever, suspected of heresy, did not clear himsel
after a year's trial was to be treated as a heretic. Ever

Laws against heretics.

---

[1] Constit. Frederici II. in Corp. Jur. tit. i. Bullar. Roman. l. 63.
[2] This law was renewed and made more severe, 1224. Raynald. sub ann. 123

magistrate on entering upon office must himself take an oath of orthodoxy, and swear to punish all whom the Church might denounce as heretics. If any temporal lord did not rid his lands of heretics, the true believers might take the business into their own hands, and seize the goods of the delinquent, provided that the rights of an innocent lord were not thereby impeached. All who concealed, aided, protected heretics were under ban and interdict; if they did not make satisfaction within two years, under outlawry; they could hold no office, nor inherit, nor enter any plea, nor bear testimony.

Three other laws, based on the eternal principles of morality, accompanied these acts of ecclesiastical legislation, or of temporal legislation in the spirit of the Church. One prohibited the plundering of wrecks, excepting the ships of pirates and infidels. Another protected pilgrims; they were to be received with kindness; if they died, their property was to be restored to their rightful heirs. The third protected the persons and labours of the cultivators of the soil.   <small>Other laws.</small>

The Pope and the Emperor, notwithstanding some trifling differences, parted in perfect amity. "Never," writes Honorius, "did Pope love Emperor as he loved his son Frederick." Each had obtained some great objects; the Pope the peaceable surrender of the Mathildine territories, and the solemn oath that Frederick would speedily set forth on the Crusade. The Emperor retired in peace and joy to the beloved land of his youth. The perilous question of his right to the kingdom of Sicily had been intentionally or happily avoided; he had been recognised by the Pope as Emperor and King of Sicily. There were still brooding   <small>Sept. 8.</small>

causes of mutual suspicion and dissatisfaction. Frederick pursued with vigour his determination of repressing the turbulent nobles of Apulia; the castles of the partisans of Otho were seized; they fled, and, he bitterly complained, were received with more than hospitality in the Papal dominions. He spared not the inimical bishops; they were driven from their sees; some imprisoned. The Pope loudly protested against this audacious violation of the immunities of Churchmen. Frederick refused them entrance into the kingdom; he had rather forfeit his crown than the inalienable right of the sovereign, of which he had been defrauded by Innocent III., of visiting treason on all his subjects.^m

Then in the next year came the fatal news from the East—the capture, the disasters which followed the capture of Damietta. The Pope and the Emperor expressed their common grief; the Pope was bowed with dismay and sorrow;ⁿ the tidings pierced as a sword to the heart of Frederick.^o Frederick had sent forty triremes, under the Bishop of Catania and the Count of Malta; they had arrived too late. But this dire reverse showed that nothing less than an overwhelming force could restore the Christian cause in the East; and in those days of colder religious zeal, even the Emperor and King of Sicily could not at once summon such overwhelming force. Frederick was fully occupied in the Sicilian dominions. During his minority, and during his absence, the powerful Germans, Normans, Italians, even Churchmen, had

A.D. 1221.
Loss of
Damietta.

---

^m "Chè prima si lascierrebbe torre la corona, chè derogar in un punto da questi suoi diritti."—Giannone, l. xvi. c. 1.

ⁿ Letter of Pope Honorius, Nov. 1221.

^o Epist. Honor. apud Raynald. Aug. 10, 1221.

usurped fiefs, castles, cities:[p] he had to resume by force rights unlawfully obtained, to dispossess men whose only title had been open or secret leanings to the Emperor Otho; to punish arbitrary oppression of the people; to destroy strong castles built without licence; to settle ancient feuds and suppress private wars: it needed all his power, his popularity, his firmness, to avert insurrection during these vigorous but necessary measures. Two great assizes held at Capua and Messina showed the confusion in the affairs of both kingdoms. *Dec. 1220 to May, 1221.* But from such nobles he could expect no ready obedience to assemble around his banner for an expedition to the Holy Land. Instead of a great fleet, suddenly raised, as by the wand of an enchanter (this the Pope seemed to expect), and a powerful army, in April in the year 1222 the Pope and the Emperor met at Veroli to deliberate on the Crusade. *Meeting at Veroli.* They agreed to proclaim a great assembly at Verona in the November of that year, at which the Pope and the Emperor were to be present. All princes, prelates, knights, and vassals were to be summoned to unite in one irresistible effort for the relief of the East. The assembly at Verona did not take place; the illness of the Pope, the occupations of the Emperor, were alleged as excuses for the further delay. A second time the Pope and the Emperor met at Ferentino; with them King John of Jerusalem, the Patriarch, the Grand Master of the Knights Templars. *At Ferentino, March, 1223.* Frederick explained the difficulties which had impeded his movements, first in Germany, now in Sicily. To the opposition of his turbulent barons was now added the danger of an insurrection of the Saracens in Sicily.

---

[p] Letter of Frederick to the Pope from Trani, March 3, 1221.

Frederick himself was engaged in a short but obstinate war.[q] Even the King of Jerusalem deprecated the despatch of an insufficient force. Two full years were to be employed, by deliberate agreement, in awakening the dormant zeal of Christendom; but Frederick, now a widower, bound himself, it might seem, in the inextricable fetters of his own personal interest and ambition by engaging to marry Iolante, the beautiful daughter of King John.

Two years passed away; King John of Jerusalem travelled over Western Christendom, to England, France, Germany, to represent in all lands the state of extreme peril and distress to which his kingdom was reduced. Everywhere he met with the most courteous and royal reception; but the days of Peter the Hermit and St. Bernard were gone by. France, England, Germany, Spain, were involved in their own affairs; a few took the Cross, and offered sums of money to no great amount; and this was all which was done by the royal preacher of the Crusade. Tuscany and Lombardy were almost as indifferent to the expostulations of Cardinal Ugolino, who had for some years received full power from the Emperor to awaken, if possible, the sluggish ardour of those provinces. King John and the Patriarch, after visiting Apulia, reported to the Pope the

---

[q] The two following passages show that this was no feigned excuse:— "Imperator in Sicilia de Mirabello triumphavit, et de ipso et suis fecit quod eorum meruerat exigentia commissorum." — Richd. San. Germ. "Dominus Fredericus erat cum magno exercitu super Saracenos Jacis, et cepit Benavith cum filiis suis, et suspendit apud Panormum."—Anon. Sic. Ile afterwards transplanted many of them to Lucera. So far was Frederick a yet from any suspicious dealings with the Saracens. The Parliament a Messina had passed persecuting law against the Jews. A law of the same year protected the churches and the clergy from the burthens laid upon them by the nobles.

absolute impossibility of raising any powerful armament by the time appointed in the treaty of Ferentino.

Honorius was compelled to submit; at San Germano was framed a new agreement, by two Cardinals commissioned by the Pope, which deferred for two years longer (till August, 1227) the final departure of the Crusade.[r] Frederick permitted himself to be bound by stringent articles. In that month of that year he would proceed on the Crusade, and maintain one thousand knights at his own cost for two years: for each knight who was deficient he was to pay the penalty of fifty marks, to be at the disposal of the King, the Patriarch, and the Master of the Knights Templars, for the benefit of the Holy Land. He was to have a fleet of 150 ships to transport 2000 knights, without cost, to Palestine. If so many knights were not ready to embark, the money saved was to be devoted to those pious interests. He was to place in the hands of the same persons 100,000 ounces of gold, at four several periods, to be forfeited for the same uses, if in two years he did not embark on the Crusade. His successors were bound to fulfil these covenants in case of his death. If he failed to perform any one of these covenants; if at the appointed time he did not embark for the Holy Land; if he did not maintain the stipulated number of knights; if he did not pay the stipulated sums of money; he fell at once under the interdict of the Church: if he left unfulfilled any other point, the Church, by his own free admission, had the power to pronounce the interdict.

Personal ambition, as well as religious zeal, or the policy of keeping on good terms with the spiritual power, might seem to mingle with the aspirations of the

marginal note: At San Germano, July, 1225.

[r] Ric. San. Germ., sub ann.

Emperor Frederick for the Holy Land; to his great Empire he would add the dominions of the East. In the November of the same year, after the signature of the treaty in San Germano, he celebrated his marriage with Iolante, daughter of the King of Jerusalem. No sooner had he done this, than he assumed to himself the title of King of Jerusalem: he caused a new great seal to be made, in which he styled himself Emperor, King of Jerusalem and Sicily. John of Jerusalem was King, he asserted, only by right of his wife; on her death, the crown descended to her daughter; as the husband of Iolante he was the lawful sovereign.* King John, by temperament a wrathful man, burst into a paroxysm of fury; high words ensued; he called the Emperor the son of a butcher; he accused him of neglecting his daughter, of diverting those embraces due to his bride to one of her attendants. He retired in anger to Bologna. Frederick had other causes for suspecting the enmity of his father-in-law. He was the brother of Walter of Brienne; and rumours had prevailed that he intended to claim the inheritance of his brother's wife, the daughter of the Norman Tancred. But John filled Italy with dark stories of the dissoluteness of the gallant Frederick: that he abstained altogether from the bed of Iolante is refuted by the fact that two years after she bore him a son, which Frederick acknowledged as his own. They appeared even during that year, at least with all outward signs of perfect harmony.

Marginal note: Frederick marries Iolante. A.D. 1225.

---

* "Desponsatâ puellâ Imperator patrem requisivit; ut regna et regalia jura resignet—stupefactus ille obedit."—Jord. apud Raynald. Yet if we are to believe the Chronicle of Tours, he just at that time threw Iolante into prison, and ravished her cousin, the daughter of Walter of Brienne. Was this one of the tales told by the King of Jerusalem?

Nor was this the only event which crossed the designs of Frederick, if he ever seriously determined to fulfil his vow (where is the evidence, but that of his bitter enemies, that he had not so determined?). Throughout all his dominions, instead of that profound peace and established order which might enable him, at the head of the united knighthood of the Empire and of Italy, to break with irresistible forces upon the East; in Germany the assassination of the wise and good Engelbert, Archbishop of Cologne,[1] to whom Frederick had entrusted the tutelage of his son Henry, and the administration of the Empire, threatened the peace of the realm. In Lombardy, Guelf and Ghibelline warred, intrigued; princes against princes, Bonifazio of Montferrat and the house of Este against the Salinguerra, and that cruel race of which Eccelin di Romano was the head, Venice and Genoa, Genoa and Pisa, Genoa and Milan, Asti and Alexandria, Ravenna and Ferrara, Mantua and Cremona, even Rome and Viterbo, were now involved in fierce hostility, or pausing to take advantage each of the other; and each city had usually a friendly faction within the walls of its rival. Frederick, who held the lofty Swabian notion as to the prerogative of the Emperor, had determined with a high hand to assert the Imperial rights. He hoped, with his Ghibelline allies, to become again the Sovereign of the north of Italy. He was prepared to march at the head of his Southern forces; a Diet had been summoned at Verona. Milan again set herself at the head of a new Lombard League. In Milan the internal strife between the nobles and the people, between the Archbishop and the Podestà, had been allayed

State of Italy.

[1] Godfred. Monach. apud Boehmer Fontes, Nov. 7, 1225.

by the prudent intervention of the Pope, to whom the peace of Milan was of infinite importance, that the republic might put forth her whole strength as head of the Lombard League.* Milan was joined by Bologna, Piacenza, Verona, Brescia, Faenza, Mantua, Vercelli, Lodi, Bergamo, Turin, Alessandria, Vicenza, Padua, Treviso.* The mediation of Honorius averted the threatening hostilities. Yet the Imperialists accuse Honorius as the secret favourer of the League.⁷

With Honorius himself a rupture seemed to be imminent. The Emperor, even before the treaty of San Germano, had done the Pope the service of maintaining him against his hostile subjects, compelling the Capitunata and the Maremma to return to their allegiance, coercing the populace of Rome, who in one of their usual outbursts, had driven the Pontiff from the city. The deep murmurs of a coming storm might be heard by the sagacious ear. Frederick, in his determination to reduce his Apulian kingdom to subjection, had still treated the ecclesiastical fiefs as he did the civil; he retained the temporalities in his possession during vacancies, so that five of the largest bishoprics, Capua, Aversa, Brundusium, Salerno, and Cosensa, were without bishops. Honorius, soon after the treaty of San Germano, wrote to inform the Emperor that for the good of his soul and the souls of his subjects, he had

---

* The annual income of the Archbishop of Milan, according to Giulini, was 80,000 golden florins (Giulini, Memorie, l. xlviii.). This Giulini estimates at, in the 13th century, nearly 10 millions of lire Milanese. Cherrier reckons this sum at more than 7½ millions of francs.—Cherrier, ii. p. 299.

* Compare the Chronicon Placentinum, particularly the strange poem, p. 69.

⁷ "Cujus suggestione multæ civitates contra imperatorem conjuraverunt facientes collegium."—God. Monach. p. 595. Compare Chronicon Placentinum, p. 75.

appointed five learned and worthy Prelates to these
sees, natives of the kingdom of Naples, and who could
not, therefore, but be acceptable to the King. Frederick,
indignant at this compulsory nomination, without, as
was usual, even courteous consultation of the Sovereign,
refused to receive the Bishops, and even repelled the
Legates of the Pope from his court. He summoned, it
might seem in reprisal, the inhabitants of Spoleto to his
banner, to accompany him in his expedition to Lombardy.
The Spoletines averred that, by the late treaty,
which the Emperor was thus wantonly violating, they
owed allegiance only to the Pope.

The correspondence betrayed the bitterness and rising
wrath on both sides. Even Honorius <small>Letter of Honorius.</small>
seemed about to resume the haughty tone of
his predecessors. "If our writing hath filled you with
astonishment, how much more were we amazed by
yours! You boast that you have been more obedient
to us than any of the Kings of your race. Indeed, no
great boast! But if you will compare yourself with
those godly and generous Sovereigns, who have in word
and deed protected the Church, you will not claim superiority;
you will strive to approach more nearly to
those great examples. You charge the Church with
treachery, that while she pretended to be your guardian,
she let loose your enemies on Apulia, and raised Otho
to the throne of your fathers: you venture on these
accusations, who have so repeatedly declared that to
the Church you owe your preservation, your life. Providence
must have urged you to these rash charges that
the care and prudence of the Church may be more
manifest to all men." To the Church, he in- <small>June 6, 1234.</small>
sinuates, Frederick mainly owes the crown of
Germany, which he has no right to call hereditary

in his family. "In all our negotiations with you we have respected your dignity more than our own." "Whatever irregularity there might be in the appointment of the bishops, it was not for the King's arbitrary will to decide; and Frederick had been guilty of far more flagrant encroachments on the rights of bishops and of the lower clergy." Honorius exculpates himself from having received the rebellious subjects of the King in the territories of the See. "You accuse us of laying heavy burdens on you, which we touch not ourselves with the tip of our finger. You forget your voluntary taking up the Cross, our prolongation of the period, our free gifts of the tithes of all ecclesiastical property; our own contributions in money, the activity of our brethren in preaching the Holy Vow. In fine, the hand of the Lord is not weakened in its power to humble the haughty: be not dazzled by your prosperity, so as to throw off the lowliness which you professed in times of trouble. It is the law of true nobility not to be elated by success, as not to be cast down by adversity."

Honorius no doubt felt his strength; the Pope at the head of the Guelfic interest in Lombardy had been formidable to the designs of Frederick. The Emperor, indeed, had assumed a tone of command, which the forces which he could army would hardly maintain. At Borgo St. Domnino he had placed all the contumacious cities under the ban of the Empire; the Papal Legate, the Bishop of Hildesheim, had pronounced the interdict of the Church, as though their turbulent proceedings impeded the Crusade. Both parties submitted to the mediation of Honorius; Frederick condescended to receive the intrusive bishops whom he had repelled: he declared himself ready to accept

July 11, 1224.

the terms most consistent with the honour of God, of the Church, of the Empire, and of the Holy Land. The Pope, whose whole soul was absorbed in the promotion of his one object, the Crusade, pronounced his award, in which he treated the Emperor and his rebellious subjects as hostile powers contending on equal terms. Each party was to suspend hostilities, to restore the prisoners taken, to forswear their animosities. The King annulled the act of the Imperial ban, and all penalties incurred under it; the Lombards stipulated to maintain at their own cost four hundred knights for the service of the Holy Land during two years, and rigidly to enforce all laws against heretics. This haughty arbitration, almost acknowledging the absolute independence of the Republics, was the last act of Honorius III.; he died in the month of March, a few months before the term agreed on in the treaty of San Germano was to expire, and the Emperor, under pain of excommunication, to embark for the Holy Land. The Apostolic tiara devolved on the Cardinal Ugolino, of the noble house of Conti, which had given to the Holy See Innocent III. The more lofty churchmen felt some disappointment that the Papacy was declined by Cardinal Conrad, the Count of Urach, the declared enemy of Frederick. They mistrusted only the feebleness of age in the Cardinal Ugolino. A Pope eighty years old, might seem no fitting antagonist for a Prince like Frederick, as yet hardly in the full maturity of his years. In all other respects the Cardinal Ugolino, in learning, in ability, in activity, in the assertion of the loftiest hierarchical principles, stood high above the whole conclave. Frederick himself, on a former occasion, had borne testimony to the distinguished character

of the Cardinal Ugolino. " He is a man of spotless
reputation, of blameless morals, renowned for piety,
erudition, and eloquence. He shines among the rest
like a brilliant star." The emperor's political astrology had not calculated the baleful influence of that
disastrous planet on his fortunes, his fame, and his
peace.

CHAPTER II.

Honorius III. and England.

THE relations of Honorius III. to the Empire and the Emperor Frederick II. were no doubt of the most profound importance to Christendom; yet those to England must find their place in an English history.* We revert to the commencement of his Papacy. The first care, indeed, of Pope Honorius was for the vassal kingdom of England. The death of King John, three months after that of Innocent III., totally changed the position of the Pontiff. On his accession Honorius had embraced with the utmost ardour the policy of Innocent. King John, the vassal of the Papacy, must be supported against his rebellious barons, and against the invasion of Louis of France, by all the terrors of the Papal power. Louis and all his army, the Barons and all their partisans, were under the most rigorous form of excommunication. But on John's death, the Pope is no longer the haughty and unscrupulous ally and protector of an odious, feeble, and irreligious tyrant; of one whose lusts had wounded

---

* Mr. Wm. Hamilton, when ambassador at Naples, rendered to the country the valuable service of obtaining transcripts of the documents in the Papal archives relating to Great Britain and the See of Rome. These documents, through the active zeal of M. Punizzi, are now deposited in the British Museum. They commence, after one or two unimportant papers, with the first year of Honorius. They are not very accurately copied; many are repetitions; whether they are full and complete no one can know. Many have been already printed in Rymer, in Raynaldus, and elsewhere. Prynne had seen some of the originals, some which do not appear, in the Tower. I cite these documents as MS. B. M.

the high chivalrous honour of many of the noblest families; whose perfidy, backed by the absolving power of the Pope, had broken the most solemn engagements, and revoked the great Charter to which he had submitted at Runnymede; who was ravaging the whole realm with wild foreign hordes, Brabanters, Poitevins, freebooters of all countries, and had driven the nobles of England into an unnatural alliance with Louis of France, and a transference of the throne to a foreign conqueror. The Pope was no longer the steadfast enemy of the liberties of the realm. He assumed the lofty ground of guardian, as liege lord, of the young heir to the throne (Henry III. was but nine years old), the protector of a blameless orphan whom a rebellious baronage and an alien usurper were endeavouring to despoil of his ancestral crown. Honorius throughout speaks of the young Henry as the vassal of the Church of Rome; of himself as the suzerain of England.[b] English loyalty and English independence hardly needed the Papal fulminations to induce them to abandon the cause into which they had plunged in their despair,[c] the cause of a foreign prince, whose accession to the throne of England would have reduced the realm to a province of France. Already their fidelity to Louis had been shaken by rumours, or

---

[b] John he describes as "carissimum in Christo filium nostrum J., Angliæ regem illustrem crucesignatum et vassallum nostrum."—p. 15. The kingdom of England "specialis juris apud, sedis existit."—p. 27. The Bulls of Honorius have been printed in an appendix to the Royal Letters of the time of Henry III., by Mr. Shirley. Rolls Publications, 1862.

[c] Honorius admits that the Barons might have had some cause for their wickedness (malitia) in resisting under John what they called the intolerable yoke of servitude. Now that John is dead, they have no excuse if they do not return to their allegiance. He gives power to the Legates, to the Bishops of Winchester, Worcester, Exeter, the Archbishops of Dublin and Bordeaux (the Primate was still in Rome), to absolve the Barons from their oaths to Prince Louis.

more than rumours, that the ambitious and unscrupulous Louis intended, so soon as he had obtained the crown, to rid himself by banishment and by disinheritance of his dangerous partisans; to expel the barons from the realm.⁴ The desertion of the nobles, the decisive battle of Lincoln, seated Henry III. on the throne of the Plantagenets. The Pope had only to reward with his praises, immunities, grants, and privileges the few nobles and prelates faithful to the cause of John and of his son, W. Mareschal Earl of Pembroke, the Earl of Arundel, Savary de Mauleon, Hubert de Burgh the Justiciary, the Chancellor R. de Marisco, who became Bishop of Durham.⁵ He had tardily, sometimes ungraciously, to relieve from the terrible penalties of excommunication the partisans of Louis;⁶ to persuade or to force the King of France to withdraw all support from the cause of his son, who still continued either in open hostility or in secret aggression on the continental dominions of Henry III.; and to maintain his lofty position as Liege Lord and Protector of the King and of the realm of England. .

The Legate Gualo, the Cardinal of St. Marcellus, had conducted this signal revolution with consummate address

---

⁴ Shakespeare has given this plot, with its groundwork in the confession of the Count of Melun.—King John, Act v. Sc. 4.

⁵ There are several letters (MS. B.M.) to these English nobles; one to Robert de Marisco empowered him to hold the chancellorship with the bishopric of Durham, and excused him from 'the fulfilment of his vow to take the cross in the Holy Land, his services being wanted in England. On R. de Marisco compare Collier, i. p. 430.

⁶ There are some curious instances (MS. B. M.) of the terror of the excommunications. One of the subjects of France, in fear of his life from a fall from his horse, implores absolution for having followed his sovereign's son to the English war: the Pope would hardly excuse him from a journey to Rome. The Chancellor of the King of Scotland is excommunicate for obeying his King. So too the Archbishop of Glasgow.

and moderation.ᶠ From the coronation of Henry III. at Gloucester by his hands, the Cardinal took the lead in all public affairs: he was virtual if not acknowledged Protector of the infant King. Before the battle of Lincoln the Legate harangued the royal army, lavished his absolutions, his promises of eternal reward; under the blessing of God, bestowed by him, the army advanced to victory.ʰ In the settlement of the kingdom, in the reconciliation of the nobles, he was mild if lofty, judicious if dictatorial. England might have owed a deep debt of gratitude to the Pope and to the Legate, if Gualo's fame had not been tarnished by his inordinate rapacity.ⁱ To the nobles he was liberal of his free absolution; the clergy must pay the penalty of their rebellion, and pay that penalty in forfeiture, or the redemption of forfeiture by enormous fines to the Pope and to his Legate. Inquisitors were sent through the whole realm to investigate the conduct of the clergy.ᵏ The lower ecclesiastics, even canons, under the slightest suspicion of the rebellion, were dispossessed of their benefices to make room for foreign priests; the only way to elude degradation was by purchasing the favour of the Legate at a vast price. The Bishop of Lincoln

---

ᶠ Letter to the Abbots of Citeaux and Clairvaux (MS. B. M. L. p. 43). They are to use all mild means of persuasion, to threaten stronger measures.
ʰ Wendover, p. 18.
ⁱ Compare the verses of Giles de Corbeil, p. 66, on the avarice of Gualo in France.
ᵏ Wendover, p. 33. The Inquisitors sent some "suspensos ad legatum et ab omni beneficio spoliatos, qui illorum beneficia suis clericis abundanter distribuit atque de damnis aliorum suos omnes divites fecit." Wendover gives the case of the Bishop of Lincoln, whose example was followed by others, who "sumptibus nimis damnosis gratiam sibi reconciliabant legati. Clericorum vero et canonicorum sæcularium ubique haustu tam immoderato loculos evacuavit," &c. See also Math. Westm. ann. 1218, who describes Gualo returning to Rome, "clitellis auro et argento refertis," having disposed ad libitum of the revenues (redditus) of England.

for his restoration to his see paid 1000 marks to the Pope, 100 to the Legate.[m]

Throughout the long reign of Henry III. England was held by successive Popes as a province of the Papal territory. The Legate, like a prætor or proconsul of old, held or affected to hold an undefined supremacy: during the Barons' wars the Pope with a kind of feudal as well as ecclesiastical authority condemned the rebels, not only against their Lord, but against the vassal of the Holy See. England was the great tributary province, in which Papal avarice levied the most enormous sums, and drained the wealth of the country by direct or indirect taxation. There were four distinct sources of Papal revenue from the realm of England.

I. The ancient payment of Peter's Pence;[n] this

---

[m] Pope Honorius was not well informed on the affairs of England. When Henry was counselled to take up arms to reduce the castles held by the ruffian Falk de Breauté in defiance of the King and the peace of the realm, the Primate had supported the King and the nobles in this act of necessary justice and order by ecclesiastical censures. The Pope wrote a furious letter of rebuke to Langton (MS. B. M. ix. Aug. 1224), espousing the cause of Fulk, who had through his wealth influence at Rome. Still later Gregory IX. reproves and revokes certain royal grants to Bishops and Barons, as "in grave prejudicium ecclesiæ Romanæ ad quam Regnum Angliæ pertinere dinoscitur, et enormem læsionem ejusdem regni."— MS. B. M. ad regem, vol. xiv. p. 77.

[n] The account of Cencius, the Pope's chamberlain, of the assessment of Peter's pence in the dioceses of England, has been published before by Dr. Lingard, but may be here inserted from MS. B. M.:—

De Cantuarvensi Ecclesia	vii. libras et xviii. solidos.			
De Roffensi	v.	"	xii.	"
De Londoniensi	xvi.	"	x.	"
De Norwicensi	xxi.	"	x.	"
De Eliensi	v.	"		
De Lincolniensi	xlii.	"		
De Cicestriensi	viii.	"		
De Wintoniensi	xvii.	"	vi.	et viii. denarios.
De Exoniensi	ix.	"	v.	"
De Wigorniensi	v.	"	v.	"
In H refordensi	vi.	"		
De Bathoniensi	vi.	"	v.	"
De Sarisberiensi	xvii.	"		
De Coventriensi	x.	"	v.	"
De Eboracensi	xi.	"	x.	"

subsidy to the Pope, as the ecclesiastical sovereign, acknowledged in Saxon times, and admitted by the Conqueror, was regularly assessed in the different dioceses, and transmitted to Rome. Dignitaries of the Church were usually the treasurers who paid it over to Italian bankers in London, the intermediate agents with Rome.

II. The 1000 marks—700 for England, 300 for Ireland—the sign and acknowledgment of feudal vassalage, stipulated by King John, when he took the oath of submission, and made over the kingdom as a fief. Powerful Popes are constantly heard imperiously, necessitous Popes more humbly, almost with supplication, demanding the payment of this tribute and its arrears (for it seems to have been irregularly levied);° but during the whole reign of Henry III. and later, no question seems to have been raised of the Pope's right.

III. The benefices held by foreigners, chiefly Italians, and payments to foreign churches out of the property of the English church;ᴾ the invasion of the English sees by foreign prelates, with its inevitable consequences (or rather antecedents, for John began the practice of purchasing the support of Rome by enriching her Italian clergy), in crowding the English benefices with strangers, and burdening them with persons who never came near them. These abuses as yet only raised deep and suppressed murmurs, ere long to break out into fierce and obstinate resistance. Pandulph, the Papal Legate, be-

---

° Urban IV., MS. B. M. x. p. 29, Dec. 1261. Clement IV., ibid. 12, June 8, 1266.

ᴾ The convent of Viterbo has a grant of 30 marks from a moiety of the living of Holkham in Norfolk, l. 278; 50 marks from church of Wing-ham to convent of M. Aureo in Anagni, iii. 110. Claims of another convent in Anagni on a benefice in diocese of Winchester, vol. iv. 50. See the grants to John Pier Leone, and others, in Prynne, p. 23. MS. B. M.

came Bishop of Norwich. Pope Honorius writes to
Pandulph not merely authorising but urging him to
provide a benefice or benefices in his diocese of Norwich
for his own (the Bishop's) brother, that brother (a
curious plurality) being Archdeacon of Thessalonica.*
These foreigners were of course more and more odious
to the whole realm: to the laity as draining away their
wealth without discharging any duties; still more to
the clergy as usurping their benefices; though ignorant
of the language, affecting superiority in attainments;
as well as from their uncongenial manners, and, if they
are not belied, unchecked vices. They were blood-
suckers, drawing out the life, or drones fattening on the
spoil of the land. All existing documents show that the
jealousy and animosity of the English did not exag-
gerate the evil.ʳ At length, just at the close of his
Pontificate, even Pope Honorius, by his Legate Otho,
made the bold and open demand that two prebends in
every cathedral and conventual church (one from the
portion of the Bishop or Abbot, one from that of the
Chapter), or the sustentation of one monk, should be
assigned in perpetuity to the Church of Rome. On
this the nobles interfered in the King's name, inhibiting
such alienation. When the subject was brought before
a synod at Westminster by the Archbishop, the pro-

* Pandulph is by mistake made cardinal; he was sub-deacon of the Roman Church. He is called in the documents Master Pandulph. Many letters to and from Pandulph, showing his great power and influence, may be read in the Royal Letters among the Rolls Publications.

ʳ MS. B. M. E. g., grant of a church to a consanguineus of the Pope, one Gervaise, excommunicated for favour-ing the Barons, having been ejected from it, I. p. 233. Transfer from one Italian to another, 235. Grant from Bishop of Durham to Peter Saracen (Civis Romanus) of 40 marks, charged on the See for services done, II. 158. Requiring a canonry of Lincoln for Thebaldus, scriptor noster, 166. Canonry of Chichester for a son of a Roman citizen.

posal was received with derisive laughter at the avarice of the see of Rome. Even the King was prompted to this prudent resolution: "When the rest of Christendom shall have consented to this measure, we will consult with our prelates whether it be right to follow their example." The Council of Bourges, where the Legate Otho urged the same general demand, had eluded it with the same contemptuous disregard. It was even more menacingly suggested that such general oppression from Rome might lead to a general withdrawal of allegiance from Rome.*

A.D. 1226.

Five years after, the people of England seemed determined to take the affair into their own hands. Terrible letters were distributed by unseen means, and by unknown persons, addressed to the bishops and chapters, to the abbots and friars, denouncing the insolence and avarice of these Romans; positively inhibiting any payments to them from the revenues of their churches; threatening those who paid to burn their palaces and barns over their heads, and to wreak the same vengeance on them which would inevitably fall on the Italians.† Cencius, the Pope's collector of Peter's Pence, a Canon of St. Paul's, was suddenly carried off by armed men, with their faces hid under vizors: he returned with his bags well rifled, after five weeks' imprisonment. John of Ferentius, Archdeacon of Norwich, escaped the same fate, and concealed himself in London. Other aggressive measures followed. The barns of the Italian clergy were attacked; the corn sold or distributed to the poor.

---

* Wendover, p. 114, 121, 124. "Quia si omnium esset universalis oppressio, posset timeri ne immineret generalis dissessio, quod Deus avertat."

† Gregory writes to the Archbishop of Canterbury (1234) that the English "ægre non ferant si inter ipsos morantes extranei, honores ibidem et beneficia consequantur, cum apud Deum non est acceptio personarum."—MS. B. M.

It might seem almost a simultaneous rising: though the active assailants were few, the feelings of the whole people were with them.* At one place (Wingham) the sheriff was obliged, as it appeared, to raise an armed force to keep the peace; the officers were shown letters-patent (forged as was said) in the King's name, authorising the acts of the spoiler: they looked on, not caring to examine the letters too closely, in quiet unconcern at the spoliation. The Pope (Gregory IX.) issued an angry Bull,ˣ which not only accused the Bishops of conniving at these enormities, and of making this ungrateful return for the good offices which he had shown to the King; he bitterly complained of the ill usage of his Nuncios and officers. One had been cut to pieces, another left half dead; the Pope's Bulls had been trampled under foot. The Pope demanded instant, ample, merciless punishment of the malefactors, restoration of the damaged property. Robert Twenge, a bold Yorkshire knight, who under a feigned name had been the ringleader, appeared before the King, owned himself to have been the William Wither who had headed the insurgents: he had done all this in righteous vengeance against the Romans, who by a sentence of the Pope, fraudulently obtained, had deprived him of the right of patronage to a benefice. He had rather be unjustly excommunicated than despoiled of his right. He was recommended to go to Rome with testimonials from the King for absolution, and this was all.ʸ The abuse, however, will appear

A.D. 1232

---

* The Pope so far admitted the justice of these complaints as to issue a bull allowing the patrons to present after the death of the Italian incumbents.—MS. B. M. lii. 138. Gregory IX. said that he had less frequently used this power of granting benefices in England.—Wilkin's Concilia, i. 269.

ˣ Apud Rymer, dated Spoleto.

ʸ Wendover, 292.

yet rampant, when we return to the history of the English Church.

IV. The taxation of the clergy (a twentieth, fifteenth, or tenth) as a subsidy for the Holy Land; but a subsidy grudgingly paid, and not devoted with too rigid exclusiveness to its holy purpose. Some portion of this was at times thrown, as it were, as a boon to the King (in general under a vow to undertake a Crusade), but applied by him without rebuke or remonstrance to other purposes. This tax was on the whole property of the Church, of the secular clergy and of the monasteries. Favour was sometimes (not always) shown to the Cistercians, the Præmonstratensians, the Monks of Sempringham—almost always to the Templars and Knights of St. John. Other emoluments arose out of the Crusades; compositions for vows not fulfilled; besides what arose out of bequests, the property of intestate clergy, and other sources. The Popes seem to have had boundless notions of the wealth and weakness of England. England paid, murmured, but laid up deep stores of alienation and aversion from the Roman See.[s]

---

[s] Clement IV. (Viterbo, May 22, 1268) orders his collector to get in all arrears "de censibus, denariis Sancti Petri, et debitis quibuscunque." Of these debts there is a long list. "Aut ex voto seu promisso, decimâ vel vicesimâ, seu redemptionibus votorum tam crucesignatorum quam aliorum, vel depositis vel testamentamentis (sic) aut bonis clericorum decedentium ab intestato seu aliâ quâcunque ratione modo vel causâ eisdem sedi Apostolicæ et terræ sanctæ vel alteri earum a quibuscunque personis debentur." The collectors had power to excommunicate for non-payment. MS. B. M. iii.

CHAPTER III.

Frederick II. and Gregory IX.

THE Empire and the Papacy were now to meet in their last mortal and implacable strife; the two first acts of this tremendous drama, separated by an interval of many years, were to be developed during the Pontificate of a prelate who ascended the throne of St. Peter at the age of eighty. Nor was this strife for any specific point in dispute like the right of investiture, but avowedly for supremacy on one side, which hardly deigned to call itself independence; for independence, on the other, which remotely at least aspired after supremacy. Cæsar would bear no superior, the successor of St. Peter no equal. The contest could not have begun under men more strongly contrasted, or more determinedly oppugnant in character than Gregory IX. and Frederick II. Gregory retained the ambition, the vigour, almost the activity of youth, with the stubborn obstinacy, and something of the irritable petulance of old age. He was still master of all his powerful faculties; his knowledge of affairs, of mankind, of the peculiar interests of almost all the nations in Christendom, acquired by long employment in the most important negotiations both by Innocent III. and by Honorius III.; eloquence which his own age compared to that of Tully; profound erudition in that learning which, in the mediæval churchman, commanded the highest admiration. No one was his superior in the science of the canon law; the Decretals to which he afterwards gave a more full and authoritative form, were at his command, and they were to him as much the law of God as the Gospels themselves or the primary principles of morality. The jealous reverence and attachment of a great lawyer to his science strengthened the lofty pretensions of the churchman.*

Frederick II. with many of the noblest qualities which could captivate the admiration of his own age, in some respects might appear misplaced, and by many centuries prematurely born. Frederick having crowded into his youth adventures, perils, successes, almost unparalleled in history, was now only expanding into the prime of manhood. A parentless orphan he had struggled upward into the actual reigning monarch of his hereditary Sicily; he was even then rising above the yoke of the turbulent magnates of his realm, and the depressing tutelage of the Papal See. He had crossed the Alps a boyish adventurer, and won, so much through his own valour and daring that he might well ascribe to himself his conquest, the kingdom of Germany, the imperial crown; he was in undisputed possession of the Empire, with all its rights in Northern Italy; King of Apulia, Sicily, and Jerusalem. He was beginning to be at once the Magnificent Sovereign, the knight, the poet, the lawgiver, the patron of arts, letters, and science; the Magnificent Sovereign now holding his court in one of the old barbaric and feudal cities of

---

* Epist. Honor., 14th March, 1221. He is described as "Forma decorus et venustus aspectu, perspicuus ingenii et fidelis memoriæ prerogativâ donatus, liberalium artium et utriusque juris peritiâ eminenter instructus, fluvius eloquentiæ Tullianæ, sacræ paginæ diligens observator et doctor, zelator fidei."—Cardin. Arragon. Vit. Greg. IX.

Germany among the proud and turbulent princes of the
Empire, more often on the sunny shores of Naples or
Palermo, in southern and almost Oriental luxury; the
gallant Knight and troubadour Poet not forbidding himself those amorous indulgences which were the reward
of chivalrous valour, and of the "gay science;" the
Lawgiver, whose far-seeing wisdom seemed to anticipate
some of those views of equal justice, of the advantages of
commerce, of the cultivation of the arts of peace, beyond
all the toleration of adverse religions, which even in a
more dutiful son of the Church would doubtless have
seemed godless indifference. Frederick must appear
before us in the course of our history in the full development of all these shades of character; but, besides
all this, Frederick's views of the temporal sovereignty
were as imperious and autocratic as those of the
haughtiest churchman of the spiritual supremacy. The
ban of the Empire ought to be at least equally awful
with that of the Church; disloyalty to the Emperor was
as heinous a sin as infidelity to the head of Christendom;
the independence of the Lombard republics was as a great
and punishable political heresy. Even in Rome itself, as
head of the Roman Empire, Frederick aspired to a
supremacy which was not less unlimited because vague
and undefined, and irreconcileable with that of the
Supreme Pontiff. If ever Emperor might be tempted
by the vision of a vast hereditary monarchy to be perpetuated in his house, the princely house of Hohenstaufen, it was Frederick. He had heirs of his greatness; his eldest son was King of the Romans; from his
loins might yet spring an inexhaustible race of princes:
the failure of his imperial line was his last fear. The
character of the man seemed formed to achieve and
to maintain this vast design; he was at once terrible

and popular, courteous, generous, placable to his foes; yet there was a depth of cruelty in the heart of Frederick towards revolted subjects, which made him look on the atrocities of his allies, Eccelin da Romano, and the Salinguerras, but as legitimate means to quell insolent and stubborn rebellion.

The loftier churchmen, if for a moment they had misgivings on account of his age, hailed the election of Cardinal Ugolino with the utmost satisfaction. The surpassing magnificence of his coronation attested the unanimous applause of the clergy, and even of the people of Rome.[b] Gregory had in secret murmured against the gentler and more yielding policy of Honorius III. Of such weakness he could not accuse himself. The old man at once threw down the gauntlet; on the day of his accession[c] he issued an energetic proclamation to all the sovereigns of Christendom announcing his election to the pontificate, and summoning them to enter on a new Crusade. That addressed to Frederick was more direct, vehement, and imperative, and closed not without some significant hints that he would not long brook the delay with which the Emperor had beguiled his predecessor.[d] The King's disobedience might involve him in difficulties from which the Pope himself, even if he should so will, could hardly extricate him.[e]

Gregory IX.

Gregory's first act.

Frederick, in the height of their subsequent contest,

---

[b] "Tunc lugubres vestes mutavit Ecclesia, et urbis semiruta mœnia pristinum recepere fulgorem."—Cardin. Arragon. in Vit. See description of the inauguration.

[c] 1227, March 18. Raynaldi Annal.

[d] "Alioquin quantumcunque te sincerâ diligamus in Domino charitate, et tibi quantum in Domino possumus deferre velimus, id dissimulare nullâ poterimus ratione."—Epistol. ad Frederic. apud Raynaldi, March 23.

[e] "Nequaquam nos et teipsum in illam necessitatem induces, de quâ forsan te de facili non poterimus, etiamsi voluerimus, expedire."—Ibid.

reproached the Pope as having been, while in the lower
orders of the Church, his familiar friend, but that no
sooner had he reached the summit of his ambition than
he threw off all gratitude, and became his determined
enemy.¹ Yet his congratulations on the accession of
Gregory were expressed in the most courtly tone. The
Bishop of Reggio, and Herman of Salza, the Grand
Master of the Teutonic order, were his ambassadors to
Rome. Gregory, on his side, with impartial severity,
compelled the Lombards to fulfil and ratify the treaty
which had been agreed to through the mediation of
Honorius. Frederick had already transmitted to Rome
the documents which were requisite for the full execution of the stipulations on his part, the general amnesty,
the revocation of the Imperial ban, the release of the
prisoners, the assent of King Henry. The Lombards
were not so ready or so open in their proceedings.
Gregory was constrained to send a strong
summons to the Lombards declaring that he *March 24.*
would no longer be tampered with by their idle and
frivolous excuses: "If in this important affair ye despise,
mock, or elude our commands and those of God, nothing
remains for us but to invoke heaven and earth against
your insolence."² The treaty arrived in Rome the day
after this summons had been despatched, wanting the
seal of the Marquis of Montferrat, and of many of the
cities; but Gregory would not be baffled; the Archbishop of Milan received orders to menace the cities

---

¹ " Iste novus athleta, sinistris auspiciis factus Pontifex Generalis, amicus noster præcipuus dum in minoribus ordinibus constitutus, beneficiorum emulum quibus Imperium Christianum sacrosanctam ditavit Ecclesiam oblitus, statim post assumptum suum fidem cum tempore varians et mores cum dignitate commutans."— Petr. de Vineâ, Epistol. L. xvi.

² Regest. Gregor., quoted by Von Raumer, p. 416.

with ecclesiastical censures, and the treaty came back with all the necessary ratifications. In this Gregory pursued the politic as well as the just course. The Emperor must not have this plausible excuse to elude his embarkation on the Crusade at the appointed day in August. The Lombards themselves were imperatively urged to furnish their proper contingent for the Holy War. Gregory IX. knew Lombardy well, it had been the scene of his own preaching of the Cross; and the sagacious fears of the Church (the stipulations in the treaty of Honorius betrayed this sagacity and these fears) could not but discern that however these proud republics might be heartily Guelfic, cordially on the side of the Church, they were only so from their common jealousy of the Empire. But there was that tacit understanding, or at least unacknowledged sympathy, between civil and religious liberty, which must be watched with vigilant mistrust. It was manifest that the respect for their bishops in all these republics depended entirely on the political conduct of the prelates, not on the sanctity of their office. There was a remissness or reluctance in the suppression of heresy, and in the punishment of heretics, which required constant urgency and rebuke on the part of the Pope: "Ye make a great noise," writes Gregory, "about fines imposed, and sentences of exile against heretics; but ye quietly give them back their fines, and admit them again into your cities. In the mean time ye regard not the immunities of the clergy, neither their exemption from taxation nor their personal freedom; ye even permit enactments injurious to their defence of their liberties, enactments foolish and culpable, even to their banishment by the laity. Take heed, lest a more fearful interdict than that with which you have been punished

GREGORY'S LETTER OF ADMONITION.

(the ban of the Empire) fall upon you, the interdict of the Church."[b]

But the Pope was not content with general exhortations to the Emperor to embark on the Crusade: he assumed the privilege of his holy office and of his venerable age to admonish the young and brilliant Frederick on his life, and on the duties of his imperial dignity. The address was sent from Anagni, to which the Pope had retired from the heats of Rome, by the famous Gualo, one of the austere Order of Friar Preachers instituted by St. Dominic.[i] The letter dwelt in the highest terms on the wonderful mental endowments of Frederick, his reason quickened with the liveliest intelligence, and winged by the brightest imagination. The Pope entreats him not to degrade the qualities which he possesses in common with the angels, nor to sacrifice them to the lower appetites, which he has in common with the beasts and the plants of the earth. The love of sensual things debases the intellect, the pampering of the delicate body corrupts the affections. If knowledge and love, those twin lights, are extinguished; if those eagles which should soar in triumph stoop and entangle themselves with earthly pleasures, how canst thou show to thy followers the way of salvation? "Far be it from thee to hold up this fatal example of thraldom to the sensual life. Your justice should be the pillar of fire, your mercy the cooling cloud to lead God's chosen people into the land of promise." He proceeds to a strange mystic interpretation of the five great ensigns of the imperial power; the

June 8.

Gregory's letter of admonition.

---

[b] Regesta, ibid. p. 417.
[i] The Cardinal Ugolino had been the first to foresee the tremendous power of the new Orders. He had been their firm protector: they were bound to him, especially the Franciscans, not only by profound reverence, but by passionate personal attachment.

inward meaning of all these mysterious symbols, the cross, the lance, the triple crown, the sceptre, and the golden apple: this he would engrave indelibly with an iron pen on the adamantine tablets of the king's heart.[k]

It were great injustice to the character of Gregory to attribute this high-toned, however extravagantly mystic, remonstrance to the unworthy motives of ambition or animosity. The severe old man might, not without grounds, take offence at the luxury, the splendour, the sensuality of Frederick's Sicilian court, the freedom at least, if not licence, of Frederick's life. It was the zeal, perhaps of a monk, but yet the honest and religious zeal. Frederick's predilection for his native kingdom, for the bright cities reflected in the blue Mediterranean, over the dark barbaric towns of Germany, of itself characterises the man. The summer skies, the more polished manners, the more elegant luxuries, the knowledge, the arts, the poetry, the gaiety, the beauty, the romance of the South, were throughout his life more congenial to his mind than the heavier and more chilly climate, the feudal barbarism, the ruder pomp, the coarser habits of his German liegemen. Among the profane sayings attributed to Frederick (who was neither guarded nor discreet in his more mirthful conversation, and as his strife with the Church grew fiercer would not become more reverential), sayings caught up, and no doubt sharpened by his enemies, was that memorable one—that God would never have chosen the barren land of Judæa for his own people if he had seen his beautiful and fertile Sicily. And no doubt that delicious climate and lovely land, so highly appreciated by the gay sovereign, was not without influ-

Court of Frederick.

---

[k] Epistola Gregor. apud Raynaldi. Anagni, June 8

ence on the state, and even the manners of his court, to which other circumstances contributed to give a peculiar and romantic character. It resembled probably (though its full splendour was of a later period) Granada in its glory, more than any other in Europe, though more rich and picturesque from the variety of races, of manners, usages, even dresses, which prevailed within it. Here it was that Southern and Oriental luxury began to impart its mysteries to Christian Europe. The court was open to the mingled population which at that time filled the cities of Southern Italy. If anything of Grecian elegance, art, or luxury survived in the West, it was in the towns of Naples and Sicily. There the Norman chivalry, without having lost their bold and enterprising bearing, had yielded in some degree to the melting influence of the land, had acquired Southern passions, Southern habits. The ruder and more ferocious German soldiery, as many as were spared by the climate, gradually softened, at least in their outward demeanour. The Jews were numerous, enlightened, wealthy. The Mohammedan inhabitants of Sicily were neither the least polished, nor the least welcome at the court of Frederick: they were subsiding into loyal subjects of the liberal Christian King; and Frederick was accused by his enemies, and even then believed by the Asiatic and Egyptian Mussulmen, to have approximated more closely to their manners, even to their creed, than became a Christian Emperor. He spoke their tongue, admired and cultivated their science, caused their philosophy to be translated into the Latin language. In his court their Oriental manners yielded to the less secluded habits of the West. It was one of the grave charges, at a later period, that Saracen women were seen at the court of Palermo, who by their licentiousness corrupted the morals of his Christian subjects. Frederick admitted the truth of the charge, but asserted the pure demeanour and chastity of these Mohammedan ladies: nevertheless, to avoid all future scandal, he consented to dismiss them. This at a time when abhorrence of the Mohammedan was among the first articles of a Christian's creed; when it would have been impious to suppose a Mohammedan man capable of any virtue except of valour, a Mohammedan female of any virtue at all! The impression made by this inclination for the society of miscreant ladies, its inseparable connexion with Mohammedan habits, transpires in the Guelfic character of Frederick by Villani. The Florentine does ample justice to his noble and kingly qualities, to the universality of his genius and knowledge, "but he was dissolute and abandoned to every kind of luxury. After the manner of the Saracens he had many concubines, and was attended by Mamelukes; he gave himself up to sensual enjoyments, and led an epicurean life, taking no thought of the world to come, and this was the principal reason of his enmity to Holy Church and to the hierarchy, as well as his avarice in usurping the possessions and infringing on the jurisdiction of the clergy."[m]

It was in this Southern kingdom that the first rude notes of Italian poetry were heard in the soft Sicilian dialect. Frederick himself, and his Chancellor Peter de Vineâ, were promising pupils in the gay science. Among the treasures of the earliest Italian song are several compositions of the monarch and of his poetic rival. One sonnet indeed of Peter de Vineâ is perhaps equal to anything of the kind before the time when

---

[m] Istorie Fiorentin. vi. c. 1.

Petrarch set the common thoughts of all these amorous Platonists in the perfect crystals of his inimitable language. Of these lays most which survive are amatory, but it is not unlikely that as the kindred troubadours of Provence, the poets did not abstain from satiric touches on the clergy. How far Frederick himself indulged in more than poetic licence, the invectives of his enemies cannot be accepted as authority. It was during his first widowhood that he indulged the height of his passion for the beautiful Bianca Lancia; this mistress bore him two sons, his best beloved Enzio, during so many years of his more splendid career the pride, the delight of his heart, unrivalled for his beauty, the valiant warrior, the consummate general, the cause, by his imprisonment, of the bitterest grief, which in the father's decline bowed down his broken spirit. Enzio was born at the close of the year in which Frederick wedded Iolante of Jerusalem. The fact that Iolante died in childbed giving birth to his son Conrad, is at least evidence that he had not altogether estranged her from his affections. In public she had all the state and splendour of his queen; nor is it known that during her lifetime her peace was embittered by any more cherished rivals.

Still if this brilliant and poetic state of society (even if at this time it was only expanding to its fulness of luxury and splendour) must appear dubious at least to the less severe Christian moralist, how must it have appeared to those who had learned their notions of morals from the rule of St. Benedict rather than the Gospel; the admirers of Francis and of Dominic; men in whom human affections were alike proscribed with sensual enjoyments, and in whose religious language, to themselves at least, pleasure bore the same meaning as sin; men, who had prayed, and fasted, and scourged out of themselves every lingering sympathy of our common nature? How, above all, to one in whom, as in Gregory IX., age had utterly frozen up a heart, already hardened by the austerest discipline of monkhood? It is impossible to conceive a contrast more strong or more irreconcileable than the octogenarian Gregory, in his cloister palace, in his conclave of stern ascetics, with all but severe imprisonment within conventual walls, completely monastic in manners, habits, views, in corporate spirit, in celibacy, in rigid seclusion from the rest of mankind, in the conscientious determination to enslave, if possible, all Christendom to its inviolable unity of faith, and to the least possible latitude of discipline; and the gay, and yet youthful Frederick, with his mingled assemblage of knights and ladies, of Christians, Jews and Mohammedans, of poets and men of science, met, as it were, to enjoy and minister to enjoyment; to cultivate the pure intellect: where, if not the restraints of religion, at least the awful authority of churchmen, was examined with freedom, sometimes ridiculed with sportive wit.

A few months were to put to the test the obedience of Frederick to the See of Rome, perhaps his Christian fidelity. By the treaty of San Germano, the August of the present year had been fixed for his embarkation for the Holy Land. Gregory, it is clear, mistrusted his sincerity; with what justice it is hard to decide. However Frederick might be wanting in fervent religious zeal, he was not in the chivalrous love of enterprise; however he might not abhor the Mohammedans with the true Christian cordiality of his day, he would not decline to meet them in arms as brave and generous foes; however the recovery of the

A.D. 1227.

Saviour's tomb might not influence him with the fierce enthusiasm which had kindled the hearers of Peter the Hermit or St. Bernard, or perhaps that which sent forth his grandsire Barbarossa: yet an Oriental kingdom, which he claimed in the right of his wife, a conquest which would have commanded the grateful admiration of Christendom, was a prize which his ambition would hardly disdain, or rather at which it would grasp with bold eagerness. Frederick was personally brave; but neither was his finer, though active and close-knit frame, suited to hew his way through hosts of unbelievers; he aspired not, and could not hope, to rival the ferocious personal prowess of our Richard Cœur de Lion, or to leave his name as the terror of Arabian mothers. Nor would his faith behold Paradise as the assured close of a battle-field with the Infidels, the remission of sins as the sure reward of a massacre of the believers in Islam. Frederick was not averse to obtain by negotiation (and surely, with the warnings of all former Crusades, especially that of his grandsire Barbarossa, not unwisely), and by taking advantage of the feuds between the Saracen princes, those conquests which some would deem it impious to strive after but by open war. Frederick had already received an embassy from Sultan Malek-al-Kameel of Egypt (of this the Pope could hardly be ignorant). Between the Egyptian and Damascene descendants of the great Saladin there was implacable hostility. Kameel had now recovered Damietta;[a] he had made a treaty with the discomfited

---

[a] In the fierce invectives of their later controversy, the Papal party attributed to the tardiness, even to the treachery of Frederick, the disastrous loss of Damietta. If he had accompanied the first German division of the German Crusaders, the Christians would not have been without a leader; and with his fame and power he might, by the conquest of Egypt, have re-

Crusaders. He hated his rival of Damascus even more bitterly than he did the Christians. His offers to Frederick were the surrender of the kingdom of Jerusalem, on condition of close alliance against the Sultan of Damascus. Frederick had despatched to the East an ambassador of no less rank than the Archbishop of Palermo. The Prelate bore magnificent and acceptable presents, horses, arms, it was said the Emperor's own palfrey.° In the January of the following year the Archbishop had returned to Palermo, with presents, according to the Eastern authority, of twice the value of his own; many rare treasures from India, Arabia, Syria, and Irak. Among these, to the admiration of the Occidentals, was a large elephant.ᵖ To the Pope, the negotiations themselves were unanswerable signs of Frederick's favour to the Infidels, and his perfidy to the cause of the Christians.ᑫ

Yet Frederick seemed earnestly determined to fulfil his vow. Though the treaty with the Lombard cities was hardly concluded, he had made vast preparations. He had levied a large tax from the whole kingdom of Sicily for the maintenance of his forces;ʳ a noble fleet

---

established, and for ever, the Christian dominion in the East. But Frederick certainly could not have gone at that time with a force equal to this great enterprise.

° Ebn Ferah, quoted in Michaud's Bibliographie des Croisades, p. 727.

ᵖ Richd. de S. German. p. 1604. Makrisi apud Reinaud. Hugo Plagon.

ᑫ The letter of Gregory IX. in Matth. Paris. "Quod detestabilius est, cum Soldano et aliis Saracenis nefandas (Fredericus) contrahens pactiones, illis favorem, Christianis odium exhibuit manifestum." — Sub ann. 1226, p. 348. On these rumours of the understanding between the Emperor and Sultan Kameel no doubt Gregory founded his darker charge of Frederick's having compelled the surrender of Damietta, not only by withholding all relief from the Christians when masters of it, but by direct and treacherous intercourse with the Soldan.

ʳ Richard de S. German. p. 1103. Alberic, ad ann. 1227. The monastery of San Germano was assessed at 450 ounces.

rode in the harbour of Brundusium: Frederick himself, with his Empress Iolante, passed over from Sicily and took up his abode in Otranto.

Pilgrims in the mean time had been assembling from various quarters. In Germany, at a great Diet at Aix-la-Chapelle, in the presence of King Henry, many of the Princes and Prelates had taken the Cross. Some of these, especially the Duke of Austria, alleged excuses from their vow. But the Landgrave of Thuringia, the husband of Elizabeth of Hungary, afterwards sainted for her virtues, tore himself from his beloved wife in the devotion to what both esteemed the higher duty.* The Bishops of Augsburg, Bamberg, and Ratisbon accompanied the Landgrave to Italy. France seemed for once to be cold in the Holy cause (Louis IX. was in his infancy), but in England there had been a wide-spread popular movement. On the vigil of John the Baptist's day it was rumoured abroad, that the Saviour himself had appeared in the heavens, bleeding, pierced with the nails and lance, on a cross which shone like fire.¹ It was to encourage forty thousand pilgrims, who were said already to have taken the Cross. This was seen more than once in different places, in order to confute the incredulous gainsayers. But of those forty thousand who were enrolled, probably no large proportion reached Southern Italy.

Preparations for Crusade.

England.

The Emperor, hardly released from the affairs of Northern Italy, was expected to have provisions and ships ready for the transport of all this vast undisciplined rout, of which no one could calculate the numbers.

---

* Montalembert, Vie de St. Elizabeth de Hongrie.
¹ Wendover, p. 144. The reading in Paris for quadraginta is sexaginta. Ed. Coxe p 144.

Delays took place, which the impatient Pope, ignorant no doubt of the difficulties of maintaining and embarking a great armament, ascribed at once to the remissness or the perfidy of Frederick. The heats came on with more than usual violence, they were such, it is said, as might have melted solid metal.^a A fever broke out fatal, as ever, to the Germans.^a The Landgrave of Thuringia, the Bishops of Augsburg and of Angers were among its victims; the pilgrims perished by thousands. The death of the Landgrave was attributed not only to the wanton delay, but even to poison administered by the orders of Frederick, who, in his insatiate rapacity, coveted the large possessions of the Prince. About the appointed day Frederick himself embarked; the fleet set sail; it lost sight of the shore;—but three days after the Imperial ship was seen returning hastily to the haven of Otranto; Frederick, alleging severe illness, returned to the baths of Pozzuoli, to restore his strength. The greater part of the fleet either dispersed or, following the Emperor's example, returned to land.

Gregory heard at Anagni (the year of Gregory's accession had not yet expired) the return of Frederick, the dissolution of the armament. On St. Michael's Day, surrounded by his Cardinals and Prelates, he delivered a lofty discourse, on the text, "It must needs be that offences come, but woe unto him through whom they come." He pronounced the excommunication, which Frederick had incurred by his breach of the agreement at San Ger-

Excommunication of Frederick. Sept. 30.

---

^a "Cujus ardoribus ipsa ferè solida metalla liquescunt."—Card. Arragon. in Vit. Greg. IX.

^a An impostor placed himself on the steps of St. Peter's, in the attire and character of the Pope, and publicly sold indulgences, releasing the pilgrims from their vows. After carrying on this strange bold fraud for some days, he was apprehended, and paid the penalty of his imposture.—Raynald. sub ann.

mano. Nothing was wanting to the terror. All the bells joined their most dissonant peals; the clergy, each with his torch, stood around the altar. Gregory implored the eternal malediction of God against the Emperor. The clergy dashed down their torches: there was utter darkness. The churchmen saw in this sentence the beginning of the holy strife, of the triumph of St. Michael over the subtle and scaly dragon. The sentence was followed by an address to the Apulian bishops, the subjects of Frederick. "The little bark of St. Peter, launched on the boundless ocean, though tossed by the billows, is submerged but never lost, for the Lord is reposing within her: he is awakened at length by the cries of his disciples; he commands the sea and the winds, and there is a great calm. From four quarters the tempests are now assailing our bark; the armies of the Infidels are striving with all their might that the land, hallowed by the blood of Christ, may become the prey of their impiety; the rage of tyrants, asserting their temporal claims, proscribes justice and tramples under foot the liberties of the Church: the folly of heretics seeks to rend the seamless garment of Christ, and to destroy the Sacraments of the faith; false brethren and wicked sons, by their treacherous perversity, disturb the bowels and tear open the sides of their mother." "The Church of Christ, afflicted by so many troubles, while she thinks that she is nursing up her children, is fostering in her bosom fire and serpents and basilisks,[f] which would destroy everything by their breath, their bite, and their burning. To combat these monsters, to triumph over hostile armies, to appease these restless tempests, the Holy

---

[f] Regulos.

Apostolic See reckoned in these latter times on a nursling whom she had brought up with the tenderest care. The Church had taken up the Emperor Frederick, as it were, from his mother's womb, fed him at her breasts, borne him on her shoulders; she had often rescued him from those who sought his life; instructed him, educated him with care and pain to manhood; invested him with the royal dignity; and to crown all these blessings, bestowed on him the title of Emperor, hoping to find in him a protecting support, a staff for her old age. No sooner was he King in Germany than, of his own accord, unexhorted, unknown to the Apostolic See, he took the Cross and made a vow to depart for the Holy Land; he even demanded that himself and all other Crusaders should be excommunicated if they did not set forth at the appointed time. At his coronation as Emperor we ourselves, then holding an inferior office under the most Holy Honorius, gave him the Cross, and received the renewal of his vows. Three times at Veroli, at Ferentino, at San-Germano, he alleged delays; the Church in her indulgence accepted his excuses. At San Germano he made a covenant, which he swore by his soul to accomplish; if not, he incurred by his own consent the most awful excommunication. How has he fulfilled that covenant? When many thousands of pilgrims, depending on his solemn promises, were assembled in the port of Brundusium, he detained the armament so long, under the burning summer heats, in that region of death, in that pestilent atmosphere, that a great part of the pilgrims perished, the noble Landgrave of Thuringia, the Bishops of Augsburg and Angers. At length, when the ships began to return from the Holy Land, the pilgrims embarked on board of them, on the Nativity of the Blessed

Virgin, expecting the Emperor to join their fleet. But he, breaking all his promises, bursting every bond, trampling under foot the fear of God, despising all reverence for Christ Jesus, scorning the censures of the Church, deserting the Christian army, abandoning the Holy Land to the Unbelievers, to his own disgrace and that of all Christendom, withdrew to the luxuries and wonted delights of his kingdom, seeking to palliate his offence by frivolous excuses of simulated sickness.*

"Behold, and see if ever sorrow was like unto the sorrow" of the Apostolic Pontiff. The Pope describes in pathetic terms the state of the Holy Land; attributes to the base intrigues of Frederick with the Unbelievers, the fatal issue of the treaty of Damietta; "but for him, Jerusalem might have been recovered in exchange for that city. That we may not be esteemed as dumb dogs, who dare not bark, or fear to take vengeance on him, the Emperor Frederick, who has caused such ruin to the people of God, we proclaim the said Emperor excommunicate; we command you to publish this our excommunication throughout the realm; and to declare, that in case of his contumacy, we shall proceed to still more awful censures. We trust, however, that he will see his own shame; and return to the mercy of his mother the Church, having given ample satisfaction for all his guilt."

---

* Compare with this statement Frederick's own account, published to the world three months after. Both he and the Landgrave had been ill; both had a relapse; both returned to Otranto, where the Landgrave died. "Præterea nondum resumptâ convalescentiâ, galeas ingressi sumus, nos et dilectus consanguineus noster Lant- gravius, vestigia præcedentium secuti. Ubi tanta subito invasit utrumque turbatio, quod et nos in graviorem decidimus recidivam, et idem Lantgravius post accessum nostrum apud Idrontum de medio, proh dolor! est ereptus."—Epist. Frederic. If this was untrue, it was a most audacious and easily confuted untruth.

Gregory IX. had been on the throne of St. Peter not eight months before he uttered the fulminating decree; in which some truth is so confounded and kneaded up with falsehood and exaggeration; and there is so much of reckless wrath, such want of calm, statesman-like dignity, such deliberate, almost artful determination to make the worst of everything. The passionate old man might seem desperately to abandon all hopes of future success in the Holy Land; and to take vindictive comfort in heaping all the blame on Frederick.[a]

Gregory returned to Rome; Frederick had already sent ambassadors solemnly to assert that his illness was real and unfeigned, the Bishops of Bari and Reggio, and Reginald of Spoleto. By one account, the Pope refused to admit them to his presence: at all events he repelled them with the utmost scorn, and so persisted in branding the Emperor in the face of Christendom as a hypocrite and a liar.[b]

Twice again, on St. Martin's Day and on Christmas Day, the Pope, amid all the assembled hierarchy, renewed and confirmed the excommunication. Frederick treated the excommunication itself with utter contempt; either through love or fear the clergy of the kingdom of Naples performed as usual all the sacred offices. At Capua he held a Diet of all the Barons of Apulia; he assessed a tax on both the kingdoms for an expedition to the Holy Land, appointed for the ensuing May. He

---

[a] "Hic (Gregorius IX.) tanquam superbus primo anno pontificatus sui cœpit excommunicare Fredericum Imperatorem pro causis frivolis et falsis."—Abb. Urspergens. p. 247.

[b] There is a letter to Frederick, quoted in Raynaldus, in the milder tone, declaring that the Pope had been blamed for the mansuetude of his proceedings; because he had not also censured him for many acts of tyranny and invasion on the rights of the Church in Naples and Sicily.

summoned an assemblage of all his Italian subjects to meet at Ravenna, to take counsel for this common Crusade. From Capua came forth his defiant appeal to Christendom.* In this appeal Frederick replied to the unmeasured language of the Pope in language not less unmeasured. He addressed all the Sovereigns of Christendom; he urged them to a league of all temporal Kings to oppose this oppressive league of the Pope and the Hierarchy. He declared that he had been prevented from accomplishing his vow, not, as the Pope falsely averred, by frivolous excuses, but by serious illness; he appealed to the faithful witness in Heaven for his veracity; he declared his fixed determination, immediately that God should restore him to health, to proceed on that holy expedition. "The end of all is at hand; the Christian charity which should rule and maintain all things is dried up in its fountain not in its streams, not in its branches, but in its stem. Has not the unjust interdict of the Pope reduced the Count of Toulouse and many other princes to servitude? Did not Innocent III. (this he especially addressed to King Henry of England) urge the noble Barons of England to insurrection against John, as the enemy of the Church? But no sooner had the humiliated King subjected his realm, like a dastard, to the See of Rome, than, having sucked the fat of the land, he abandoned those Barons to shame, ruin, and death. Such is the way of Rome, under words as smooth as oil and honey lies hid the rapacious blood-sucker: the Church of Rome, as though she were the true Church, calls herself my mother and my nurse, while all her acts have been those of a stepmother. The whole world pays tribute

---

* Rich. de San Germ.

to the avarice of the Romans. Her Legates travel about through all lands, with full powers of ban and interdict and excommunication, not to sow the seed of the word of God, but to extort money, to reap what they have not sown. They spare not the holy churches, nor the sanctuary of the poor, nor the rights of the prelates. The primitive Church, founded on poverty and simplicity, brought forth numberless Saints: she rested on no foundation, but that which had been laid by our Lord Jesus Christ. The Romans are now rolling in wealth; what wonder that the walls of the Church are undermined to the base, and threaten utter ruin?"[d] The Emperor concluded with the solemn admonition to all temporal Sovereigns to make common cause against the common adversary: "Your house is in danger when that of your neighbour is on fire." But in all this strife of counter proclamations, the advantage was with the Pope. Almost every pulpit in Christendom might propagate to the end of the earth the Papal fulminations: every wandering friar might repeat them in the ears of men. The Emperor's vindication, the Imperial ban against the Pope, might be transmitted to Imperial officers, to municipal magistrates, even to friendly prelates or monks: they might be read in diets or burgher meetings, be affixed on town-halls or market places, but among a people who could not read; who would tremble to hear them.[e]

---

[d] Matth. Paris, sub ann. 1228. Written no doubt at the end of 1227, Dec. 6; received in England in 1228.

[e] "D'ailleurs les moyens de publicité faciles et puissans dans les mains du Pape, étaient presque nuls dans celles des princes séculiers, qui avant l'imprimerie ne pouvaient que difficilement se faire entendre des masses populaires. Dans cette lutte de paroles l'avantage devoit rester au Saint Siège, puisque la chaire dont il disposait était la seule tribune de ce temps."— Cherrier, Lutte des Papes et des Empereurs, ii. p. 239.

Yet the Emperor had allies, more dangerous to the Pope than the remote Sovereigns of Christendom. Gregory, on his return from Anagni, had been received in Rome with the acclamations of the clergy, and part at least of the people. But in Rome there had always been a strong Imperialist party, a party hostile to the ruling Pontiff. Gregory had already demolished the palaces and castle towers of some of the Roman nobles, which obstructed his view, and no doubt threatened his security in the Lateran:[1] he had met with no open resistance, but such things were not done in Rome without more dangerous secret murmurs. Frederick, by timely succours during a famine in the last winter, had won the hearts of many of the populace. He had made himself friends, especially among the powerful Frangipani, by acts of prodigal generosity. He had purchased the lands of the heads of that family, and granted them back without fine as Imperial fiefs. The Frangipanis became the sworn liegemen of the Emperor's family. Roffrid of Benevento, a famous professor of Jurisprudence in Bologna, appeared in Rome and read in public, with the consent of the Senate and people of Rome, the vindication of the Emperor.

On Thursday in the Holy Week the Pope proceeded to his more tremendous censures on the impenitent Frederick. "His crimes had now accumulated in fearful measure. To the triple offence, which he had committed in the breach of the treaty of San Germano—that he had neither passed the sea to the Holy Land, nor armed and despatched the stipulated number of knights at his own cost, nor furnished the sums of money according to his obligation

March 21. Second excommunication. A.D. 1239.

---

[1] Card. Arragon. in Vita.

—were added other offences. He had prevented the Archbishop of Tarento from entering his See; he had seized all the estates held by the Knights Templars and Knights of St. John within his realm; he had broken the treaty entered into and guaranteed by the See of Rome with the Count of Celano and Reginald of Acerra; he had deprived the Count Roger, though he had taken the Cross, of his followers and of his lands, and thrown his son into prison, and had refused to release him at the representation of the Holy See." All these were, in Frederick's estimation, his rebellious subjects, visited with just and lawful penalties. These aggravated crimes —for crimes they were assumed to be on the irrefragable grounds of Papal accusation—called for aggravated censures. The Pope declared every place in which Frederick might be, under interdict; all divine offices were at once to cease; all who dared to celebrate such offices were deprived of their functions and of their benefices. If he himself should dare to force his way into the ceremonies of the Church he was threatened with something worse. If he did not desist from the oppression of the churches and of ecclesiastical persons, if he did not cease from trampling under foot the ecclesiastical liberties, and from treating the excommunication with contempt, all his subjects were at once absolved from their allegiance. He was menaced with the loss of his fief, the kingdom of Naples, which he held from, and for which he had done homage to, the See of Rome. The holy ceremonies passed away undisturbed; but on the Wednesday in Easter week, while the Pope was celebrating the mass, there was suddenly heard a fierce cry, a howl as Gregory describes it; and the whole populace rose in insurrection. The storm was for a time allayed; but after

Gregory driven from Rome.

some weeks Gregory found it necessary to leave Rome. He retired first to Rieti, afterwards to Perugia.*

Frederick, in the mean time, although under excommunication, celebrated his Easter with great pomp and rejoicing at Baroli. Tidings had arrived of high importance from the Holy Land. Gregory had received, and had promulgated throughout Christendom, the most doleful accounts of the state of the Christians in Palestine. A letter addressed to the Pope by Gerold the Patriarch, Peter Archbishop of Cæsarea (the Pope's Legate), the Archbishop of Narbonne, the Bishops of Winchester and Exeter, the Grand Masters of the Templars and of St. John, announced, that no sooner had the news of the Emperor's abandonment of the Crusade arrived in Syria, than the pilgrims, to the number of forty thousand, re-embarked for the West. Only eight hundred remained, who were retained with difficulty, and were only kept up to the high pitch of enthusiasm by the promise of the Duke of Limbourg, then at the head of the army, to break the existing treaties, and march at once upon Jerusalem. On the other hand, a letter from Thomas Count of Acerra, the Lieutenant of Frederick in the Holy Land, who now held the city of Ptolemais, announced the death of the Sultan Moadhin of Damascus.[b] Moadhin was the most formidable enemy of the Christians; he had been at the head of a powerful army; his implacable hatred of the Christians had brought all the more warlike Saracens under his banner: he had destroyed many of the strongholds, which, if in the power of the Crusaders,

[March 28.]

---

[f] Rich. San Germ. "Quocirca lidem (the Frangipanis) reversi cum Papa rursus excommunicaret imperatorem, fecerunt ut a populo pelleretur turpiter extra civitatem."—Conrad. Urnsperg. Compare Vit. Greg. IX.

[b] The Christians called him Conradin.—Rich. San Germ.

might be of military importance: he had subjected Jerusalem itself to further ravage.

All the acts of Frederick now showed his determination to embark before the spring was passed for the Holy Land. He would convince the world, the Pope himself, of his sincerity. Already had he despatched considerable reinforcements to the Count of Acerra; the taxes for the armament were levied with rigour; the army which was to accompany him was drawn together from all quarters. The death of the Empress Iolante in childbirth did not delay these warlike proceedings. To Baroli he summoned all the magnates of the kingdom, to hear his final instructions, to witness his last will and testament, in case he should not return alive from his expedition. No building could contain the vast assemblage: a tribune was raised in the open air, from which the Imperial mandates were read aloud. He exhorted all the barons and prelates with their liegemen to live at peace among themselves, as in the happy days of William II. Reginald Duke of Spoleto was appointed Bailiff of the realm; his elder son Henry was declared heir both of the Empire and of the kingdom of Sicily;[1] if he died without heirs, then Conrad; afterwards any surviving son of Frederick by a lawful wife. This, his last will, could only be annulled by a later authentic testament. The Duke of Spoleto, the Grand Justiciary Henry de Morro, and others of the nobles, swore to the execution of this solemn act.

The more determined Frederick appeared to fulfil his vow, the more resolute became the Pope in his hostility. He had interdicted the payment of all taxes to the ex-

---

[1] Bla. de San Germ. p. 1005.

communicated sovereign by all the prelates, monasteries, and ecclesiastics of his realm.[k] Pilgrims who passed the Alps to join the army were plundered by the Lombards; at the instigation (so, no doubt, it was falsely rumoured, but the falsehood is significant) of the Pope himself.[m] The border of the Neapolitan kingdom was violated by the Pope's subjects of Rieti; the powerful Lords of Polito in the Capitanata renounced their allegiance to the King. Frederick went down to Brundusium; his fleet, only of twenty galleys, rode off the island of St. Andrew.[n] Messengers from the Pope arrived peremptorily inhibiting his embarkation on the Crusade till he should have given satisfaction to the Church, and been released from her ban. Frederick paid no attention to the mandate; he sailed to Otranto; as he left that harbour, he sent the Archbishop of Bari and Count Henry of Malta to the Pope, to demand the abrogation of the interdict: they were rejected with scorn by Gregory.[o]

Frederick set sail with his small armament of twenty galleys, which contained at most six hundred knights, more, the Pope tauntingly declared, like a pirate than a great sovereign. He could not await, perhaps he had no inclination to place himself at the head of a great Crusade, assembled from all quarters of the world, and so involve himself in a long war which he could not abandon without disgrace. He could not safely withdraw the main part of his forces, and expose his kingdom of Naples to the undisguised hostility of the Pope, with malcontents of all classes,

---

[k] Ric. de San Germ.   [m] Urspergen. sub ann. 1228.
[n] Jordanus, in Raynald. sub ann. Andreas Dandolo, apud Muratori, ill. 344. June or July.
[o] Reg. Gregor., quoted by Von Raumer, p. 445.

especially the clergy, whom he had been forced to keep down with a strong hand. He was still in secret intelligence with the Sultan of Egypt, still hoped to acquire by peaceful negotiations what his predecessors had not been able to secure by war.[p] Frederick, after a prosperous voyage, landed at Cyprus: there, by acts of violence and treachery (the only account of these transactions is from hostile writers) he wrested the tutelage of the young King from John of Ibelin, whom he invited to a banquet, treated with honour as his own near kinsman, and then compelled to submit to his terms. But as the young King was cousin to his Empress Iolante, his interference, which was solicited by some of the leading men in the island, may have rested on some asserted right as nearest of kin.[q] From Cyprus he sailed to Ptolemaïs (Acre): he was received with the utmost demonstrations of joy. The remnant of the pilgrims who had not returned to Europe welcomed their tardy deliverer as about to lead them to conquest; the clergy and the people came forth in long processions; the Knights of the Temple and St. John knelt before the Emperor and kissed his knee; but (inauspicious omen!) the clergy refused the kiss of peace, and declined all intercourse with one under the ban of the Church.[r] At the head of a great force Frederick might have found it difficult to awe into concord the conflicting factions which divided the Christians in the Holy Land: they seemed to suspend their mutual animosities in their common jealousy of Frederick. The old estrangement of the clergy quickened rapidly into open hostility. The

In Cyprus.

At Ptolemaïs Sept. 7.

Frederick landed Sept. 7.

---

[p] See above, p. 100.
[q] The mother of Henry of Cyprus was half-sister to Maria Iolante, the mother of the Empress.
[r] Matth. Paris. Unspagena. sub ann.

active hatred of the Pope had instantly pursued the Emperor, even faster than his own fleet, to the Holy Land. Two Franciscan friars had been despatched in a fast sailing bark, to proclaim to the Eastern Christians that he was still under excommunication; that all were to avoid him as a profane person. The Patriarch, the two Grand Masters of the Orders, were to take measures that the Crusade was not desecrated by being under the banner of an excommunicated man, lest the affairs of the Christians should be imperilled. The Master of the Teutonic Order was to take the command of the German and Lombard pilgrims; Richard the Marshal and Otho Peliard of the troops of the kingdoms of Jerusalem and Cyprus; in his own camp the Emperor was to be without power, nothing was to be done in his name.*

The Knights Templars and Knights of the Hospital hardly required to be stimulated by the Papal censures to the hatred of Frederick. These associations, from bands of gallant knights vowed to protect the pilgrims to the Holy Sepulchre, and to perform other Christian services, had rapidly grown into powerful Orders, with vast possessions in every Christian kingdom; and, themselves not strong enough to maintain the kingdom of Jerusalem, were jealous of all others. As yet they were stern bigots, and had not incurred those suspicions which darkened around them at a later period in their history. Frederick had placed them under severe control, with all the other too zealous partisans of the Church, in his realm of Naples and Sicily. This was one of the acts which appears throughout among the charges of tyran-

* Richard de San Germano, p. 1005.

nical maladministration in the Apulian kingdom. These religious Orders claimed the same exemptions, the same immunities, with other ecclesiastics: the mere fact that they were submitted to the severe and impartial taxation of Frederick would to them be an intolerable grievance. Their unruly murmurs, if not resistance, would no doubt provoke the haughty sovereign; his haughtiness would rouse theirs to still more inflexible opposition. Perhaps Frederick's favour to the Teutonic Order might further exasperate their jealousy. They had already filled the ears of the Pope with their clamours against Thomas of Acerra, the Lieutenant of Frederick. Gregory had proclaimed to Christendom, to France where the Templars were in great power, that "the worthy vicegerent of Frederick, that minister of Mahomet who scrupled not to employ his impious Saracens of Nocera against Christians and Churchmen in his Apulian kingdom, had openly taken part with the unbelievers against these true soldiers of the Cross." The Saracens, when the suspension of arms was at an end, had attacked a post of the Knights Templars, and had carried off a rich booty. The Templars had pursued the marauders, and rescued part of the spoil; when Thomas of Acerra appeared at the head of his troops, and, instead of siding with the Christians, had compelled them to restore the booty to the Infidels. Such was their version of this affair,[1] eagerly accredited by the Pope. It is more probable that the Lieutenant of the Emperor acted as General of the Christian forces; and that this whole proceeding was in violation of his orders,

---

[1] Letter of Gregory to the Legate in France, in Matth. Paris. Compare Hugo Plagon. where the Marshal Richard is represented as in command of the pilgrims.

as it clearly was on both sides, of the existing treaty. The Knights Templars and Hospitallers held themselves as entirely independent powers; fought or refused to fight according to their own will and judgement; formed no part of one great Christian army: were amenable, in their own estimation, to no superior military rule. If they had refused obedience to the Lieutenant of the Emperor or the King of Jerusalem, they were not likely to receive commands from one under excommunication. Frederick himself soon experienced their utter contumacy. He commanded them to evacuate a castle called the Castle of the Pilgrims, which he wished to garrison with his own troops. The Templars closed the gates in his face, and insultingly told him to go his way, or he might find himself in a place from whence he would not be able to make his way.[a]

Frederick, however, with the main army of the pilgrims was in high popularity; they refused not to march under his standard; he appeared to approve of their determination to break off the treaty, and to advance at once upon Jerusalem. Frederick, to avoid this perpetual collision with his enemies, pitched his camp at Recordana, some distance without the gates of Ptolemaïs. He then determined to take possession of Joppa (Jaffa), and to build a strong fortress in that city. He summoned all the Christian forces to join him in this expedition. The Templars peremptorily refused, if the war was to be carried on, and the orders issued to the camp, in the name of the excommunicated Emperor. Frederick commenced his march without them; but mistrusting the small number of his forces, was obliged to submit that all orders should be issued in the name of God and of

---

[a] Hugo Plagon.

Christianity. Frederick's occupation of Joppa, the port nearest to Jerusalem, was not only to obtain possession of a city in which he should be more completely master than in Ptolemais, and to strengthen the Christian cause by the erection of a strong citadel; but as the jealous vigilance of his enemies discerned, to bring himself into closer neighbourhood with the Sultan of Egypt. Kameel, the Babylonian Sultan, as he was called from the Egyptian Babylon (Cairo), was encamped in great force near Gaza. The old amity, and more than the amity, something like a close league between the Sultan of Egypt and the Emperor Frederick, now appeared almost in its full maturity. Already, soon after the loss of Damietta and its recovery from the discomfited Christians, Sultan Kameel had sent his embassy to Frederick, avowedly because he was acknowledged to be the greatest of the Christian powers, and in Sicily ruled over Mohammedan subjects with mildness, if not with favour. The interchange of presents had been such as became two such splendid sovereigns.[a] The secret of their negotiations, carried on by the mission of the Archbishop of Palermo to Cairo, of Fakreddin the favourite of Sultan Kameel to Sicily, could be no secret to the watchful emissaries of the Pope.

There had been mortal feud between Malek Kameel of Egypt and Malek Moadhin of Damascus. Malek Moadhin had called in the formidable aid of Golal-eddin, the Sultan of Kharismia, who had made great conquests in Georgia, the Greater Armenia, and Northern Syria. Sultan Kameel had not scrupled to seek the aid of the Christian against Moadhin; no doubt to Frederick the

---

[a] See the Arabian history of the Patriarchs of Alexandria.

lure was the peaceful establishment of the kingdom of Jerusalem, in close alliance with the Egyptian Sultan.[y] On the death of Moadhin the Damascene, Sultan Kameel had marched at once into Syria, occupied Jerusalem, and the whole southern district: he threatened to seize the whole dominions of Moadhin. But a third brother, Malek Ashraf, Prince of Khelath, Edessa, and Haran on the Euphrates, took up the cause of David, the young son of Moadhin. The Christians, reinforced by Frederick's first armament under Thomas of Acerra, upon this had taken a more threatening attitude; had begun to rebuild Sidon, to man other fortresses, and to make hostile incursions. Sultan Kameel affected great dread of their power: he addressed a letter to his brother Ashraf, expressing his fears lest, to the disgrace of the Mohammedan name, the Christians should wrest Jerusalem, the great conquest of Saladin, from the hands of the true believers. Ashraf was deceived, or chose to be deceived; he abandoned the cause of the young Sultan of Damascus; he agreed to share in his spoils; Sultan Kameel was to remain in Palestine master of Jerusalem, to oppose the Christians; while Ashraf undertook the siege of Damascus. Such was the state of affairs when Frederick suddenly landed at Ptolemaïs. Sultan Kameel repented that he had invited him; he had sought an ally, he feared a master. The name of the Great Christian Emperor spread terror among the whole Mohammedan population.[z] Had Frederick, even though he had brought so inconsiderable a force, at once been recognised as the head of the Crusade; had he been joined cordially by the Knights of the Temple and of the Hospital, his name had still been imposing.

---

[y] Abulfeda.   [z] Ibid.

he might have dictated his own terms. The dissensions of the Christians were fatal—dissensions which could not be disguised from the sagacious Mohammedans.

Almost the first act of King Frederick on his arrival in Palestine was an embassy, of Balian Prince of Tyre and Thomas of Acerra his Lieutenant, to the camp of his old ally Sultan Kameel; they were received with great pomp; the army drawn up in array. The embassy returned to Ptolemais with a huge elephant and other costly presents. The negotiations began at the camp of Recordana; they were continued at Joppa. The demands of Frederick were no less than the absolute surrender of Jerusalem and all the adjacent districts; the restoration of his kingdom to its full extent. The Sultan, as much in awe of the zealots of Mohammedanism as Frederick of the zealots of Christianity, alleged almost insuperable difficulties. The Emir Fakreddin, the old friend of Frederick, and another named Shems Eddin, were constantly in the Christian camp. They not merely treated with the accomplished Emperor, who spoke Arabic fluently, on the subjects of their mission, but discussed all the most profound questions of science and philosophy. Sultan Kameel affected the character of a patron of learning; Frederick addressed to him a number of those philosophic enigmas which exercise and delight the ingenious Oriental mind. Their intercourse was compared to that of the Queen of Sheba and Solomon. There were other Eastern amusements not so becoming the Christian Emperor. Christian ladies met the Mohammedan delegates at feasts, it was said with no advantage to their virtue. Among the Sultan's presents was a bevy of dancing girls, whose graceful feats the Emperor beheld with too great interest, and was not, it was said, insensible to their beauty.

NEGOTIATIONS WITH SULTAN KAMEEL.

The Emperor wore the Saracen dress; he became, in the estimation of the stern Churchmen, a Saracen.[a]

The treaty dragged slowly on. Sultan Kameel could not be ignorant of the hostility against Frederick in the Christian camp: if he had been ignorant, the knowledge would have been forced upon him. The Emperor, by no means superior even to the superstition of the land, had determined to undertake a pilgrimage almost alone, and in a woollen robe, to bathe in the Jordan. The Templars wrote a letter to betray his design to the Sultan, that he might avail himself of this opportunity of seizing and making Frederick prisoner, or even of putting him to death. The Sultan sent the letter to the Emperor.[b] From all these causes, *Negotiations with Sultan Kameel.* the tone of the Sultan naturally rose, that of Frederick was lowered, by the treason of which he was obliged to dissemble his knowledge, as he could not revenge it. Eastern interpreters are wont to translate all demands made of their sovereigns into humble petitions. The Arabian historian has thus, perhaps, selecting a few sentences out of a long address, toned down the words of Frederick to Sultan Kameel to abject supplication. "I am thy friend. Thou art not ignorant that I am the greatest of the Kings of the West. It is thou that hast invited me to this land; the Kings and the Pope are well informed of my journey. If I return having obtained nothing, I shall forfeit all consideration with

---

[a] "Quod cum maximâ verecundiâ referimus et rubore, Imperatori Soldanus audiens quod secundam morem Saracenicum se haberet, misit cantatrices quæ et saltatrices dicuntur, et joculatores, personas quidem non solum infames rerum etiam de quibus inter Christianos haberi mentio non debebat, Cum quibus idem princeps hujus mundi vigiliis, potationibus, et indumentis, et omni modo Saracenus se gerebat."—Epist. Gerold. apud Reynald. 1229, v.

[b] Matthew Paris, and the Arabian historians in Reinaud, p. 429. Addition to Michaud.

them. And after all, Jerusalem, is it not the birthplace of the Christian religion? and have you not destroyed it? It is in the lowest state of ruin; out of your goodness surrender it to me as it is, that I may be able to lift up my head among the kings of Christendom. I renounce at once all advantages which I may obtain from it." To Fakreddin, in more intimate converse, he acknowledged, according to another Eastern account, "My object in coming hither was not to deliver the Holy City, but to maintain my estimation among the Franks." He had before made large demands of commercial privileges, the exemption of tribute for his merchants in the ports of Alexandria and Rosetta. The terms actually obtained, at their lowest amount, belie this humiliating petition. The whole negotiation was a profound secret to all but Frederick and the immediate adherents to whom he condescended to communicate it.

At length Frederick summoned four Syrian Barons;
Feb. 11. he explained to them that the state of his affairs, the utter exhaustion of his finances, made it impossible for him to remain in the Holy Land. There were still stronger secret reasons for hastening the conclusion of the treaty. A fast-sailing vessel had been despatched to Joppa, which announced that the Papal army had broken into Apulia, and were laying waste the whole land, and threatened to wrest from Frederick his beloved kingdom of Sicily. The Sultan of Babylon, he told the Barons, had offered to surrender Jerusalem, and other advantageous conditions. He demanded their advice. The Barons replied that under
Terms of treaty. such circumstances it might be well to accept the terms; but they insisted on the right of fortifying the walls of Jerusalem. The Emperor then

summoned the Grand Masters of the Temple and the
Hospital and the English Bishops of Winchester and
Exeter; he made the same statement to them. They
answered that no such treaty could be made without
the assent of the Patriarch of Jerusalem, in his double
capacity as head of the Syrian Church and Legate of
the Pope. Frederick superciliously replied that he
could dispense with the assent of the Patriarch. Gerold,
before his adversary, became his most implacable foe.

One week after the first interview the treaty was
signed: there is much discrepancy in the articles between the Mohammedan and Christian   Feb. 18.
accounts; the Mohammedans restrict, the Christians
enlarge the concessions. The terms transmitted by the
Patriarch to the Pope, translated from the Arabic into
the French, were these:—I. The entire surrender of
Jerusalem to the Emperor and his Prefects. II. Except
the site of the Temple, occupied by the Mosque of Omar,
which remained absolutely in the power of the Saracens:
they held the keys of the gates. III. The Saracens were
to have free access as pilgrims to perform their devotions at Bethlehem. IV. Devout Christians were only
permitted to enter and pray within the precincts of the
Temple on certain conditions. V. All wrong committed
by one Saracen upon another in Jerusalem was to be
judged before a Mussulman tribunal. VI. The Emperor was to give no succour to any Frank or Saracen,
who should be engaged in war against the Saracens, or
suffer any violation of the truce. VII. The Emperor
was to recall all who were engaged in any invasion of
the territory of the Sultan of Egypt, and prohibit to the
utmost of his power every violation of such territory.
VIII. In case of such violation of the treaty, the Emperor was to espouse and defend the cause of the Sultan

of Egypt. IX. Tripoli, Antioch, Karak, and their dependencies were not included in this treaty.*

The German pilgrims rejoiced without disguise at this easy accomplishment of their vows; they were eager to set out to offer their devotions in the Holy Sepulchre. Frederick himself determined to accomplish his own pilgrimage, and to assume in his capital the crown of the kingdom of Jerusalem. Attended by the faithful Master of the Teutonic Knights, Herman of Salza, and accompanied by Shems Eddin, the Saracen Kadi of Naplous, he arrived on the eve of Sunday, the 19th of March, in Jerusalem: he took up his lodging in the neighbourhood of the Temple, now a Mohammedan mosque, under the guardianship of the Kadi; there were fears lest he should be attacked by some Mohammedan fanatic. But the Emperor had not arrived in Jerusalem before the Archbishop of Cæsarea appeared with instructions from the Patriarch of Jerusalem to declare him under excommunication, and to place the city of Jerusalem under the ban. Even the Sepulchre of the Lord was under interdict; the prayers of the pilgrims even in that holiest place were forbidden, or declared unholy. No Christian rite could be celebrated before the Christian Emperor, and that disgrace was inflicted in the face of all the Mohammedans!

Immediately on his arrival the Emperor visited the Church of the Holy Sepulchre. The church was silent:

---

* These articles are obviously incomplete; they do not describe the extent of the concessions, which, according to other statements, included, with Jerusalem, Bethlehem, Nazareth, and the whole district between Joppa and Jerusalem. There is nothing said, if anything was definitively agreed, as to the right of the Emperor to rebuild the walls of Jerusalem; nor of the condition that the Saracens were only to enter Jerusalem unarmed, and not to pass the night within the walls. The important stipulation of the surrender of all Christian prisoners without ransom is altogether omitted.

not a priest appeared: during his stay no mass was celebrated within the city or in the suburbs. An English Dominican, named Walter, performed one solitary service on the morning of the Sunday. Frederick proceeded again in great pomp and in all his imperial apparel to the Church of the Sepulchre. No prelate, no priest of the Church of Jerusalem was there who ventured to utter a blessing. The Archbishops of Palermo and of Capua were present, but seem to have taken no part in the ceremony. The imperial crown was placed on the high altar; Frederick took it up and with his own hands placed it on his head. The Master of the Teutonic Order delivered an address in the name of the Emperor, which was read in German, in French, in Latin, and in Italian. It ran in this strain: "It is well known that at Aix-la-Chapelle I took the Cross of my own free will. Hitherto insuperable difficulties have impeded the fulfilment of my vow. I acquit the Pope for his hard judgement of me and for my excommunication: in no other way could he escape the blasphemy and evil report of men. I exculpate him further for his writing against me to Palestine in so hostile a spirit, for men had rumoured that I had levied my army not against the Holy Land, but to invade the Papal States. Had the Pope known my real design, he would have written not against me, but in my favour: did he know how many are acting here to the prejudice of Christianity, he would not pay so much respect to their complaints and representations. . . . . I would willingly do all which shall expose those real enemies and false friends of Christ who delight in discord, and so put them to shame by the restoration of peace and unity. I will not now think of the high estate which is my lot on earth, but humble myself

Coronation of Frederick.

before God to whom I owe my elevation, and before him who is his Vicar upon earth."[a] The Emperor returned through the streets wearing the crown of Jerusalem. The same day he visited the site of the Temple, whereon stood the Mosque of Omar.

The zealous Mohammedans were in bitter displeasure with Frederick, as having obtained from their easy Sultan the possession of the Holy City; yet their religious pride watched all his actions, and construed every word and act into a contempt of the Christian faith, and his respect, if not more than respect, for Islam. The Emir Shems Eddin, so writes the Arabic historian, had issued rigid orders that nothing should be done which could offend the Emperor. The house where the Emperor slept was just below the minaret from which the Muezzin was wont to proclaim the hour of prayer. But in Jerusalem the Muezzin did more. He read certain verses of the Korân; on that night the text, "How is it possible that God had for his son Jesus the son of Mary?" The Kadi took alarm; he silenced altogether the officious Muezzin. The Emperor listened in vain for that sound which in the silent night is so solemn and impressive. He inquired the reason of this silence, which had continued for two days. The Kadi gave the real cause, the fear of offending the Christian Emperor. "You are wrong," said Frederick, "to neglect on my account your duty, your law, and your religion. By God, if you should visit me in my realm,

---

[a] If this is the genuine speech, quoted by Von Raumer from the unpublished Regesta in the Papal archives, it may show the malice of the Patriarch Gerold, who thus describes it :—" Ita coronatus resedit in cathedrâ Patriar- chatus excusando malitiam suam et accusando ecclesiam Romanam, imponens ei quod injustè procosserat contra eum; et notabilem sum fecerat Invectivè et reprehensivè de insatiabili et simoniali avaritiâ."

you will find no such respectful deference." The Emperor had declared that one of the chief objects of his visit to the Holy Land was to behold the Mohammedans at prayer. He stood in wondering admiration before the Mosque of Omar; he surveyed the pulpit from which the Imaun delivered his sermons. A Christian priest had found his way into the precincts with the book of the Gospels in his hand; the Emperor resented this as an insult to the religious worship of the Mohammedans, and threatened to punish it as a signal breach of the treaty. The Arabic historian puts into his mouth these words: "Here we are all the servants of the Sultan; it is he that has restored to us our Churches." So writes the graver historian.* There is a description of Frederick's demeanour in the Temple by an eye-witness, one of the ministering attendants, in which the same ill-suppressed aversion to the uncircumcised is mingled with the desire to claim an imperial proselyte. "The Emperor was red-haired and bald, with weak sight; as a slave he would not have sold for more than 200 drachms."

Frederick's language showed (so averred some Mohammedans) that he did not believe the Christian religion; he did not scruple to jest upon it. He read without anger, and demanded the explanation of the inscription in letters of gold, "Saladin, in a certain year, purified the Holy City from the presence of those who worship many Gods."† The windows of the Holy Chapel were closely barred to keep out the defilements of the birds. "You may shut out the birds," said Frederick, "how will ye keep out the swine?" At noon, at the hour of prayer, when all the faithful fall on

* Makrisi, in Reinaud.
† The Mohamedans so define the worshippers of the Trinity.

their knees in adoration, the Mohammedans in attendance on Frederick did the same; among the rest the aged preceptor of Frederick, a Sicilian Mussulman who had instructed him in dialectics. Frederick, in this at least not going beyond the bounds of wise tolerance, betrayed neither surprise nor dissatisfaction.

After but two days the Emperor retired from the interdicted city; if he took no steps to restore the walls, some part of the blame must attach to his religious foes, who pursued him even into the Holy City with such inexorable hostility.

Both the Emperor and the Sultan had wounded the pride and offended the religious prejudices of the more zealous among their people. To some the peaceful settlement of the war between Christian and Mussulman was of itself an abomination, a degenerate infringement of the good old usage, which arrayed them against each other as irreclaimable enemies: the valiant Christians were deprived of the privilege of obtaining remission of their sins by the pillage and massacre of the Islamites: the Islamites of winning Paradise by the slaughter of Christians. The Sultan of Egypt, so rude was the shock throughout the world of Islam, was obliged to send ambassadors to the Caliph of Bagdad and to the Princes on the Euphrates to explain his conduct. The surrender of Jerusalem was the great cause of affliction and shame. The Sultan in vain alleged that it was but the unwalled and defenceless city that he yielded up; there were bitter lamentations among all the Moslems, who were forced to depart from their homes; sad verses were written and sung in the streets. The Imauns of the Mosque of Omar went in melancholy procession to the Sultan to remonstrate. They attempted to overawe him by proclaiming an

Unpopularity of the treaty.

unusual hour of prayer. Kameel treated them with great indignity, and sent them back stripped of their silver lamps and other ornaments of the Mosque. In Damascus was the most loud and bitter lamentation. The Sultan of Damascus was besieged in his capital by Malek el Ashraf. The territory, now basely yielded to the Christians, was part of his kingdom; he was the rightful Lord of Jerusalem. There an Imaun of great sanctity, the historian Ibn Dschusi himself, was summoned to preach to the people on this dire calamity. The honour of Islam was concerned; he mounted the pulpit: " So then the way to the Holy City is about to be closed to faithful pilgrims: you who love communion with God in that hallowed place can no longer prostrate yourself, or water the ground with your tears. Great God! if our eyes were fountains, could we shed tears enough? If our hearts were cloven, could we be afflicted enough?" The whole assembly burst into a wild wail of sorrow and indignation.[f]

Frederick announced this treaty in Western Christendom in the most magnificent terms. His letter to the King of England bears date on the day of his entrance into Jerusalem. He ascribes his triumph to a miracle wrought by the Lord of Hosts, who seemed no longer to delight in the multitude of armed men. In the face of two great armies, that of the Sultan of Egypt and of Sultan Ashraf encamped near Gaza, and that of the Sultan (David) of Damascus at Naplous, Jerusalem, Bethlehem, Nazareth, the district of Sharon, and Sidon, had been freely ceded to him: the Mohammedans were only by sufferance to enter the Holy City. The Sultan had bound himself to surrender all prisoners, whom he

---

[f] Reinaud. Extrait des Auteurs Arabes.—Wilken, vi. p. 493.

ought to have released by the treaty of Damietta, and all who had been taken since.[b] The seal of this letter bore a likeness of the Emperor, with a scroll: over his head "the Emperor of the Romans," on the right shoulder "the King of Jerusalem," on the left "the King of Sicily."

Far different was the reception of the treaty by the Pope, and by all who sided with, or might be expected to side with, the Pope. It was but a new manifestation of the perfidy, the contumacy, the ingratitude to the Church, the indifference of the Emperor to religion, if not of his apostasy. A letter arrived, and was actively promulgated through Western Christendom, from Gerold, Patriarch of Jerusalem, describing in the blackest colours every act of the Emperor. In the treaty the dignity, the interests of religion and of the Church, the dignity and interests of the Patriarch, had been, it might seem studiously neglected; even in the territory conceded by the Sultan some of the lands belonging to the Knights Templars were comprehended, none of those claimed by the Patriarch. Gerold overlooked his own obstinate hostility to Frederick, while he dwelt so bitterly on that of Frederick to himself. The letter began with Frederick's occupation of Joppa; his avowed partiality to the interests of the Mohammedans, his neglect, or worse, of the Christians. At least five hundred Christians had fallen since his arrival, not ten Saracens. All excesses, all breaches of the truce were visited severely on the Christians, connived at or disregarded in the Mohammedans. A Saracen who had been plundered was sent back in splendid apparel to the Sultan. All the

Letter of the Patriarch.

---
[b] The letter in Matthew Paris.

Emperor's suspicious intercourse with the Saracens, his Mohammedan luxuries, his presents of splendid arms to be used by Infidels against true Believers, were recounted; the secrecy of the treaty and its acceptance, with the signature of the Sultan as its sole guarantee. The Master of the Teutonic Order had insidiously invited him (the Patriarch) to accompany the Emperor to Jerusalem. He had demanded first to see the treaty. There he found that the Sultan of Damascus, the true Lord of Jerusalem, was no party to the covenant; "there were no provisions in favour of himself or of the Church; how could he venture his holy person within the power of the treacherous Sultan and his unbelieving host?" The letter closed with a strong complaint that the Emperor had left the city without rebuilding the walls. But the Patriarch admitted that Frederick had consulted the Bishops of Winchester and Exeter, the Master of the Hospitallers, the Praeceptor of the Temple, to advise and aid him in this work: their reply had been cold and dilatory; and Frederick departed from the city.[1]

Even before the arrival of Gerold's letters, the Pope, in a letter to the Archbishop of Milan and his suffragans, all liegemen of the Emperor, had denounced the treaty as a monstrous reconciliation of Christ and Belial; as the establishment of the worship of Mohammed in the Temple of God; and thus "the antagonist of the Cross, the enemy of the faith, the foe of all chastity, the condemned to hell, is lifted up for adoration, by a perverse judgement, to the intolerable contumely of the Saviour, the inexpiable disgrace of the Christian name, the contempt of all

Letter of Gregory to Archbishop of Milan.

---

[1] Epist. Gerold. Patriarchæ, apud Matth. Paris.

the martyrs who have laid down their lives to purify the Holy Land from the worldly pollutions of the Saracens."*

Albert of Austria was the most powerful enemy who might be tempted to revolt against Frederick in his German dominions, the greatest and most dangerous vassal of the Empire. Him the Pope addressed at greater length, and with a more distinct enumeration of four flagitious enormities with which he especially charged the Emperor. First, he had shamelessly presented the sword and other arms which he had received from the altar of St. Peter, blessed by the Pope himself, for the defence of the faith, and the chastisement of the wicked, to the Sultan of Babylon, the enemy of the faith, the adversary of Christ Jesus, the worshipper of Mohammed the son of Perdition; he had promised not to bear arms against the Sultan, against whom as Emperor he was bound to wage implacable war. The second was a more execrable and more stupendous offence. In the Temple of God, where Christ made his offering, where he had sat on his cathedral throne in the midst of the doctors, the Emperor had cast Christ forth, and placed Mohammed, that son of Perdition; he had commanded the law of God to keep silence, and permitted the free preaching of the Korân: to the Infidels he had left the keys of the Sanctuary, so that no Christian might enter without their sufferance. Thirdly, he had excluded the Eastern Christians of Antioch, Tripoli, and other strong places, from the benefit of the treaty, and so betrayed the Christian cause in the East to the enemy. Lastly, he had so bound himself by this wicked league, that if

marginal notes: June 18. Letter to Albert of Austria.

---

* Ad Epise. Mediol. June 13, 1229.

CHAP. III. LAST ACTS OF FREDERICK IN PALESTINE. 135

the Christian army should attempt to revenge the insult done to the Redeemer, to cleanse the Temple and the City of God from the defilements of the Pagans, the Emperor had pledged himself to take part with the foe. Albert of Austria was exhorted to disclaim all allegiance to one guilty of such capital treason against the majesty of God, to hold himself ready at the summons of the Church to take up arms against the Emperor.

The last acts of Frederick in Palestine are dwelt upon both by the Patriarch and the Pope; they are known almost entirely by these unfriendly representations. Frederick returned from Joppa to Ptolemais in no placable mood with his implacable enemies leagued against him in civil war.[m] The Patriarch had attempted to raise an independent force at his own command: if the pilgrims should retire from the Holy Land he would need a body-guard for his holy person. He proposed, out of some large sums of money left for the benefit of the sacred cause by Philip-Augustus of France, to enrol a band of knights, a new Order, for this end. Frederick declared that no one should levy or command soldiers within his realm without his will and consent. With the inhabitants of Ptolemais Frederick had obtained, either by his affable demeanour or by his treaty, great popularity. He summoned a full assembly of all Christian people on the broad sands without the city. There he arose and arraigned the Patriarch and the

---

[m] "Præterea qualiter contra ipsum Imperatorem, apud Acon, postmodum redeuntem, prædicti Patriarchæ, Magistri domuum hospitalis et templi se gesserint, utpote qui contra ipsum, intestina bella moverint in civitate prædicta, his qui interfuerunt luce clarius extitit manifestum." — Rich. San Germ. It is remarkable how many privileges and grants he made to the Teutonic Order: it is manifest that his object was to raise up a loyal counterpoise to the Templars and Hospitallers. — Buehmer, Regesta, sub ann.

Master of the Templars as having obstinately thwarted all his designs for the advancement of the Christian Cause, and having pursued him with their blind and obstinate hostility. He summoned all the pilgrims, having now fulfilled their vows, to depart from the Holy Land, and commanded his Lieutenant, Thomas de Acerra, to compel obedience to these orders. He was deaf to all remonstrance; on his return to the city he seized all the gates, manned them with his crossbowmen, and while he permitted all the Knights Templars to leave the city, he would admit none. He took possession of the churches, and occupied them with his archers. The Patriarch assembled all his adherents and all the Templars still within the city, and again thundered out his excommunication. Frederick kept him almost as a prisoner in his palace; his partisans were exposed to every insult and attack, even those who were carrying provisions to the palace. Two bold Franciscans, who on Palm Sunday denounced Frederick in the Church, were dragged from the pulpit, and scourged through the streets. But these violences availed not against the obstinate endurance of the Churchmen. After some vain attempts at reconciliation, the Patriarch placed the city of Ptolemais under interdict. These are not all the charges against Frederick; it was made a crime that he destroyed some of his ships, probably unserviceable: his arms and engines of war he is said to have sent to the Sultan of Egypt.

Palm Sunday. April 2.

On the day of St. Peter and St. Paul the Emperor set sail for Europe; his presence was imperiously required. In every part of his dominions the Pope, with the ambitious activity of a temporal sovereign, and with all the tremendous arms wielded by

May 2.

the spiritual power, was waging a war either in open day, or in secret intrigues with his unruly and disaffected vassals. The ostensible cause of the war was the aggression of Frederick's vicegerent in Apulia, Reginald Duke of Spoleto. Frederick had left Reginald to subdue the revolt of the powerful family of Polito. These rebels had taken refuge in the Papal territory: they were pursued by Reginald. But once beyond the Papal frontier the Duke of Spoleto extended his ravages, it might seem reviving certain claims of his own on the Dukedom of Spoleto. Frederick afterwards disclaimed these acts of his lieutenant, and declared that he had punished him for the infringement of his orders.[a] But the occasion was too welcome not to be seized by the Pope. He levied at once large forces, placed them under the command of Frederick's most deadly enemies, his father-in-law, John de Brienne, the ejected King of Jerusalem, and the Cardinal John Colonna, with the King's revolted subjects, the Counts of Celano and of Aquila; the martial Legate Pelagius, who had commanded the army of Damietta, directed the whole force. A report of Frederick's death in Palestine (a fraud of which he complains with the bitterest indignation) was industriously disseminated. John de Brienne even ventured to assert that there was no Emperor but himself. The Papal armies at first met with great success; many cities from fear, from disaffection to Frederick, from despair of relief, opened their gates. The soldiers of the Church committed devastations almost unprecedented even in these rude wars. But Gregory was not content with this limited war; he strove to arm all

War in Apulia.

---

[a] The most particular account of these wars is in Rich. de San Germano, apud Muratori, t. vii.

Christendom against the contumacious Emperor who defied the Church. From the remotest parts, from Wales, Ireland, England, large contributions were demanded, and in many cases extorted, for this holy war. Just at this juncture England contributed in a peculiar manner, even beyond her customary tribute, to the Papal treasury: the whole of such revenue was devoted to this end.

Election to Arch- bishopric of Canterbury. July 1228.
A dispute was pending in the Court of Rome concerning the See of Canterbury. On the death of Archbishop Stephen, the monks of Canterbury elected Walter of Hevesham to the primacy. The King refused his assent, and the objections urged were sufficiently strange, whether well-founded or but fictitious, against a man chosen as the successor of Becket. The father of Walter, it was said, had been hanged for robbery, and Walter himself, during the interdict, had embraced the party opposed to King John. The suffragan bishops (they always resented their exclusion from the election) accused Walter of having debauched a nun, by whom he had several children. Appeal was made to Rome; the Pope delayed his sentence for further inquiry. The ambassadors of the King, the Bishops of Chester and Rochester, and John of Newton in vain laboured to obtain the Papal decision. One only argument would weigh with the Pope and the Cardinals. At length they engaged to pay for this tardy justice the tenth of all moveable property in the realm of England and Ireland in order to aid the Pope in his war against the Emperor. Even then the alleged immoralities were put out of sight; the elected Primate of England was examined by three Cardinals on certain minute points of theology, and condemned as unworthy of so august a see, "which

ought to be filled by a man noble, wise, and modest."[o] Richard, Chancellor of Lincoln, was proposed in the name of the King and the suffragan bishops, and received his appointment by a Papal Bull. In France, besides the exertions of the Legate, the Archbishops of Sens and of Lyons were commanded by the Pope himself to publish the grave offences of Frederick against the Holy See, and to preach the Crusade against him. In Germany, Albert of Austria had been urged to revolt; in the North and in Denmark the Legate, the Cardinal Otho, preached and promulgated the same Crusade.[p] He laid Liège under an interdict, and King Henry raised an army to besiege the Cardinal in Strasburg. The Pope praised, as inspired by the Holy Ghost, the chivalrous determination of the Prince of Portugal, to take up arms in defence of the Church of Christ. The Lombards, on the other hand, were sternly rebuked for their tardiness in sending aid against the common enemy, the Pope gave them a significant hint that the deserters of the cause of the Church might be deserted in their turn in their hour of need.

The rapid return of the Emperor disconcerted all these hostile measures. With two well-armed barks he landed at Astore, near Brundusium; many of the brave German pilgrims followed after and rapidly grew to a formidable force. His first act was to send ambassadors to the Pope, the Archbishop of Bari, the Bishop of Reggio and Herman de

May 10 and July 13, 1779. Return of Frederick.

---

[o] He was asked whether our Lord descended into hell, in the flesh or not in the flesh; on the presence of Christ in the sacrament; how Rachel, being already dead, could weep for her children; on the power of an excommunication, unrightly pronounced; on a case of marriage, where one of the parties had died in infidelity. To all these questions his answers were wrong.

[p] Raynald. in not.

Salza, the master of the Teutonic order. The overtures were rejected with scorn. An excommunication even more strong and offensive had been issued by the Pope at Perugia.* The first clause denounced all the heretics with names odious to all zealous believers. After the Cathari, the Publicans, the Poor Men of Lyons, the Arnoldists, and under the same terrific anathema as no less an enemy of the Church, followed the Emperor Frederick; his contumacious disregard of the excommunication pronounced by the Cardinal of Albano was thus placed on the same footing with the wildest opinions and those most hostile to the Church. After the recital of his offences, the release of all his subjects from their allegiance, came the condemnation of his adherents, Reginald of Spoleto and his brother Bertoldo. With the other enemies of the Church were mingled up the Count de Foix, and the Viscount of Beziers; the only important names which now represented the odious heresy of Southern France. Some lesser offenders were included under the comprehensive ban. These were all, if not leagued together under the same proscription, alike denounced as enemies of God and of the Church. The conquering army of the Pope was on all sides arrested, repelled, defeated; the rebellious barons and cities returned to their allegiance; Frederick marched to the relief of Capua; the strength of the Papal force broke up in confusion. Frederick moved to Naples where he was received in triumph. In Capua he had organised the Saracens whom he had removed from Sicily, where they had been a wild mountain people, untameably and utterly lawless, to Nocera: there he

---

* This bull must have been issued in June, not in August. See Boehmer, p. 335. Raynaldus, sub ann.

had settled them, foreseeing probably their future use as inhabitants of walled cities and cultivators of the soil. This was a force terrible to the rebellious churchmen who had espoused the Papal cause. From San Germano Frederick sent forth his counter appeal to the Sovereigns of Europe, representing the violence, the injustice, the implacable resentment of the Pope. The appeal could not but have some effect.

Christendom, even among the most devout adherents of the Papal supremacy, refused to lend itself to the fiery passions of the aged Pontiff. The Pope was yet too awful to be openly condemned, but the general reluctance to embrace his cause was the strongest condemnation. Men throughout the Christian world could not but doubt by which party the real interests of the Eastern Christians had been most betrayed and injured. The fierce enthusiasm which would not receive advantages unless won from the unbeliever at the point of the sword had died away: men looked to the effect of the treaty, they compared it with the results of all the Crusades since that of Godfrey of Bouillon. Jerusalem, the Holy Sepulchre, were in the power of the Christians: devout pilgrims might perform unmolested their pious vows; multitudes of Christians had taken up their abode in seeming security in the city of Sion. But if, thus trammelled, opposed, pursued by the remorseless excommunication into the Holy Sepulchre itself, Frederick by the awe of his imperial name, by his personal greatness, had obtained such a treaty; what terms might he not have dictated, if supported by the Pope, the Patriarch, and Knights Templars.* Treaties with the Mohammedan

Christendom against the Pope.

---

* It has been observed that the three contemporary historians, Matthew Paris, the Abbot Urspergensis, and Richard of San Germano, are all

powers were nothing new; they had been lately made by Philip Augustus, and by the fierce Richard Cœur de Lion. The Christians had never disdained the policy of taking advantage of the feuds among the Mohammedan sovereigns and allying themselves with the Sultan of Egypt or the Sultan of Damascus. Even the Pope himself had not disdained all peaceful intercourse with the Unbelievers. Frederick positively asserted that he had surprised and had in his possession letters addressed by the Pope to Sultan Kameel, urging him to break off his negotiations with the Emperor. Gregory afterwards denied the truth of this charge; but it was publicly averred, and proof offered, in the face of Christendom.* Frederick had appealed to witnesses of all his acts, and they, at all events the English Bishops of Winchester and Exeter, the Master of the Hospitallers, the Master of the Teutonic Order, had given no countenance to the envious and rancorous charges of the Patriarch.

There was a deeper cause of dissatisfaction throughout that Hierarchy, to which the Pope had always looked for the most zealous and self-sacrificing aid. The clergy felt the strongest repugnance to the levy of a tenth demanded by the Pope throughout Christendom, to maintain wars, if not unjust, unnecessary, against the Emperor. No doubt the lavish and partial favour with

---

against the Pope. "Verisimile enim videtur, quod si tunc Imperator cum gratiâ ac pace Romanæ Ecclesiæ transisset, longe melius et efficacius prosperatum fuisset negotium Terræ Sanctæ."—Richard de San Germano adds, that if the Sultan had not known that Frederick was excommunicated by the Pope, and hated by the Patriarch, he would have granted much better terms. Compare Muratori, Annal. d'Italia, sub ann.; and in Wilken the extract from Theuerdank:—

* Waren dem Kaiser die gestanden,
Die ihm ain Ehre wandten (-ntwandten)
Das Grab und alle diese Land,
Die munden gar in seiner Hand:
Nazareth und Bethlem,
Der Jordan und Jerusalem,
Jesu manig heilig Stat,
In Gott mitt seinem Fussen trat,
Syria und Juda," &c.
—Wilken, vi. p. 509.

* Epist. Petr. de Vineâ.

which he treated the Preaching and Begging Friars had already awakened jealousy. Gregory had sagaciously discerned the strength which their influence in the lowest depths of society would gain for the Papal cause. He had solemnly canonised Francis of Assisi —one of his most confidential counsellors was the Dominican Gualo.¹ So active had the Friars been in stirring up revolt in the kingdom of Naples, that the first act of Reginald of Spoleto had been their expulsion from the realm.

Oct. 4, 1228.

Christendom had eagerly rushed into a Crusade against the unbelievers; it had not ventured to disapprove a Crusade against the heretics of Languedoc; but a Crusade (for under that name Gregory IX. levied this war) against the Emperor, and that Emperor the restorer of the Kingdom of Jerusalem, was encountered with sullen repugnance or frank opposition. It was observed as a strange sight that when Frederick's troops advanced against those of the Pope, they still wore the red crosses which they had worn in Palestine. The banner of the Cross, under which Mohammedans fought for Frederick, met the banner with the keys of St. Peter."

The disapprobation of silent disobedience, at best of sluggish and tardy sympathy if not of rude disavowal and condemnation, could not escape the all-watchful ear of Rome. Gregory had no resource but in his own dauntless and unbroken mind, and in the conviction of his power. The German Princes had refused to dethrone King Henry: some of the greatest influence,

---

¹ Gualo was his emissary, if not his Legate, in Lombardy. He was active in framing the peace of San Germano. —Epist. Gregor., Oct. 9, 1226.

" "Imperator cum crucesignatis contra claviggeros hostes proporat.' — Rich. de San Germano, p. 1013.

Leopold Duke of Austria, the Duke of Moravia, the Archbishops of Saltzburg and of Aquileia, the Bishop of Ratisbon, were in Italy endeavouring to mediate a peace. The Lombards did not move; even if the Guelfs had been so disposed, they were everywhere controlled by a Ghibelline opposition. One incident alone was of a more encouraging character. Gregory was still at Perugia an exile from rebellious Rome. But a terrific flood had desolated the city. The religious fears of the populace beheld the avenging hand of God for their disobedience to their spiritual father; the Pope returned to Rome in triumph.[x]

Peace was necessary to both parties, negotiations were speedily begun. The Pope was suddenly seized with a sacred horror of the shedding human blood. A treaty was framed at San Germano which maintained unabased the majesty of the Pope.[y] In truth, by the absolution of the Emperor with but a general declaration of submission to the Church, without satisfaction for the special crime for which he had undergone excommunication, the Pope, virtually at least, recognised the injustice of his own censures. Of the affairs of the Holy Land, of the conduct of the Emperor, of the treaty with the Sultan, denounced as impious, there was a profound and cautious silence. In other respects the terms might seem humiliating to the Emperor; he granted a complete amnesty to all his rebellious subjects, the Archbishop of Tarentum and all the bishops and churchmen who had

---

[x] Not only was there a great destruction of property, of corn, wine, cattle, and of human life, but a great quantity of enormous serpents were cast on shore, which rotted and bred a pestilence. This is a story more than once repeated in the later annals of Rome —on what founded?—Gregor. Vit.

[y] Albanensi Episcopo, apud Raynald. 1229.

fled the realm; even the reinstatement of the insurgent Counts of Celano and Aversa in their lands and domains in Germany, in Italy, in Sicily; he consented to restore all the places he occupied in the Papal dominions, and all the estates which he had seized belonging to churches, monasteries, the Templars, the Knights of the Hospital, and generally of all who had adhered to the Church. He renounced the right of judging the ecclesiastics of his realm by the civil tribunals, excepting in matters concerning royal fiefs; he gave up the right of levying taxes on ecclesiastical property, as well that of the clergy as of monasteries. It is said, but it appears not in the treaty, that he promised to defray the enormous charges of the war, variously stated at 120,000 crowns and 120,000 ounces of gold; but in those times promises to pay such debts by no means ensured their payment. Frederick never fulfilled this covenant. If to obtain absolution from the Papal censures Frederick willingly yielded to these terms, it shows either that his firm mind was not proof against the awe of the spiritual power which enthralled the rest of Europe, or that he had the wisdom to see that the time was not come to struggle with success against such tyranny. He might indeed hope that, ere long, to the stern old man who now wielded the keys of St. Peter with the vigour of Hildebrand or Innocent III., might succeed some feebler or milder Pontiff. Already was Gregory approaching to or more than ninety years old.[1] He was himself in the strength and prime of manhood, nor could he expect that this same aged Pontiff would rally again for a contest, more long, more obstinate, and though not

---

[1] I confess that this extreme old age of Gregory IX. does not seem to me quite clearly made out. At all events, after every deduction, he was of an extraordinary age to display such activity and firmness.

terminated in his lifetime, more fatal to the Emperor and to the House of Hohenstaufen. Frederick had been released from the ban of excommunication at Ceperano by the Cardinal John of St. Sabina; he visited the Pope at Anagni. They met, Frederick with dignified submission, the Pope with the calm majesty of age and position, held a conference of many hours, appeared together at a splendid banquet, and interchanged the kiss of peace; the antagonists whose mortal quarrel threatened a long convulsion throughout Christendom proclaimed to the world their mutual amity.*

Aug. 28.
Sept. 1, 1230.

Nearly nine years elapsed before these two antagonists, the Pope Gregory IX. and the Emperor Frederick II. resumed their immitigable warfare,—years of but dubious peace, of open amity yet secret mistrust, in which each called upon the other for aid against his enemies; the Pope on Frederick against the unruly Romans, Frederick on the Pope against the rebellious Lombards and his rebellious son; but

Sept. 1, 1230. to 1239, Palm Sunday.

---

* Frederick describes the interview—"Deinde ut post absolutionem ex præsentia corporum mentium serenitas sequeretur, primo Septembris apostolicam sedem adivimus, et sanctissimum patrem dominum Gregorium, Dei gratiâ summum Pontificem, vidimus reverenter. Qui affectione paternâ nos recipiens, et pace cordium sacris osculis fœderatâ, tam benevole, tam benigne propositum nobis suæ intentionis aperuit de ipsis quæ præcesserant nil omittens, et singula prosequens evidentis judicio rationis, quod etsi non præcedens causam commoverit, vel rancorem potuerit aliquem attulisse, sic benevolentia, quam persensimus in eodem, omnem motum lenivit animi, et nostrum amoto rancore serenavit adeo voluntatem, ut non velimus ulterius præterita memorari quæ necessitas intulit, ut virtus ex necessitate prodens operaretur gratiam ampliorem."—Monument. Germ. iv. 275. There is something very striking in this. The generous awe and reverence of Frederick for the holy old man, considering his deep injuries (I envy not those who can see nothing but specious hypocrisy in Frederick), and the Christian amenity of the Pope, considering that Frederick, a short time before, had been called a godless heretic, almost a Mohammedan. Their mutual enmity is lost in mutual respect.

where each suspected a secret understanding with those enemies. It is remarkable that both Frederick and the Pope betook themselves in this interval of suspended war to legislation. Frederick to the promulgation of a new jurisprudence for his kingdom of Naples and Sicily; Gregory of a complete and authoritative code of the Decretals which formed the statute law by which the Papacy and the sacerdotal order ruled the world, and administered the internal government of the Church. During the commencement of this period Frederick left the administration of affairs in Germany, though he still exercised an imperial control, to his son Henry. The rebellion of Henry alone seemed to compel him to cross the Alps and resume the sway. His legislation aspired to regulate the Empire; but in Germany from the limits imposed on his power, it was not a complete and perfect code, it was a succession of remedial laws. His earliest and most characteristic work of legislation was content to advance the peace, prosperity, and happiness of his own Southern realm.

The constitution of his beloved kingdom was thus the first care of Frederick. As a legislator he commands almost unmingled admiration; and the aim and temper of his legislation whether emanating from himself, or adopted from the counsel of others, may justly influence the general estimate of a character so variously represented by the passions of his own age, passions which have continued to inflame, and even yet have not died away from the heart of man.[b] The object of Frederick's

---

[b] Even in our own day M. Höfler, for instance, seems to revive all the rancour of the days of Innocent IV. Even Boehmer is not above this fatal influence. This part of my work was finished before the publication of the "Regesta Imperii," to which, nevertheless, I am bound to acknowledge much obligation.

jurisprudence was the mitigation, as far as possible the suppression, of feudal violence and oppression; the assertion of equal rights, equal justice, equal burthens; the toleration of different religions; the promotion of commerce by wise, almost premature regulations; the advancement of intellectual culture among his subjects by the establishment of universities liberally endowed, and by the encouragement of all the useful and refined arts. It is difficult to suppose a wise, equitable and humane legislator, a blind, a ruthless tyrant; or to reconcile the careful and sagacious provision for the rights and well-being of all ranks of his subjects with the reckless violation of those rights, and with heavy and systematic oppression; more especially if that jurisprudence is original and beyond his age. The legislator may himself be in some respects below the lofty aim of his laws; Frederick may have been driven to harsh measures to bring into order the rebellious magnates of the realm, whom his absence in Asia, the invasion and the intrigues of the Papal party, cast loose from their allegiance; the abrogation of their tyrannical privileges may have left a deep and brooding discontent, ready to break out into revolt and constantly enforcing still more rigorous enactments. The severe guardian of the morals of his subjects may have claimed to himself in some respects a royal, an Asiatic indulgence; he may have been compelled by inevitable wars to lay onerous burthens on the people, he may have been compelled to restrict or suspend the rights of particular subjects, or classes of subjects, by such determined hostility as that of the clergy to himself and to all his house; but on the whole the laws and institutions of the kingdom of Naples are an unexceptionable and imperishable testimony at least to his lofty designs for the good of mankind; which history cannot decline, or rather receives with greater respect and trust than can be claimed by any contemporary view of the acts or of the character of Frederick II. It is in this light only as illustrating the life of the great antagonist of the Church that they belong to Christian history, beyond their special bearing on religious questions, and the rights and condition of the clergy.[c]

The groundwork of Frederick's legislation was the stern supremacy of the law; the submission of all, even the nobles, who exercised the feudal privilege of separate jurisdictions, to a certain extent of the clergy, to the king's sole and exclusive justice. This was the great revolution through which every feudal kingdom must inevitably pass sooner or later.[d] The crown must become the supreme fountain of justice and law. The first, and most difficult, but necessary step was the uniformity of that law. There was the most extraordinary variety of laws and usages throughout the realm, Roman, Greek, Gothic, Lombard, Norman, Imperial-German institutes; old municipal and recent seignorial rights.[e] The Jews had their special privileges, the Saracens their own customs and forms of procedure. The majestic law had to overawe to one system of obedience, with due maintenance of their proper rights, the nobles, the clergy, the burghers, and the peasants, even the Jews

---

[c] The constitutions of the Emperor Frederick may be read in Canciani, vol. I. sub fine. I am much indebted for a brief, It appears to me very sensible and accurate comment in the Considerazioni sopra la Storia di Sicilia, by the Canonico Gregorio (Palermo, 1805), and to my friend M. von Raumer's earliest and best work, Geschichte der Hohenstaufen.

[d] King Roger (see the Canonico Gregorio, L. iii.) had already vindicated a certain supremacy for the King's Justiciary. King Roger's legislation is strikingly analogous to, Gregorio thinks borrowed from, that of his remote kinsman William, our Norman Conqueror. In France this was among the great steps first decisively taken by St. Louis.

[e] Canciani, Preface.

and the Mohammedans. Frederick wisely determined not to aspire so much to be the founder of an absolutely new jurisprudence, as to select, confirm, and harmonise the old institutions.⁴

The religious ordinances of the Sicilian constitution demand our first examination. Frederick maintained the immunities of the worshippers of other religions, of the Jews and the Arabians, with such impartial equity, as to incur for this and other causes the name of Jew and Saracen. But the most faithful son of the Church could not condemn the heretic with more authoritative severity, or visit his offence with more remorseless punishment.⁵ Heresy was described as a crime against the offender himself, against his neighbour, and against God, a more heinous crime even than high treason. The obstinate heretic was condemned to be burned, his whole property confiscated, his children were incapable of holding office or of bearing testimony. If such child should merit mercy by the denunciation of another heretic, or of a concealer of heretics, the Emperor might restore him to his rank. Schismatics were declared outlaws, incapable of inheriting, liable to forfeiture of their goods. No one might petition in favour of a heretic: yet the repentant heretic might receive pardon; his punishment, after due investigation of the case by the ecclesiastical power, was to be adjudged by the secular authority. But these laws were

<small>*Laws relating to religion.*</small>

---

⁴ The code was published at Amalfi, Sept. 1231: Rich. San Germ. sub ann. 1231; in Sicily by Richard de Montenegro, High Justiciary, during the same year. Apprnd. ad Malater. p. 251. Gregorio, III. 14.

⁵ Compare the edicts issued at Ravenna, Feb. 22, 1232, and March, against the Lombard heretics. They might have satisfied S. Dominic or Simon de Montfort. Re-enacted at Cremona, 1238; at Padua, 1239.— Monument. Germ. iv. 287, 288. Also letter of June 15, ex Regest. Greg. IX. in Höfler, p. 344.

directed against a particular class of men, dangerous it
was thought no less to the civil than to the religious
power; actual rebels against the Church, rebels likewise
against the Emperor, who was still the conservator of
pure orthodoxy, and betraying at least rebellious inclinations, if not designs hostile towards all power. They
were neither enacted nor put in force against the Greek
Christians who were still in considerable numbers in the
kingdom of Sicily, had their own priests, and celebrated
undisturbed their own rites. They were those heretics
which swarmed under various denominations, Cathari
or Paterina, from rebellious and republican Lombardy,
the hated and suspected source of all these opinions.
In all the states of the Pope, in Rome itself, not merely
were there hidden descendants of the Arnoldists, but
all the wild sects which defied the most cruel persecutions in the North of Italy, spread their doctrines even
within the shadow of the towers of St. Peter. Naples
and Aversa were full of them,[b] and derived them from
rebellious Lombardy; and Frederick, whose notions of
the imperial power were as absolute as Gregory's of the
Papal, not only would not incur by their protection such
suspicions, as would have inevitably risen, of harbouring
or favouring heretics, he scrupled not to assist in the
extermination of these insolent insurrectionists against
lawful authority.[i]

---

[b] "Adeo quod ab Italiæ finibus, præsertim a partibus Longobardiæ in quibus pro certo perpendimus ipsorum nequitiam amplius abundare, jam usque ad regnum nostrum usus perfidiæ rivulos derivarunt."—l. l. tit. l. "Quod dolentes referimus, in regno nostro Siciliæ Neapolin, et Aversam, partesque vicinas dicitur infecisse."— Frederic. Epist. apud Epist. Gregor. iv. 131.

[i] Gregor. Vit. Richard de San Germ. See also the Edict of the Senator and people of Rome.—Apud Raynald. 1231. Compare (afterwards) Frederick's letter commanding the heretics throughout Lombardy to be committed to the flames.

The Constitution of Frederick endeavoured to reduce the clergy into obedient and loyal subjects at once by the vigorous assertion of the supreme and impartial law, and by securing and extending their acknowledged immunities. The clergy were amenable to the general law of the realm as concerned fiefs, could be impleaded in the ordinary courts concerning occupancy of land, inheritances, and debts: they had jurisdiction over their own body, with the right of inflicting canonical punishments: but besides this they were amenable to the secular laws, especially for treason, or all crimes relating to the person of the King.[k] They were not exempt from general taxation; they were bound to discharge all feudal obligations for their fiefs. On the other hand, the crown abandoned its claim to the revenues of vacant bishoprics and benefices:[m] three unexceptionable persons belonging to the Church were appointed receivers on behalf of the successor. On the election of bishops the law of Innocent III. was recognised; the chapter communicated the vacancy to the Crown, and proceeded to elect a fit successor; that successor could not be inaugurated without the consent of the King, nor consecrated without that of the Pope. Tithes were secured to the Church from all lands, even from the royal domains:[n] the Crown only enforced the expenditure of the appointed third on the sacred edifices, the churches and chapels. All special courts of the higher ecclesiastics as of the barons were abrogated; the crown would be the sole fountain of justice: but the holders of the great spiritual fiefs sat with the great Barons under the presidency of the high Chancellor. Except-

---

[k] L. 43. A law of King William.
[m] iii. 28. Serfs and villains were not to be ordained, iii. 1, 3.   [n] i. 7.

ing in cases of marriage, no separate jurisdiction of the clergy was recognised over the laity.* Appeals to Rome were allowed, but only on matters purely ecclesiastical; and these during wars with the Pope were absolutely forbidden. The great magnates of the realm received likewise substantial benefits in lieu of the privileges wrested from them, which were perilous to the public peace.ᵖ All their separate jurisdictions of noble or prelate were abolished; the King's justiciary was alone and supreme. But their fiefs were made hereditary, and in the female line and to collaterals in the third degree.ᵍ

The cities were emancipated from all the jurisdictions of nobles or of ecclesiastics; but the municipal authorities were not absolutely left to their free election. The Sicilian King dreaded the fatal example of the Lombard Republics: all the superior governors were nominated by the Crown; the cities only retained in their own hands the inferior appointments, for the regulation of their markets and havens.ʳ The law overlooked not the interest of the free peasants, who constituted the chief cultivators of the soil; or that of the serfs attached to the soil. Absolute slavery was by no means common in Sicily; the serfs could acquire and hold property. The free peasants were numerous; the measures of Frederick tended to raise the serfs to the same condition. He absolutely emancipated all those on the royal domain.

Cities.

Peasants.

---

* Frederick asserted and exercised the right of declaring the children of the clergy, who by the canon law were spurious, legitimate, with full title to a share in all the inheritances of all the goods of their parents, unless they were fiefs; and capability of attaining to all civil offices and honours. For this privilege they paid an annual tax of five per cent. to the royal exchequer. This implied the marriage of the clergy to a great extent.—Pet. de Vin. vi. 16. Constitut. lii. 25.

ᵖ L. 46. ᵍ id. 23, 24. ʳ L. 47.

The establishment of his courts enabled all classes to obtain justice at an easy and cheap rate against their lords; the extraordinary aids to be demanded by the lord were limited by law, that of the lay feudal superior, to aids on the marriage of a daughter or sister, the arming the son when summoned to the service of the King, and his ransom in captivity; that of the higher ecclesiastics and monasteries, to the summons to the King's service, and receiving the King at free quarters; journeys to Church Councils summoned by the Pope, and Consecrations. Frederick was so desirous to promote the cultivation of the soil, that he exempted new settlers in Sicily from taxes for ten years; only the Jews, who took refuge from Africa, were obliged to pay such taxes, and compelled to become cultivators of the land.

But of all institutions, the most advanced was the system of representative government, for the first time regularly framed by the laws of the realm. Besides the ancient Parliaments, at which the magnates of the realm, the great ecclesiastical and secular vassals of the Crown assembled when summoned by the King's writs, two annual sessions took place, on the 1st of March and the 1st of August, of a Parliament constituted from the different orders of the realm.* All the Barons and Prelates appeared in person; each of the larger cities sent four representatives, each smaller city two, each town or other place one; to these were joined all the great and lesser Bailiffs of the Crown. The summons to the Barons and Prelates was directly from the King, that of the cities and towns from the

<small>Parliaments.</small>

---

* One of the cities appointed for the meeting of Parliament in Apulia was Lentini; in Sicily, Piazza. Compare Gregorio, iii. p. 82.

judge of the province. They were to choose men of probity, good repute, and impartiality. A Commissioner from the Crown opened the Parliament, and conducted its proceedings, which lasted from eight to ten days. Every clerk or layman might arraign the conduct of any public officer, or offer his advice for the good of his town or district. The determinations which the royal Commissioner, with the advice of the most distinguished spiritual and temporal persons, approved, were delivered signed and sealed by him directly to the King, excepting in unimportant matters, which might be regulated by an order from the Justiciary of the Province.

The criminal law of Frederick's constitution was, with some remarkable exceptions, mild beyond precedent; and also administered with a solemnity, impartiality, and regularity, elsewhere unknown. The Chief Justiciary of the realm, with four other judges, formed the great Court of Criminal Law; and the Crown asserted itself to be the exclusive administrator of criminal justice.[1] Besides its implacable abhorrence of heresy, it was severe and inexorable against all disturbers of the peace of the realm, and those who endangered the public security. Private war,[2] and the execution of the law by private hands, was rigidly forbidden. Justice must be sought only in the King's courts. The punishment for every infringement of this statute was decapitation and forfeiture of goods. Arms were not to be borne except by the King's officers, employed in the court or on the royal affairs,[3] or by knights, knights' sons, and burghers, riding abroad from

---

[1] Gregorio, l. iii. c. iv. "Nobis aliquando, quibus solum ordinationem Justitiariorum, ubicunque fuerimus, reservamus."—L. l. t. 95. This was part of the "merum imperium" of the sovereign.—l. t. 49.
[2] l. 8.
[3] l. 9.

their own homes. Whoever drew his sword on another paid double the fine imposed for bearing it; whoever wounded another lost his hand; whoever killed a man if a knight, was beheaded, if of lower rank, hanged. If the homicide could not be found, the district paid a heavy fine, yet in proportion to the wehrgeld of the slain man; but Christians paid twice as much as Jews or Saracens, as, no doubt, bound more especially to know and maintain the law. The laws for the preservation of female chastity were singular and severe. Even rape upon a common prostitute was punished by beheading, if the charge was brought within a certain time:[7] whoever did not aid a woman suffering violence was heavily fined. But in these cases a false accusation was visited with the same punishment. Mothers who betrayed their daughters to whoredom had their noses cut off;[8] men who connived at the adultery of their wives were scourged. A man caught in adultery might be slain by the husband; if not instantly slain, he paid a heavy fine. The trials by battle and ordeal were abolished as vain and superstitious: the former allowed only in cases of murder, poisoning, or high treason, where there was strong suspicion but not full proof. It was designed to work on the terror of the criminal; but if the accuser was worsted, he was condemned in case of high treason to the utmost penalty; in other cases to proportionate punishment. Torture was only used in cases of heavy suspicion against persons of notoriously evil repute.[9]

---

[7] I. 20. [8] III. 48, 50.

[9] Frederick's legislation was not content with abolishing these barbarous forms of testimony, almost the only available testimony in rude unlettered times. He laid down rules on written evidence; documents must be on parchment, not on perishable paper; he prohibited a certain kind of obscure and intricate writing, in use at Naples, Amalfi, and Sorrento; and ordered the notaries to write all deeds legibly and

These are but instances of the spirit in which Frederick framed his legislation, which aimed rather to advance, enrich, enlighten his subjects than to repress their free development by busy and perpetual interference. His regulations concerning commerce were almost prophetically wise: he laid down the great maxim that commercial exchange benefited both parties; he permitted the export of corn as the best means of fostering its cultivation. He entered into liberal treaties with Venice, with Asia, Genoa, and the Greek Empire, and even with some of the Saracen powers in Africa. By common consent, both parties condemned the plundering of wrecks, and pledged themselves to mutual aid and friendly reception into their harbours. The King himself was a great merchant; the royal vessels traded to Syria, Egypt, and other parts of the East. He had even factors who traded to India.[b] He encouraged internal commerce by the establishment of great fairs and markets;[c] manufactures of various kinds began to prosper.

But that which—if the constitution of Frederick had continued to flourish, if the institutions had worked out in peace their natural consequences—if the house of Hohenstaufen had maintained their power, splendour and tendencies to social and intellectual advancement—if they had not been dispossessed by the dynasty of Charles of Anjou, and the whole land thrown back by many centuries—might have enabled the Southern kingdom

---

clearly. The Emperor himself laid down regulations to test the authenticity of a certain document.—Gregorio, iii. p. 61.

[b] "Fredericus II. erat omnibus Soldanis Orientis particeps in mercimoniis et amicissimus, ita ut uaque ad Indos currebant ad commodum suum, tam per mare, quam per terras, institores."—Matth. Par. 544.

[c] See edict for annual fairs at Sulmona, Capua, Lucera, Bari, Tarentum, Cosenza, Reggio, Jan. 1234.—Rich. San Germ.

to take the lead, and anticipate the splendid period of Italian learning, philosophy, and art, was the Universities; the establishments for education; the encouragements for all learned and refined studies, imagined by this accomplished King. Even the revival of Greek letters might not have awaited the conquest of Constantinople by the Turks two centuries later. Greek was the spoken language of the people in many parts of the kingdom; the laws of Frederick were translated into Greek for popular use; the epitaph of the Archbishop of Messina in the year 1175 was Greek.ᵈ There were Greek priests and Greek congregations in many parts of Apulia and Sicily; the privileges conferred by the Emperor Henry VI. on Messina had enacted that one of the three magistrates should be a Greek. Hebrew, and still more Arabic, were well known, not merely by Jews and Arabians but by learned scholars. Frederick himself spoke German, Italian, Latin, Greek, Arabic, and Hebrew. He declared his own passionate love for learned and philosophical studies. Nothing after the knowledge of affairs, of laws and of arms, became a monarch so well; to this he devoted all his leisure hours, these were the liberal pursuits which adorned and dignified human life.ᵉ In Syria, and in his intercourse with the Eastern monarchs, he had obtained great collections of books; he caused translations to be made from the Arabic, and out of Greek into Latin, of some of the philosophic works of Aristotle and the Almagest of Ptolemy.ᶠ The University of Naples was his great

---

ᵈ Von Raumer, p. 556.
ᵉ Peter de Vineâ, iii. 67.
ᶠ He employed the celebrated Michael Scott (the fabled magician) in the translation of Aristotle. Among the Papal documents relating to England in the British Museum are several letters concerning this remarkable man, patronised alike by Frederick and by the Popes. Honorius III. writes

foundation; Salerno remained the famous school of medicine; but the University in the capital was encouraged by liberal endowments, and by regulations with regard to the relations of the scholars and the citizens; the price of lodgings was fixed by royal order; sums of money were to be advanced to youths at low interest, and could not be exacted during the years of study. The King held out to the more promising students honourable employments in his service. Philosophical studies appeared most suited to the genius of Frederick; natural history and the useful sciences he cultivated with success; but he had likewise great taste for the fine arts, especially for architecture, both ornamental and military. He restored the walls of many of the greatest cities; built bridges and other useful works. He had large menageries, supplied from the East and from Africa. He sometimes vouchsafed to send some of the more curious animals about for the instruction and amusement of his subjects. The Ravennese were delighted with the appearance of some royal animals. He was passionately fond of field sports, of the chase with the hound and the hawk; his own book on falconry is not merely instructive on that sport, but is a scientific treatise on the nature and habits of those birds, and of many other animals. The first efforts of Italian sculpture and painting rose under his auspices; the beautiful Italian language began to form itself in his court: it has been said above that the earliest strains of Italian

---

(Jan. 16, 1225, p. 214) to the Archbishop of Canterbury to bestow preferment on Michael Scott. "Quod inter literatos dono vigeat scientiæ singulari." M. Scott (p. 229) has a licence to hold pluralities. (P. 246) he is named by the Pope Archbishop of Cashel, and to hold his other benefices. (P. 253) he refuses the Archbishopric: "Dum linguam terræ illius se ignorare diceret." He is described as not only a great Latin scholar, but as familiar with Hebrew and Arabic.

poetry were heard there: Peter de Vineâ, the Chancellor of Frederick, the compiler of his laws, was also the writer of the earliest Italian sonnet. Nor was Peter de Vineâ the only courtier who emulated the King in poetry: his beloved son Enzio, many of his courtiers, vied with their King and his ministers in the cultivation of the Italian language; and its first fruits the rich harmonious Italian poetry.*

His own age beheld with admiring amazement the magnificence of Frederick's court, the unexampled progress in wealth, luxury, and knowledge. The realm was at peace, notwithstanding some disturbance by those proud barons, whose interest it was to maintain the old feudal and seignorial rights; the reluctance of the clergy to recede from the complete dominion over the popular mind; and the taxation, which weighed, especially as Frederick became more involved in the Lombard war, on all classes. The world had seen no court so splendid, no system of laws so majestically equitable; a new order of things appeared to be arising; an epoch to be commencing in human civilisation. But this admiration was not universal: there was a deep and silent jealousy, an intuitive dread in the Church,[b] and in all

---

* Some of these poems I have read in a collection of the Poeti del Primo Secolo, Firenze, 1814. A small volume has been published by the Literary Union of Stuttgard (1543), Italienische Lieder des Hohenstaufischen Hofes in Sicilien. It contains lays by thirteen royal and noble authors. Dante, in his book De Vulgari Eloquentia, traces to the court of Frederick the origin of the true and universal Italian language. We return to this subject.

[b] The Pope seemed to consider that Frederick's new constitutions must be inimical to the Church. "Intelleximus siquidem quod vel proprio motu, vel seductus inconsultis consiliis perversorum, novas adere constitutiones intendis ex quibus necessario sequitur ut dicaris Ecclesiae persecutor et obrutor publicae libertatis."—lib. v. Epist. 91, apud Raynald. 1231. He reproaches the Archbishop of Capua as " Fredericæ constitutiones destructivas salutis et institutivas enormium scandalorum edenti voluntarius obsequens."—Apud Hofler ii. p. 333.

the faithful partisans of the Church of remote, if not
immediate danger; of a latent design, at least a latent
tendency in the temporal kingdom to set itself apart,
and to sever itself from the one great religious Empire,
which had now been building itself up for centuries.
There was, if not an avowed independence, a threatening disposition to independence. The legislation, if it
did not directly clash, yet seemed to clash, with the
higher law of the Church; if it did not make the clergy
wholly subordinate, it degraded them in some respect to
the rank of subjects; if it did not abrogate, it limited
what were called the rights and privileges, but which
were in fact the separate rule and dominion of the
clergy; at all events, it assumed a supremacy, set itself
above, admitted only what it chose of the great Canon
Law of the Church; it was self-originating, self-asserting,
it had not condescended to consult those in whom for
centuries all political as well as spiritual wisdom had
been concentered: it was a legislation neither emanating
from, nor consented to by, the Church. If every nation
were thus to frame its own constitution, without regard
to the great unity maintained by the Church, the vast
Christian confederacy would break up, Kings might
assume the power of forbidding the recurrence to Rome
as the religious capital of the world; independent kingdoms might aspire to found independent churches. This
new knowledge too was not less dangerous because its
ultimate danger was not clearly seen; at all events, it
was not knowledge introduced, sanctioned, taught by
the sole great instructress, the Church. Theology, the
one Science, was threatened by a rival, and whence did
that rival profess to draw her wisdom? from the Heathen,
the Jew, the Unbeliever; from the Pagan Greek, the
Hebrew, the Arabic. That which might be in itself

harmless, edifying, improving, when taught by the Church, would but inflame the rebellious pride of the human intellect. What meant this ostentatious toleration of other religions, if not total indifference to Christ and God; if not a secret inclination to apostasy? What was all this splendour, but Epicurean or Eastern luxury? What this poetry, but effeminate amatory songs? Was this the life of a Christian King, of a Christian nobility, of a Christian people? It was an absolute renunciation of the severe discipline of the Church, of that austere asceticism, which however the clergy and religious men alone could practise its angelic, its divine perfection, was the remote virtue after which all, even Kings (so many of whom had exchanged their worldly robes for the cowl and for sackcloth) ought to aspire, as to the ultimate culminating height of true Christianity. It was Mohammedan not merely in its secret indulgences, its many concubines, in which the Emperor was still said to allow himself Mohammedan licence; some of his chosen companions, his trusted counsellors, at least his instructors in science and philosophy were Mohammedans; ladies of that race and religion appeared, as has been said, at his court (in them virtue was a thing incredible to a sound churchman). The Saracens whom he had transplanted to Nocera were among his most faithful troops, followed him in his campaigns; it was even reported, that after his marriage with Isabella of England, he dismissed her English ladies, and made her over to the care of Moorish eunuchs.

Such to the world was the fame, such to the Church the evil fame of Frederick's Sicilian court; exaggerated no doubt as to its splendour, luxury, licence, and learning, as well by the wonder of the world, as by the abhorrence of the Church. Yet, after all, out of his long life (long if considered not by years but by events, by the civil acts, the wars, the negotiations, the journeyings, the vicissitudes, crowded into it by Frederick's own busy and active ambition and by the whirling current of affairs) the time during which he sunned himself in this gorgeous voluptuousness must have been comparatively short, intermittent, broken. At eighteen years of age Frederick left Sicily to win the Imperial crown; he had then eight years of the cold German climate and the rude German manners during the establishment of his Sovereignty over the haughty German Princes and Prelates. Then eight years in the South, but during the first four the rebellious Apulian and Sicilian nobles were to be brought under control, the Saracens to be reduced to obedience, and transported to Apulia: throughout the later four, was strife with the Lombard cities, strife about the Crusade, and preparation for the voyage. Then came his Eastern campaign, his reconciliation with the Church. Four years followed of legislation; and perhaps the nearest approach to indolent and luxurious peace. Then succeeded the revolt of his son. Four years more to coerce rebellious Germany, to attempt in vain to coerce rebellious Lombardy: all this was to close, with his life, in the uninterrupted immitigable feud with Gregory IX. and Innocent IV.

A.D. 1220 to 1224.

A.D. 1225 to 1228.

A.D. 1230 to 1234.

A.D. 1234 to 1238.

The Pope Gregory IX. (it is impossible to decide how far influenced by the desire of overawing this tendency of temporal legislation to assert its own independence) determined to array the higher and eternal law of the Church in a more august and authoritative form. The great code of the Papal Decretals constituted this law; it had now long recog-

The Decretals.

nised and admitted to the honours of equal authority the bold inventions of the book called by the name of Isidore; but during the Pontificate of Innocent III. there had been five distinct compilations, conflicting in some points, and giving rise to intricate and insoluble questions.[1] Gregory in his old age aspired to be the Justinian of the Church. He entrusted the compilation of a complete and regular code to Raimond da Pennaforte, a noble Spaniard, related to the royal house of Arragon, of the Dominican Order, and now the most distinguished jurist in the University of Bologna. Raimond da Pennaforte was to be to the Canon what Irnerius of Bologna had been to the revived Roman Law. It is somewhat singular that Raimond had been the most famous antagonist of the Arabian school of learning, the most admired champion of Christianity, in his native Spain.

The first part of these Decretals comprehended the whole, in a form somewhat abbreviated; abbreviations which, as some complained, endangered the rights of the Church on important points; but were defended by the admirers of Raimond of Pennaforte, who declared that he could not err, for an angel from Heaven had constantly watched over his holy work.[k] The second contained the Decretals of Gregory IX. himself. The whole was promulgated as the great statute law of Christendom, superior in its authority to all secular laws as the interests of the soul were to those of the

---

[1] "Sane diversas constitutiones, et decretales epistolas, praedecessorum nostrorum in diversa sparsas volumina, quarum aliquae propter nimiam similitudinem, et quaedam propter contrarietatem, nonnullae etiam propter suam prolixitatem, confusionem inducere videbantur; aliquae vero vagabantur extra volumina supradicta, quae tanquam incertae frequenter in judiciis vacillabant."—In Praefat.

[k] Chiflet, quoted by Schroeck, xxvii. 64. Raimond da Pennaforte was canonised by Clement VIII., in 1601.

body, as the Church was of greater dignity than the State; as the Pope higher than any one temporal sovereign, or all the sovereigns of the world. Though especially the law of the clergy, it was the law binding likewise on the laity as Christians, as religious men, both as demanding their rigid observance of all the rights, immunities, independent jurisdictions of the clergy, and concerning their own conduct as spiritual subjects of the Church. All temporal jurisprudence was bound to frame its decrees with due deference to the superior ecclesiastical jurisprudence; to respect the borders of that inviolable domain; not only not to interfere with those matters over which the Church claimed exclusive cognisance, but to be prepared to enforce by temporal means those decrees which the Church, in her tenderness for human life, in her clemency, or in her want of power, was unwilling or unable herself to carry into execution. Beyond that sacred circle temporal legislation might claim the full allegiance of its temporal subjects; but the Church alone could touch the holy person, punish the delinquencies, control the demeanour of the sacerdotal order; could regulate the power of the superior over the inferior clergy, and choose those who were to be enrolled in the order. The Church alone could administer the property of the Church; that property it was altogether beyond the province of the civil power to tax; even as to feudal obligations, the Church would hardly consent to allow any decisions but her own: though compelled to submit to the assent of the crown in elections to benefices which were temporal fiefs, yet that assent was, on the other hand, counterbalanced by her undoubted power to consecrate or to refuse consecration. The Book of Gregory's Decretals was ordered to be the authorised text in all courts and in all schools of law; it was to be, as it were, more and more deeply impressed into the minds of men. Even in its form it closely resembled the Roman law yet unabrogated in many parts of Europe; but of course it comprehended alike those who lived under the different national laws, which had adopted more or less of the old Latin jurisprudence; it was the more universal statute-book of the more wide-ruling, all-embracing Rome.

CHAPTER IV.

Renewal of hostilities between Gregory IX. and Frederick II.

DURING the nine years of peace between the Empire and the Papacy, Pope Gregory IX. at times poured forth his flowery eloquence in the praise, almost the adulation, of the Emperor; the Emperor proclaimed himself the most loyal subject of the Church. The two potentates concurred only with hearty zeal in the persecution of those rebels against the civil and ecclesiastical power, the heretics.[a]

<small>Peace of nine years, Aug. 1230 to 1239, Palm Sunday.</small>

---

[a] During this period of peace an obscure heresy, that of the Stadinger, appeared or grew to its height in the duchy of Oldenburg; the Pope and the Emperor would concur in inflicting summary punishment on these rebels. Hartung, the Archbishop of Bremen, had long appealed to Rome. On one occasion he returned with full power to subdue his refractory spiritual subjects, bearing, as he boasted, a singular and significant relique,—the sword with which Peter had struck off the ear of Malchus. More than thirty years after, Archbishop Gerhard, Count de la Lippe, a martial prelate, turned not his spiritual but his secular arms against them. Among their deadly tenets was the refusal to pay tithes. The Pope recites the charges against them, furnished of course by their mortal enemies. They worshipped the Evil One now as a toad, which they kissed behind and on the mouth, and licked up its foul venom; now as a man, with a face wonderfully pale, haggard, with coal-black eyes. They kissed him; his kiss was cold as ice, and with his kiss oozed away all their Catholic faith. The Pope would urge the Emperor to take part in the war against these wretches. Conrad of Marburg, the hateful persecutor of the saintly Elizabeth of Hungary, now the Holy Inquisitor, was earnest and active in the cause. The Stedinger withstood a crusading army of 40,000 men; were defeated with the loss of 6000. Many fled to other lands; the rest submitted to the Archbishop. The Pope released them from the excommunication; but it is curious to observe, he only censures their disobedience and insurrection

At Rome multitudes of meaner religious criminals were burned; many priests and of the lower orders of clergy degraded and sent to Monte Casino and other rigid monasteries as prisoners for life.[b] The Pope issued an act of excommunication rising in wrath and terror above former acts. Persons suspected of heresy were under excommunication; if within a year they did not prove themselves guiltless, they were to be treated as heretics. Heretics were at once infamous; if judges, their acts were at once null; if advocates, they could not plead; if notaries, the instruments which they had drawn were invalid. All priests were to be publicly stripped of their holy dress and degraded. No gifts or oblations were to be received from them; the clerk who bestowed Christian burial on a heretic was to disentomb him with his own hands, and cast him forth from the cemetery, which became an accursed place unfit for burial. No lay person was to dispute in public or in private concerning the Catholic faith: no descendant of a heretic to the second generation could be admitted to holy orders. Annibaldi, the senator of Rome and the Roman people, passed a decree enacting condign punishment on all heretics. The Emperor, not content with suppressing these insurgents in his hereditary dominions, had given orders that throughout Lombardy, their chief seat, they should be sought out, delivered to the Inquisitors,[c] and there punished by the secular arm.[d] One of his own most useful allies, Eccelin da Romano,

---

he is silent of their heresy.—Raynaldus, sub ann. 1233; Schroeck, xxix. 641, &c. The original authorities are Albert. Stad. Ger. Monach. apud Boehmer—above all the Papal letters.

[b] Vit. Gregor. IX. Rich. San German. Raynald. sub ann. 1231.

[c] Gregory in one letter insinuates that Frederick had burned some good Catholics, his enemies, as pretending that they were or had been heretics.—Epist. 244. Raynald. p. 85.

[d] See ante, note, p. 151.

was in danger. Eccelin's two sons, Eccelin and Alberic, offered to denounce their father to the Inquisition. There was, what it is difficult to describe but as profound hypocrisy, or worse, on the part of the Pope: he declared his unwillingness to proceed to just vengeance against the father of such pious sons, who by his guilt would forfeit, as in a case of capital treason, all their inheritance; the sons were to persuade Eccelin to abandon all connexion with heresy or with heretics: if he refused, they were to regard their own salvation, and to denounce their father before the Papal tribunal.* It is strange enough that the suspected heretic, suspected perhaps not unjustly, took the vows, and died in the garb of a monk; the pious son became that Eccelin da Romano whose cruelty seems to have defied the exaggeration of party hatred.

But in all other respects the Pope and the Emperor were equally mistrustful of each other; peace was disguised war. Each had an ally in the midst of the other's territory whom he could not avow, yet would not abandon. Even in these perverse times the conduct of the Romans to the Pope is almost inexplicable. No sooner had the Pope, either harassed or threatened by their unruly proceedings, withdrawn in wrath, or under the pretext of enjoying the purer and cooler air, to Rieti, Anagni, or some other neighbouring city, than Rome began to regret his absence, to make overtures of submission; and still received him back with more rapturous demonstrations of joy.ᶠ In a few months they began to be

---

* The age may be pleaded in favour of Gregory IX. What is to be said of the comment of the Papal annalist, Raynaldus?—" Nec mirum cuiquam videri potest datum hoc filiis adversus parentem consilium, cum nominis, a quo descendit omnis paternitas, causa humanis affectibus debet anteferri." —p. 41. Raynald. 1231.

ᶠ Rich. de S. Germ., sub ann. 1231,

weary of their quiet: his splendid buildings for the defence and ornament of the city lost their imposing power, or became threatening to their liberties; he was either compelled or thought it prudent to retire. Viterbo had become to the Romans what Tusculum had been in a former century; the Romans loved their own liberty, but their hate of Viterbo was stronger than their love; the fear that the Pope might take part with Viterbo brought them to his feet; that he did not aid them in the subjugation of Viterbo rekindled their hostility to him. More than once the Pope called on the Emperor to assist him to put down his insurgent subjects: Frederick promised, eluded his promise;[a] his troops were wanted to suppress rebellions not feigned, but rather of some danger, at Messina and Syracuse. He had secret partisans everywhere: when Rome was Papal, Viterbo was Imperialist; when Viterbo was for the Pope, Rome was for the Emperor. If Frederick was insincere in his maintenance of the Pope against his domestic enemies, Gregory was no less insincere in pretending to renounce all alliance, all sympathy with the Lombards.[b] But this connexion of the Pope with the Lombard League required infinite management and

---

1233. He returned to Rome, March, 1233. He was again in Anagni in August!

[a] Rebellion, reconciliation, 1233. New rebellion, beginning of 1234. "Quo Fredericus imperator apud sanctum Germanum certa relatione comperto, qui fidele defensionis presidium ecclesiæ Romanæ promiserat, et fidei et majestatis oblitus, Messanam properans, nullo persequente decessit, hostibus tanti favoris auxilium ex amissione datorum."—Vit. Greg. Compare Pope's letter (Feb. 3, from Anagni, and Feb. 10). But in fact there was a dangerous insurrection in Messina; the King's Justiciary had been obliged to fly. Frederick had to put down movements also at Syracuse and Nicosia.—Ann. Sicul. Rich. San Germano.

[b] The Chronicon Placentinum has revealed a renewal of the Lombard League at Bologna, Oct. 26, 1231, and a secret mission to the Pope. p. 98.

dexterity: the Lombard cities swarmed with heretics, and so far were not the most becoming allies of the Pope.¹ Yet this alliance might seem an affair, not of policy only, but of safety. Gregory could not disguise to himself that so popular, so powerful a sovereign had never environed the Papal territories on every side. If Frederick (and Frederick's character might seem daring enough for so impious an act) should despise the sacred awe which guarded the person of the Pope, and scorn his excommunications, he was in an instant at the gates of Rome, of fickle and treacherous Rome. He had planted his two colonies of Saracens near the Apulian frontier; they at least would have no scruple in executing his most irreverent orders. The Pope was at his mercy, and friendless, as far as any strong or immediate check on the ambition or revenge of the Emperor. The Pope in supporting the Lombard republics, assumed the lofty position of the sacred defender of liberty, the asserter of Italian independence, when Italy seemed in danger of lying prostrate under one stern and despotic monarchy, which would extend from the German Ocean to the further shore of Sicily. At first his endeavours were wisely and becomingly devoted to the maintenance of peace—a peace which, so long as the Emperor refrained from asserting his full imperial rights, so long as the Guelfs ruled undisturbed in those cities in which their interests predominated, the republics were content to

---

¹ A modern writer, rather Papal, thus describes the state of Italy at that time: "Alle Kreise und Stände derjenigen Theile der Nation, den man als den eigentlichen Träger der Intelligenz in Italien betrachten müsste, waren geistig frei und mächtig genug, wo ihre Interessen denen der Kirche entgegen waren, die letzeren mit Füssen zu treten, nicht bloss einzelne Podestaten, oder das Geld-Interesse des gemeinen Volkes, sondern oft alle gebildeten Städtebewohner wagten so keck den Bannstrahlen des Papstes hohn zu sprechen."—Leo, Geschichte der Italien, II. 234.

observe; the lofty station of the mediator of such peace became his sacred function, and gave him great weight with both parties.[k] But nearly at the same time an insurrection of the Pope's Roman subjects, more daring and aggressive than usual, compelled him to seek the succour of Frederick, and Frederick was threatened with a rebellion which the high-minded and religious Pope could not but condemn, though against his fearful adversary.

Affairs of Rome.

For the third or fourth time the Pope had been compelled to retire to Rieti. Under the senatorship of Luca di Sabelli the senate and people of Rome had advanced new pretensions, which tended to revolutionise the whole Papal dominions. They had demolished part of the Lateran palace, razed some of the palaces of the cardinals, proclaimed their open defiance of the Pope's governor, the Cardinal Rainier. They had sent justiciaries into Tuscany and the Sabine country to receive oaths of allegiance to themselves, and to exact tribute. The Pope wrote pressing letters addressed to all the princes and bishops of Christendom, imploring succour in men and money; there was but one near enough at hand to aid, had all been willing. The Pope could not but call on him whose title as Emperor was protector of the Church, who as King of Naples was first vassal of the papal see. Frederick did not disobey the summons: with his young son Conrad he visited the Pope at Rieti. The Cardinal Rainier had thrown himself with the Pope's forces into Viterbo; the army of Frederick sat down before Respampano, a strong castle which the

May, 1234.

May 30, 1234.

---

[k] See the letter to Frederick, in which he assumes the full power of arbitration between the Emperor and the League.—Monument. Germ. iv. 299, dated June 5, 1233.

Romans occupied in the neighbourhood as an annoyance, and as a means, it might be, of surprising and taking Viterbo. But Respampano made resistance; Frederick himself retired, alleging important affairs, to his own dominions. The Papalists burst into a cry of reproach at his treacherous abandonment of the Pope. Yet it was entirely by the aid of some of his German troops that the Papal army inflicted a humiliating defeat on the Romans, who were compelled to submit to the terms of peace dictated by the Pope,[m] and enforced by the Emperor, who was again with the Pope at Rieti. Angelo Malebranca, "by the grace of God the illustrious senator of the gentle city" (such were the high-sounding phrases), by the decree and authority of the sacred senate, by the command and instant acclamation of the famous people, assembled in the Capitol at the sound of the bell and of the trumpet, swore to the peace proposed by the three cardinals, between the Holy Roman Church, their Father the Supreme Pontiff, and the Senate and people of Rome. He swore to give satisfaction for the demolition of the Lateran palace and those of the cardinals, the invasion of the Papal territories, the exaction of oaths, the occupation of the domains of the Church. He swore that no clerks or ecclesiastical persons belonging to the families of the Pope or cardinals should be summoned before the civil tribunals (thus even in Rome there was a strong opposition to those immunities of the clergy from temporal jurisdiction for temporal offences).

Sept. 1231.

April 14, 17.b.

---

[m] "Milites in civitate Viterbio collocavit, quorum quotidianis insultibus et depredationibus Romani adeo sunt vexati, ut non multo post cum Papâ pacem subirent."—God. Colon. The author of the life of Gregory says that the Emperor, instead of aiding the Pope, killed his time away in hunting: "Majestatis titulum in officium venaturæ commutans.... in exptorum avium sollicitabat aquilas triumphales."

This did not apply to laics who belonged to such households. He swore to protect all pilgrims, laymen as well as ecclesiastics, who visited the shrines of the Apostles.[a] The peace was re-established likewise with the Emperor and his vassals—with Anagni, Segni, Velletri, Viterbo, and other cities of the Papal territories. But even during this compulsory approximation to the Emperor, the Pope, to remove all suspicion that he might be won to desert their cause, wrote to the Lombards to reassure them. However, he might call upon them not to impede the descent of the Imperial troops from the Alps, those troops were not directed against their liberties, but came to maintain the liberties of the Church.

But if the rebels against the Pope were thus his immediate subjects the Romans, the rebel against Frederick was his own son. Henry had been left to rule Germany as king of the Romans; the causes and indeed the objects of his rebellion are obscure.[c] Henry appears to have been a man of feeble character; so long as he was governed by wise counsellors, filling his high office without blame; released from their control, the slave of his own loose passions, and the passive instrument of low and designing men. The only impulse to which the rebel son could appeal was the pride of Germany, which would no longer condescend to be governed from Italy, and to

Rebellion of King Henry.

---

[a] Apud Raynald. ann. 1235.

[c] In the year 1232 Frederick began to entertain suspicions of his son, and to be discontented with his conduct. Henry (but 20 years old) met his father at Aquileia, promised amendment, and to discard his evil counsellors.—Hahn. Collect. Monument. i. 223. Frederick might remember the fatal example of the Franconian house; the conduct of Henry V. to Henry IV. The chief burthen of Henry's vindication, addressed, Sept. 1234, to Bishop Conrad of Hildesheim, is that the Emperor had annulled some of his grants, interfered in behalf of the house of Bavaria (Louis of Bavaria had been guardian of the realm during his minority).

be a province of the kingdom of Apulia. Unlike some of his predecessors, Pope Gregory took at once the high Christian tone: he would seek no advantage from the unnatural insurrection of a son against his father. All the malicious insinuations against Gregory are put to silence by the fact that, during their fiercest war of accusation and recrimination, Frederick never charged the Pope with the odious crime of encouraging his son's disobedience. Frederick passed the Alps with letters from the Pope, calling on all the Christian prelates of Germany to assert the authority of the King and of the parent. Henry had held a council of princes [p] at Boppart to raise the standard of revolt, and had entered into treasonable league with Milan and the Lombard cities. The rebellion was as weak as wanton and guilty; Frederick entered Germany with the scantiest attendance; the affrighted son, abandoned by all his partisans, met him at Worms, and made the humblest submission.[q] Frederick renewed his pardon; but probably some new detected intrigues, or the refusal to surrender his castles, or meditated flight,[r] induced the Emperor to send his son as a prisoner to the kingdom of Naples. There he remained in such obscurity that his death might have been unnoticed but for a passionate lamentation which Frederick himself sent forth, in which he adopted the language of King David on the loss of his ungrateful but beloved Absalom.[s]

May, 1235.

July, 1235.

[p] God. Colon. Chron. Erphurd. apud Boehmer Fontes R. G.

[q] "Ipso mense, nullo obstante, Alemanniam intrans, Henricum regem filium suum ad mandatum suum recepit, quem duci Bavariæ custodiendum commisit."—Rich. San Germ.

[r] God. Col. Annal. Erphurdt. Quotation from Ann. Argentin. in Boehmer's Regesta, p. 254.

[s] Besides this pathetic letter in Peter de Vineâ, iv. 1, see the more extraordinary one, quoted by Höfler, addressed to the people of Messina.

Worms had beheld the sad scene of the ignominious arrest and imprisonment of the King of the Germans: that event was followed by the splendid nuptials of the Emperor with Isabella of England.

But though the Pope was guiltless, we believe he was guiltless, the Lombards were deep in this conspiracy against the power and the peace of Frederick. They, if they had not from the first instigated, had inflamed the ambition of Henry:[1] they had offered, if he would cross the Alps, to invest him at Monza with the iron crown of Italy." Frederick's long-suppressed impatience of Lombard freedom had now a justifiable cause for vengeance. The Ghibelline cities—Cremona, Parma, Pisa, and others; the Ghibelline Princes Eccelin and Alberic, the two sons of the suspected heretic Eccelin II. (who had now descended from his throne, and taken the habit of a monk, though it was rumoured that his devotion was that of an austere Paterin rather than that of an orthodox recluse) summoned the Emperor to relieve them from the oppressions of the Guelfic league, and to wreak his just revenge on those aggressive rebels. Frederick's declaration of war was drawn with singular subtlety. His chief object, he declared, was the suppression of heresy. The wide prevalence of heresy the Pope could not deny; to espouse the Lombard cause was to espouse that at least of imputed heresy; it was

Marginal notes: Lombards concerned in King Henry's rebellion. May 1, 1235. Aug. 1235.

---

[1] Galvaneo Fiamma has these words: "Henricus comporuit cum Mediolanensibus ad petitionem Domini Papæ,"—c. 264. "Et tunc facta est liga fortis inter Henricum et Mediolanenses ad petitionem Papæ contra Imperatorem patrem suum."—Annal. Mediolan., Muratori, xvi. 624. These are Milanese, certainly not Ghibelline writers!

" During this year (1235) Frederick assisted with seemingly deep devotion at the translation to Marburg of the remains of St. Elizabeth of Hungary. 1,200,000 persons are said to have been present.—Montalembert, Vie de St. Elisabeth d'Hongrie.

to oppose the Emperor in the exercise of his highest imperial function, the promotion of the unity of the Church. The Emperor could not leave his own dominions in this state of spiritual and civil revolt to wage war in foreign lands: so soon as he had subdued the heretic he was prepared to arm against the Infidel. Lombardy reduced to obedience, there would be no obstacle to the reconquest of the Holy Land. Yet though thus embarrassed, the Pope, in his own defence, could not but interpose his mediation; he commanded both parties to submit to his supreme arbitration. Frederick yielded, but resolutely limited the time; if the arbitration was not made before Christmas, he was prepared for war. To the most urgent remonstrances for longer time he turned a deaf and contemptuous ear: he peremptorily challenged the Legate whom the Pope had appointed, the Cardinal Bishop of Præneste, and refused to accept as arbiter his declared enemy.[a] Frederick had already begun the campaign: Verona had opened her gates; he had stormed Vicenza, and laid half the city in ashes. He was recalled beyond the Alps by the sudden insurrection of the Duke of Austria. Gregory so far yielded, that in place of the obnoxious Cardinal of Præneste, he named as his Legates the Cardinals of Ostia and of San Sabina. He commended them with high praise to the Patriarchs of Aquileia and of Grado, to the Archbishops of Genoa and Ravenna, whom, with the suffragans and all the people of Northern Italy, he exhorted to join in obtaining the blessings of peace. But already he began to murmur his complaints of those

Nov. 1, 1236.

March, 1237.

---

[a] Compare the letter, apud Raynald. sub ann. 1236; more complete in Höfler, p. 357, and 360.

grievances which afterwards darkened to such impious crimes. The Frangipanis were again breaking out into turbulence in Rome:[y] it was suspected and urged that they were in the pay of Frederick. Taxes had been levied on the clergy in the kingdom of Naples; they had been summoned before civil tribunals; the old materials of certain churches had been profanely converted by the Saracens of Nocera to the repair of their mosques. The answer of Frederick was lofty and galling. He denied the truth of the Pope's charges; he appealed to the conscience of the Pope. Gregory demanded by what right he presumed to intrude into that awful sanctuary.[z] "Kings and princes were humbly to repose themselves on the lap of priests; Christian Emperors were bound to submit themselves not only to the supreme Pontiff, but even to other bishops. The Apostolic See was the judge of the whole world; God had reserved to himself the sole judgement of the manifest and hidden acts of the Pope. Let the Emperor dread the fate of Uzzah, who laid his profane hands on the ark of God." He urged Frederick to follow the example of the great Constantine, who thought it absolutely wicked that, where the Head of the Christian religion had been determined by the King of Heaven, an earthly Emperor should have the smallest power, and had therefore surrendered Italy to

---

[y] "Hoc anno Petrus Frangipane, 1236, in urbe Româ pro parte Imperatoris guerram movit contra Papam et Senatorem."—Rich. San Germ.

[z] "Quod nequaquam Incauta ad judicanda secreta conscientiæ nostræ ... evolasses; cum regum colla et principum videas genibus sacerdotum, et Christiani Imperatores subdere debeant executiones suas non solum Romano Pontifici, quin etiam aliis præsulibus non præferre, nec non Dominus sedem apostolicam, cujus judicio orbem terrarum subjicit, in occultis et manifestis a nemine judicandam, soli suo judicio reservavit."—Greg. Epist. 10, 253, Oct. 23, 1236, apud Raynald.

the Apostolic government, and chosen for himself a new residence in Greece.*

Frederick returned from Germany victorious over the rebellious Duke of Austria; his son Conrad had been chosen King of the Romans. He crossed the Alps with three thousand German men-at-arms, besides the forces of the Ghibelline cities: he was joined by ten thousand Saracens from the South. His own ambassadors, Henry the Master of the Teutonic Order and his Chancellor Peter de Vineâ, by whom he had summoned the Pope to his aid against the enraged Lombards, had returned from Rome without accomplishing their mission. At the head of his army he would not grant audience to the Roman legates, the Cardinal Bishop of Ostia and the Cardinal of St. Sabina, who peremptorily enjoined him to submit to the arbitration of the Pope. The great battle of Corte Nuova might seem to avenge the defeat of his ancestor Frederick Barbarossa at Legnano. The Lombard army was discomfited with enormous loss; the Carroccio of Milan, defended till nightfall, was stripped of its banners, and abandoned to the conqueror. Frederick entered Cremona, the palaces of which city would hardly contain the captives, in a splendid ovation. The Podestà of Milan, Tiepolo, son of the Doge of Venice, was bound on the captive Carroccio; which was borne, as in the pomp of an Eastern potentate, on an elephant, followed by a wooden tower, with trumpeters and the Imperial standard. The pride of Frederick at this victory was at its height; he supposed that it would prostrate at once the madness of the rebels; he called upon the world to rejoice at the resto-

Second descent on Italy.
Aug. 1237.
Nov. 27, 1237.

---

* Ibid.

ration of the Roman Empire to all its rights.[b] The Caroccio was sent to Rome as a gift to the people of the gentle city: it was deposited in the Capitol, a significant menace to the Pope.[c] But where every city was a fortress, inexpugnable by the arts of war then known, a battle in the open field did not decide the fate of a league which included so many of the noblest cities of Italy. Frederick had passed the winter at Cremona; the terror of his arms had enforced at least outward submission from many of the leaguers. Almost all Piedmont, Alexandria, Turin, Susa, and the other cities raised the Ghibelline banner. Milan, Brescia, Piacenza, Bologna, remained alone in arms; even they made overtures for submission. Their offers were in some respects sufficiently humiliating; to acknowledge themselves rebels, to surrender all their gold and silver, to place their banners at the feet of the Emperor, to furnish one thousand men for the Crusades; but they demanded in return a general amnesty and admission to the favour of the Emperor, the maintenance of the liberties of the citizens and of the cities. Frederick haughtily de-

---

[b] See the letter in Peter de Vineâ. "Exultet jam Romani Imperii culmen ... mundus gaudeat universus ... confundatur rebellis insania."—Frederick disguised not, he boasted of the aid of his Saracens. He describes the Germans reddening their swords with blood, Pavia and Cremona wreaking vengeance on the tyrannous Milanese, "et suas evacuaverunt pharetras Saraceni."

[c] "Quando illum ad alma urbis populum destinavit." A marble monument of this victory was shown in 1727.—Muratori, Dissert. xxvi. t. ii. p. 491. The inscription was:—

"Ergo triumphorum urbis memor esto priorum, Quos tibi militabant reges qui bella gerebant."

—Francisc. Pipin. apud Muratori.—Compare the (Ghibelline) Chronicon de Rebus in Italia gestis, discovered by M. Panizzi in the British Museum, and printed with the Chronicon Placentinum at Paris, 1856. "Quod carocciam cum apud Romam duxissent, domious papa usque ad mortem doluit." The Pope would have prevented its admission into the city, but was overawed by the Imperialist party.—p. 172.

manded absolute and unconditional surrender. They
feared, they might well fear, Frederick's severity
against rebels. With mistimed and impolitic rigour he
had treated the captive Podestà of Milan as a rebel;
Tiepolo was sent to Naples, and there publicly executed.
The Republics declared that it was better to die by the
sword than by the halter, by famine, or by fire.[d] Frederick, in the summer of the next year, under- _{Aug. 2 to Oct.}
took the siege of Brescia; at the end of two ^{1238.}
months, foiled by the valour of the citizens and the skill
of their chief engineer, a Spaniard, Kalamandrino, he
was obliged to burn his besieging machines, and retire
humiliated to Padua.[e] But without aid the Lombard
liberties must fall: the Emperor was master of Italy
from the Alps to the straits of Messina; the knell of
Italian independence was rung; the Pope a vassal at
the mercy of Frederick.

The dauntless old man rose in courage with the
danger. Temporal allies were not absolutely wanting.
Venice, dreading her own safety, and enraged at the
execution of her noble son, Tiepolo, sent proposals for
alliance to the Pope. The treaty was framed; Venice
agreed to furnish 25 galleys, 300 knights, 2000 foot-
soldiers, 500 archers; she was to obtain, as the price of
this aid, Bari and Salpi in Apulia, and all that she could
conquer in Sicily.[f]

The Pope wrote to the confederate cities of Lombardy
and Romagna, taking them formally under the protection of the Holy See.[g] Genoa, under the same fears as
Venice, and jealous of Imperialist Pisa, was prepared
with her fleets to join the cause. During these nine

---

[d] Rich. de San Germ.
[e] Dandolo, 350. Marin. lv. 223.
[f] See B. Museum Chronicon, p. 177.
[g] Greg. Epist. apud Hahn. xviii.

years of peace, even if the former transgressions of Frederick were absolutely annulled by the treaty and absolution of San Germano, collisions between two parties both grasping and aggressive, and with rights the boundaries of which could not be precisely defined, had been inevitable: pretexts could be found, made, or exaggerated into crimes against the spiritual power, which would give some justification to that power to put forth, at such a crisis, its own peculiar weapons; and to recur to its only arms, the excommunication, the interdict, the absolution of subjects from their allegiance. Over this power Gregory had full command, in its employment no scruple.

On Palm Sunday, and on Thursday in Holy week, with all the civil and ecclesiastical state which he could assemble around him, Gregory pronounced excommunication against the Emperor; he gave over his body to Satan for the good of his soul, absolved all his subjects from their allegiance, laid under interdict every place in which he might be, degraded all ecclesiastics who should perform the services of the Church before him, or maintain any intercourse with him; and commanded the promulgation of this sentence with the utmost solemnity and publicity throughout Christendom. These were the main articles of the impeachment published some months before:—I. That in violation of his oath, he had stirred up insurrection in Rome against the Pope and the Cardinals. II. That he had arrested the Cardinal of Præneste while on the business of the Church among the Albigenses. III. That in the kingdom of Sicily he had kept benefices vacant to the ruin of men's souls; unjustly seized the goods of churches and monasteries, levied taxes on the clergy, imprisoned, banished, and even punished them with death. IV. That he had not restored their lands or goods to the Templars and Knights of St. John. V. That he had ill-treated, plundered, and expelled from his realm all the partisans of the Church. VI. That he had hindered the rebuilding of the church of Sora, favoured the Saracens, and settled them among Christians. VII. That he had seized and prevented the nephew of the King of Tunis from proceeding to Rome for baptism, and imprisoned Peter, Ambassador of the King of England. VIII. That he had taken possession of Massa, Ferrara, and especially Sardinia, being part of the patrimony of St. Peter. IX. That he had thrown obstacles in the way of the recovery of the Holy Land and the restoration of the Latin Empire in Constantinople, and in the affairs of the Lombards rejected the interposition of the Pope.

Frederick was at Padua, of which his most useful ally, Eccelin da Romano, had become Lord by all his characteristic treachery and barbarity. There were great rejoicings and festivities on that Palm Sunday; races and tournaments in honour of the Emperor. But some few Guelfs were heard to murmur bitterly among themselves, "This will be a day of woe to Frederick; this day the Holy Father is uttering his ban against him, and delivering him over to the devil!" On the arrival of the intelligence from Rome, Frederick for a time restrained his wrath. Peter de Vineâ, the great Justiciary of the realm of Naples, pronounced in the presence of Frederick, who wore his crown, a long exculpatory sermon to the vast assembly, on a text out of Ovid—"Punishment when merited is to be borne with patience, but when it is undeserved, with sorrow."[b]

---

[b] "Leniter ex merito quicquid patiare ferendum est
Quæ venit indigno pœna dolenda venit."

He declared, "that since the days of Charlemagne, no Emperor had been more just, gentle, and magnanimous, or had given so little cause for the hostility of the Church." The Emperor himself rose and averred, that if the excommunication had been spoken on just grounds, and in a lawful manner, he would have given instant satisfaction. He could only lament that the Pope had inflicted so severe a censure, without grounds and with such precipitate haste; even before the excommunication he had refuted with the same quiet arguments all these accusations. His first reply had been in the same calm and dignified tone.[1] The Pope had commissioned the Bishops of Wurtzburg, Worms, Vercelli, and Parma to admonish the Emperor previous to the excommunication. In their presence, and in that of the Archbishops of Palermo and Messina, the Bishops of Cremona, Lodi, Novara, and Mantua, many abbots, and some Dominican and Franciscan friars, he had made to all their charges a full and satisfactory answer, and delivered his justification to the Bishops:—I. He had encouraged no insurrection in Rome; he had assisted the Pope with men and money; he had no concern in the new feuds. II. He had never even dreamed of arresting the Cardinal of Præneste, though he might have found just cause, since the Cardinal, acting for the Pope, had inflamed the Lombards to disobedience and rebellion. III. He could give no answer to the vague and unspecified charges as to the oppression of the clergy in the realm of Naples; and as to particular churches he entered into long and elaborate explanations.[2] IV. He

Frederick's confutation of the charges.

Nov. 1238.

---

[1] Peter de Vineâ, l. 21, p. 156. The refutation of the charges, according to Matthew Paris (sub ann. 1239), was anterior to the excommunication.

[2] See especially, in a letter to

had restored all the lands to which the Templars and Knights of St. John had just claim; all but those which they had unlawfully received from his enemies during his minority; they had been guilty of aiding his enemies during the invasion of the kingdom, and some had incurred forfeiture: their lands, in certain cases, were assessable; were this not so, they would soon acquire the whole realm, and that exempt from all taxation. V. No one was condemned as a partisan of the Pope; some had abandoned their estates from fear of being prosecuted for their crimes. VI. No church had been desecrated or destroyed in Lucera; that of Sora was an accident, arising out of the disobedience of the city; he would rebuild that, and all which had fallen from age. The Saracens, who lived scattered over the whole realm, he had settled in one place, for the security of the Christians, and to protect rather than endanger the faith. VII. Abdelasis had fled from the court of the King of Tunis; he was not a prisoner, but living a free and pleasant life, furnished with horses, clothes, and money by the Emperor. He had never (he appealed to the Archbishops of Palermo and Messina) expressed any desire for baptism. Had he done so, no one would have rejoiced more than the Emperor. Peter was no Ambassador of the King of England. VIII. The pretensions of the Pope to Massa and Ferrara were groundless, still more to Sardinia, his son Enzio had married Adelasia, the heiress of that island; he was the rightful King. IX. The King prevents no one from preaching the Crusade; he only interferes with

---

Höfler, his justification for the refusal to rebuild the church at Sora. The city had rebelled, had been razed, church and all, and sown with salt. | Frederick. had sworn that the city should never be again inhabited: why build a church for an uninhabited wilderness?

those who, under pretence of preaching a Crusade, preach rebellion against the Sovereign, or, like John of Vicenza, usurp civil power. As to the affairs of Lombardy, the Pope had but interposed delays, to the frustration of his military plans. He would willingly submit to just terms; but after the unmeasured demands of the Lombards, and such manifest hostility on the part of the Pope, it would be dangerous and degrading to submit to the unconditional arbitration of the Pope.

The indignation of Frederick might seem to burst out with greater fury from this short, stern suppression. He determined boldly, resolutely, to measure his strength, the strength of the Emperor, the King of Sicily, so far the conqueror (notwithstanding the failure before Brescia) of the Lombard republics, against the strength of the Popedom. The Pope had declared war on causes vague, false or insignificant; the true cause of the war, Frederick's growing power and his successes in Lombardy, the Pope could not avow; Frederick would appeal to Christendom, to the world, on the justice of his cause and the unwarranted enmity of the Pope. He addressed strong and bitter remonstrances to the Cardinals, to the Roman people, to all the Sovereigns of Christendom. To the Cardinals he had already written, though his letter had not reached Rome before the promulgation of the excommunication, admonishing them to moderate the hasty resentment of the Pope. He endeavoured to separate the cause of the Pope from that of the Church; but vengeance against Gregory and the family of Gregory could not satisfy the insulted dignity of the Empire; if the authority of the Holy See, and the weight of their venerable college, thus burst all restraint, he must use all measures of

March 10.

defence; injury must be repelled with injury." Some
of the Cardinals had endeavoured to arrest the precipitate wrath of Gregory; he treated their timid prudence with scorn. To the Romans the Emperor expressed his indignant wonder that Rome being the head
of the Empire, the people, without reverence for his
majesty, ungrateful for all his munificence, had heard
tamely the blasphemies of the Roman Pontiff against
the Sovereign of Rome; that of the whole tribe of
Romulus there was not one bold patrician, of so many
thousand Roman citizens not one, who uttered a word of
remonstrance, a word of sympathy with their insulted
Lord. He called on them to rise and to revenge the
blasphemy upon the blasphemer, and not to allow him to
glory in his presumption, as if they consented to his audacity.* As he was bound to assert the honour of Rome,
so were they to defend the dignity of the Roman Emperor.

Before all the temporal Sovereigns of the world, the
Emperor entered into a long vindication of all his acts towards the Church and the Pope; he appealed to their justice against the unjust and tyrannous hierarchy. "Cast your eyes around! lift up your ears, O sons of men, that ye may hear! behold the universal scandal of the world, the dissensions of nations, lament the utter extinction of justice! Wickedness has gone out from the Elders of Babylon, who hitherto appeared to rule the people, whilst judgement is turned into bitterness, the fruits of justice into wormwood. Sit in judgement, ye Princes, ye People

Appeal to the Princes of Christendom, April 20.

---

* Apud Petrum de Vineâ, l. vi.
* "Quia cum idem blasphemator noster ausus non fuisset in nostri nominis blasphemiam prorumpere, de tantâ præsumptione gloriari non possit, quod valentibus et volentibus Romanis, contra nos talia perpetrasset," &c.— Apud Petr. de Vin. l. vii. Matth. Par. 332.

take cognisance of our cause; let judgement go forth from the face of the Lord and your eyes behold equity." The Papal excommunication had dwelt entirely on occurrences subsequent to the peace of San Germano. The Emperor went back to the commencement of the Pope's hostility: he dwelt on his ingratitude, his causeless enmity. "He, who we hoped thought only of things above, contemplated only heavenly things, dwelt only in heaven, was suddenly found to be but a man; even worse, by his acts of inhumanity is not only a stranger to truth, but without one feeling of humanity." He charged the Pope with the basest duplicity;° he had professed the firmest friendship for the Emperor, while by his letters and his Legates he was acting the most hostile part.ᵖ This charge rested on his own letters, and the testimony of his factious accomplices. The Pope had called on the Emperor to defy, and wage war against, the Romans on his behalf, and at the same time sent secret letters to Rome that this war was waged without his knowledge or command, in order to excite the hatred of the Romans against the Emperor. Rome, chiefly by his power, had been restored to the obedience of the Pope; what return had the Pope made?—befriending the Lombard rebels in every manner against their rightful Lord!ᑫ No sooner had

---

° "Asserens quod nobis omnia planissima faciebat, cujus contrarium per nuncios et literas manifeste procuraret; prout constat testimonio plurium nostrorum fidelium qui tunc temporis erant omnium consilii velut ex eis quidam participes, et alii principes factionis."

ᵖ He brought the charge against the Pope of writing letters to the Sultan, dissuading him from making peace, letters which he declared had fallen into his hands.

ᑫ "Audite mirabilem circumventionis modum ad depressionem nostræ justitiæ excogitatum. Dum pacem cum nobis habere velle se simularet ot Lombardos ad tempus, per treuguarum suffragia, respirantes, contra nos fortius postmodum in rebellione confirmet."—Epist. ad H. R. Angliæ. Rymer, sub ann. 1236.

he raised a powerful army of Germans to subdue these rebels, than the Pope inhibited their march, alleging the general truce proclaimed for the Crusade. The Legate, the Cardinal of Præneste, whose holy life the Pope so commended, had encouraged the revolt of Piacenza. Because he could find no just cause for his excommunication, the Pope had secretly sent letters and Legates through the Empire, through the world, to seduce his subjects from their allegiance. He had promised the ambassadors of Frederick, the Archbishop of Palermo, the Bishops of Florence and Reggio, the Justiciary Thaddeus of Suessa, and the Archbishop of Messina, that he would send a Legate to the Emperor to urge the Lombards to obedience; but in the mean time he sent a Legate to Lombardy to encourage and inflame their resistance. Notwithstanding his answer to all the charges against him, which had made the Bishops of the Papal party blush by their completeness;* notwithstanding this unanswerable refutation, the Pope had proceeded on Palm Sunday, and on Thursday in the Holy Week, to excommunicate him on these charges; this at the instigation of a few Lombard Cardinals, most of the better Cardinals, if report speaks true, remonstrating against the act. "Be it that we had offended the Pope by some public and singular insult, how violent and inordinate those proceedings, as though, if he had not vomited forth the wrath that boiled within him, he must have burst! We grieve from our reverence for our Mother the Church! Could we accept the Pope, thus our avowed enemy, no equitable judge, to arbitrate in our dispute with Milan;

---

* "Quanquam de patris instabilitate confusos as filii reputarent, ac verecundiâ capitis rubor ora perfunderet."—p. 156.

Milan, favoured by the Pope, though by the testimony of all religious men, swarming with heretics?"*. "Wo hold Pope Gregory to be an unworthy Vicar of Christ, an unworthy successor of St. Peter; not in disrespect to his office, but of his person, who sits in his court like a merchant weighing out dispensations for gold, himself signing, writing the bulls, perhaps counting the money. He has but one real cause of enmity against me, that I refused to marry to his niece my natural son Enzio, now King of Sardinia. But ye, O Kings and Princes of the earth, lament not only for us, but for the whole Church; for her head is sick; her prince is like a roaring lion; in the midst of her sits a frantic prophet, a man of falsehood, a polluted priest!" He concludes by calling all the princes of the world to his aid; not that his own forces are insufficient to repel such injuries, but that the world may know that when one temporal prince is thus attacked the honour of all is concerned.

Another Imperial address seems designed for a lower class, that class whose depths were stirred to hatred of the Emperor by the Preachers and the Franciscans. Its strong figurative language, its scriptural allusions, its invective against that rapacity of the Roman See which was working up a sullen discontent even among the clergy, is addressed to all Christendom. Some passages must illustrate this strange controversy. "The Chief Priests and the Pharisees have met in Council against their Lord, against the Roman Emperor. 'What shall we do,' say they, 'for this man is triumphing over all his enemies? If we let him alone, he will subdue the glory of the Lom-

<small>Appeal to the commonalty.</small>

---

* This very year Frederick renewed his remorseless edicts against the Lombard heretics.—Feb. 22. Monument. Germ. l. 396, 7, 8.

bards; and, like another Cæsar, he will not delay to take away our place and destroy our nation. He will hire out the vineyard of the Lord to other labourers, and condemn us without trial, and bring us to ruin.' . . . 'Let us not await the fulfilment of these words of our Lord, but strike him quickly,' say they, 'with our tongues; let our arrows be no more concealed, but go forth; so go forth as to strike, so strike as to wound; so be he wounded as to fall before us, so fall as never to rise again; and then will he see what profit he has in his dreams.'" Thus speak the Pharisees who sit in the seat of Moses. . . . "This father of fathers, who is called the servant of servants, shutting out all justice, is become a deaf adder; refuses to hear the vindication of the King of the Romans; hurls malediction into the world as a stone is hurled from a sling; and sternly, and heedless of all consequences, exclaims, 'What I have written, I have written.'"

In better keeping Frederick alludes to the words of our Lord to his disciples after his resurrection, "That Master of Masters said not, 'Take arms and shield, the arrow, and the sword;' but, 'Peace be with you.'" On the avarice of the Pope he is inexhaustible. "But thou having nothing, but possessing all things, art ever seeking what thou mayest devour and swallow up; the whole world cannot glut the rapacity of thy maw, for the whole world sufficeth thee not. The Apostle Peter, by the Beautiful Gate, said to the lame man, 'I have neither silver nor gold;' but thou, if thy heap of money, which thou adorest, begins to dwindle, immediately beginnest to limp with the lame man, seeking anxiously what is of this world.' . . . Let our Mother

---

¹ In one place he calls him "Gregorius gregis disgregator potius."

Church then bewail that the shepherd of the flock is become a ravening wolf, eating the fatlings of the flock; neither binding up the broken, nor bringing the wanderer home to the fold; but a lover of schism, the head and author of offence, the father of deceit; against the rights and honour of the Roman King he protects heretics, the enemies of God and of all the faithful in Christ; having cast aside all fear of God, all respect of man. But that he may better conceal the malice of his heart, he cherishes and protects these enemies of the Cross and of the faith, under a certain semblance of piety, saying that he only aids the Lombards lest the Emperor should slay them, and should judge more rigorously than his justice requires. But this fox-like craft will not deceive the skilful hunter. . . . O grief! rarely dost thou expend the vast treasures of the Church on the poor! But, as Anagni bears witness, thou hast commanded a wonderful mansion, as it were the Palace of the Sun, to be built, forgetful of Peter, who long had nothing but his net; and of Jerusalem, which lies the servant of dogs, tributary to the Saracens; 'All power is from God,' writes the Apostle; 'whoso resists the power resists the authority of God.' Either receive, then, into the bosom of the Church her elder son,° who without guile incessantly demands pardon; otherwise, the strong lion, who feigns sleep, with his terrible roar will draw all the fat bulls from the ends of the earth, will plant justice, take the rule over the Church, plucking up and destroying the horns of the proud."ˣ

The Pope, in his long and elaborate reply, exceeded even the violence of this fierce Philippic. It is thus

---

" Filium singularem."   ˣ Peter de Vineâ, l. 1.

that the Father of the Faithful commences his manifesto against the Emperor in the words of the Apocalypse: "Out of the sea is a beast arisen, *Pope's reply.* whose name is all over written 'Blasphemy;' he has the feet of a bear, the jaws of a ravening lion, the mottled limbs of the panther. He opens his mouth to blaspheme the name of God; and shoots his poisoned arrows against the tabernacle of the Lord, and the saints that dwell therein. . . . Already has he laid his secret ambush against the Church; he openly sets up the battering engines of the Ishmaelites; builds schools for the perdition of souls;' lifts himself up against Christ the Redeemer of man, endeavouring to efface the tablets of his testament with the pen of heretical wickedness. Cease to wonder that he has drawn against us the dagger of calumny, for he has risen up to extirpate from the earth the name of the Lord. Rather, to repel his lies by the simple truth, to refute his sophisms by the arguments of holiness, we exorcise the head, the body, the extremities of this beast, who is no other than the Emperor Frederick."

Then follows a full account of the whole of Frederick's former contest with Gregory, in which the Emperor is treated throughout as an unmeasured liar. "This shameless artisan of falsehood lies when he says that I was of old his friend." The history of the preparation for the Crusade, and the Crusade is related with the blackest calumny. To Frederick is attributed the death of the Crusaders at Brundusium, and the poisoning of the Landgrave of Thuringia insinuated as the general belief. The suppression of heresy in Lombardy could not be entrusted to one himself tainted by heresy.

---

⁷ Gregory no doubt alludes to the universities founded by Frederick.

The insurrections in Lombardy are attributed to the Emperor's want of clemency; the oppressions of the Church are become the most wanton and barbarous cruelties; "the dwellings of Christians are pulled down to build the walls of Babylon; churches are destroyed that edifices may be built where divine honours are offered to Mohammed." The kingdom of Sicily, so declares the Pope, is reduced to the utmost distress.[1] By his unexampled cruelties, barons, knights, and others have been degraded to the state and condition of slaves; already the greater part of the inhabitants have nothing to lie upon but hard straw, nothing to cover their nakedness but the coarsest clothes; nothing to appease their hunger but a little millet bread. The charge of dilapidation of the Papal revenues, of venal avarice, the Pope repels with indignation: "I, who by God's grace have greatly increased the patrimony of the Church. He falsely asserts that I was enraged at his refusing his consent to the marriage of my niece with his natural son.[2] He lies more impudently when he says that I

---

[1] Read the Canonico Gregorio's sensible account of the taxation of Sicily by Frederick II. "Occupato di continuo nelle guerre Italiane, intento a reprimere nei suoi stati i movimenti dei fazioni, e dalla implacabile ira dei suoi nemici oppresso e dai Romani Pontefici sempre costernato, ebbe così varia e travagliata fortuna, e fu in tali angustie di continuo ridotto, ed ai suoi molti e pressanti e sempre nuovi bisogni più non trovò gli ordinari proventi della corona, e le antiche rendite del regno sufficienti. Indi avvenne, chè da qual tempo in poi fu costretto ad ordinare i più sottili modi, perchè accrescence le pubbliche entrate, e nuove contribuzioni, comecchè fosse, si procacciasse: anzi le cose in processo di tempo supramente e per molta irritazion di animo si esacerbarono."—t. iii. p. 110. No doubt, as his finances became more and more exhausted by war, the burthens must have been heavier. But the flourishing state of Sicilian commerce and agriculture during the peaceful period but now elapsed, confutes the virulent accusation of the Pope.

[2] This is not strictly a denial of the fact of such proposals, or at least of advances by the Pope. This charge of early nepotism is curious.

have in return pledged my faith to the Lombards against the Empire." Throughout the whole document there is so much of the wild exaggeration of passion, and at the same time so much art in the dressing out of facts; such an absence of the grave majesty of religion and the calm simplicity of truth, as to be surprising even when the provocations of Frederick's addresses are taken into consideration. But the heaviest charge was reserved for the close. "In truth this pestilent King maintains to use his own words, that the world has been deceived by three impostors;[b] Jesus Christ, Moses, and Mahomet: the two of these died in honour, the third was hanged on a tree. Even more, he has asserted distinctly and loudly that those are fools who aver that God, the Omnipotent Creator of the world, was born of a Virgin."

Charge about the three impostors.

Such was the blasphemy of which the Pope arraigned the Emperor before Christendom. Popular rumour had scattered abroad through the jealousy of the active priesthood, and still more through the wandering Friars, many other sayings of Frederick equally revolting to the feelings of the age; not merely that which contrasted the fertility of his beloved Sicily with the Holy Land, but sayings which were especially scornful as to the presence of Christ in the sacrament. When he saw the host carried to a sick person, he is accused of saying, "How long will this mummery last?"[c] When a Saracen prince was present at the mass, he asked what was in the monstrance: "The people fable that it is our God." Passing once through a corn-field, he said,

---

[b] A book was said to have existed at this time, with this title; it has never been discovered. I have seen a vulgar production with the title, of modern manufacture.

[c] "Quam diu durabit Truffa ista?"

"How many Gods might be made out of this corn?" "If the princes of the world would stand by him he would easily make for all mankind a better faith and better rule of life."[a]

Frederick was not unconscious of the perilous workings of these direct and indirect accusations upon the popular mind. He hastened to repel them; and to turn the language of the Apocalypse against his accuser. He thus addressed the bishops of Christendom.

Frederick's rejoinder.

After declaring that God had created two great lights for the guidance of mankind, the Priesthood and the Empire:—" He, in name only Pope, has called us the beast that arose out of the sea, whose name was Blasphemy, spotted as the panther. We again aver that he is the beast of whom it is written, 'And there went out another horse that was red, and power was given to him that sat thereon to take away peace from the earth, that the living should slay each other.' For from the time of his accession this Father, not of mercies but of discord, not of consolation but of desolation, has plunged the whole world in bitterness. If we rightly interpret the words, he is the great anti-Christ, who has deceived the whole world, the anti-Christ of whom he declares us the forerunner. He is a second Balaam hired by money to curse us; the prince of the princes of darkness who have abused the prophecies. He is the angel who issued from the abyss having the vials full of wormwood to waste earth and heaven." The Emperor disclaims in the most emphatic terms the speech about the three impostors; rehearses his creed, especially concern-

---

[a] Peter de Vineâ, l. 31. He was said also to have laid down the maxim, "Homo nihil aliud debet credere, nisi quod potest vi et ratione naturæ probare."—Apud Raynald.

ing the Incarnation, in the orthodox words; expresses the most reverential respect for Moses: "As to Mahomet, we have always maintained that his body is suspended in the air, possessed by devils, his soul tormented in hell, because his works were works of darkness and contrary to the laws of the Most High." The address closed with an appeal to the sounder wisdom of the Prelates, and significant threats of the terrors of his vengeance.

The effect of this war of proclamations, addressed, only with a separate superscription, to every King in Christendom, circulated in every kingdom, was to fill the hearts of the faithful with terror, amazement, and perplexity. Those who had espoused neither the party of the Emperor nor of the Pope fluctuated in painful doubt. The avarice of the Roman See had alienated to a great extent the devotion of mankind, otherwise the letter of the Pope would have exasperated the world to madness; they would have risen in one wide insurrection against the declared adversary of the Church, as the enemy of Christ. "But alas!" so writes a contemporary historian, "many sons of the Church separated themselves from their father the Pope, and joined the Emperor, well knowing the inexorable hatred between the Pope and the Emperor, and that from that hatred sprung these fierce, indecent and untrustworthy invectives. The Pope, some said, pretends that from his love to Frederick he had contributed to elevate him to the Empire, and reproaches him with ingratitude. But it is notorious that this was entirely out of hatred to Otho, whom the Pope persecuted to death for asserting the interests of the Empire, as Frederick now asserts them. Frederick fought the battle of the Church in Palestine,

July 1.

Public opinion in Christendom.

which is under greater obligation to him than he to the Church. The whole Western Church, especially the monasteries, are every day ground by the extortions of the Romans; they have never suffered any injustice from the Emperor. The people subjoined, 'What means this? A short time ago the Pope accused the Emperor of being more attached to Mohammedanism than to Christianity, now he is accused of calling Mohammed an impostor. He speaks in his letters in the most Catholic terms. He attacks the person of the Pope, not the Papal authority. We do not believe that he has ever avowed heretical or profane opinions; at all events he has never let loose upon us usurers and plunderers of our revenues.'"*

This was written in an English monastery. In England as most heavily oppressed, there was the strongest discontent. The feeble Henry III., though brother-in-law of the Emperor, trembled before the faintest whisper of Papal authority. But the nobles, even the Churchmen, began to betray their Teutonic independence. Robert Twenge, the Yorkshire knight, the ringleader of the insurrection against the Italian intruders into the English benefices, ventured to Rome, not to throw himself at the Pope's feet and to entreat his pardon, but with a bold respectful letter from the Earls of Chester, Winchester, and other nobles, remonstrating against the invasion of their rights of patronage. Gregory was compelled to condescend to a more moderate tone; he renounced all intention of usurpation on the rights of the barons. Robert Twenge received the acknowledgment of his right to present to the church of Linton. All the Prelates of the realm, assembled at London,

---

* Matt. Paris, sub ann. 1239.

disdainfully rejected the claim made for procurations for the Papal Legate Otho, whom two years before they had allowed to sit as Dictator of the Church in the council of London.ᶠ "The greedy avarice of Rome," they said, "has exhausted the English Church; it will not give it even breathing time; we can submit to no further exactions. What advantage have we from the visitation of this Legate? Let him that sent him here uninvited by the native clergy, maintain him as long as he remains here." The Legate, finding the Prelates obstinate, extorted a large sum for his procurations from the monasteries.

The Emperor highly resented the publication of the sentence of excommunication in the realm of the brother of his Empress Isabella. He sent a haughty message,ᵍ expostulating with the King for permitting this insult upon his honour; he demanded the dismissal of the Legate, no less the enemy of the kingdom of England than his own;ʰ the Legate who was exacting money from the whole realm to glut the avarice of the Pope, and to maintain the Papal arms against the Emperor. Henry III. sent a feeble request to Rome, imploring the Pope to act with greater mildness to Frederick; the Pope treated the message with sovereign contempt. Nor did the Legate behave with less insolent disdain to the King. Henry advised him to

---

[f] Wilkins, Concilia, 1237. Compare page 216.

[g] Letters to the Barons of England (Boehmer, Oct. 29, 1239), Rymer, 1238? To the King, March 16, 1240. Matt. Paris, 1239.

[h] Henry, before the declaration of the Pope against the Emperor, had sent a small force, under Henry de Turberville and the Bishop Elect of Valence, to aid Frederick against the insurgent Lombards. The army was accompanied by a citizen and a clerk of London, John Mansel and W. Hardel, with money.—Paris, sub ann. 1238, Matt. West. The Pope broke out into fury against the King.

quit the kingdom; "You invited me here, find me a safe-conduct back." In the mean time he proceeded again to levy his own procurations, to sell (so low was the Pope reduced), by Gregory's own orders, dispensations to those who had taken on them vows to proceed to the Holy Land. At length, at a council held at Reading, he demanded a fifth of all the revenues of the English clergy, in the name of the Pope to assist him in his holy war against the Emperor. Edmund Rich the Primate yielded to the demand, and was followed by others of the bishops.[1] But Edmund, worn out with age and disgust, abandoned his see, withdrew into France, and in the same monastery of Pontigny, imitated the austerities and prayers, as he could not imitate the terrors, of his great predecessor Becket. The lower clergy were more impatient of the Papal demands. A crafty agent of the Pope, Pietro Rosso,[k] (Peter the Red), travelled about all the monasteries extorting money; he falsely declared that all the bishops, and many of the higher abbots, had eagerly paid their contributions. But he exacted from them, as if from the Pope himself, a promise to keep his assessment secret for a year. The abbots appealed to the King, who treated them with utter disdain. He offered one of his castles to the Legate and Peter the Red, and to imprison two of the appellants, the Abbots of St. Edmundsbury and of Beaulieu. At Northampton the Legate and Peter again assembled the bishops, and demanded the fifth from all the possessions of the Church. The bishops declared that they must consult their archdeacons. The clergy refused altogether this new levy; they

---

[1] Edmund had aspired to be a second Becket; he had raised a quarrel with the King on the nomination to the benefices; but feebly supported by Gregory in his distress, he recoiled from the contest. [k] De Rubeis.

would not contribute to a fund raised to shed Christian blood. The rectors of Berkshire were more bold; their answer has a singular tone of fearless English freedom; "they would not submit to contribute to funds raised against the Emperor as if he were a heretic; though excommunicated he had not been condemned by the judgement of the Church; even if he does occupy the patrimony of the Church, the Church does not employ the secular arm against heretics. The Church of Rome has its own patrimony, it has no right to tax the churches of other nations. The Pope has the general care over all churches, but no property in their estates. The Lord said to Peter, 'What you bind on earth shall be bound in heaven;' not 'What you exact on earth shall be exacted in heaven.' The revenues of the Church were assigned to peculiar uses, for the relief of the poor, not for maintenance of war, especially among Christians. Popes, even when they were exiles and the Church of England was at its wealthiest, had made no such demands." Yet partly by sowing discord among his adversaries, partly by flattery, partly by menace, the Legate continued, to the great indignation of the Emperor, to levy large sums for the Papal Crusade in the dominions of his brother-in-law.[m]

All Saints, 1240.

In France Pope Gregory attempted to play a loftier game by an appeal to the ambition of the royal house; he would raise up a new French Pepin or Charlemagne to the rescue of the endangered Papacy. He sent ambassadors to the court of St. Louis with this message:—"After mature deliberation with our brethren the Cardinals we have deposed from the imperial throne the reigning Emperor

Offer of Imperial Crown to Robert of France.

---
[m] M. Paris, sub ann. 1240.

Frederick; we have chosen in his place Robert, brother of the King of France. Delay not to accept this dignity, for the attainment of which we offer all our treasures, and all our aid." The Pope could hardly expect the severe rebuke in which the pious King of France couched his refusal of this tempting offer. "Whence this pride and audacity of the Pope, which thus presumes to disinherit and depose a King who has no superior, nor even an equal, among Christians; a King neither convicted by others, nor by his own confession, of the crimes laid to his charge? Even if those crimes were proved, no power could depose him but a general council. On his transgressions the judgement of his enemies is of no weight, and his deadliest enemy is the Pope. To us he has not only thus far appeared guiltless, he has been a good neighbour; we see no cause for suspicion either of his worldly loyalty, or his Catholic faith. This we know, that he has fought valiantly for our Lord Jesus Christ both by sea and land. So much religion we have not found in the Pope, who endeavoured to confound and wickedly supplant him in his absence, while he was engaged in the cause of God."[a] The nobles of France did more, they sent ambassadors to Frederick to inform him of the Pope's proceedings, and to demand account of his faith. Frederick was moved by this noble conduct. He solemnly protested his orthodox belief. "May Jesus Christ grant that I never depart from the faith of my magnanimous ancestors, to follow the ways of perdition. The Lord judge between me and the man who has thus defamed me before the world." He lifted his hands to heaven, and said in a passion of tears: "The

---

[a] Paris, sub ann. 1239.

God of vengeance recompense him as he deserves. If," he added, " you are prepared to war against me, I will defend myself to the utmost of my power." "God forbid," said the ambassadors, "that we should wage war on any Christian without just cause. To be the brother of the King of France is sufficient honour for the noble Robert."

In Germany the attempt of the Pope to dethrone the Emperor awoke even stronger indignation. Two princes to whom Gregory made secret overtures refused the perilous honour. An appeal to the Prelates of the Empire was met even by the most respectful with earnest exhortations to peace. In one address they declared the universal opinion that the whole quarrel arose out of the unjustifiable support given by the Pope to the Milanese rebels; and they appealed to the continued residence of the Papal Legate, Gregory of Monte Longo, in Milan as manifesting the Pope's undeniable concern in that obstinate revolt.° Popular German poetry denounced the Pope as the favoured of the Lombard heretics, who had made him drunk with their gold.ᵖ Gregory himself bitterly complains " that the German princes and prelates still adhered to Frederick, the oppressor, the worse than assassin, who imprisons them, places them under the ban of the Empire, even puts them to death. Nevertheless they despise the Papal anathema, and maintain his cause."ᵍ Gregory was not fortunate or not wise in the choice of his

* Apud Hahn, Monument. t. I. p. 234. "Testimonium generalis opinionis quod in favorem Mediolanensium, et suorum sequacium processerit taliter contra eum ... quod G. de Monte Longo legatus vester, apud Mediolanenses continuam moram trahens, fideles im-
perti modis omnibus, quibus potest, a fide et devotione debita altitur revocare."

ᵖ See the quotation from Bruder Weinher, the Minnesinger, in Giesler.

ᵍ Dumont apud Von Raumer.

partisans. One of those partisans, Rainer of St. Quentin, presumed to summon the German prelates to answer at Paris for their disloyal conduct to the Pope. The Pope had invested Albert von Beham Archdeacon of Passau, a violent and dissolute man, with full power; he used it to threaten bishops and even archbishops, he dared to utter sentences of excommunication against them. He alarmed the Duke of Bavaria into the expression of a rash desire that they had another Emperor. It was on Otho of Bavaria that Albert strove to work with all the terrors of delegated papal power. There was a dispute between the Archbishop of Mentz and Otho concerning the convent of Laurisheim. Albert as Papal Legate summoned the Primate to appear at Heidelberg. The archbishop not appearing was declared contumacious; an interdict was laid on Mentz. In another quarrel of Otho with the Bishop of Freisingen the imperialist judges awarded a heavy fine against Otho. Von Beham, irritated by songs in the streets, "The Pope is going down, the Emperor going up,"[r] rescinded the decree on the Pope's authority, and commanded the institution of a new suit. Von Beham ordered the Archbishop of Saltzburg and the Bishop of Passau to excommunicate Frederick of Austria for his adherence to the Emperor; summoned a council at Landshut; placed Siegfried Bishop of Ratisbon, the Chancellor of the Empire, under the ban; threatened to summon the Archbishop of Saltzburg and the Bishop to arraign them under processes of treason; "he would pluck their mitres from their heads." The Bishop of Passau, in his resentment, threatened to arm his men in a Crusade against Albert

---

[r] "Ruit pars Papalis, prævaluit Imperialis."

von Beham. Albert did not confine himself to Bavaria, he threatened the Bishops of Augsburg, Wurtzburg, Eichstadt, with the same haughty insolence. The consequence of all this contempt thus thrown on the greatest prelates was, that the imperialists everywhere gained courage. The Emperor, the Landgrave of Thuringia, the Marqnis of Meissen, Frederick of Austria, treated the excommunication as a vulgar ghost, an old wives' tale.* But the great prelates did not disguise their wrath; their dislike and contempt for Von Beham was extended to his master. "Let this Roman priest," said Conrad Bishop of Freisingen, "feed his own Italians; we who are set by God as dogs to watch our own folds, will keep off all wolves in sheep's clothing." Eberhard Archbishop of Saltzburg not only applied the same ignominious term to the Pope, but struck boldly at the whole edifice of the Papal power; we seem to hear a premature Luther. He describes the wars, the slaughters, the seditions, caused by these Roman Flamens, for their own ambitious and rapacious ends. "Hildebrand, one hundred and seventy years ago, under the semblance of religion, laid the foundations of Antichrist. He who is the servant of servants would be the Lord of Lords. . . . This accursed man, whom men are wont to call Anti-

---

* "Ut tremendum olim excommunicationis nomen, non magis quam capitalem larvam, aut nutricularum narnias metuerent, probrosum rati croda militarium hominum pectora capi, angique religionibus, quae sacrificali ut vanissimus superstitiones desperarent."—Brunner, xll, quoted in the preface to the curious publication of Höfler, "Albert von Beham," Stuttgard, 1847. Frederick of Austria held a grave assembly of Teutonic Knights, Templars, and Hospitallers, three abbots, five myrtæ. By these "Alberti impudentia irrisa; exsibilati qui huic misero nundinatori operam præstarent cujus mercem fumosque præter Bohemum Regem, et Bavariæ Ducem nemo æstimaret." — Ibid. "Neque deerant inter sacrificulos scurræ qui omnia Alberti fulmina, negarent se vel una piaculari faba procuraturos,"—p. xix. Albert was in poverty and disgrace about the time of Gregory's death, May 6, 1241.— Höfler, p. 30.

christ, on whose contumelious forehead is written, 'I am God, I cannot err,' sits in the temple of God and pretends to universal dominion."[t] Frederick himself addressed a new proclamation to the princes of Germany. Its object was to separate the interests of the Church from those of the Pope; those of the Bishop of Rome from Gregory. "Since his ancestors the Cæsars had lavished wealth and dignity on the Popes, they had become the Emperor's most implacable enemies. Because I will not recognise his sole unlimited power and honour him more than God, he, Antichrist himself, brands me, the truest friend of the Church, as a heretic. Who can wish more than I that the Christian community should resume its majesty, simplicity, and peace? but this cannot be, until the fundamental evil, the ambition, the pride, and prodigality of the Bishop of Rome, be rooted up. I am no enemy of the priesthood; I honour the priest, the humblest priest, as a father, if he will keep aloof from secular affairs. The Pope cries out that I would root out Christianity with force and by the sword. Folly! as if the kingdom of God could be rooted out by force and by the sword; it is by evil lusts, by avarice and rapacity, that it is weakened, polluted, corrupted. Against these evils it is my mission of God to contend with the sword. I will give back to the sheep their shepherd, to the people their bishop, to the world its spiritual father. I will tear the mask from the face of this wolfish tyrant, and force him to lay aside worldly affairs and earthly pomp, and tread in the holy footsteps of Christ."[u]

---

[t] Aventinus, Annal. Brunner doubts the authenticity of this speech of the Archbishop of Saltzburg. It rests on the somewhat doubtful authority of Aventinus. It sounds rather of a later date.

[u] Frederick wrote to Otho of Bavaria (Oct. 4, 1240) to expel Albert von Beham from his dominions.—Aventin. Ann. Boior. v. 3, 5.

On the other hand, the Pope had now a force working in every realm of Christendom, on every class of mankind, down to the very lowest, with almost irresistible power. The hierarchical religion of the age, the Papal religion, with all its congenial imaginativeness, its burning and unquestioning faith, its superstitions, was kept up in all its intensity by the preachers and the mendicant friars. Never did great man so hastily commit himself to so unwise a determination as Innocent III., that no new Orders should be admitted into that Church which has maintained its power by the constant succession of new Orders. Never was his greatness shown more than by his quick perception and total repudiation of that error. Gregory IX. might indeed have more extensive experience of the use of these new allies: on them he lavished his utmost favour; he had canonised both St. Dominic and St. Francis with extraordinary pomp; he entrusted the most important affairs to their disciples. The Friars. May 6, 1241. The Dominicans, and still more the Franciscans, showed at once the wisdom of the Pope's conduct and their own gratitude by the most steadfast attachment to the Papal cause. They were the real dangerous enemies of Frederick in all lands. They were in kings' courts; the courtiers looked on them with jealousy, but were obliged to give them place; they were in the humblest and most retired villages. No danger could appal, no labours fatigue their incessant activity. The first act of Frederick was to expel, imprison, Nov. 1240 or take measures of precaution against those of the clergy who were avowed or suspected partisans of the Pope. The friars had the perilous distinction of being cast forth in a body from the realm, and forbidden under the severest penalties to violate its borders." In every Guelfic city they openly, in every Ghibelline city, if they dared not openly, they secretly preached the crusade against the Emperor.' Milan, chiefly through their preaching, redeemed herself from the charge of connivance at the progress of heresy by a tremendous holocaust of victims, burned without mercy. The career of John of Vicenza had terminated before the last strife;* but John of Vicenza was the type of the friar preachers in their height of influence; that power cannot be understood without some such example; and though there might be but one John of Vicenza, there were hundreds working, if with less authority, conspiring to the same end, and swaying with their conjoint force the popular mind.

Assuredly, of those extraordinary men who from time to time have appeared in Italy, and by their passionate religious eloquence seized and for a time bound down the fervent Italian mind, not the least extraordinary was Brother John (Fra Giovanni), of a noble house in Vicenza. He became a friar preacher: he appeared in Bologna. Before long, not only did the populace crowd in countless multitudes to his pulpit; the authorities, with their gonfalons and crosses, stood around him in mute and submissive homage. In a short time he preached down every feud in the city, in the district, in the county of Bologna. The women threw aside their ribbons, their flowers—their modest heads

John of Vicenza.

---

* "Capitula edita sunt, in primis ut Fratres Prædicatores et Minores, qui sunt oriundi de terris Infidelium Lombardiæ expellantur de regno."— Rich. de San Germ. Gregory asserts that one Friar Minor was burned.—Greg. Bull. apud Raynald. p. 220.

▼ It is, however, very remarkable that even now the second Great Master of the Franciscans, expelled or having revolted from his Order, Brother Elias, a most popular preacher, was on the side of Frederick.

‡ There is an allusion to John of Vicenza in a letter of Frederick.—Höfler, p. 363.

were shrouded in a veil. It was believed that he wrought daily miracles.* Under his care the body of St. Dominic was translated to its final resting-place with the utmost pomp. It was said, but said by unfriendly voices, that he boasted of personal conversation with Christ Jesus, with the Virgin Mary, and with the angels. The friar preachers gained above twenty thousand marks of silver from the prodigal munificence of his admirers. He ruled Bologna with despotic sway; released criminals; the Podestà stood awed before him; the envious Franciscans alone (their envy proves his power) denied his miracles, and made profane and buffoonish verses against the eloquent Dominican.[b]

But the limits of Bologna and her territory were too narrow for the holy ambition, for the wonderful powers of the great preacher. He made a progress through Lombardy. Lombardy was then distracted by fierce wars—city against city; in every city faction against faction. Wherever John appeared was peace. Padua advanced with her carroccio to Monselice to escort him into the city. Treviso, Feltre, Belluno, Vicenza, Verona, Mantua, Brescia, heard his magic words, and reconciled their feuds. On the shores of the Adige, about three miles from Verona, assembled the whole of Lombardy, to proclaim and to swear to a solemn act of peace. Verona, Mantua, Brescia, *August 28, 1233.*

---

* But, says an incredulous writer, "Dicevasi ancora ch' egli curasse ogni malattia, e che cacciasse i demoni; ma Io non potei vedere alcuno da lui liberato, benchè pure usassi ogni mezzo per vederlo; nè potei parlare con alcuno che affermasse con sicurezza di aver veduto qualche miracolo da lui operato."—Salimbeni.

[b] "Et Johannes Johannissat Et saltando chorizat: Modo salta, modo salta, Qui coriorum petis alta. Saltat laic, saltat ille, Resultant cohortes mille; Saltat chorus Dominarum, Saltat Dux Venetiarum."
—from Salimbeni, Von Raumer, iii. p. 656.

Padua, Vicenza, came with their carroccios; from Treviso, Venice, Ferrara, Bologna, thronged numberless votaries of peace. The Bishops of Verona, Brescia, Mantua, Bologna, Modena, Reggio, Treviso, Vicenza, Padua, gave the sanction of their sacred presence. The Podestàs of Bologna, Treviso, Padua, Vicenza, Brescia, Ferrara, appeared, and other lords of note, the patriarch of Aquileia, the Marquis of Este. It was asserted that 400,000 persons stood around. John of Vicenza ascended a stage sixty feet high; it was said that his sermon on the valedictory words of the Lord, "My peace I leave with you," was distinctly heard, wafted or echoed by preternatural powers to every ear.* The terms of a general peace were read, and assented to by one universal and prolonged acclamation. Among these was the marriage of Rinaldo, son of the Marquis of Este, with Adelaide daughter of Alberic, brother of Eccelin da Romano. This was the gage of universal amity; these two great houses would set the example of holy peace. Men rushed into each other's arms; the kiss of peace was interchanged by the deadliest enemies, amid acclamations which seemed as if they would never cease.

But the waters of the Po rise not with more sudden and overwhelming force, ebb not with greater rapidity, than the religious passions of the Italians, especially the passion for peace and concord. John of Vicenza split on the rock fatal always to the powerful spiritual demagogues, even the noblest demagogues, of Italy. He became a politician. He retired to his native Vicenza; entered into the Council, aspired to be Lord and Count;

---

* Even the Franciscans were carried away by the enthusiasm; they preached upon his miracles; they averred that he had in one day raised ten dead bodies to life.

all bowed before him. He proceeded to examine and
reform the statutes of the city. He passed to Verona,
demanded and obtained sovereign power; introduced
the Count Boniface, received hostages for mutual peace
from the conflicting parties. He took possession of some
of the neighbouring castles; waged fierce war with heretics; burned sixty males and females of some of the
noble families; published laws. Vicenza became jealous
of Verona; Padua leagued with Vicenza to throw off
the yoke. The Preacher, at the head of an armed force,
appeared at the gates, demanded the unconditional surrender of the walls, towers, strongholds of the city. He
was repelled, discomfited, by the troops of Padua and
Vicenza, taken, and cast into prison.

He was released by the intercession of Pope Gregory
IX.[d] The peace of Lombardy was then accordant to
the Papal policy, because it was embarrassing to Frederick II. He returned to Verona; but the spell of his
power was broken. He retired to Bologna, to obscurity.
Bologna even mocked his former miracles. Florence
refused to receive him: "Their city was populous
enough; they had no room for the dead which he would
raise."[e]

Christendom awaited in intense anxiety the issue of
this war—a war which, according to the declaration
of the Emperor, would not respect the sacred person

[d] It is said that he was afterwards commissioned by Innocent IV. to proclaim the Papal absolution in Vicenza, from excommunication incurred by the succours furnished by that city to Frederick II. and Ezzelin da Romano. Tiraboschi has collected all the authorities on John of Vicenza with his usual industry.—Storia della Lit. Ital. vol. xiv. p. 2.

[e] See in Von Raumer how the Grammarian Buoncompagnol assembled the people to see him fly, on wings which he had prepared. After keeping them some time in suspense, he coolly said, "This is a miracle after the fashion of John of Vicenza."—Von Raumer, from Salimbeni.

of the Pope, and would enforce, if Frederick were victorious, the absolute, unlimited supremacy of the temporal power. This war was now proclaimed and inevitable. The Pope must depend on his own armies and on those of his Italian allies. The tenths and the fifths of England and of France might swell the Papal treasury, and enable him to pay his mercenary troops; but there was no sovereign, no army of Papal partisans beyond the Alps which would descend to his rescue. The Lombards might indeed defend their own cities against the Emperor,[1] and his son King Enzio,

May 25, 1239.

who was declared imperial vicar in the north of Italy, was at the head of the Germans and Saracens of the Imperial army, and had begun to display his great military skill and activity. The strength of the maritime powers, who had entered into the league, was in their fleets; though at a later period Venetian forces appeared before Ferrara. The execution of Tiepolo the podestà of Milan, taken at the battle of Corte Nuova, had enflamed the resentment of that republic: they seemed determined to avenge the insult and wrong to that powerful and honoured family. But the Pope, though not only his own personal dignity, but even the stability of the Roman See was on the hazard, with the calm dauntlessness which implied his full reliance on his cause as the cause of God, confronted the appalling crisis. Some bishops sent to Rome by Frederick were repelled with scorn. The Pope, as the summer heats came on, feared not to leave fickle Rome: he retired, as

---

[1] The legate of the Pope, Gregory of Monte Longo, at Milan, raised the banner of the Cross—"sumpto mandato ejus signo crucis, et paratis duobus vexillis cum crucibus et clavibus intus"—marched towards Lodi, destroying church towers (turres ecclesiarum) and ravaging the harvests.—B. Museum Chronicon, p. 177.

usual, to his splendid palace at Anagni. During the rest of that year successes and failures seemed nearly balanced.* Treviso threw off the imperial yoke; even Ravenna, supported by a Venetian fleet, rebelled. The Emperor sat down before Bologna, obtained some great advantages humiliating to the Bolognese, but, as usual, failed in his attempt to capture the town. These successes before Bologna were balanced by failure, if not defeat, before Milan. Bologna was not so far discomfited but that she could make an attack on Modena. In November the Pope returned to Rome: he was received with the utmost honour, with popular rejoicings. He renewed in the most impressive form the excommunication of the Emperor and all his sons, distinguishing with peculiar rigour the King Enzio.

<small>April, 1239.</small>
<small>September.</small>
<small>Nov. 1239.</small>

The Emperor passed the winter in restoring peace in Ghibelline Pisa. The feud in Pisa was closely connected with the affairs of Sardinia.[b] Pisa claimed the sovereignty of that island, which the all-grasping Papacy declared a fief of the Roman See. Ubaldo, of the noble Guelfic house of Visconti, had married Adelasia, the

---

<small>* The castles of Piumazzo and Cravacoore were taken. Piumazzo was burned; the captain of the garrison was burned in the castle: 500 taken prisoners.—July.

[b] The Sardinian affair was another instance of the way in which an assertion once made that a certain territory or right belonged to the See of St. Peter, grew up into what was held to be an indefeasible title. The Popes had made themselves the successors of the Eastern Emperors. Their own declaration that Naples was a fief of the Holy See (having been acknowledged by the Normans to piece out their own usurpation) became a legal inalienable dominion. The claim to Sardinia rested on nothing more than the assertion that it was a part of the territory of the Roman See (it was no acknowledged part of the inheritance of the Countess Matilda).—Rich. de San Germ. The strange pretension that all islands belonged to the See of Rome, as well as all lands conquered from heretics, if already heard, was not yet an axiom of the canon law.</small>

heiress of the native Judge or Potentate of Gallura and of Tura: he bought the Papal absolution from a sentence of excommunication and the recognition of his title by abandoning the right of Pisa, and acknowledging the Papal sovereignty. Pisa heard this act of treason with the utmost indignation. The Gherardesci, the rival Ghibelline house, rose against the Visconti. Ubaldo died; and Frederick (this was among the causes of Gregory's deadly hatred) married the heiress Adelasia to his natural son, whom he proclaimed king of Sardinia. The Ghibellines of Pisa recognised his title.

1240.

With the early spring the Emperor, at the head of an imposing, it might seem irresistible force, advanced into the territories of the Church. Foligno threw open her gates to welcome him. Other cities from fear or affection, Viterbo from hatred of Rome, hailed his approach. Ostia, Civita Castellana, Corneto, Sutri, Montefiascone, Toscanella received the enemy of the Pope. The army of John of Colonna, which during the last year had moved into the March against King Enzio, was probably occupied at some distance: Rome might seem to lie open; the Pope was at the mercy of his foe. Could he depend on the fickle Romans, never without a strong Imperial faction? Gregory, like his predecessors, made his last bold, desperate, and successful appeal to the religion of the Romans. The hoary Pontiff set forth in solemn procession, encircled by all the cardinals, the whole long way from the Lateran to St. Peter's. The wood of the true cross, the heads of St. Peter and St. Paul were borne before him; all alike crowded to receive his benediction. The Guelfs were in a paroxysm of devotion, which spread even among the overawed and unresisting

February.

Ghibellines.[1] In every church of the city was the solemn mass; in every pulpit of the city the friars of St. Dominic and St. Francis appealed to the people not to desert the Vicar of Christ, Christ himself in his Vicar; they preached the new Crusade, they distributed crosses to which were attached the same privileges of pardon, and so of eternal life, if the wearers should fall in the glorious conflict, awarded to those who fought or fell for the holy sepulchre of Christ.

To these new crusaders Frederick showed no compassion; whoever was taken with the cross was put to death without mercy, even if he escaped more cruel and ignominious indignities before his death.

The Emperor was awed, or was moved by respect for his venerable adversary: he was either not strong enough, or not bold enough to march at once on Rome, and so to fulfil his own menaces. He retired into Apulia; some overtures for reconciliation were made; Frederick endeavoured to detach the Pope from his allies, and to induce him to make a separate peace. But the Pope, perhaps emboldened by the return of some of his legates with vast sums of money from England and other foreign countries, resolutely refused to abandon the Lombard League.[k] Up to this time he had affected to disavow his close alliance, still to hold the lofty tone of a mediator; now he nobly determined to be true to their cause. He bore the remonstrances, on this, perhaps on some other cause of quarrel, of his ablest general, the Cardinal John

March, 1240.

---

[1] According to the B. Museum Chronicle, he laid down his crown on the reliques and appealed to them — "Vos, Sancti, defendite Romam, si homines Romani nollunt defendere." The greater part of the Romans at once took the Cross, p. 182.

[k] Peter de Vineis, l. 36. Cant. Lect. Œfele Script. Bohem. i. 668.

Colonna. Colonna had agreed to a suspension of arms, which did not include the Lombards; this the Pope refused to ratify. Colonna declared that he would not break his plighted faith to the Emperor. "If thou obeyest not," said the angry Pope, "I will no longer own thee for a cardinal." "Nor I thee," replied Colonna, "for Pope." Colonna joined the Ghibelline cause, and carried over the greater part of his troops.[m]

Ferrara in the mean time was for ever lost to the Imperialist side. Salinguerra, the aged and faithful partisan of the Emperor, was compelled to capitulate to a strong force, chiefly of Venetians. They seized his person by an act of flagrant treachery: for five years Salinguerra languished in a Venetian prison.

April.

The Emperor advanced again from the South, wasted the Roman territory, and laid siege to Benevento, which made an obstinate resistance. The Emperor was at San Germano; but instead of advancing towards Rome, he formed the siege of Faenza.

May.

August.

The Pope meditated new means of defence. Imperial armies were not at his command; he determined to environ himself with all the majesty of a spiritual sovereign; he would confront the Emperor at the head of the hierarchy of Christendom; he issued a summons to all the prelates of Europe for a General Council to be held in the Lateran palace at Easter in the ensuing year; they were to consult on the important affairs of the Church.

A.D. 1241.

The Emperor and the partisans of the Emperor had appealed to a general Council against the Pope; but a

---

[m] This quarrel was perhaps rather later in point of time.

Council in Rome, presided over by the Pope, was not
the tribunal to which they would submit. Frederick
would not permit the Pope, now almost in his power,
thus to array himself in all the imposing dignity of the
acknowledged Vicar of Christ. He wrote a Sept. 13,
circular letter to the Kings and Princes of 1240.
Europe, declaring that he could not recognise nor suffer
a Council to assemble, summoned by his arch-enemy,
to which those only were cited who were his declared
foes, either in actual revolt, or who, like the English
prelates, had lavished their wealth to enable the Pope
to carry on the war. "The Council was convened not
for peace but for war." Nor had the summons been
confined to hostile ecclesiastics. His temporal enemies,
the Counts of Provence and St. Bonifazio, the Marquis
of Este, the Doge of Venice, Alberic da Romano, Paul
Traversaria, the Milanese, were invited to join this un-
hallowed assembly. So soon as the Pope would abandon
the heretical Milanese, reconciliation might at once
take place; he was prepared to deliver his son Conrad
as hostage for the conclusion of such peace. He called
on the Cardinals to stand forth; they were bound by
their duty to the Pope, but not to be the slaves of his
passion. He appealed to their pride, for the Pope, not
content with their counsel, had summoned prelates from
all, even the remotest parts of the world,. to sit in
judgement on affairs of which they knew nothing." To
the Prelates of Europe he issued a more singular warning. All coasts, harbours, and ways were beset by his
fleet, which covered the seas: "From him who spared
not his own son, ye may fear the worst. If ye reach

---

[a] Quoted from Pet. de Vin. in Bibl. Barberina, No. 2136, by Von Raumer, p. 96.

Rome, what perils await you! Intolerable heat, foul water, unwholesome food, a dense atmosphere, flies, scorpions, serpents, and men filthy, revolting, lost to shame, frantic. The whole city is mined beneath, the hollows are full of venomous snakes, which the summer heat quickens to life. And what would the Pope of you? Use you as cloaks for his iniquities, the organ-pipes on which he may play at will. He seeks but his own advantage, and for that would undermine the freedom of the higher clergy; of all these perils, perils to your revenues, your liberties, your bodies, and your souls, the Emperor, in true kindness, would give you this earnest warning." Many no doubt were deterred by these remonstrances and admonitions. Yet zeal or fear gathered together at Genoa a great concourse of ecclesiastics. The Legate, Cardinal Otho, brought many English prelates; the Cardinal of Palestrina appeared at the head of some of the greatest dignitaries of France; the Cardinal Gregory, of Monte Longo, with some Lombard Bishops, hastened to Genoa, to urge the instant preparation of the fleet, which was to convey the foreign prelates to Rome.* Frederick was seized with apprehension at the meeting of the Council. He tried to persuade the prelates to pass by land through the territories occupied by his forces; he offered them safe conduct. The answer was that they could have no faith in one under excommunication. They embarked on board the hostile galleys of Genoa. But Frederick had prepared a powerful fleet in Sicily and Apulia, under the command of his son Enzio. Pisa joined him with all her galleys. The Genoese

---

* The Pope expressed great anger against the Cardinal Gregory of Monte Longo, for not having provided a fleet of overwhelming force. See his consolatory letter to the captive bishops, Raynald. p. 273.

Admiral, who had the ill-omened name Ubbriaco, the Drunkard, was too proud or too negligent to avoid the hostile armament. They met off May 3, 1241. the island of Meloria; the heavily-laden Genoese vessels were worsted after a sharp contest; three galleys were sunk, twenty-two taken, with four thousand Genoese.[p] Some of the prelates perished in the sunken galleys; among the prisoners were three Cardinals, the Archbishops of Rouen, Bordeaux, Auch, and Besançon; the Bishops of Carcassonne, Agde, Nismes, Tortona, Asti, Pavia, the Abbots of Clairvaux, Citeaux, and Clugny; and the delegates from the Lombard cities, Milan, Brescia, Piacenza, Genoa.[q] The vast wealth which the Cardinal Otho had heaped up in England was the prize of the conqueror. The Prelates, already half dead with sea-sickness and fright, no doubt with very narrow accommodation, crowded together in the heat and closeness of the holds of narrow vessels, exposed to the insults of the rude seamen and the lawless Ghibelline soldiery, had to finish their voyage to Naples, where they were treated with greater or less hardship, according as they had provoked the animosity of the Emperor. But all were kept in rigid custody.[r] Letters from Louis of France, almost rising to menace, and afterwards an embassy, at the head of which was the Abbot of Clugny (who himself was released before), demanded and obtained at length the liberation of the

---

[p] The battle was not likely to be fought without fury. The Genoese boasted to the Pope that they had taken three galleys before the battle began, beheaded all the men, and sunk the ships. They then complain of the barbarity of Frederick's sailors, not only to the innocent prelates, but to their conductors.

[q] The Archbishops of St. James (of Compostella), of Arles, of Tarragona, of Braga, the Bishops of Placentia, Salamanca, Orense, Astorga, got back safely to Genoa.—Epist. Laurent. apud Raynald. p. 270.

[r] Matth. Paris, sub ann. 1241.

French prelates; but the cardinals still languished in prison till the death of Gregory.

Faenza and Benevento had withstood the Imperial arms throughout the winter. Faenza had now fallen; the inhabitants had been treated with unwonted clemency by Frederick. Benevento too had fallen. The Papal malediction might seem to have hovered in vain over the head of Frederick; Heaven ratified not the decree of its Vicar on earth. On one side the victorious troops of Frederick, on the other those of John of Colonna, were wasting the Papal dominions; the toils were gathering around the lair of the imprisoned Pope. At that time arrived the terrible tidings of the progress made by the Mongols in Eastern Europe: already the appalling rumours of their conquests in Poland, Moravia, Hungary, had reached Italy. The Papal party were loud in their wonder that the Emperor did not at once break off his war against the Pope, and hasten to the relief of Christendom. So blind was their animosity that he was actually accused of secret dealings with the Mongols; the wicked Emperor had brought the desolating hordes of Zengis-Khan upon Christian Europe.* But Frederick would not abandon what now appeared a certain, an immediate triumph.

Even this awful news seemed as unheard in the camp of the Emperor, and in the city where the unsubdued Pope, disdaining any offer of capitulation, defied the terrors of capture and of imprisonment; he was near one hundred years old, but his dauntless spirit dictated these words: "Permit not yourselves, ye faithful, to be cast down by the unfavourable appearances of the

---

* Matth. Paris, sub ann.

present moment; be neither depressed by calamity nor
elated by prosperity. The bark of Peter is for a time
tossed by tempests and dashed against breakers; but
soon it emerges unexpectedly from the foaming billows,
and sails in uninjured majesty over the glassy surface."[t]
The Emperor was at Fano, at Narni, at Rieti, at Tivoli:
Palestrina submitted to John of Colonna. Even then
the Pope named Matteo Rosso Senator of Rome in place
of the traitor Colonna. Matteo Rosso made a sally
from Rome, and threw a garrison into Lagosta. The
fires of the marauders might be seen from the walls of
Rome; the castle of Monteforte, built by Gregory from the contributions of the Crusaders *July.*
and of his own kindred, as a stronghold in which the
person of the Pope might be secure from danger, fell
into the hands of the conqueror; but still no sign of
surrender; still nothing but harsh defiance. The Pope
was released by death from this degradation.
His death has been attributed to vexation; but *August 21.*
extreme age, with the hot and unwholesome air of
Rome in August, might well break the stubborn frame
of Gregory at that advanced time of life. Frederick, in
a circular letter addressed to the Sovereigns of Europe,
informed them of the event. "The Pope Gregory IX.
is taken away from this world, and has escaped the
vengeance of the Emperor, of whom he was the implacable enemy. He is dead, through whom peace was
banished from the earth, and discord prospered. For
his death, though so deeply injured and implacably persecuted, we feel compassion; that compassion had been
more profound if he had lived to establish peace between

---

[t] See letter to the Venetians, Lombards, and Bolognese.—Apud Raynald. p. 271.

the Empire and the Papacy. God, we trust, will raise up a Pope of more pacific temper; whom we are prepared to defend as a devout son, if he follows not the fatal crime and animosity of his predecessor. In these times we more earnestly desire peace, when the Catholic Church and the Empire are alike threatened by the invasion of the Tartars; against their pride it becomes us, the monarchs of Europe, to take up arms."* Frederick acted up to this great part of delivering Christendom from the yoke of these terrible savages. Immediately on the death of Gregory he detached King Enzio with four thousand knights, to aid the army of his son Conrad, King of the Romans. The Mongols were totally defeated near the Delphos, a stream which flows into the Danube; to the house of Hohenstaufen Europe and civilisation and Christendom owed this great deliverance.

Frederick suspended the progress of his victorious arms in the Roman territory that the Cardinals might proceed to the election of a new Pope. There were but six Cardinals in Rome; Frederick consented to their supplication that the two imprisoned Cardinals, James and Otho, giving hostages for their return to captivity, should join the conclave. There were fierce dissensions among these eight churchmen; five were for Godfrey of Milan, favoured by the Emperor, three for Romanus. One died, not without suspicion of poison; the Cardinal Otho returned to his captivity; the Emperor, delighted with his honourable conduct, treated him with respectful lenity.* In September, the choice to which the Cardinals were compelled by famine, sickness and violence, fell on Godfrey of Milan, a prelate of

Sept. 21.

---

* Peter de Vin. l. 11.   * Raynald. p. 377.

gentle character and profound learning; in October Cœlestine IV. was dead. The few remaining cardinals left Rome and fled to Anagni.   <small>Oct. 6, 1241.</small>

For nearly two years the Papal throne was vacant. The King of England remonstrated with the Emperor, on whom all seemed disposed to throw the blame; the ambassadors returned to England, if not convinced of the injustice, abashed by the lofty tone of Frederick. The King of France sent a more singular menace. He signified his determination, by some right which he asserted to belong to the Church of France, through St. Denys, himself to proceed to the election of a Pope. Frederick became convinced of the necessity of such election; none but a Pope could repeal the excommunication of a Pope. In addresses, which rose above each other in vehemence, he reproached the cardinals for their dissensions. "Sons of Belial! animals without heads! sons of Ephraim who basely turned back in the day of battle! Not Jesus Christ the author of Peace, but Satan the Prince of the North, sits in the midst of their conclave, inflaming their discords, their mutual jealousies. The smallest creatures might read them a salutary lesson; birds fly not without a leader; bees live not without a King. They abandon the bark of the Church to the waves, without a pilot."[y] In the mean time, he used more effective arguments; <small>July, 1242.</small> he advanced on Rome, seized and ravaged the estates, even the churches, belonging to the Cardinals. At length they met at Anagni, and in an evil hour for Frederick the turbulent conclave closed its labours. The choice fell on a cardinal once connected with the interests, and supposed to be attached to the person

---

[y] Pet. de Vin. xiv. 17.

of Frederick, Sinibald Fiesco, of the Genoese house of Lavagna. He took the name of Innocent IV., an omen and a menace that he would tread in the footsteps of Innocent III. Frederick was congratulated on the accession of his declared partisan; he answered coldly, and in a prophetic spirit: "In the Cardinal I have lost my best friend; in the Pope I shall find my worst enemy. No Pope can be a Ghibelline."

June, 1243.

CHAPTER V.

Frederick and Innocent IV.

YET Frederick received the tidings of the accession of Innocent IV. with all outward appearance of joy. He was at Amalfi; he ordered Te Deum to be sung in all the churches: he despatched the highest persons of his realm, the Archbishop of Palermo, the Chancellor Peter de Vincâ, Thaddeus of Sucesa, and the Admiral Ansaldo, to bear his congratulations to the Pope. "An ancient friend of the noble sons of the Empire, you are raised into a Father, by whom the Empire may hope that her earnest prayers for peace and justice may be fulfilled."

June 26.

Innocent could not reject these pacific overtures; he sent as his ambassadors to Frederick at Amalfi, the Archbishop of Rouen, William formerly Bishop of Modena, and the Abbot of St. Facundus. They were to demand first the release of all the captive prelates and ecclesiastics; to inquire what satisfaction the Emperor was disposed to offer for the crimes, on account of which he lay under excommunication; if the Church (this could scarcely be thought) had done him any wrong, she was prepared to redress such wrong; they were to propose a General Council of temporal and spiritual persons, Kings, Princes, and Prelates. All the adherents of the Church were to be included in the peace. Frederick demanded the withdrawal of the Papal Legate, Gregory di Monte Longo, from Lom-

Offers of peace.

bardy; he demanded the release of Salinguerra, the Lord of Ferrara; he complained that honour was shown to the Archbishop of Mentz, who was under the ban of the Empire (he had been appointed Papal Legate in Germany); that the Pope took no steps to suppress heresy among the Lombards; that the Imperial ambassadors were not admitted to the presence of the Pope. It was answered by Innocent, that the Pope had full right to send his Legates into every part of Christendom; Salinguerra was the prisoner of the Venetians, not of the Pope; the Archbishop of Mentz was a prelate of the highest character, one whom the Pope delighted to honour; the war waged by the Emperor prevented the Church from extirpating the Lombard heretics; it was not the usage of Rome to admit persons under excommunication to the holy presence of the Pope.

Aug. 25.

Frederick might seem now at the summit of his power and glory: his fame was untarnished by any humiliating discomfiture; Italy unable to cope with his victorious armies: the Milanese had suffered a severe check in the territory of Pavia: King Enzio had displayed his great military talents with success: the Papal territories were either in his occupation, or with Rome itself were seemingly capable of no vigorous resistance: his hereditary dominions were attached to him by affection, the Empire by respect and awe. He might think that he had full right to demand, full power to enforce, in the first place, the repeal of his excommunication. But the star of the Hohenstaufen had reached its height; it began to decline, to darken; its fall was almost as rapid and precipitate as its rise had been slow and stately.

Frederick's power.

The first inauspicious sign was the defection of Viterbo. The Cardinal Rainier, at the head of the Guelfic party, drove Frederick's garrison into the citadel, destroyed the houses of the Ghibellines, and gathered all the troops which he could to defend the city. Frederick was so enraged at this revolt, that he declared, "if he had one foot in Paradise, he would turn back to avenge himself on the treacherous Viterbans."* He immediately, unwarned by perpetual failures, formed the siege. The defence was stubborn, obstinate, successful; his engines were burned, he was compelled to retire, stipulating only for the safe retreat of his garrison from the citadel. Notwithstanding the efforts of Cardinal Otho of Palestrina, who had guaranteed the treaty, the garrison was assailed, plundered, massacred. To the remonstrance of Frederick, the Pope, who was still under a kind of truce with the Emperor, coldly answered, that he ought not to be surprised if a city returned to its allegiance to its rightful Lord. The fatal example of the revolt of Viterbo spread in many quarters: the Marquises of Montferrat and Malespina, the cities of Vercelli and Alexandria deserted the Imperial party. Even Adelasia, the wife of King Enzio, sought to be reconciled with the Holy See. Innocent himself ventured to leave Anagni, and to enter Rome; the Imperialists were awed at his presence; his reception, as usual, especially with newly crowned Popes, was tumultuously joyful. The only sullen murmurs, which soon after almost broke out into open discontent, were among the wealthy, it was said mostly the Jews, who demanded the payment of 40,000 marks, borrowed in his distress by Gregory IX. Innocent had authority enough to wrest

Defection of Viterbo.

Sept. 9 to Nov. 13.

Nov. 18.

---

* Von Raumer, iv. 128.

from the Frangipanis half of the Colosseum, and parts of the adjacent palace, where they no doubt hoped to raise a strong fortress in the Imperial interest.

The Emperor again inclined to peace, at least to negotiations for peace. The Count of Toulouse, the Chancellor Peter de Vineâ, and Thaddeus of Sucssa, appeared in Rome with full powers to conclude, and even to swear and guarantee the fulfilment of a treaty. The terms were hard and humiliating. The Emperor was to restore all the lands possessed by the Pope and the Pope's adherents at the time of the excommunication; the Emperor was to proclaim to all the sovereigns of Christendom that he had not scorned the Papal censure out of contempt for the Pope's predecessor, or the rights of the Church; but, by the advice of the prelates and nobles of Germany and Italy, treated it as not uttered, since it had not been formally served upon him; he owned his error on this point, and acknowledged the plenitude of the Papal authority in spiritual matters. For this offence he was to make such compensation in men or money as the Pope might require; offer such alms and observe such fasts as the Pope should appoint; and respect the excommunication until absolved by the Pope's command. He was to release all the captive Prelates, and compensate them for their losses. These losses and all other damages were to be left to the estimation of three Cardinals. Full amnesty was to be granted, the imperial ban revoked against all who had adhered to the Church since the excommunication. This was to be applied, as far as such offences, to all who were in a state of rebellion against the Emperor. The differences between the Emperor and his revolted subjects were to be settled by the Pope and the College of Cardinals within a limited time to be

Treaty. March 31, 1244.

fixed by the Pope. But there was a saving clause, which appeared to extend over the whole treaty, of the full undiminished rights of the Empire.[b] The Emperor was to be released from the excommunication by a public decree of the Church. To these and the other articles the imperial ambassadors swore in the presence of the Emperor Baldwin of Constantinople, the Cardinals, the Senators, and people of Rome. The Emperor did not disclaim the terms proposed by his ambassadors; but in the treaty there were some fatal flaws, which parties each so mistrustful, and justly mistrustful of the other, could not but discern, and which rendered the fulfilment of the treaty almost impossible. Was the Emperor to abandon all his advantages, to release all his prisoners (one of the stipulations), surrender all the fortresses he held in the Papal dominions, grant amnesty to all rebels, fulfil in short all these hard conditions at once, and so leave himself at the mercy of the Pope: then and not till then, not till the Pope had exacted the scrupulous discharge of every article, was he to receive his tardy absolution? Nor was the affair of the Lombards clearly defined. Innocent (perhaps the Emperor knew this) had from the first declared that he would not abandon their cause. Was the Emperor to be humiliated before the Lombards as he had been before the Pope, first to make every concession, with the remote hope of regaining his imperial rights by the Papal arbitration?[c]

March 31, 1214.

[b] "Jurabit præcise stare mandatis domini Papæ; salva tamen sint ei honores et jura quoad conservationem integram sine aliqua diminutione Imperii et honorum suorum."—If these undefined rights were to be respected, the Pope's decisions concerning the Lombards were still liable to be called in question.

[c] "Si latenti morbo, videlicet de negotio Lombardorum, medicina non esset opposita, pax omnino præcedere non valebat."—Cod. Epist. Vatic. MS., quoted by Von Raumer.

According to the Papal account, Frederick began to shrink back from the treaty to which he had sworn; the Pope was fully prepared on his part for the last extremity.[4] He left Rome, where his motions had perhaps been watched; he advanced to Civita Castellana under the pretext of approaching the Emperor. The bickerings, however, still continued; the Emperor complained that all the secret terms agreed on with the Pope were publicly sold for six pennies in the Lateran; the Pope demanded 400,000 marks as satisfaction for the imprisonment of the Prelates. The Lombard affairs were still in dispute. The Pope having seemingly made some slight concession, proceeded still further to Sutri. There at midnight he suddenly rose, stole out of the town in disguise, mounted a powerful horse, like the proud Sinibald the Genoese noble, he pressed its reeking flanks, so as to escape a troop of 300 cavalry which the Emperor—to whom perhaps his design had been betrayed—sent to intercept him, outrode all his followers, and reached Civita Vecchia, where the Genoese fleet of twenty-three well-armed galleys, which had been long prepared for his flight (so little did Innocent calculate on a lasting treaty), was in the roads.[*] He was in an instant on board one of the galleys. The

Flight of the Pope.

June 28.

June 29.

---

[4] See Matth. Paris, sub ann. 1244. "Imperator, illo instigante, qui primus superbivit, a forma Jurata et humiliate satisfactionis compromissa superbiendo penitens infeliciter resiluit." Of course, the biographers of Pope Innocent are loud on the deceit and treachery of Frederick (Vit. Innocent. IV.). But if Innocent resolutely refused (and this seems clear) to revoke the excommunication until Frederick had absolutely fulfilled all the stipulations, the charge of duplicity must be at least equally shared. In truth, if Frederick was not too religiously faithful to his oaths, the Pope openly asserted his power of annulling all oaths.

[*] It was given out that he fled to avoid being captured by these 300 Tuscan horse, who were sent to seize him. But the flight must have been pre-arranged with the Genoese fleet.

next morning, before the anchor was weighed, arrived
five cardinals, who had been outstripped by the more
active Pope. Seven others made their way to the north
of Italy. The Pope's galleys set sail, a terrible storm
came on, which threatened to cast them on an
island which belonged to Pisa. After seven July 7.
days they entered the haven of Genoa. The Genoese
had heard of the arrival of their illustrious fellow-
citizen at Porto Venere. They received him with a
grand procession of the nobles with the Podestà, the
clergy with the Archbishop at their head. The bells
clanged, music played, the priests chanted "Blessed is
he that cometh in the name of the Lord." The Pope's
followers replied, "Our soul is escaped, even as a bird
out of the snare of the fowler: the snare is broken, and
we are delivered." †

The Emperor was furious at this intelligence: he too
had his scriptural phrase—"The wicked flees when no
man pursueth." He complained bitterly of the negligent watch kept up by his armies and his fleets. He
sent the Count of Toulouse to invite, to press the Pope
to return, and to promise the fulfilment of all the conditions of the truce. Innocent replied that after such
flagrant violations of faith, he would not expose himself
or the Church to the imminent perils escaped with such
difficulty. Frederick, in an address to Mantua, denounced the flight of the Pope as a faithless revolt to
the insurgents against the Empire, as though he supposed that Innocent at Genoa, where he remained three
months, would place himself at the head of his Lombard
League.

But he was not safe in Genoa. The Emperor was in

† Psalm cxxiv. 7.

Pisa. Through the revolted cities of Asti and Alexandria, by secret ways Innocent crossed the Alps, and on the 2nd of December arrived at Lyons.

July 1.

The Pope at Lyons became an independent potentate. Lyons was not yet within the realm of France, though to a certain degree under her protection. It belonged in name to the Roman Empire; but it was almost a free city, owning no authority but that of the Archbishop. It was proud to become the residence of the Supreme Pontiff.

His reception in France was somewhat more cool than his hopes might have anticipated from the renowned piety of Queen Blanche and her son Saint Louis. The King with his mother visited the monastery of Citeaux; as they approached the church they were met by a long procession of five hundred monks from the convent of that saintly Order, entreating the King with tears and groans to aid the Holy Father of the Faithful against that son of Satan his persecutor, as his ancestor Louis VII. had received Pope Alexander. The first emotion of the King was to kneel in the profoundest reverence. But his more deliberate reply was, that he was prepared to protect the Pope against the Emperor so far as might seem fit to the nobles, his counsellors. The counsellors of Louis refused at once to grant permission that so dangerous and costly a guest should take up his residence in Rheims. The King of Arragon repelled the advances of the Pope. We shall hereafter see the conduct of Henry and the Barons of England. Innocent remained at Lyons; though thus partially baffled, he lost no time in striking at his foe. He summoned all kings, princes, and prelates to a Council on St. John the Baptist's day, upon the weighty

August. Innocent in France.

affairs of Christendom; he cited Frederick to appear
in person, or by his representatives, to hear the
charges on which he might be arraigned, and $^{\text{Dec. 27, 1244.}}$
to give the satisfaction which might be demanded. In
the mean time meditating a still heavier
penalty, and without awaiting the decree of $^{\text{A.D. 1245.}}$
the Council, he renewed the excommunication, and
commanded it to be published again throughout Christendom. In France, Spain, and England many of the
clergy obeyed, but a priest in Paris seems to have
created a strong impression on men's wavering minds.
"The Emperor and the Pope mutually condemn each
other; that one then of the two who is guilty I excommunicate, that one who is guiltless I absolve."[s] But
even in Lyons the haughty demeanour, the immoderate
pretensions, and the insatiable rapacity of Innocent IV.
almost endangered his safety. It is the greatest proof of
the deep-rooted strength of the Papal power, that with
a sullen discontent throughout Christendom, with a
stern impatience of the intolerable burthens imposed on
the Church as well as on the laity, with open menaces
of revolt, it still proceeded and successfully proceeded
to the most enormous act of authority, the deposition of
the Emperor in what claimed to be a full Council of the
Church.

In the short period, since the Pontificate of Innocent
III., a great but silent change had taken place in the
Papacy. Innocent III. was a mighty feudal monarch
at the head of a loyal spiritual aristocracy: the whole
clergy rose, with their head, in power; they took pride
in the exaltation of the Pope; the Pope not merely
respected but elevated the dignity of the bishops and

---

[s] Matt. Paris. Fleury, lxxix. c. 17.

abbots; each in his sphere displayed his pomp, exercised his power, enjoyed his wealth, and willingly laid his unforced, unextorted benevolences at the foot of the Papal throne. But already the Pope had begun to be— Innocent IV. aspired fully to become—an absolute monarch with an immense standing army, which enabled him to depress, to humiliate, to tax at his pleasure the higher feudatories of the spiritual realm. That standing army was the two new Orders, not more servilely attached to the Pope than encroaching on the privileges as well as on the duties of the clergy. The elevation of an Italian noble to the Papacy already gave signs of that growing nepotism which at last sunk the Head of Christendom in the Italian sovereign.[h] Throughout the contest Pope Innocent blended with the inflexible haughtiness of the Churchman[i] the inexorable passionate hatred of a Guelfic Burgher towards a rival Ghibelline, the hereditary foe of his house, that of the Sinibaldi of Genoa. There had been rumours at least that Gregory IX. resented the scornful rejection of his niece as a fit bride for a natural son of the Emperor. It was now declared that Frederick had offered to wed his son Conrad to a niece of Sinibald Fiesco, the Pope Innocent IV. That scheme of Papal ambition was afterwards renewed.

Among the English clergy the encroachments of the Pope, especially in two ways, the direct taxation and usurpation of benefices for strangers, had kindled such violent resentment, alike among the Barons and

[h] Nic. de Carbio, in Vit. Innocent. IV.

[i] Innocent held high views of the omnipotence of the Papacy:—" Cum teneat omnium credulitas pia fidelium quod apostolicæ sedis auctoritas in ecclesiis universis liberam habeat a Dei providentia potestatem; nec arbitrio principum stare cogitur, ut eorum in electionem vel postulationem negotiis requirat assensum."—Ad Regem Henric. MS. B. M. v. 19. Lateran, Feb. 1244.

the Prelates, as almost to threaten that the realm would altogether throw off the Papal yoke. It was tauntingly said that England was the Pope's farm. At this time the collector of the Papal revenues, Master Martin, was driven ignominiously, and in peril of his life, from the shores of the kingdom. Martin had taken up his residence in the house of the Templars in London. Fulk Fitzwarenne suddenly appeared before him, and, with a stern look, said, "Arise—get thee forth! Depart at once from England!" "In whose name speakest thou?" "In the name of the Barons of England assembled at Luton and at Dunstable. If you are not gone in three days, you and yours will be cut in pieces." Martin sought the King: "Is this done by your command, or by the insolence of your subjects?" "It is not by my command; but my Barons will no longer endure your depredations and iniquities. They will rise in insurrection, and I have no power to save you from being torn in pieces." The trembling priest implored a safe-conduct. "The devil take thee away to hell," said the indignant King, ashamed of his own impotence. One of the King's officers with difficulty conveyed Martin to the coast; but Martin left others behind to insist on the Papal demands. Yet so great was the terror, that many of the Italians, who had been forced (this was the second grievance) into the richest benefices of England, were glad to conceal themselves from the popular fury. The Pope, it is said, gnashed his teeth at the report from Martin of his insulting expulsion from England. Innocent, once beyond the Alps, had expected a welcome reception from all the great monarchs except his deadly foe. But to the King of England the Cardinal had made artful suggestions of the honour and benefit which his presence might confer on the realm. "What an immortal glory for your reign, if (unexampled honour!) the Father of Fathers should personally appear in England! He has often said that it would give him great pleasure to see the pleasant city of Westminster, and wealthy London." The King's Council, if not the King, returned the ungracious answer, "We have already suffered too much from the usuries and simonies of Rome; we do not want the Pope to pillage us."[k] More than this, Innocent must listen in patience, with suppressed indignation, to the "grievances" against which the Nobles and whole realm of England solemnly protested by their proctors: the subsidies exacted beyond the Peter's-pence, granted by the generosity of England; the usurpation of benefices by Italians, of whom there was an infinite number; the insolence and rapacity of the Nuncio Martin.[m]

The King of France, as has been seen, and the King of Arragon courteously declined this costly and dangerous visit of the fugitive Pope. The Pope, it was reported, was deeply offended at this stately and cautious reserve; on this occasion he betrayed the violence of his temper: "We must first crush or pacify the great dragon, and then we shall easily trample these small basilisks under foot." Such at least were the rumours spread abroad, and believed by all who were disposed to assert the dignity of the temporal power, or who groaned under the heavy burthens of the Church. Even Lyons had become, through the Pope's ill-timed favouritism, hardly a safe refuge.

Church of Lyons.

---

[k] Matth. Paris, however in some respects not an absolutely trustworthy authority for events which happened out of England, is the best unquestionably for the rumours and impressions prevalent in Christendom—rumours, which as rumours, and showing the state of the public mind, are not to be disdained by history.

[m] Matth. Paris, 1245.

He had endeavoured to force some of his Italian followers into the Chapter of Lyons; the Canons swore in the face of the Pope that if they appeared, neither the Archbishop nor the Canons themselves could prevent their being cast into the Rhone. Some indeed of the French prelates and abbots (their enemies accused them of seeking preferment and promotion by their adulatory homage) hastened to show their devout attachment to the Pope, their sympathy for his perils and sufferings, and their compassion for the destitution of which he loudly complained. The Prior of Clugny astonished even the Pope's followers by the amount of his gifts in money. Besides these he gave eighty palfreys splendidly caparisoned to the Pope, one to each of the twelve Cardinals. The Pope appointed the Abbot to the office, no doubt not thought unseemly, of his Master of the Horse: he received soon after the more appropriate reward, the Bishopric of Langres. The Cistercian Abbot would not be outdone by his rival of Clugny. The Archbishop of Rouen for the same purpose loaded his see with debts: he became Cardinal Bishop of Albano. The Abbot of St. Denys, who aspired to and attained the vacant Archbishopric, extorted many thousand livres from his see, which he presented to the Pope. But the King of France, the special patron of the church of St. Denys, forced the Abbot to regorge his exactions, and to beg them in other quarters. Yet with all these forced benevolences and lavish offerings it was bruited abroad that the Church of Rome had a capital debt, not including interest, of 150,000*l.*

The Council met at Lyons, in the convent of St. Just, on the Nativity of St. John the Baptist. Around the Pope appeared his twelve Cardinals, two Patriarchs, the Latin of Constantinople, who claimed

<small>Council of Lyons, June 24.</small>

likewise to be Patriarch of Antioch, and declared that the heretical Greeks had reduced by their conquests his suffragans from thirty to three, and the Patriarch of Aquileia, who represented the church of Venice; the Emperor of Constantinople, the Count of Toulouse, Roger Bigod and other ambassadors of England who had their own object at the Council, the redress of their grievances from Papal exactions, and the canonisation of Edmund Archbishop of Canterbury. Only one hundred and forty prelates represented the whole of Christendom, of whom but very few were Germans. The Council and the person of the Pope were under the protection of Philip of Savoy at the head of a strong body of men-at-arms, of Knights of the Temple and of the Hospital. Philip, brother of the Count of Savoy, was in his character a chief of Condottieri, in his profession an ecclesiastic; he enjoyed vast riches from spiritual benefices, was high in the confidence of the Pope. Aymeri Archbishop of Lyons, a pious and gentle prelate, beheld with deep sorrow the Pope as it were trampling upon him in his own diocese, despoiling his see, as he was laying intolerable burthens on the whole church of Christ. He resigned his see and retired into a convent. Philip of Savoy, yet but in deacon's orders, was advanced to the metropolitan dignity; he was at once Archbishop of Lyons, Bishop of Valence, Provost of Bruges, Dean of Vienne. Of these benefices he drained with remorseless rapacity all the rich revenues, and remained at the head of the Papal forces. And this was the act of a Pope who convulsed the world with his assertion of ecclesiastical immunities, of the sacrilegious intrusion of secular princes into the affairs of the Church. During four pontificates Philip of Savoy enjoyed the title, and spent the revenues of the Archbishopric of Lyons. At length Clement IV. insisted on his ordination and on his consecration. Philip of Savoy threw off, under this compulsion, the dress (he had never even pretended to the decencies) of a bishop, married first the heiress of Franche Comté, and afterwards a niece of Pope Innocent IV., and died Duke of Savoy. And the brother of Philip and of Amadeus Duke of Savoy, Boniface, was Primate of England.[a]

This then was the Council which was to depose the Emperor, and award the Empire. Even before the opening of the Council the intrepid, learned, and eloquent jurisconsult Thaddeus of Suessa, the principal proctor of the Emperor,[o] advanced and made great offers in the name of his master: to compel the Eastern Empire to enter into the unity of the Church: to raise a vast army and to take the field in person against the Tartars, the Charismians, and the Saracens, the foes which threatened the life of Christendom; at his own cost, and in his own person, to re-establish the kingdom of Jerusalem; to restore all her territories to the See of Rome; to give satisfaction for all injuries. "Fine words and specious promises!" replied the Pope. "The axe is at the root of the tree, and he would avert it. If we were weak enough to believe this deceiver, who would guarantee his truth?" "The Kings of France and England," answered Thaddeus. "And if he violated the treaty, as he assuredly would, we should have instead of one, the three greatest monarchs of Christendom for our enemies." At the next session the Pope in full attire mounted the pulpit; this was his text: "See,

---

[a] Gallia Christiana, iv. 144. M. Paris, sub ann. 1251.

[o] Sismondi says that Peter de Vineâ was one of the Emperor's representatives; that his silence raised suspicion of his treason. Was he there? The whole defence seems to have been entrusted to Thaddeus.

ye who pass this way, was ever sorrow like unto my sorrow." He compared his five afflictions to the five wounds of the Lord: the desolations of the Mongols; the revolt of the Greek Church; the progress of heresy, especially that of the Paterins in Lombardy; the capture and destruction of Jerusalem and the devastation of the Holy Land by the Charismians; the persecutions of the Emperor. He wept himself; the tears of others interrupted his discourse. On this last head he enlarged with bitter eloquence; he accused the Emperor of heresy and sacrilege, of having built a great and strong city and peopled it with Saracens, of joining in their superstitious rites; of his close alliance with the Sultan of Egypt; of his voluptuous life, and shameless intercourse with Saracen courtesans; of his unnumbered perjuries, his violation of treaties: he produced a vast number of letters, sealed with the imperial seal, as irrefragable proofs of these perjuries.

Thaddeus of Suessa rose with calm dauntlessness. He too had letters with the Papal seal, damning proofs of the Pope's insincerity. The assembly professed to examine these conflicting documents; they came to the singular conclusion that all the Pope's letters, and all his offers of peace were conditional; those of the Emperor all absolute. But Thaddeus was not to be overawed; he alleged the clashing and contradictory letters of the Pope which justified his master in not observing his promises. On no point did the bold advocate hesitate to defend his sovereign; he ventured to make reprisals. "My lord and master is arraigned of heresy; for this no one can answer but himself; he must be present to declare his creed: who shall presume to read the secrets of his heart? But there is one strong argument that he is not guilty of heresy (he fixed his

eyes on the prelates); he endures no usurer in his
dominions." The audience knew his meaning
—that was the heresy with which the whole
world charged the Court of Rome. The orator justified
the treaties of the Emperor with the Saracens as entered
into for the good of Christendom; he denied all criminal
intercourse with the Saracen women; he had permitted
them in his presence as jongleurs and dancers, but on
account of the offence taken against them he had
banished them for ever from his court. Thaddeus
ended by demanding delay, that the Emperor his
master might appear in person before the Council. The
Pope shrunk from this proposal: "I have hardly escaped
his snares. If he comes hither I must withdraw. I
have no desire for martyrdom or for captivity."
But the ambassadors of France and England
insisted on the justice of the demand: Innocent was
forced to consent to an adjournment of fourteen days.
The Pontiff was relieved of his fears. Frederick had
advanced as far as Turin. But the hostile character of
the assembly would not allow of his appearance. "I
see that the Pope has sworn my ruin; he would revenge
himself for my victory over his relatives, the pirates of
Genoa. It becomes not the Emperor to appear before
an assembly constituted of such persons." On the next
meeting this determination encouraged the foes of Frederick. New accusers arose to multiply charges against
the absent sovereign: many voices broke out against the
contumacious rebel against the Church. But Thaddeus,
though almost alone, having stood unabashed before the
Pope, was not to be silenced by this clamour of accusations. The Bishop of Catana ? was among the loudest;

---

* Carinola in Giannone.

he charged Frederick with treason against the Church for his imprisonment of the Prelates, and with other heinous crimes. "I can no longer keep silence," broke in Thaddeus, "thou son of a traitor, who was convicted and hanged by the justiciary of my Lord, thou art but following the example of thy father." Thaddeus took up the desperate defence, before such an assembly, of the seizure of the Prelates. The Pope again mingled in the fray; but Thaddeus assumed a lofty tone.

June 29.

"God delivered them into the hands of my master; God took away the strength of the rebels, and showed by this abandonment that their imprisonment was just." "If," replied the Pope, "the Emperor had not mistrusted his own cause, he would not have declined the judgement of such holy and righteous men: he was condemned by his own guilty conscience." "What could my lord hope from a council in which presided his capital enemy, the Pope Gregory IX., or from judges who even in their prison breathed nothing but menace?" "If one has broken out into violence, all should not have been treated with this indignity. Nothing remains but ignominiously to depose a man laden with such manifold offences."

Thaddeus felt that he was losing ground. At the third sitting he had heard that the daughter of the Duke of Austria, whom Frederick proposed to take as his fourth wife (the sister of the King of England had died in childbed), had haughtily refused the hand of an Emperor tainted with excommunication, and in danger of being deposed. The impatient Assembly would hardly hear again this perilous adversary; he entered therefore a solemn appeal: "I appeal from this Council, from which are absent so many great prelates and secular sovereigns, to a general and impartial

July 17.

Council. I appeal from this Pope, the declared enemy of my Lord, to a future, more gentle, more Christian Pope."ᵃ This appeal the Pope haughtily overruled· "it was fear of the treachery and the cruelty of the Emperor which had kept some prelates away: it was not for him to take advantage of the consequences of his own guilt." The proceedings were interrupted by a long and bitter remonstrance of England against the Papal exactions. The Pope adjourned this question as requiring grave and mature consideration.

With no further deliberation, without further investigation, with no vote, apparently with no participation of the Council, the Pope proceeded *Sentence of deposition.* at great length, and rehearsing in the darkest terms all the crimes at any time charged against Frederick, to pronounce his solemn, irrefragable decree: "The sentence of God must precede our sentence: we declare Frederick excommunicated of God, and deposed from all the dignity of Empire, and from the kingdom of Naples. We add our own sentence to that of God: we excommunicate Frederick, and depose him from all the dignity of the Empire, and from the kingdom of Naples." The Emperor's subjects in both realms were declared absolved from all their oaths and allegiance. All who should aid or abet him were by the act itself involved in the same sentence of excommunication. The Princes of Germany were ordered to proceed at once to the election of a new Emperor. The kingdom of Naples was reserved to be disposed of, as might seem to them most fit, by the Pope and the Cardinals.

The Council at this sentence, at least the greater

ᵃ Annal. Cassin. Concil. sub ann.

part, sat panic-stricken; the imperial ambassadors uttered loud groans, beat their heads and their breasts in sorrow. Thaddous cried aloud, "Oh, day of wrath, of tribulation, and of agony! Now will the heretics rejoice, the Charismians prevail; the foul Mongols pursue their ravages." "I have done my part," said the Pope, "God must do the rest." He began the hymn, "Wo glorify thee, O God!" His partisans lifted up their voices with him; the hymn ended, there was profound silence. Innocent and the prelates turned down their blazing torches to the ground till they smouldered and went out. "So be the glory and the fortune of the Emperor extinguished upon earth."

Frederick received at Turin the report of his dethronement; he was seated in the midst of a splendid court. "The Pope has deprived me of my crown? Whence this presumption, this audacity? Bring hither my treasure chests." He opened them. "Not one of my crowns but is here." He took out one, placed it on his own head, and with a terrible voice, menacing gesture, and heart bursting with wrath, exclaimed, "I hold my crown of God alone; neither the Pope, the Council, nor the devil shall rend it from me! What! shall the pride of a man of low birth degrade the Emperor, who has no superior nor equal on earth? I am now released from all respect; no longer need I keep any measure with this man."[r]

July 3L

Frederick addressed his justification to all the kings and princes of Christendom, to his own chief officers and justiciaries. He called on all temporal princes to make common cause against this common enemy of the temporal power. "What might not all Kings fear

---

[r] Peter de Vineâ, i. 3.

from the presumption of a Pope like Innocent IV.?" He inveighed against the injustice of the Pope in all the proceedings of the Council. The Pope was accuser, witness, and judge. He denounced crimes as notorious which the Emperor utterly denied. "How long has the word of an Emperor been so despicable as not to be heard against that of a priest?" "Among the Pope's few witnesses one had his father, son and nephew convicted of high treason. Of the others, some came from Spain to bear witness on the affairs of Italy. The utter falsehood of all the charges was proved by irrefragable documents. But were they all true, how will they justify the monstrous absurdity, that the Emperor, in whom dwells the supreme majesty, can be adjudged guilty of high treason? that he who as the source of law is above all law, should be subject to law? To condemn him to temporal penalties who has but one superior in temporal things, God! We submit ourselves to spiritual penances, not only to the Pope, but to the humblest priest; but, alas! how unlike the clergy of our day to those of the primitive church, who led Apostolic lives, imitating the humility of the Lord! Then were they visited of angels, then shone around by miracles, then did they heal the sick and raise the dead, and subdue princes by their holiness not by arms! Now they are abandoned to this world, and to drunkenness; their religion is choked by their riches. It were a work of charity to relieve them from this noxious wealth; it is the interest of all princes to deprive them of these vain superfluities, to compel them to salutary poverty."[a]

The former arguments were addressed to the pride of

---

[a] Peter de Vin. lib. I. 8.

France; the latter to England, which had so long groaned under the rapacity of the clergy. But it was a fatal error not to dissever the cause of the Pope from that of the clergy. To all the Emperor declared his steadfast determination to resist with unyielding firmness: "Before this generation and the generation to come I will have the glory of resisting this tyranny; let others who shrink from my support have the disgrace as well as the galling burthen of slavery." The humiliation of Pope Innocent might have been endured even by the most devout sons of the Church; his haughtiness and obstinacy had almost alienated the pious Louis; his rapacity forced the timid Henry of England to resistance. Perhaps the Papacy itself might have been assailed without a general outburst of indignation; but a war against the clergy, a war of sacrilegious spoliation, a war which avowed the necessity, the expediency of reducing them to Apostolic simplicity and Apostolic poverty, was in itself the heresy of heresies. To exasperate this indignation to the utmost, every instance of Frederick's severity, doubtless of his cruelty, to ecclesiastics, was spread abroad with restless activity. He is said to have burned them by a slow fire, drowned them in the sea, dragged them at the tails of horses. No doubt in Apulia and Sicily Frederick kept no terms with the rebellious priests and friars who were preaching the Crusade against him; urging upon his subjects that it was their right, their duty to withdraw their allegiance. But under all circumstances the violation of the hallowed person of a priest was sacrilege; while they denounced him as a Pharaoh, a Herod, a Nero, it was an outrage against law, against religion, against God, to do violence to a hair of their heads. And all these rumours, true or untrue, in their terrible simplicity, or in the gathered blackness of rumour, propagated by hostile tongues, confirmed the notion that Frederick contemplated a revolution, a new æra, which by degrading the Clergy would destroy the Church.[t]

The Pope kept not silence; he was not the man who would not profit to the utmost by this error. He replied to the Imperial manifesto: "When the sick man who has scorned milder remedies is subjected to the knife and the cautery, he complains of the cruelty of the physician: when the evil doer, who has despised all warning, is at length punished, he arraigns his judge. But the physician only looks to the welfare of the sick man, the judge regards the crime, not the person of the criminal. The Emperor doubts and denies that all things and all men are subject to the See of Rome. As if we who are to judge angels are not to give sentence on all earthly things. In the Old Testament priests dethroned unworthy kings; how much more is the Vicar of Christ justified in proceeding against him who, expelled from the Church as a heretic, is already the portion of hell! Ignorant persons aver that Constantine first gave temporal power to the See of Rome; it was already bestowed by Christ himself, the true king and priest, as inalienable from its nature and absolutely unconditional. Christ founded not only a pontifical but a royal sovereignty, and committed to Peter the rule both of an earthly and a heavenly kingdom, as is indicated and visibly proved by the plurality of the keys." 'The power of the

---

[t] " De hærrsi per id ipsum se reddens suspectum, merito omnem quem hactenus habebat in omnes populos igniculos famæ propriæ et sapientiæ impudenter et imprudenter extinxit atque deleverit."—Matt. Par. p. 450. Höfler quotes Albert of Beham's MS.

" Non solum pontificalem, sed

sword is in the Church and derived from the Church;' she gives it to the Emperor at his coronation, that he may use it lawfully and in her defence; she has the right to say, 'Put up thy sword into its sheath.' He strives to awaken the jealousy of other temporal kings, as if the relation of their kingdoms to the Pope were the same as those of the electoral kingdom of Germany and the kingdom of Naples. The latter is a Papal fief; the former inseparable from the Empire, which the Pope transferred as a fief from the East to the West." To the Pope belongs the coronation of the Emperor, who is thereby bound by the consent of ancient and modern times to allegiance and subjection."

War was declared, and neither the Emperor nor the Pope now attempted to disguise their mutual immitigable hatred. Everywhere the Pope called on the subjects of the Emperor to revolt from their deposed and excommunicated monarch. He assumed the power of dispensing with all treaties; he cancelled that of the city of Treviso with the Emperor as extorted by force; thus almost compelling a war of extermination;' for if treaties with a conqueror were thus to be cast aside, what opening remained for mercy? In a long and solemn address, he called on the bishops, barons, cities, people of the kingdom of Naples and Sicily to throw off the yoke under which they had so long groaned of the tyrant Frederick. Two Cardinals, Rainier Capoccio and Stephen de Romanis, had full

April 24.

---

regalem constituit principatum, beato Petro ejusque successoribus terreni simul ac cœlestis imperii commissis habenis, quod in pluralitate clavium competenter innuitur." This passage is quoted by Von Raumer from the Vatican archives, No. 4957, 47, and from the Codex Vindobon. Philol. p. 178. See also Höfler, Albert von Beham.

" " In feodum transtulit occidentale."
ʸ Raynald. sub ann.

powers to raise troops, and to pursue any hostile measures against the King. The Crusade was publicly preached throughout Italy against the enemy of the Church. The Emperor on his side levied a third from the clergy to relieve them from the tyranny of the Pope. He issued inflexible orders that every clerk or religious person who, in obedience to the command of the Pope or his Legate, should cease to celebrate mass or any other religious function, should be expelled at once from his place and from his city, and despoiled of all his goods, whether his own or those of the Church. He promised his protection and many advantages to all who should adhere to his party; he declared that he would make no peace with the Pope till all those ecclesiastics who might be deposed for his cause should be put in full possession of their orders, their rank, and their benefices.ᵃ The Mendicant Friars, as they would keep no terms of peace with Frederick, could expect no terms from him; they were seized and driven beyond the borders. The summons of the Pope to the barons of the realm of Sicily to revolt found some few hearers. A dark conspiracy was formed in which were engaged Pandolph of Fasanella, Frederick's vicar in Tuscany, Jacob Morra of the family of the great justiciary, Andrew of Ayala, the Counts San Severino, Theobald Francisco, and other Apulian barons. It was a conspiracy not only against the realm, but against the life of Frederick. On its detection Pandolph of Fasanella and De Morra, the leaders of the plot, fled to, and were received by, the Pope's Legate. The Cardinal Rainier, Theobald and San Severino seized the castles of Capoccio and of Scala, and stood on their defence. The

---

ᵃ Peter de Vin. l. 4.

loyal subjects of Frederick instantly reduced Scala; Capoccio with the rebels fell soon after. Frederick arraigned the Pope before the world, he declared him guilty on the full and voluntary avowal of the rebels,[a] as having given his direct sanction not only to the revolt, but to the murder of the Emperor.[b] "This they had acknowledged in confession, this in public on the scaffold. They had received the cross from the hands of some Mendicant Friars; they were acting under the express authority of the See of Rome." Frederick at first proposed to parade the chief criminals with the Papal bull upon their foreheads through all the realms of Christendom as an awful example and a solemn rebuke of the murtherous Pope; he found it more prudent to proceed to immediate execution, an execution with all the horrible cruelty of the times; their eyes were struck out, their hands hewn off, their noses slit, they were then broken on the wheel.[c] The Pope denied in strong terms the charge of meditated assassination; on the other hand, he declared to Christendom that three distinct attempts had been designed against his life, in all which Frederick was the acknowledged accomplice. On both sides probably these accusations were groundless. On one part, no doubt, fanatic Guelfs might think themselves called upon even by the bull of excommunication, which was an act of outlawry, to deliver the Church, the Pope, and the world from a monster of perfidy and iniquity such as Frederick was

July 18.

---

[a] See in Höfler the letter of the Pope to Theobald Francisco, and all the others of the kingdom of Sicily who returned to their loyalty to the Roman See: "God has made his face to shine upon you, by withdrawing your persons from the dominion of Pharaoh. From the soldiers of the reprobate tyrant, you have become champions of our Lord Jesus Christ."—Appendix. p. 372.

[b] "Et prædictæ mortis et exhæredita tionis nostræ summum pontificem asseruunt authorem."—Peter de Vin. il. z.

[c] Matth. Paris. sub ann. 1246, 7.

described in the manifestoes of the Pope. Fanatic Ghibellines might in like manner think that they were doing good service, and would meet ample even if secret reward, should they relieve the Emperor from his deadly foe. They might draw a strong distinction between the rebellious subject of the Empire, and the sacred head of Christendom.

The Pope pledged himself solemnly to all who would revolt from Frederick never to abandon them to his wrath, never on any terms to make peace with the perfidious tyrant; "no feigned penitence, no simulated humility shall so deceive us, as that, when he is cast down from the height of his imperial and royal dignity, he should be restored to his throne. His sentence is absolutely irrevocable! his reprobation is the voice of God by his Church: he is condemned and for ever! His viper progeny are included under this eternal immitigable proscription. Whoever then loves justice should rejoice that vengeance is thus declared against the common enemy, and wash his hands in the blood of the transgressor." So wrote the Vicar of Christ![a]

Frederick took measures to relieve himself from the odious imputation of heresy. The Archbishop of Palermo, the Bishop of Pavia, the Abbots of Monte Casino, Cava, and Casanova, the Friar Preachers Roland and Nicolas, men of high repute, appeared before the Pope at Lyons, and declared themselves ready to attest on oath the orthodox belief of the Emperor. Innocent sternly answered, that they deserved punishment for holding conference with an excommunicated person, still severer penalty for treating him as

A.D. 1246.

---

[a] Apud Höfler, p. 383.

Emperor. They rejoined in humility, "Receive us then as only representing a Christian."

The Pope was compelled to appoint a commission of three cardinals. These not only avouched the report of the ambassadors, but averred the Emperor prepared to assert his orthodoxy in the presence of the Pope. Innocent extricated himself with address: he declared the whole proceeding, as unauthorised by himself, hasty, and presumptuous: "If he shall appear unarmed, and with but few attendants before us, we will hear him, if it be according to law, according to law."* Even the religious Louis of France could not move the rigid Pope. In his own crusading enthusiasm, as strong as that of his ancestors in the days of Urban, Louis urged the Pope to make peace with the Emperor, that the united forces of Christendom might make head in Europe and in Palestine against the unbelieving enemies of the Cross. He had a long and secret interview with the Pope in the monastery of Clugny. Innocent declared that he could have no dealings with the perfidious Frederick. Louis retired, disgusted at finding such merciless inflexibility in the Vicar of Christ.† But not yet had the spell of the great magician begun to work. The conspiracy in the kingdom of Sicily was crushed; Frederick did not think it wise to invade the territories of Rome, where the Cardinal Rainier kept up an active partisan war. But even Viterbo yielded; the Guelfs were compelled to submit by the people clamouring for bread. Prince Theodore of Antioch entered Florence in triumph. The Milanese had suffered discomfiture; Venice had become more amicable. Inno-

May 22, 1246.

---

* "Ipsum super hoc, si de jure, et sicut de jure fuerit audiamus."—Apud Raynald. 1246. † Matt. Paris, 1246.

cent had not been wanting in attempts to raise up a rival sovereign in Germany to supplant the deposed Emperor. All the greater princes coldly, almost contemptuously, refused to become the instruments of the Papal vengeance: they resented the presumption of the Pope in dethroning an Emperor of Germany.

The Papal Legate, Philip Bishop of Ferrara, in less troubled times would hardly have wrought powerfully on the minds of Churchmen. He was born of poor parents in Pistoia, and raised himself by extraordinary vigour and versatility of mind. He was a dark, melancholy, utterly unscrupulous man, of stern and cruel temper; a great drinker;[a] even during his orisons he had strong wine standing in cold water by his side. His gloomy temperament may have needed this excitement. But the strength of the Papal cause was Albert von Beham.[b] Up to the accession of Innocent IV., if not to the Council of Lyons, the Archbishops of Saltzburg, the Bishops of Freisingen and Ratisbon and Passau, had been the most loyal subjects of Frederick. They had counteracted all the schemes of Albert von Beham, driven him, amid the universal execration for his insolence in excommunicating the highest prelates, and rapacity in his measureless extortions, from Southern Germany. We have heard him bitterly lamenting his poverty. Otho of Bavaria, who when once he embraced

---

[a] "Multæ crudelitates exercuit. Melancholicus, et tristis et furiosus, et filius Belial. Magnus potator."—Salimbeni, a Papal writer quoted by Von Raumer, p. 212.

[b] Höfler affirms that because Albert von Beham, in one of his furious letters to Otho, calls Frederick the parricide, the murderer of Otho's father, that it is a striking proof that Frederick was guilty of that murder.—p. 118. The letter is a remarkable one. Höfler's is one of those melancholy books, showing how undying is religious hatred. Innocent himself might be satisfied with the rancour of his apologist, and his merciless antipathy to Frederick.

the cause of the Hohenstaufen adhered to it with honourable fidelity, had convicted him of gross bribery, and hunted him out of his dominions. Albert now appeared again in all his former activity. He had been ordained priest by the Cardinal Albano; he was nominated Dean of Passau; but the insatiable Albert knew his own value, or rather the price at which the Pope and his cardinals calculated his services: he insisted on receiving back all his other preferments. The Pope and the Cardinals held it as a point of honour to maintain their useful emissary.[1]

Already before the elevation of Innocent, at a meeting at Budweis, a league of Austria, Bohemia, and Bavaria, had proposed the nomination of a new Emperor. Eric King of Denmark had refused it for his son, in words of singular force and dignity. At Budweis Wenceslaus of Bohemia had fallen off to the interests of the Emperor: there were fears among the Papalists, fears speedily realised, of the Imperialism of Otho of Bavaria. A most audacious vision of Poppo, the Provost of Munster, had not succeeded in appalling Otho into fidelity to the Pope. The Queen of Heaven and the Twelve Apostles sent down from Heaven ivory statues of themselves, which contained oracles confirming all the acts of Albert; writings were shown with the Apostolic seals, containing the celestial decree.[k] Albert had threatened, that if the electors refused, the Pope

Sept. 1241.

---

[1] He complains that they prevented him from collecting 300 marks of silver, which otherwise he might have obtained. Höfler cannot deny the venality of Albert von Beham, but makes a long apology, absolutely startling in a respectable writer of our own day. The new letters of Albert seem to me more fatal to his character than the partial extracts in Aventinus.

[k] "Quorum decreta cum divinæ mentis decretis examussim conspirantia, ambobus cælestis senatus-consulti in eburneis descripta sigillis, inspiciendi copiam factam." The sense is not quite clear; I doubt my own rendering.

would name a French or Lombard King or Patrician, without regard to the Germans.

The meeting at Budweis so far had failed; but a dangerous approximation had even then been made between Sifried of Mentz, hitherto loyal to Frederick, who had condemned and denounced the rapacious quæstorship of Albert von Beham, and Conrad of Cologne, a high Papalist.* This approximation grew up into an Anti-Imperialist League, strengthened as it was, before long, by the courageous demeanour, the flight, the high position taken by Innocent at Lyons; still more by the unwise denunciations against the whole hierarchy by Frederick in his wrath. Now the three great rebellious temporal princes—Otho of Bavaria, the King of Bohemia, the Duke of Austria— are the faithful subjects of Frederick; his loyal prelates, Saltzburg, Freisingen, Ratisbon, are his mortal enemies. Not content with embracing the Papal cause, they endeavoured by the most stirring incitements to revenge for doubtful or mendaciously asserted wrongs, by the dread of excommunication, by brilliant promises, to stir up Otho of Bavaria to assume the Imperial crown. Otho replied, "When I was on the side of the Pope you called him Antichrist; you declared him the source of all evil and all guilt: by your counsels I turned to the Emperor, and now you brand him as the most enormous transgressor. What is just to-day is unjust to-morrow: in scorn of all principle and all truth, you blindly follow your selfish interests. I shall hold to my pledges and my oaths, and not allow myself to be blown about by every changing wind." Otho of Bavaria persisted in his agreement to wed his daughter with Conrad, son of

April 20.

---

* Boehmer, p. 390. See citations.

Frederick. Every argument was used to dissuade him from this connexion. Three alternatives were laid before him: I. To renounce the marriage of his daughter with Conrad, Frederick's son; if so, the Pope will provide a nobler bridegroom, and reconcile him fully with Henry, elected King of the Romans. II. To let the marriage proceed if Conrad will renounce his father. Albert von Beham was busy in inciting the unnatural revolt of Conrad from his father. III. The third possibility was the restoration of Frederick to the Pope's favour: he must await this; but in the mean time bear in mind that the victory of the Church is inevitable.ª The King of Bohemia, the Dukes of Austria, Brabant, and Saxony, the Margraves of Meissen and Brandenburg, repelled with the same contemptuous firmness the tempting offer of the Imperial crown. At last an Emperor was found in Henry Raspe, Landgrave of Thuringia. Henry of Thuringia was a man of courage and ability; but his earlier life did not designate him as the champion of Holy Church.º He was the brother-in-law of the sainted Elizabeth of Hungary, now the object of the most passionate religious enthusiasm, sanc-

---

ª "Quia si omne aurum haberetis, quod Rex Solomon habuit, ordinationi Sanctæ Romanæ Ecclesiæ et divinæ potentiæ non poteritis repugnare, quia necesse est, ut in omni negotio semper Ecclesia Dei vincat."—p. 120. The marriage took place, Sept. 6, 1246. The rhetorical figures in this address of Albert of Beham, if it came not from the Pope himself, were sufficiently bold: "The Pope would not swerve from his purpose though the stars should fall from their spheres, and rivers be turned into blood. Angels and archangels would in vain attempt to abrogate his determination." "Nec credo angelos aut archangelos sufficere illi articulo, ut eum possint ad vestrum bene placitum inclinare."

º The electors to the Kingdom of Germany were almost all ecclesiastics. The Archbishops of Mentz, Cologne, Trèves, Bremen; the Bishops of Wurtzburg, Naumbourg, Ratisbon, Strasburg, Henry (Elect) of Spires; Dukes Henry of Brabant, Albert of Saxony; with some Counts.—May 22.

tioned by the Pope himself. To her, in her desolate widowhood, Henry had shown little of the affection of a brother or the reverence of a worshipper; dark rumours charged him with having poisoned her son, his nephew, to obtain his inheritance. He had been at one time the Lieutenant of the Emperor in Germany. Even Henry at first declined the perilous honour. He yielded at length as to a sacrifice: "I obey, but I shall not live a year."

Innocent issued his mandate,[p] his solemn adjuration to the prelates to elect, with one consent, Henry of Thuringia to the Imperial crown. He employed more powerful arguments: all the vast wealth which he still drew, more especially from England, was devoted to this great end. The sum is variously stated at 25,000 and 50,000 marks, which was spread through Germany by means of letters of exchange from Venice. The greater princes still stood aloof; the prelates espoused, from religious zeal, the Papal champion; among the lower princes and nobles the gold of England worked wonders. On Ascension Day the Archbishops of Mentz, Cologne, Trèves, and Bremen, the Bishops of Metz, Spires, and Strasburg, anointed Henry of Thuringia as King of Germany at Hochem, near Wurtzburg. His enemies called him in scorn the priest king.[q] The sermons of the prelates and clergy, who preached the Crusade against the godless Frederick, and the money of the Pope, raised a powerful army. King Conrad was worsted in a great battle near Frankfort; two thousand of his own Swabian soldiers passed over to the enemy. But the

---

[p] See the very curious letter in Höfler, p. 195, on the determination of the Pope.
[q] Matt. Paris. Chronic. Erphurt. Ann. Argentin. apud Boehmer, Font.

cities, now rising to wealth and freedom, stood firm to Frederick: they defied, in some cases expelled, their bishops. Henry of Thuringia attempted to besiege first Reutlingen, then Ulm; was totally defeated near that city, fled to his Castle of Wartburg, and died of grief and vexation working on a frame shattered by a fall from his horse.

Feb. 17, 1247.

Frederick was still in the ascendant, the cause of the Pope still without prevailing power. The indefatigable Innocent sought throughout Germany, throughout Europe: he even summoned from the remote and barbarous North Hakim King of Norway to assume the crown of Germany.* At last William of Holland, a youth of twenty years of age, under happier auspices, listened to the tempting offers of the Pope; but even Aix-la-Chapelle refused, till after a siege of some length, to admit the Papal Emperor to receive the crown within her walls: he was crowned, however, by the Papal Legate, the Cardinal of St. Sabina.

Oct. 3, 1247.

From this time till Frederick lay dying, four years after, at Fiorentino, some dire fatality seemed to hang over the house of Hohenstaufen. Frederick had advanced to Turin; his design no one knew; all conjectured according to their wishes or their fears. It was rumoured in England that he was at the head of a powerful force, intending to dash down the Alps and seize the Pope at Lyons. The Papalists gave out that he had some dark designs, less violent but more treacherous, to circumvent the Pontiff. Innocent had demanded succour from Louis, who might, with his brothers and the nobles of France, no doubt have been moved by the personal danger of the Pope to take up

---

* Letter to William of Holland.

arms in his cause.* Frederick had succeeded, by the
surrender of the strong castle of Rivoli to Thomas Duke
of Savoy, in removing the obstructions raised by that
prince to the passage of the Alps. The Duke of Savoy
played a double game: he attacked the Cardinal
Octavian, who was despatched by the Pope with a strong
chosen body of troops and 15,000 marks to aid the
Milanese. The Cardinal reached Lombardy with hardly
a man; his whole treasure fell into the hands of the
Duke of Savoy. Others declared that Frederick was
weary of the war, and had determined on the humblest
submission. He himself may have had no fixed and
settled object. He declared that he had resolved to
proceed to Lyons to bring his cause to issue in the face
of the Pope, and before the eyes of all mankind.[1] He
was roused from his irresolution by the first of those
disasters which went on darkening to his end.
The Pope was not only Pope; he had powerful   June, 1247.
compatriots and kindred among the great Guelfic houses
of Italy. This, not his spiritual powers alone, gave the
first impulse to the downfall of Frederick. In Parma
itself the Rossi, the Corroggi, the Lupi, connected with
the Genoese family of the Sinibaldi, maintained a
secret correspondence with their party within the city.
The exiles appeared before Parma with a strong force;
the Imperialist Podestà, Henry Testa of Arezzo, sallied
forth, was repulsed and slain; the Guelfs entered the
city with the flying troops, became masters of the
citadel: Gherardo Correggio was Lord of Parma.

---

* Matt. Paris. In the letters to
Louis and to his mother Blanche the
Pope intimates that they were ready to
march an army not only to defend him
in Lyons, but to cross the Alps.

[1] Nicolas de Carbio, in Vit. Innoc. IV. "Causae nostrae justitiam praesentialiter et potenter in adversarii nostri facie, coram transalpinis gentibus ponituri."—Petr. de Vin. ii. 49.

This was the turning point in the fortunes of Frederick; and Frederick, by the horrible barbarity of his revenge against the revolted Parmesans, might seem smitten with a judicial blindness, and to have laboured to extinguish the generous sympathies of mankind in his favour. His wrath against the ungrateful city, which he had endowed with many privileges, knew no bounds. He had made about one thousand prisoners: on one day he executed four, on the next two, before the walls, and declared that such should be the spectacle offered to the rebels every day during the siege. He was with difficulty persuaded to desist from this inhuman warfare. Parma became the centre of the war; on its capture depended all the terrors of the Imperial arms, on its relief the cause of the Guelfs. Around Frederick assembled King Enzio, Eccelin da Romano, Frederick of Antioch, Count Lancia, the Marquis Pallavicini, Thaddeus of Suessa, and Peter de Vineâ. On the other hand, the Marquis Boniface threw himself with a squadron of knights into the city. The troops of Mantua, the Marquis of Este, Alberic da Romano, the martial Cardinal Gregory of Monte Longo at the head of the Milanese; the Count of Lavagna, the Pope's nephew, at the head of four hundred and thirty crossbow men of Genoa and three hundred of his own, hovered on all sides to aid the beleaguered city. Parma endured the storm, the famine. Frederick had almost encircled Parma by his works, and called the strong point of his fortifications by the haughty but ill-omened name of Vittoria. After many months' siege, one fatal night the troops of Parma issued from the city, and surprised the strong line of forts, the Vittoria, which contained all the battering engines, stores, provisions, arms, tents, treasures, of the Imperial forces. So little alarm was at first caused, that Thaddeus of Suessa, who commanded in Vittoria, exclaimed, "What! have the mice left their holes?" In a few moments the whole fortress was in flames, it was a heap of ashes, the Imperial garrison slain or prisoners; two thousand were reckoned as killed, including the Marquis Lancia; three thousand prisoners.[u] Among the inestimable booty in money, jewels, vessels of gold and silver, were the carroccio of Cremona, the Imperial fillet, the great seal, the sceptre and the crown. The crown of gold and jewels was found by a mean man, called in derision "Short-legs." He put the crown on his head, was raised on the shoulders of his comrades, and entered Parma, in mockery of the Emperor. Among the prisoners was the faithful and eloquent Thaddeus of Suessa. The hatred of his master's enemies was in proportion to his value to his master. Already both his hands were struck off; and in this state, faint with loss of blood, he was hewn in pieces.[x] And yet could Frederick hardly complain of the cruelty of his foes—cruelties shown when the blood was still hot from battle. Only three days before the loss of the Vittoria, Marcellino, Bishop of Arezzo, a dangerous and active partisan of the Pope, who had been taken prisoner, and confined for months in a dungeon, was brought forth to be hanged. His death was a strange wild confusion of the pious prelate and the intrepid Guelf. He was commanded to anathematise the Pope,

---

* Muratori, Annal. sub ann.
x Compare in Höfer's "Albert von Beham" the curious Latin songs on the defeat of Frederick before Parma. All the monkish bards broke out in gratulant hymns.

" Amisit astrologos et magos et vates,
Beelzebub et Astaroth proprios Penates,
Tenebrarum coaequirоs per quos potestates
Sgræverat ecclesiam, et mundi magnates."

he broke out into an anathema against the Emperor. He then began to chant the Te Deum, while the furious Saracen soldiers tied him to the tail of a horse, bound his hands, blindfolded his eyes, dragged him to the gibbet, where he hung an awful example to the rebels of Parma. He was hanged, says the indignant Legate of the Pope, "like a villain, a plebeian, a nightman, a parricide, a murderer, a slave-dealer, a midnight robber."[7]

This was but the first of those reverses, which not only obscured the fame, but wrung with bitterest anguish the heart of Frederick. Still his gallant son Enzio made head against all his father's foes: in a skirmish before Bologna Enzio was wounded and taken prisoner. Implacable Bologna condemned him to perpetual imprisonment. All the entreaties to which his father humbled himself; all his own splendid promises that for his ransom he would gird the city with a ring of gold, neither melted nor dazzled the stubborn animosity of the Guelfs. A captive at the age of twenty-four, this youth, of beauty equal to his bravery—the poet, the musician, as well as the most valiant soldier and consummate captain—pined out twenty-three years of life, if not in a squalid dungeon, in miserable inactivity. Romance, by no means improbable, has darkened his fate. The passion of Lucia Biadagioli, the most beautiful and high-born maiden of Bologna, for the captive, her attempts to release him, were equally vain: once he had almost escaped, concealed in a cask; a lock of his bright hair

May 22, 1249.

Imprisonment of Enzio.

---

[7] Matt. Paris, sub ann. 1249. Letter of Cardinal Rainier. However extravagant this letter, the fact can hardly have been invention. Compare the sermon of the Archbishop of Mentz at Wurtzburg. Ann. Erphurdt. Paris, xvi. 36.

betrayed the secret.* Nor had Frederick yet exhausted
the cup of affliction; the worst was to come: suspected,
at least, if unproved treachery in another of his most
tried and faithful servants. Thaddeus of Suessa had
been severed from him by death, his son by imprisonment, Peter de Vineâ was to be so, by the most galling
stroke of all, either foul treason in De Vineâ, or in
himself blind, ungrateful injustice. Peter de Vineâ
had been raised by the wise choice of Fre- Peter de
derick to the highest rank and influence. All Vineâ.
the acts of Frederick were attributed to his chancellor.*
De Vineâ, like his master, was a poet: he was one of
the counsellors in his great scheme of legislation.
Some rumours spread abroad that at the Council of
Lyons, though Frederick had forbidden all his representatives from holding private intercourse with the
Pope, De Vineâ had many secret conferences with
Innocent, and was accused of betraying his master's
interests. Yet there was no seeming diminution in the
trust placed in De Vineâ. Still to the end the Emperor's letters concerning the disaster at Parma are by
the same hand. Over the cause of his disgrace and
death, even in his own day, there was deep doubt and
obscurity. The popular rumour ran that Frederick was
ill; the physician of De Vineâ prescribed for him; the
Emperor, having received some warning, addressed De
Vineâ: "My friend, in thee I have full trust; art thou
sure that this is medicine, not poison?" De Vineâ
replied: "How often has my physician ministered
healthful medicines!—why are you now afraid?"
Frederick took the cup, sternly commanded the phy-

* Bologna gave him the mockery of a splendid funeral. "Sepultus est maximo cum honore."—D. Mussum

* Chronicon, p. 340.

* There is some doubt whether he was actually chancellor.

sician to drink half of it. The physician threw himself at the King's feet, and as he fell overthrew the liquor. But what was left was administered to some criminals, who died in agony. The Emperor wrung his hands and wept bitterly: "Whom can I now trust, betrayed by my own familiar friend? Never can I know security, never can I know joy more." By one account Peter de Vineâ was led ignominiously on an ass through Pisa, and thrown into prison, where he dashed his brains out against the wall. Dante's immortal verse has saved the fame of De Vineâ: according to the poet, he was the victim of wicked and calumnious jealousy.[b]

June, 1250. Death of Frederick II.

The next year Frederick himself lay dying at Fiorentino. His spirit was broken by the defeat of Parma; a strange wayward irresolution came over him: now he would march fiercely to Lyons and dethrone the Pope; now he was ready to make the humblest submission; now he seemed to break out into paroxysms of cruelty—prisoners were put to the torture, hung. Frederick, if at times rebellious against the religion, was not above the superstition of his times. He had faith in astrology: it had also been foretold that he should die in Firenze (Florence). In Fioren-

Dec. 13, 1250.

tino, a town not far from Lucera, he was seized with a mortal sickness. The hatred which pursued him to the grave, and far beyond the grave, described him as dying unreconciled to the Church, miserable, deserted, conscious of the desertion of all. The inexorable hatred pursued his family, and charged

---

[b] "I son colui, che tenne ambo le chiavi
Del cuor di Federigo, e che le volsi
Serrando e disserrando, sì soavi" * *
 * * * * *
La meretrice, che mai dal ospizio
Di Cesare non torse gli occhi putti,

Morte commune, e delle corti vizio
Infiammò contra me l' animi tutti.
E gl' infiammati infiammar sì Augusto,
Che i lieti onor tornaro in tristi lutti."
ed seqq.—Inferno, xiii. 55.

his son Manfred with hastening his death by smothering him with a pillow. By more credible accounts he died in Manfred's arms, having confessed and received absolution from the faithful Archbishop of Palermo. His body was carried to Palermo in great state, a magnificent tomb raised over his remains, an epitaph proclaiming his glory and his virtues was inscribed by his son Manfred.* In his last will he directed that all her rights and honours should be restored to the Holy Church of Rome, his mother; under the condition that the Church should restore all the rights and honours of the Empire. In this provision the Church refused to see any concession, it was the still stubborn and perfidious act of a rebel. All his other pious legacies for the rebuilding and endowment of churches passed for nothing.

The world might suppose that with the death of Frederick the great cause of hostility had been removed; but he left to his whole race the inheritance of the implacable hatred of the Papal See; it was extinguished only in the blood of the last of the house of Hohenstaufen on the scaffold at Naples.

It might indeed seem as if, in this great conflict, each had done all in his power to justify the extreme suspicion, the immitigable aversion, of his adversary; to stir up the elements of strife, so that the whole world was arrayed, one half against the other, in defence of vital and absorbing principles of action. It was a war of ideas, as well as of men; and those ideas, on each side, maintained to the utmost imaginable height. That the justice of Frederick was a stern absolutism

---

* "Si probitas, sensus, virtutum gratia, census,
Nobilitas orti posssent sinistere morti
Non foret extinctus Fredericus qui jacet intus."

cannot be denied; that his notion of the Imperial power was not merely irreconcileable with the fierce and partisan liberties of the Italian republics, but with all true freedom; that he aspired to crush mankind into order and happiness with the iron hand of autocracy. Still no less than autocracy in those times could coerce the countless religious and temporal feudal tyrannies which oppressed and retarded civilisation. The Sicilian legislation of Frederick shows that order and happiness were the ultimate aim of his rule: the assertion of the absolute supremacy of law; premature advance towards representative government; the regard to the welfare of all classes; the wise commercial regulations; the cultivation of letters, arts, natural philosophy, science; all these if despotically enforced, were enforced by a wise and beneficent despotism. That Frederick was honoured, admired, loved by a great part of his subjects; that if by one party he was looked on with the bitterest abhorrence, to others he was no less the object of wonder and of profound attachment, appears from his whole history. In Sicily and Naples, though the nobles had been held down with an inflexible hand, though he was compelled to impose still heavier taxation, though his German house had contracted a large debt of unpopularity, though there might be more than one conspiracy instantly and sternly suppressed, yet there was in both countries a fond, almost romantic attachment, to his name and that of his descendants. The crown of Germany, which he won by his gallant enterprise, he secured by his affability, courtesy, chivalrous nobleness of character. In Germany, not all the influence of the Pope could for a long time raise up a formidable opposition; the feeble rebellion of his son, unlike most parricidal rebellions of

old, was crushed on his appearance. For a long time
many of the highest churchmen were on his side: and
when all the churchmen arrayed themselves against
him, all, even his most dangerous enemies among the
temporal princes, rallied round his banner; the Empire
was one; it was difficult to find an obscure insignificant
prince, with all the hierarchy on his side, to hazard the
assumption of the Imperial crown.

The religion of Frederick is a more curious problem.
If it exercised no rigorous control over his luxurious life, there was in his day no indissoluble alliance between Christian morals and Christian religion. This holy influence was no less wanting to the religion of many other kings, who lived and died in the arms of the Church. Frederick, if he had not been Emperor and King of Sicily, and so formidable to the Papal power, might have dallied away his life in unrebuked voluptuousness. If he had not threatened the patrimony of St. Peter, he might have infringed on the pure precepts of St. Peter. Frederick was a persecutor of the worst kind—a persecutor without bigotry: but the heretics were not only misbelievers, they were Lombard rebels. How far he may have been goaded into general scepticism by the doubts forced upon him by the unchristian conduct of the great churchmen: how far, in his heart, he had sunk to the miserable mocking indifference betrayed by some of the sarcasms, current, as from his lips, and which, even if merely gay and careless words, jarred so harshly on the sensitive religion of his age, cannot be known. Frederick certainly made no open profession of unbelief; he repeatedly offered to assert and vindicate the orthodoxy of his creed before the Pope himself. He was not superior, it is manifest, to some of the superstitions of

Religion of Frederick.

his time; he is accused of studying the influence of the stars, but it may have been astrology aspiring (under Arabic teaching) to astronomy, rather than astronomy grovelling down to astrology.[d] That which most revolted his own age, his liberality towards the Mohammedans, his intercourse by negotiation, and in the Holy Land, with the Sultan and his viziers, and with his own enlightened Saracen subjects, as well as his terrible body-guard at Nocera, will find a fairer construction in modern times. How much Europe had then to learn from Arabian letters, arts and sciences; how much of her own wisdom to receive back through those channels, appeared during the present and the succeeding centuries. Frederick's, in my judgement, was neither scornful and godless infidelity, nor certainly a more advanced and enlightened Christianity, yearning after holiness and purity not then attainable. It was the shattered, dubious, at times trembling faith, at times desperately reckless incredulity, of a man for ever under the burthen of an undeserved excommunication, of which he could not but discern the injustice, but could not quite shake off the terrors: of a man, whom a better age of Christianity might not have made religious; whom his own made irreligious. Perhaps the strongest argument in favour of Frederick, is the generous love which he inspired to many of the noblest minds of his time; not merely such bold and eloquent legists as Thaddeus of Suessa, whose pride and conscious power might conspire with his zeal for the Imperial cause, to make him confront so intrepidly, so eloquently, the Council at Lyons; it was the first bold encounter of the Roman lawyer

---

[d] Read on the religion of Frederick the passage in Ernest Renan's Averroes, p. 288, et seqq.

with the host of Canon lawyers. Nor was it merely Peter de Vineâ, whose melancholy fate revenged itself for its injustice, if he ever discovered its injustice, on the stricken and desolate heart of the King: but of men, like Herman of Salza, the Grand Master of the Teutonic Order. Herman was, by all accounts, one of the most blameless, the noblest, the most experienced, most religious of men. If his Teutonic Order owed the foundation of its greatness, with lavish grants and immunities, to Frederick, it owed its no less valuable religious existence, its privileges, its support against the hostile clergy, to the Popes. Honorius and Gregory vied with the Emperor in heaping honours on De Salza and his Order. Yet throughout his first conflict, De Salza is the firm, unswerving friend of Frederick. He follows his excommunicated master to the Holy Land, adheres to his person in good report and evil report; death alone separates the friends.[a] The Archbishop of Palermo (against whom is no breath of calumny) is no less, to the close of Frederick's life, his tried and inseparable friend; he never seems to have denied him, though excommunicate, the offices of religion; buried him, though yet unabsolved, in his cathedral; inscribed on his tomb an epitaph, which, if no favourable proof of the Archbishop's poetic powers, is the lasting tribute of his fervent, faithful admiration.

On the other hand, Innocent IV. not only carried the Papal claims to the utmost, and asserted them with a kind of ostentatious intrepidity: "We are no mere man, we have the place of God upon earth!" but there was a personal arrogance in his

Pope Innocent IV.

---

[a] In Voigt, Geschichte Preussens, is a very elaborate and interesting account of Herman of Salza, and the rise of the Teutonic Order.

demeanour, and an implacability which revolted even the most awe-struck worshippers of the Papal power. Towards Frederick he showed, blended with the haughtiness of the Pope, the fierceness of a Guelfic partisan; he hated him with something of the personal hatred of a chief of the opposite faction in one of the Italian republics. Never was the rapacity of the Roman See so insatiate as under Innocent IV.; the taxes levied in England alone, her most profitable spiritual estate, amounted to incredible sums. Never was aggression so open or so daring on the rights and exemptions of the clergy (during the greater part of the strife the support of the two new Orders enabled the Pope to trample on the clergy, and to compel them to submit to extortionate contributions towards his wars): never was the spiritual character so entirely merged in the temporal as among his Legates. They were no longer the austere and pious, if haughty churchmen. Cardinal Rainier commanded the Papal forces in the state of St. Peter with something of the ability and all the ferocity and mercilessness of a later Captain of Condottieri. Albert von Beham, the Archdeacon of Passau, had not merely been detected, as we have seen, in fraudulent malversation and shamefully expelled from Bavaria, but when he appeared again as Dean of Passau, his own despatches, which describe his negotiations with the Duke of Bavaria, show a repulsive depth of arrogant iniquity. The incitement of Conrad to rebellion against his father seems to him but an ordinary proceeding. The Bishop of Ferrara, the Legate in Germany, was a drunkard, if not worse. Gregory of Monte Longo, during the whole period Papal representative in Lombardy, the conductor of all the negotiations with the republics, the republics which swarmed with heretics, was a man of notorious incontinence; Frederick himself had hardly more concubines than the Cardinal Legate.

Immediately on the death of Frederick, the Pope began to announce his intention of returning to Italy. Peter Capoccio was ordered to ascertain the state of feeling in the kingdom of Sicily. The Pope himself raised a song of triumph, addressed to all the prelates and all the nobles of the realm: "Earth and heaven were to break out into joy at this great deliverance."[f] But the greater number of both orders seem to have been insensible to the blessing; they were mourning over the grave of him whom the Pope described as the hammer of persecution. The aged Archbishop of Palermo and the Archbishop of Salerno openly espoused the cause of Conrad; the Archbishop of Bari, Frederick's deadly enemy, seemed to stand alone in the Papal interest. Strangers, the Subdeacon Matthew, and a Dominican friar, were sent into Calabria and Sicily to stir up the clergy to a sense of their wrongs. In Germany Conrad was arraigned as a rebellious usurper for presuming to offer resistance to William of Holland. He was again solemnly excommunicated; a crusade was preached against him. The Pope even endeavoured to estrange the Swabians from their liege lord: "Herod is dead; Archelaus aspires to reign in his stead." In an attempt to murder Conrad at Ratisbon, the Abbot Ulric is supposed to have been the chief actor; the Bishop of Ratisbon was awaiting without the walls the glad tidings of the accomplishment of the assassination.[g] The Archbishop of Mentz, Christian, a prelate of great piety,

The Pope after the death of Frederick.

Dec. 25, 1253.

Raynald. sub ann. 1251.

[f] "Qui episcopus foras muros civitatis cum multis armatis eventum rei solicitus expectabat."—Herm. Alt. apud Boehmer, ii. 507. See Chron. Salisb. Pez. i. 361.

broaches the unpalatable doctrine that, as far as spiritual enemies, the word of God is the only lawful sword; but as for drawing the sword of steel, he held it unbefitting his priestly character. He is deposed for these strange opinions.[h] A youth, the Subdeacon Gerard, is placed on the Primate's throne of Germany.

Monarchs, however, seemed to vie in giving honour to the triumphant Pontiff on his proposed return to Rome. The Queen-mother Blanche of France (Louis IX., her son, was now prisoner in the East) offered to accompany him with a strong body of French troops. Henry of England expressed his earnest desire to prostrate himself at the feet of the Holy Father before he departed for the south. Alphonso of Castile entreated him to trust to the arms, fleets, and protection of Spain rather than of France. Before he bade farewell to the city of Lyons, whose pious hospitality he rewarded with high praise and some valuable privileges,[i] he had an interview within the city with his own Emperor William of Holland. After that he descended the Rhone to Vienne, to Orange, and then proceeded to Marseilles. He arrived at Genoa; the city hailed her holy son with the utmost honours. The knights and nobles of the territory supported a silken canopy over his head to

The kings do honour to Innocent IV.

April 19.

---

[h] "At jure episcopatu dejectum ob principatum conjunctum exploratum est; cum non modo præsulem sed etiam principem agere, ac vim insultantium ecclesiam vi repellere oporteret." Such is the comment of the ecclesiastical annalist Raynaldus, sub ann.

[i] The morals of Lyons were not improved by the residence of the Papal court. It was openly declared by Cardinal Hugo, "Magnam fecimus, postquam in hanc urbem venimus, utilitatem et eleemosynam: quando enim primo huc venimus, tria vel quatuor prostibula invenimus; sed nunc recedentes unum solum relinquimus; verum ipsum durat continuatum ab orientali parte civitatis usque ad occidentalem."—Matt. Paris, p. 819.

protect him from the sun. On Ascension Day he received the delegates from the cities of Lombardy. Ghibellinism held down its awe-struck and discomfited head. Rome alone was not as yet thought worthy, or sought not to be admitted to the favour of his presence, or he dared not trust,[k] notwithstanding his close alliance with the Frangipani (whom he had bought), that unruly city. He visited Milan, Brescia, Mantua, Ferrara, Modena, everywhere there was tumultuous joy among the Guelfs. While he was at Milan Lodi made her submission: the Count of Savoy abandoned the party of the Hohenstaufen. On All-Saints'-Day he was at Faenza; on the 5th of November he stayed his steps, and fixed his court at Perugia. For a year and a half he remained in that city; Rome was not honoured with the presence of her Pontiff till Rome compelled that presence.

<small>May 17.</small>
<small>His return to Italy. July 24.</small>

Among the first resolutions of Innocent was the suppression of heresy, more especially in the Ghibelline cities, such as Cremona. A holocaust of these outcasts would be a fit offering of gratitude to heaven for the removal of the perfidious Frederick. It was his design to strike in this manner at the head of the Ghibelline interests in Lombardy. The sum of Eccelin da Romano's atrocities, atrocities which, even if blackened by Guelfic hatred, are the most frightful in these frightful times, must be still aggravated by the charge of hereditary heresy. It may well be doubted if such a monster could have religion enough to be a heretic; but Eccelin was dead to spiritual censures as to the reproaches of his own conscience.

But the affairs of the kingdom of Naples occupied the

---

[k] Nic. de Curbio, c. 30.

thoughts of Innocent. Though the firm hand of Manfred
had maintained almost the whole realm in allegiance,
the nominal rule was intrusted by King Conrad to his
younger brother Henry. The denunciations, intrigues,
and censures of the Pope had wrought on certain nobles
and cities. A conspiracy broke out simultaneously in
many places, at the head of which was the Count of
Aquino; in Apulia the cities of Foggia, Andrea, and
Barletta; in the Terra di Lavoro Capua and Naples
were in open rebellion. Capua and Naples defied all
the forces of Manfred. The Pope had already assumed
a sovereign power, as if the forfeited realm had reverted
to the Holy See. He had revoked all Frederick's
decrees which were hostile to the Church: he had invested Henry Frangipani with Manfred's principality of
Tarentum and the land of Otranto; he had bestowed
on the Venetian Marco Ziani, the kinsman of the captain
executed by Frederick, the principality of Lecce.

Conrad had already with some forces crossed the
Alps; he had been received by the few faithful Ghibelline cities in Lombardy, Verona, Padua,
Vicenza. But throughout Central Italy the
Guelfic faction prevailed; the Papal forces were strong.
He demanded of the Venetians, and as they were glad
to get rid of Conrad from the north of Italy, he obtained
ships to convey him to the south; he landed at Siponto,
near Manfredonia. He was received by Manfred and
by the principal nobility as their deliverer.
Aquino, Suessa, San Germano fell before him,
and Capua opened her gates; Naples was
stormed, sacked, and treated with the utmost cruelty.
Innocent beheld the son of Frederick, though under
excommunication, in full and undisturbed possession of
his hereditary kingdom. Innocent looked in vain for

aid in Italy; his own forces, those of the Guelfs, had not obeyed the summons to relieve Naples. Eccelin da Romano and the Ghibellines occupied those of Lombardy; the Guelfs of Tuscany and Romagna, now superior to the Ghibellines, had broken out into factions among themselves; the fleets of Genoa were engaged against the infidels. Innocent looked abroad; the wealth of England had been his stay in former adversities. He had already sent an offer of the kingdom of Naples to the brother of King Henry, Richard of Cornwall; but Richard, from timidity or prudence, shrunk from this remote enterprise. He alleged the power of Conrad; his own relationship with the house of Swabia: in his mistrust he went so far as to demand guarantees and hostages for the fulfilment of his contract on the part of the Pope. But his feeble brother, Henry of England, was not embarrassed by this prudence. He accepted the offer of the investiture for his second son Edmund; in his weak vanity he addressed Edmund in his court, and treated him as already the King of Sicily. The more prudent Nuncio of the Pope enjoined greater caution; but all that the King could abstract from his own exchequer, borrow of his brother Richard, extort from the Jews, exact by his justices on their circuit, was faithfully transmitted to Rome, and defrayed the cost of the Papal armament against Conrad. For this vain title, which the Pope resumed at his earliest convenience, Henry III. endangered his own throne: these exactions precipitated the revolt of his Barons, which ended in the battle of Lewes.

<small>Papal decree, May 14, 1254. Henry III. accepts the crown of Apulia for his son. Aug. 1252.</small>

But while Innocent IV. was thus triumphing over the fall of his great enemy; while he was levying taxes on the tributary world; while he was bestowing the empire

T 2

of Germany on William of Holland, assuming the kingdom of Naples as an appanage escheated to the See of Rome, and selling it to one foreign prince after another, he was himself submitting to the stern dictation of the people and the Senator of Rome. The Frangipanis could no longer repay with their vigorous support the honours bestowed upon their family by the grant of the principality of Tarentum. The popular party was in the ascendant. Brancaleone, a Bolognese of great fame as a lawyer, was summoned to assume the dignity of Senator of Rome. He refused for a time to place himself at the head of the unruly people; he consented only on the prudent condition that thirty hostages of the noblest families in Rome should be sent to Bologna. Nor would he condescend to accept the office but for the period of three years. He exacted a solemn oath of obedience from every citizen. At first the nobles as well as the people appear to have acquiesced in the stern, just rule of the Senator. No rank, no power could protect the high born; no obscurity, nor the favour of the populace, the meaner criminal. His first act was to hang from the windows of their castles some citizens notorious and convicted as homicides; other rebels he suspended on gibbets.[m] Among his first acts was to summon the Bishop of Rome to take up his residence in his diocese; it was not becoming that the Queen of cities should sit as a widow without her Pontiff. Innocent hesitated; a more imperious message summoned him to instant obedience; at the same time the Perugians received a significant menace; that if they persisted in entertaining the Pope, the Romans would treat them as they had

---

[m] Raynald. sub ann. 1254.

already treated other cities in the neighbourhood, whom
they had subdued by force of arms. Innocent trembled and complied; he entered Rome
with a serene countenance but heavy heart. He was
received with triumph by the Senator and the whole
people. In the spring Innocent again withdrew from
Rome to Assisi; the pretext was the consecration of the
magnificent church of St. Francis.[a] But the impatient
people murmured at his delay; the Senator Brancaleone
again sent messengers to expostulate in haughty humility
with the Pope; "it became not the pastor to abandon his
flock: he was the Bishop not of Lyons, of Perugia, of
Anagni, but of Rome." The people of Assisi, like those
of Perugia, were warned by the fate of Ostia, Porto,
Tusculum, Albano, Sabina, and of Tivoli, against which
last the Romans were in arms. Innocent was compelled
to return; he passed by Narni, and again he was received
with outward demonstrations of joy; but now secret
murmurs and even violent reclamations were heard that
the Pope owed the people of Rome great sums for the
losses sustained by his long absence. Pilgrims and suitors
had been few; they had let no lodgings; their shops had
been without customers; their provisions unsold; their
old usurious profits of lending money had failed. The
Pope could only take refuge in the rigid justice of the Senator; Brancaleone allayed or awed the tumult to peace.

Yet at the same time Innocent was pursuing his
schemes upon the kingdom of Naples without
fear or scruple. Conrad at first had made
overtures of submission.[c] He was strong enough to

---

[a] Matt. Paris, sub ann. 1252. Corbio, Vit. Innocent. IV. Compare Gibbon, xii. 278, ch. lxix.

[c] To the Pope's first envoy, according to Spinelli, Conrad haughtily replied, "Che farà meglio ad impacciarsi con la chierica rasa."—Diario, apud Muratori.

indulge the hereditary cruelty which he unhappily displayed in a far higher degree than the ability and splendour of his forefathers,[p] and to foster ignoble jealousy against his bastard brother, Manfred, to whom he owed the preservation of his realm, but whose fame, extraordinary powers of body and mind, influence, popularity overshadowed the authority of the King. He gradually withdrew his confidence from Manfred, and despoiled him of his power and honours.[q] With admirable prudence Manfred quietly let fall title after title, post after post, possession after possession; nothing remained to him but the principality of Tarentum, and that burthened with a heavy tax raised for the royal treasury. The King dismissed, under various pretexts, the kindred of Manfred, Galvaneo and Frederico Lancia, Bonifacio di Argoino, his maternal uncle. The noble exiles found refuge with the Empress Constantia, Manfred's sister, at Constantinople: Conrad, by his ambassadors, insisted on their expulsion from that court.

But the Pope, in his despair at this unexpected strength displayed by the House of Swabia, had recourse to new measures of hostility. Conrad, like his ally Eccelin, was attainted of heresy; both were summoned to appear before the presence of the Pope to answer these charges; and to surrender themselves unarmed, unprotected into the hands of their enemy. Conrad, whose policy it was rather to conciliate than irreconcileably to break with the Pope, condescended to make his appearance by his proctor in the Papal Court.

But death was on the house of Hohenstaufen. Henry,

---

[p] "Vi fece gran giustizia, e grande occisione."—M. Spinelli, Diario, apud Muratori, R. I. S. xli. Bartholomeo di Neocastro, c. iii. Murat., R. I. S. xiii. [q] Giannone, p. 485.

the younger son of Frederick, a youth of twelve years old, came from Sicily to visit his brother Conrad; he sickened and died.* No death could take place in this doomed family, the object of such inextinguishable hate, without being darkened from a calamity into a crime. Conrad was accused of poisoning his brother, and by the Pope himself. Even the melancholy of Conrad at the loss of his brother, perhaps a presentiment of his own approaching end, was attributed to remorse. He hardly raised his head again; he wrote letters to the court of England, full of the most passionate grief. In another year Conrad himself was in his grave: he was seized with a violent fever, and died in a few days. Of his death the guilt, for guilt the Guelfs were determined to see, was laid on Manfred.* Conradin, almost an infant, not three years old, was the one legitimate heir of Barbarossa and of Frederick II. The consummate sagacity of Manfred led him to declare that he would not accept the Regency of the realm which Conrad (perhaps in some late remorse, or in the desperate conviction enforced on his death-bed, that Manfred alone could protect his son) had thought of bequeathing to him. Manfred awaited his time: he left to Berthold, Marquis of Homburg, the commander of the German auxiliaries of Conrad, the perilous post, knowing perhaps at once the incapacity of Berthold, and the odiousness of the Germans to the subjects of Sicily. Berthold, according to the will of Conrad,

Death of Prince Henry. Dec. 1253.

Of Conrad. May 21, 1254.

Conradin.

---

* Matt. Paris, sub ann. Nic. de Jamsilla. The Pope is said to have proposed to marry his niece to Henry (Paris, p. 832). A treaty was begun. Conrad during the negotiations was poisoned, but recovered. He accused the Pope of this poisoning (ibid. 852). The Pope himself accused Conrad of poisoning Henry.

* Jamsilla, Malespini.

assumed the Regency, took possession of the royal treasures, and, in obedience to the dying instructions of Conrad, sent a humble message entreating peace and the parental protection of the Pope for the fatherless orphan. Innocent was said to have broken out into a paroxysm of joy on hearing the death of Conrad. But he assumed a lofty tone of compassion; enlarged upon his own merciful disposition; granted to Conradin the barren title of King of Jerusalem, and acknowledged his right to the Dukedom of Swabia. But the absolute dominion of the kingdom of Naples had devolved to the Roman See: when Conradin should be of age, the See of Rome might then, if he should appear not undeserving, condescend to take his claims into her gracious consideration.

June 18.

Innocent had again, perhaps on account of the summer heats, escaped from Rome, and was holding his court at Anagni. He spared no measures to become master of the kingdom of Naples. He issued extraordinary powers to William, Cardinal of St. Eustachio, to raise money and troops for this enterprise. The Cardinal was authorised to empawn as security to the Roman merchants, the Church of Rome, all the castles and possessions of the separate churches of the city, of the Campagna and the Maritima, and of the kingdom of Sicily. He was to seize and appropriate to the use of the war the possessions and revenues of all the vacant Bishoprics; and of all the Bishoprics, though not vacant, whose prelates did not espouse the Papal cause. He had power to levy taxes, and even money throughout the realm; to confiscate all the estates of the adherents of Frederick and of his son, who should not, after due admonition, return to their allegiance to the Pope. He might annul all grants, seize all fiefs, and regrant them to the partisans of Rome. By these exertions, a great army was gathered on the frontier. From Anagni the Pope issued his bull of excommunication against Manfred, the Marquis of Homburg, and all the partisans of the house of Conrad.[1] The Regent, the Marquis of Homburg, found that many of the nobles were in secret treaty with the Pope; he let the sceptre of Regency fall from his feeble hands; and amidst the general contempt abdicated his trust.

All eyes were turned on Manfred; all who were attached to the house of Swabia, all who abhorred or despised the Papal government, all who desired the independence of the realm, counts, barons, many of the higher clergy, at least in secret, implored Manfred to assume the Regency. Manfred, consummate in the art of self-command, could only be forced in these calamitous times to imperil his honour by taking up this dangerous post. Rumours indeed were abroad of the death of Conradin; and Manfred was the next successor, according to the will of his father Frederick.[2] He assumed the Regency; threw a strong force of Germans into San Germano; fortified Capua and the adjacent towns to check the progress of the Papal arms. But everywhere was rebellion, defection, treachery. The Papal agents had persuaded or bribed Pietro Ruffo, the Regent under Berthold of Homburg, of Calabria and Sicily, and raised the Papal standard. Berthold's own conduct

Manfred Regent.

Date doubtful, 1254.

---

[1] Apud Raynald. 1254, Sept. 2.
[2] Nic. Jamsilla makes Manfred legitimate; his mother, Bianca Lancia, was the *fifth* wife of Frederick. But Manfred does not seem to have asserted his own legitimacy. Malespina (though Papalist) writes, " Tanquam ex damnato coitu derivatum, defectum natalium patiatur, nobilis tamen naturæ decus utriusque parentis, qua ortus ejus esse meruerat generosus, maculam fere defectûs hujus expiabat.'—Apud Muratori, viii. 787.

indicated treachery; he sent no troops to the aid of
Manfred, but roved about with his Germans, committing
acts of plunder, and so estranging the people from the
Swabian rule. He retained possession of the royal
treasures. Richard of Monte Negro had already, in
hatred of Berthold, made his peace with the Pope; other
nobles were secretly dealing for the renewal of their
fiefs, or for the grant of escheated fiefs, with the Pope,
who claimed the right of universal sovereign. Even in
Capua a conspiracy was discovered against the power
and against the life of Manfred.

Manfred was as great a master in the arts of dissimulation as the Pope himself. He found it
necessary at least to appear to yield. Already
the Papal agents had sounded his fidelity; he now
openly appealed to the magnanimity of the Pope as the
protector of the orphan; he expressed his willingness to
admit the Pope into the realm, reserving his own rights
and those of his royal ward. Innocent was in a
transport of joy. In his most luxuriant language he
dwelt on the moderation, the delight in mercy, the
parental tenderness of the Roman See: he received
Manfred into his highest favour. Not regarding his
grant to the Frangipani, he invested Manfred (Galvaneo
Fiamma, his uncle, receiving in his name the ring of
investiture) with the Principality of Tarentum, with the
County of Gravino, Tricarico, and the Honour of Monte
St. Angelo: he added the Countship of Andrea, which
he had obtained in exchange for other territories from
the Marquis of Homburg: with this he invested Frederick Lancia, Manfred's other uncle. Manfred met all
these advances with his consummate self-command. He
received the Pope on his entrance into his kingdom at
Ceperano, prostrated himself at his feet, led his horse,

as he passed the bridge over the Garigliano.ˣ The pride of Innocent was at its height in seeing Naples in his power, the son of Frederick at his feet. He lavished honours on Manfred; proclaimed him Vicar of the realm as far as the Faro. Manfred persuaded the Pope to scatter his forces all through the provinces, and by their means controlled the Germans, whom he could not trust, and who began quietly to withdraw to their own country.ʸ The people hailed Manfred as Vicar of the Pope. They enjoyed again, and under a Swabian Prince not environed by German soldiery, their full religious ceremonies.

The Pope entered the kingdom as though to take possession of the realm; after a short delay at Teano from indisposition, he entered Capua in state; he entered Naples in still greater pomp. His nephew, William Fiesco, Cardinal of St. Eustachio, his Legate, received the homage of the prelates and the nobles, with no reservation of the rights of the King or of the Prince, but absolutely in the name of the Pope, to whom had devolved the full sovereignty. Manfred himself was summoned to take the oath of allegiance. In his deep dissimulation he might have eluded this trial; he was perhaps awaiting the death of the Pope, now old and in bad health; but an accidental circumstance compelled him prematurely to throw off the mask. Borello d'Anglone, as the reward of his revolt to the Pope, had received the grant of the county of Lesina, an under-fief of Manfred's principality. Manfred summoned him to do homage; Anglone, confident in the Pope's favour, returned a haughty denial. Manfred

The Pope in Naples. Oct. 27, 1254.

ˣ On this homage, says Spinelli, "et onneuno se ne meravigliao assai."— Apud Muratori.   ʸ Giannone, in loc.

appealed to the Pope. The oracle spoke with his usual cautious ambiguity, he had granted to Borello none of the rights of Manfred. Berthold of Homburg was on his way to do homage to the Pope; Manfred withdrew, lest he should encounter him in Capua; his guards fell in with those of Borello; strife arose, Borello, unknown <small>Death of Borello d'Anglone. Flight of Manfred.</small> to Manfred, was slain. Manfred sent his messengers, declaring himself ready to prove himself before the Pope guiltless of the death of Borello. He was summoned to answer in person. He received secret intelligence from his uncle Galvaneo Lancia, that the treacherous Berthold of Homburg, instead of espousing his cause, had secretly betrayed it; that his liberty at least was threatened, if not his life. He mounted his horse, with few followers; after many wild adventures, he reached the city of Lucera, occupied chiefly by the Saracenic allies of his father. In despite of the German knights who commanded in the city in the name of Berthold of Homburg, he was received with the loudest acclamations. He was proclaimed Prince and Sovereign. Before the people he swore to maintain and defend the rights and title of the King his nephew, and his own, the liberty and the good estate of the realm, and of the city.

In a short time he was master of Foggia, had gained a brilliant victory over the Papal troops, and those of the Marquis of Homburg.

Innocent had already entered into negotiations with that enemy afterwards so fatal to Manfred. He had once sold the realm of Sicily to Edmund of England, <small>Dec. 1254.</small> and received at least some part of the price: he had now, regardless of his former obligations, or supposing them forfeited by the inactivity or less lavish subsidies of England, offered the realm to

Charles of Anjou, the brother of the King of France. All his solemn engagements were, to Innocent IV., but means to advance his immediate interests. He might seem as if he would try to the utmost his own power of absolution, to release himself from the most sacred obligations.*

But death, which had prostrated the enemies of Innocent before his feet, and had reduced the house of Swabia to a child and a bastard, now laid his hand on Innocent himself. He died master of Naples, the city of his great adversary, in the palace of Peter de Vineâ, the minister of that adversary. He left a name odious for ambition, rapacity, implacable pride, to part, at least, of Christendom. In England, where his hand had been the heaviest, strange tales were accredited of his dying hours, and of what followed his death. It was said that he died in an agony of terror and remorse; his kindred were bitterly wailing around his bed, rending their garments and tearing their hair: he woke up from a state seemingly senseless, "Wretches, why are ye weeping? have I not made you all rich enough?" He had been, indeed, one of the first Popes, himself of noble family, who by the marriage of his nieces, by heaping up civil and ecclesiastical dignities on his relatives, had made a Papal family. On the very night of his death a monk, whose name the English historian conceals from prudence, had a vision. He was in Heaven, and saw God seated on his throne. On God's right was the Holy Virgin, on his left a stately and venerable matron, who held what seemed a temple in

Death of Innocent. Dec. 7, 1254.

---

* Petr. de Vineâ, Epist. ii. 45. I here agree with M. Cherrier : "Trop de faits attestent qu'Innocent IV. n'était alacbre avec personne; qu'il promettait et se retractait avec une égale facilité, suivant l'état de ses affaires."—t. iii. p. 394.

her outstretched hand. On the pediment of this temple was written in letters of gold, "The Church." Innocent was prostrate before the throne, with clasped and lifted hands and bowed knees, imploring pardon, not judgement. But the noble matron said, "O, equitable judge, render just judgement. I arraign this man on three charges: Thou hast founded the Church upon earth and bestowed upon her precious liberties; this man has made her the vilest of slaves. The Church was founded for the salvation of sinners; he has degraded it to a counting-house of money-changers. The Church has been built on the foundation stones of faith, justice, and truth; he has shaken alike faith and morals, destroyed justice, darkened truth." And the Lord said, "Depart and receive the recompense thou hast deserved;" and Innocent was dragged away. "Whether this was an unreal vision, we know not," adds the historian, "but it alarmed many. God grant it may have amended them."

Nor was this all. The successor of Innocent was himself warned and terrified by a dream of not less awful import. In a spacious palace sat a judge of venerable majesty; by his side a stately matron, environed by a countless company. A bier was carried out by mean-looking bearers; upon it rested a corpse of sad appearance. The dead arose, cast himself before the throne, "O God of might and mercy, have pity upon me!" The judge was silent, the matron spoke: "The time of repentance is passed, the day of judgement is come. Woe to thee, for thou shalt have justice, not mercy. Thou hast wasted the Church of God during thy life; thou hast become a carnal man; disdained, despised, annulled the acts of thy holy predecessors; therefore shall thine own acts be held annulled." The severe judge uttered his sentence! The bier was hurried away. The dead sent to a place which the Christian may charitably hope was Purgatory. Pope Alexander tremblingly inquired who was the dead man. His guide replied, "Sinibald, thy predecessor, who died of grief, not for his sins, but for the defeat of his army." The affrighted Alexander, when he awoke, ordered masses and alms to mitigate the purgatorial suffering of his predecessor; he endeavoured to retrieve Innocent's sins by cancelling some of his acts; to one who offered rich presents to buy a benefice, the Pope replied, "No, my friend, he who sold churches is dead."*

Such were the current and popular tales, which showed that even the Pope could not violate the great principles of Christian justice and generosity and mercy, with impunity, or without some strong remonstrance finding its expression. If Innocent, indeed, had not trampled on the rights of the clergy, these murmurs had not been so deep and loud: it was this that impersonated, as it were, the Church, to demand his condemnation. It was not Imperialist or Ghibelline hatred, but the hatred of churchmen which invented or propagated these legends.

In England, indeed, not only after his death, but during his life, the courageous English spirit had allied itself with the profoundest religious feeling to protest against the rapacity and usurpation of the Italian Pope. It had found a powerful and intrepid voice in Robert Grostête Bishop of Lincoln. Robert Grostête, during his life, had manfully resisted and fearlessly condemned the acts of the haughty Pontiff: after his death he had been permitted, it was believed, to appear in a vision.

---

* All these are from Matt. Paris.

Robert Grostête was of humble birth: at Oxford his profound learning won the admiration of Roger Bacon. He translated the book called the Testament of the Twelve Patriarchs. He went to France to make himself master of that language. He became Archdeacon of Leicester, Bishop of Lincoln. As Bishop of that vast diocese he began to act with a holy rigour unprecedented in his times. With him Christian morals were inseparable from Christian faith. He endeavoured to bring back the festivals of the Church, which had grown into days of idleness and debauchery, to their sacred character; he would put down the Feast of Fools, held on New Year's Day. But it was against the clergy, as on them altogether depended the holiness of the people, that he acted with the most impartial severity. He was a Churchman of the highest hierarchical notions. Becket himself did not assert the immunities and privileges of the Church with greater intrepidity: rebellion against the clergy was as the sin of witchcraft; but those immunities, those privileges, implied heavier responsibility; that authority belonged justly only to a holy, exemplary, unworldly clergy. Everywhere he was encountered with sullen, stubborn, or open resistance. He was condemned as restless, harsh, passionate: he was the Ishmael of the hierarchy, with his hand against every man, every man's hand against him. The Dean and Chapter of Lincoln were his foremost and most obstinate opponents; the clergy asserted their privileges, the monasteries their Papal exemptions; the nobles complained of his interference with their rights of patronage, the King himself that he sternly prohibited the clergy from all secular offices; they must not act as the King's justiciaries, or sit to adjudge capital offences. His allies were the new

Orders, the Preachers and Mendicants. He addressed letters of confidence to the generals of both Orders. He resolutely took his stand on his right of refusing institution to unworthy clergy.[b] He absolutely refused to admit to benefices pluralists, boys, those employed in the King's secular service, in the courts of judicature or the collection of the revenue; in many cases foreigners; he resisted alike Churchmen, the Chancellor of Exeter; nobles, he would not admit a son of the Earl of Ferrara, as under age; the King, whose indignation knew no bounds; he resisted the Cardinal Legates, the Pope himself.

As a Churchman, Grostête held the loftiest views of the power of the Pope: his earlier letters to the Pope are in the most submissive, almost adulatory tone; to the Cardinals they are full of the most profound reverence. The Canon Law is as eternal, immutable, universal as the law of God. The Pope has undoubted power to dispose of all benefices; but for the abuse of that power hell-fire is the doom.[c] The resistance of the clergy to their Bishop involved the Bishops and themselves in vast expense; there was a perpetual appeal to Rome. Twice Grostête appeared in Lyons: the second time he was received with respect and courtesy by the Pope and Cardinals. The Pope even permitted him to read in his own presence and in the full consistory, a memorial against the abuses of the Court of Rome (the Curia), of its avarice and venality, its usurpations and exemptions, hardly surpassed in its

---

[b] Godwin. de Præsul. Matt. Paris.
[c] "Scio et veraciter scio, domini Papæ et sanctæ Romanæ Ecclesiæ hanc esse potestatem, ut de omnibus beneficiis ecclesiasticis libere possit ordinare, scio quoque quod quisquis abutitur hac potestate, ... ædificat ad ignem Gehennæ."—Epist. 49, apud Brown,' Fasciculus ii. 339.

vigorous invective in later times. Grostête returned to England with a decree against the refractory Chapter of Lincoln, ample powers to reform his diocese, and the strong support of the seeming favour of the Pope. The Pope even condescended to limit to some extent the demands of the Italian clergy on English benefices. Yet on his return even the firm mind of Grostête was shaken by the difficulties of his position: he meditated retirement from the intractable world; but he shook off the unworthy sloth, and commenced and carried through a visitation of his diocese unprecedented in its stern severity. The contumacious clergy were compelled to submit, and accepted his conditions; the monasteries opened their reluctant gates, and acknowledged his authority. In the convents of nuns he is said to have put their chastity to a strange and indelicate test, which shows at once the coarseness of the times and the laxity of morals. Yet he extorted from the monkish historian, who perhaps had suffered under his rigour, the admission that his sole object was the salvation of souls.[d]

On Innocent's triumphal return to Italy he had become, as it were, wanton in his invasions on the impoverished English Church. It was rumoured, incredible as it seems, that he demanded provision for three hundred of the Roman clergy.[e] Robert Grostête was summoned to the test of his obedience to the See of Rome. He had ordered a calculation to be made of the ecclesiastical revenues possessed by strangers in Eng-

---

[d] Paris, sub ann.
[e] There are many mandates for benefices in favour of Italians.—MS. B. M. E. g. Stephen the Pope's chaplain to hold the rich archdeaconry of Canterbury with the archdeaconry of Vienne, et alia beneficia. vii. sub ann. 1252, p. 110; a Colonna, 213. An Annibaldi De ——, and John of Civitella, 289; one or more prebends, with or without cure of souls.

land. It amounted to 70,000 marks: the King's income was not one-third of the sum. Grostête received command, through his Nuncio, to confer a canonry of Lincoln on the nephew of Innocent, a boy, Frederick of Lavagna. Grostête was not daunted by the ascendant power of the Pope.[f] His answer was a firm, resolute, argumentative refusal: "I am bound by filial reverence to obey all commands of the Apostolic See; but those are not Apostolic commands which are not consonant to the doctrine of the Apostles, and the Master of the Apostles, Christ Jesus. The most holy Apostolic See cannot command that which verges on the odious detestable abomination, pernicious to mankind, opposed to the sanctity of the Apostolic See, contrary to the Catholic faith. You cannot in your discretion enact any penalty against me, for my resistance is neither strife nor rebellion, but filial affection to my father, and veneration for my mother the Church."[g]

It was reported in England, that when this letter reached the Pope, he cried out in a passion of wrath, "Who is this old dotard who presumes to judge our acts? By St. Peter and St. Paul, if we were not restrained by our generosity, we would make him a fable, an astonishment, an example, and a warning to the world. Is not the King of England our vassal, rather our slave? Would he not, at a sign from us, throw

---

[f] Paris.
[g] The letter in Brown. Fasciculus, p. 400. There is a point which I find it difficult to explain. In the former epistle to the Legate Otho (quoted above), Epist. 49—seemingly of an earlier period—Grostête writes: "Licet præ meam conservationem in Episcopum supra Domini Papæ promotus ait in unā de optimis præbendis in Lincolniensi Ecclesiā." This could not be another nephew of Innocent; at the time of his nomination he must have been a boy indeed. Another writer (Ann. Burton) calls him puerulus. Compare Grostête's Letters on the Popes in the Grostete Epistolæ (Rolls publications) page 432.

this Bishop into prison and reduce him to the lowest disgrace?" With difficulty the Cardinals allayed his wrath: they pleaded the Bishop's irreproachable life, his Catholic doctrine; they more than insinuated the truth of his charges. The condemnation of Grostête might revolt the whole clergy of France and England, "for he is held a great philosopher, deeply learned in Greek and Latin letters, a reader in theology, a devout preacher, an admirer of chastity, a persecutor of Simoniacs." The more moderate or more astute counsels prevailed. Papal letters were framed which in some degree mitigated the abuses of these Papal provisions. The Pope acknowledged, almost in apologetic tone, that he had been driven by the difficulties of the times and the irresistible urgency of partisans to measures which he did not altogether approve. All who possessed such benefices were to be guaranteed in their free enjoyment, all who had expectancies were to be preferred to other persons, but these benefices were not to go down, as it were, by hereditary descent from Italian to Italian: on decease or vacancy the patron, prelate, monastery, or layman, might at once present.[b]

On Grostête's death it was believed that music was heard in the air, bells of distant churches tolled of their

---

[b] This letter is dated Perugia, Ann. Pontific. 10, 1252. It is in the Burton Annals, and in the Additamenta to Paris. In Rymer there is another quite different in its provisions. There the Pope asserts that he has made very few appointments. But Westminster adds to Paris: "Inventum est quod nunquam aliquis predecessorum suorum in triplo aliquos sui generis vel patriae tot ditaverunt." There is a strange clause in Innocent's letter, expressive of the wild times and the exasperation of the public mind: if a papal expectant should be murdered (si perimi contigerit, as if it were an usual occurrence), no one should be appointed who had not previously cleared himself of all concern in the murder.

own accord, miracles were wrought at his grave and in his church at Lincoln. But it was said likewise that the inexorable Pontiff entertained the design of having his body disinterred and his bones scattered. But Robert Grostête himself appeared in a vision, dressed in his pontifical robes before the Pope. "Is it thou, Sinibald, thou miserable Pope, who wilt cast my bones out of their cemetery, to thy disgrace and that of the Church of Lincoln? Better were it for thee to respect after their death the zealous servants of God. Thou hast despised the advice which I gave thee in terms of respectful humility. Woe to thee who hast despised, thou shalt be despised in thy turn!" The Pope felt as if each word pierced him like a spear. From that night he was wasted by a slow fever. The hand of God was upon him. All his schemes failed, his armies were defeated, he passed neither day nor night undisturbed. Such was believed by a large part of Christendom to have been the end of Pope Innocent IV.[1]

---

[1] It is a significant fact that Grostête was never canonised. This honour was granted to the claistral virtues of his predecessor, Hugh of Lincoln; to his contemporary, Edmund Rich of Canterbury. Edmund had ingloriously retired from his difficult post of primate; his timid piety despaired of reforming his clergy; he was embarrassed between the King and his Barons; between the King compelled to resist the exactions of the Pope, and the Pope whose demands Edmund would have gratified to the full. He took refuge in the retreat of Becket, Pontigny; but with nothing of Becket's character. Yet the mild prelate shared with Becket the honours of a saint. Grostête was canonised only by the reverence of his country. Even Matthew Paris after his death found out his virtues. Of these not the least was his opposition to the King and to Rome (fuit Domini Papæ et Regis redargutor manifestus; Romanorum malleus et contemptor); the instructor of the clergy, the support of scholars; the preacher of the people; persecutor only of the incontinent. At table he was liberal, plentiful, courteous, cheerful, and affable; in church, devout, tearful, penitent; as a prelate, sedulous, venerable, indefatigable.

BOOK XI.

CONTEMPORARY CHRONOLOGY.

POPES.		EMPERORS OF GERMANY.		KINGS OF FRANCE.		KINGS OF ENGLAND.	
A.D.	A.D.	A.D.	A.D.	A.D.	A.D.	A.D.	A.D.
1254 Alexander IV.	1261	1269 William	1256				
1261 Urban IV.	1265	(Conrad)					
1265 Clement IV.	1268	1256 Interregnum	1273	Louis IX.	1270		
1268 Vacancy	1271			1270 Philip the Hardy	1285		
1271 Gregory X.	1276	1273 Rodolph of Haps-				Henry III.	1272
1276 Innocent V., Hadrian V., John XXI.		burg	1291			1272 Edward I.	1307
1277 Nicolas III.	1281					*Archbishops of Canterbury.*	
1281 Martin IV.	1285			1285 Philip the Fair	1314	1244 Boniface of Sa- voy	1270
1285 Honorius IV.	1288	1291 Adolph of Nassau	1298			1273 Robert Kil- wardby	1278
1288 Nicolas IV.	1292					1278 Robert Peck- ham	1294
1292 Vacancy	1294	1298 Albert of Austria	1308			1294 Robert Winchel- sey	1313
1294 Celestine V., Boniface VIII.	1303						
1303 Benedict X.	1304						

KINGS OF SCOTLAND.		KINGS OF SPAIN.		KINGS OF SWEDEN.		EASTERN EMPIRE.	
A.D.	A.D.	A.D.	A.D.	A.D.	A.D.	A.D.	A.D.
		Castile.				*Latin.*	
Alexander III.	1286	1252 Alfonso XI., the Wise	1284	1250 Waldemar	1276	Baldwin II.	1271
1286 Interregnum	1292	1284 Sancho IV.	1295	1276 Magnus II.	1283	*Greek.*	
1292 John Balliol		1295 Ferdinand IV.	1312	1283 Birger II.		1254 Theodorus	1259
1301 Interregnum		*Arragon.*				1259 John IV.	
		James I.		KINGS OF DENMARK.		1259 Michael (Palæ- logus)	1282
		Alfonso II.	1276	A.D.	A.D.	1282 Andronicus II. (Palæologus)	
		1276 Pedro III.	1285	1252 Christopher	1259		
		1285 Alfonso III., the Beneficent	1297	1259 Eric VII.	1283		
		1291 James II., the Just	1327	1283 Canute IV.	1290		
				1290 Eric VIII.			
		KINGS OF PORTUGAL.		1302 Hakim II.			
		A.D.	A.D.				
		Alfonso III.	1279				
		1279 Dionysius I.					

BOOK XI.

CHAPTER I.

St. Louis.

The great fabric of mediæval religion might have suffered a shock from the haughtiness, the rapacity, the implacability of Innocent IV., which had raised a deep and sullen alienation even among the clergy, in parts of Christendom, especially in England and Germany. The Teutonic pride revolted at the absolute nomination of an obscure prince to the Empire by the will of the Pope. The bold speculations, the enlightened studies, promoted by Frederick II., even the contemptuous indifference ascribed to him, though outwardly rejected, were working no doubt in the depths of many minds. Heresy, crushed in blood in Languedoc, was spreading elsewhere the more extensively in defiance of the Inquisition, which was already becoming odious throughout Europe. The strife of the new Orders with the clergy had weakened their influence over the popular mind, influence not altogether replaced by the wonderful numbers, activity, learning, ubiquity of the Mendicants. In the Franciscan Order had already begun that schism, which was of far greater importance than is commonly supposed in religious history.

But there was not wanting the great example of religion to awe and to allure mankind: it was not in the chair of St. Peter, not at the head of a new Order, but on the throne of France: the Saint of this period was a King. The unbounded admiration of St. Louis in his own days, the worship of the canonised Sovereign in later times, was a religious power, of which it is impossible to trace or define the limits. Difficult, indeed, it is to imagine that at the same historic period lived Frederick II. and Louis IX. Louis was a monk upon the throne, but a monk with none of the harshness, bitterness, or pride of monkery. His was a frank playfulness, or amenity at least of manner, which Henry IV. never surpassed, and a blamelessness hardly ever before, till very recent times never after, seen on the throne of France. Nor was he only a monk: he had kingly qualities of the noblest order, gentleness, affability, humanity towards all his believing subjects, a kind of dignity of justice, a loftiness of virtue, which prevented the most religious of men from degenerating into a slave of the clergy; a simple sincerity even in his lowest superstitions, an honest frankness, an utter absence of malignity even in his intolerance, which holds even those failings and errors high above contempt, or even aversion. Who can read the Seneschal Joinville without love and veneration of his master?

St. Louis.

Louis was ten years old at the death of his father Louis VIII. His mother, Blanche of Castile, took possession at once of the regency. Her firm demeanour awed all ranks; her vigorous administration at once established her power. Philip the Rough, the brother of Louis VIII. (the son of Philip Augustus by Agnes of Moran, but who had been acknowledged as a legitimate prince), submitted sullenly, yet submitted, to the female rule. It is strange to contrast the severe court of the Queen-mother Blanche with that

{.sidenote}
A.D. 1824.
Blanche of Castile.

of Marie de Medicis, or Anne of Austria; the youth of
Louis IX. with that of Louis XIV. or Louis XV.: and
to suppose that the same religion was preached in the
churches, then by a rude Dominican or a homely Franciscan, afterwards in the exquisite and finished language
of Bossuet and Massillon. Blanche of Castile did not
entirely escape the malicious slanders of her enemies.
She was accused of too close an intimacy with the
Legate himself. She fell under stronger suspicion as
the idol of the amorous poetry of the gallant Thiebault,
Count of Champagne, afterwards King of Navarre. But
Thiebault's Platonic raptures were breathed in vain to
the inaccessible matron ; it was the policy not the heart
of the Queen Regent which led her not to disdain the
poetic suit of a dangerous subject, constantly falling off
to the enemies of her son, and recalled to his allegiance
by the authority of his mistress. The historian guarantees her chaste and cleanly life.* Her treatment of
her son showed no indulgence for such weaknesses.
Once in his early youth he had looked with kindling
eye on some fair damsels. "I had rather he were
dead," said the rigid mother, "than that he should
commit sin." Thus bred a monk, the congenial disposition of Louis embraced with ardour the austere rule.
Had he not been early married, he would have vowed
perpetual chastity. The jealousy of his mother of any
other influence than her own was constantly watching
his most familiar intercourse with his wife, Marguerite
of Provence. He bore it, even the harshness with which
Blanche treated her daughter-in-law at times when
woman's sympathies are usually most tender, with the
meekest filial submission. At all the great religious

---

* " Sa vie bonne et nette."—Joinville.

periods, Advent, Lent, the high Festivals, and all holy
days (which now filled no small part of the
year), the youthful King denied himself all con-
nubial indulgences; he would rise from his bed, and
pace the cold chamber till he was frozen into virtue.
His other appetites he controlled with equal inflexibility.
Besides the most rigorous observance of the ordinary
fasts, once only in the year would he allow himself
to taste fruit: he wore the roughest sackcloth next to
his skin. His spiritual teachers persuaded him to less
severe observance, to deny himself only unripe fruit, to
wear haircloth of less coarse texture. On Fridays he
never laughed; if he detected himself in laughter he
repressed and mourned over the light emotion. On
Friday he never changed his raiment. In his girdle he
wore an ivory case of iron-chain scourges (such boxes
were his favourite presents to his courtiers), not for idle
display. Every Friday during the year, and in Lent on
Mondays, Wednesdays, and Fridays, he shut himself up in
his chamber, searching every corner, lest any one should
be present, with his confessor, the Dominican Godfrey of
Beaulieu. The bleeding shoulders of the King attested
his own sincerity, and the singular adulation of the confessor, who knew the King too well not to administer the
discipline with unsparing hand. These more secret acts
of holiness were no doubt too admirable for the clergy to
allow them to remain secret; but the people were no less
edified by his acts of public devotion. It was his constant
practice to visit distant churches with bare feet, or, to
disguise his piety, in sandals without soles. On every
altar he offered profuse alms. One day he walked bare-
foot from Nogent l'Erembert to the church of Our Lady
at Chartres, a distance of four leagues; he was obliged
to lean on his attendants for support. He constantly

washed the feet of beggars; he invited the poor and the
sick to his table; he attended the hospitals, and performed
the most menial and loathsome offices. A leper
on the farther side of a swamp begged of him; the King
crossed over, not only gave him alms, but kissed his
hand. He heard daily two, sometimes three or four,
masses; his whole day might seem one unbroken
service; as he rode, his chaplain chanted or recited the
offices. Even in this respect his teachers attempted to
repress his zeal. A Dominican preacher urged him
from the pulpit not to lower too much the royal dignity,
not to spend the whole day in church, to content himself
with one mass: "whoever counselled him otherwise was
a fool, and guilty of a deadly sin." "If I spent twice as
much time in dice and hawking, should I be so rebuked?"[b]
answered the gentle King. He bore even
reproach with meekness. A woman named Sarrette,
pleading in the King's court, said "Fie! you are not
King of France; you are only a king of friars, of priests,
and of clerks. It is a great pity that you are King of
France; you should be turned out of the kingship."[c]
The blessed King would not allow his attendants to
chastise the woman. "You say true! It has pleased
the Lord to make me king; it had been well if it had
pleased him to make some one who had better ruled the
realm." He then ordered his chamberlain to give her
money, as much as forty pence.

Louis had the most religious aversion for all lighter
amusements, the juggler, the minstrel. He was profoundly
ignorant of polite letters. His whole time
might seem fully occupied in rehearsing over and over

---

[b] Notices et Extraits, ix. 406.
[c] Life, by the Confessor of Queen Margaret, in Bouquet, p. 366.

the same prayers; yet he is said to have read perpetually in a Latin Bible with devotional notes, and to have been deeply versed in the writings of some of the Fathers, especially St. Augustine. But this learning, whatever it might be, he acquired with the most reverential humility; it tempted him to no daring religious speculation, emboldened him to no polemic zeal. "Even clerks, if not profoundly learned, ought to abstain from controversy with unbelievers; the layman had but one argument, his good sword. If he heard a man to be an unbeliever, he should not dispute with him, he should at once run that sword into his entrails, and drive it home."[d] He related with special approbation the anecdote of a brave old knight, who broke up a discussion on the relative excellence of their law between some Catholic doctors and some Jewish Rabbis by bringing down his mace upon the head of the principal Jew teacher. Louis loved all mankind with a boundless love except Jews, heretics, and infidels, whom he hated with as boundless hatred.

But above all these weaknesses or exaggerated virtues there were the high Christian graces, conscientiousness such as few kings are able or dare to display on the throne, which never swerved either through ambition or policy from strict rectitude. No acquisition of territory, no extension of the royal power, would have tempted Louis IX. to unjust aggression. He was strongly urged to put to death the son of the chief of the rebels in arms against him, the Count de la Marche, who had fallen into his hands; he nobly

His virtues.

---

[d] "Mais lomme loy (laic) quand il ot mesdire de la ley crestienne, ne doit desputer a eulz, ne doit pas defendre la ley crestienne, ne mais (si non) de l'espee, de quoi il doit donner parmi le ventre dedans, tant comme il peut entrer."—Joinville, in Bouquet, t. xx. p. 198.

replied: "A son could not refuse to obey his father's orders." The one great war in which he was involved, before his departure for the Crusade, which ended in the humiliation of the great vassals of the Crown and of the leader in that revolt, Henry III. of England, the chief of these great vassals, was provoked by no oppression or injustice on his part, was conducted with moderation unusual in that age; and his victory was not sullied by any act of wanton revenge or abuse of power. He had no rapacity; he coveted but one kind of treasure, reliques; and no doubt when he bought the real crown of thorns (the abbey of St. Denys had already boasted their possession of the authentic crown, but their crown sank into obscurity, when that of Constantinople arrived in Paris),* when he obtained this inestimable prize at such enormous cost, there was no abstemiousness which he would not have practised, in order so to enrich his beloved France. He plundered the Jews, but that was on religious grounds; their tainted wealth might not infect the royal treasury; he bestowed the whole on Baldwin of Constantinople.

Yet Louis was no slave of the hierarchy. His religion was of too lofty a cast to submit to the dictates of a worldly clergy. His own great objects of admiration were the yet uncorrupt Mendicants, the Preachers and Minorites; half his body he would give to St. Dominic, half to St. Francis. He once gravely meditated the abandonment of his throne to put on the weeds of one of these Orders. His laws will afterwards display him, if not as the founder, the asserter of the liberties of the Gallican Church, and of the royal power, as limiting that of the Papacy. Throughout the strife between

---

* Compare Tillemont, Vie de Saint Louis, ii. 337.

Frederick II. and Gregory IX. he maintained an impartial and dignified neutrality. He had not declined the summons of the Emperor to hold a meeting of the temporal Sovereigns of Christendom to resist in common the encroachments of the spiritual power. Nothing could surpass the calm loftiness with which he demanded the release of the French prelates taken at the battle of Meloria; he could advance the cogent argument, that he had resisted all the demands and entreaties of the Pope to be permitted to levy subsidies on the realm of France for the war against the Emperor. He had refused, as we have seen, the offer of the Imperial crown from Innocent IV. for his brother; only when Frederick threatened to march on Lyons, and crush the Pope, did Louis seem disposed to take up arms for the defence of the Pontiff.'

Louis determines on a crusade. Such a monarch could not but be seized by the yet unexpired passion for the Crusade. Urban II., two centuries before, would not have found a more ardent follower. It was in St. Louis no love, no aptitude for war, no boiling and impetuous valour. His slight frame and delicate health gave no promise of personal prowess or fame; he was in no way distinguished in, he loved not, knightly exercises. He had no conscious confidence in his military skill or talent to intoxicate him with the hopes of a conqueror; he seems to have utterly wanted, perhaps to have despised, the most ordinary acquirements of a general. He went forth simply as the servant of God; he might seem to disdain even the commonest precautions. God was to fight his own battles; Louis was assured of victory or Paradise. All depended on the faith, and the sup-

---

' Tillemont, III. p. 164.

pression of military licence, at which he laboured with fond hopes of success, not on the valour, discipline, generalship of the army. In his determination to embark on the Crusade, Louis resolutely asserted the absolute power of the monarch: in this alone he resisted the colder caution of his mother Blanche; she was obliged to yield to the pious stubbornness of her son. Louis was seized with an alarming illness, he had sunk into a profound lethargy, he was thought dead; a pious female had drawn the covering, in sad respect, over what seemed the lifeless corpse. Another gently withdrew it. The soft but hollow voice of the King was heard: "God has raised me from the dead: give me the Cross." His mother wept tears of joy; when she saw the Cross on his breast, she knew the meaning of that gesture. She shuddered as if he lay dead before her.[*] _{A.D. 1244. Dec. 10.}

No expedition to the East was so ignominiously disastrous as that of St. Louis: yet none might seem to set forth under more promising auspices. He was three years in assembling his forces, preparing arms, money, horses, soldiers. It was in October (A.D. 1245) that in the Parliament of Paris he publicly took the Cross. The princes, the nobles, vied in following his example; his brother, Robert of Artois, the Duke of Burgundy, the Duke of Brabant, the Countess of Flanders and her sons, Peter Mauclerc of Dreux and his son, the Count of Bretagne, the Counts of Bar, Soissons, St. Pol, de la Marche, Rhetel, Montfort; the Archbishops of Rheims, Sens, and Bourges, the Bishops of Beauvais, Laon, and Orleans, with countless knights and esquires. At Christmas in the same year Louis practised perhaps

---

[*] Joinville, p. 207.

the only act of treachery of which he was guilty in his life. It was the custom for the King to distribute, as his gifts on that day, new robes to the courtiers. He ordered red crosses to be secretly embroidered between the shoulders; they were lavished in more than usual numbers. The courtiers were astonished to find that the King had thus piously enlisted them; they were now warriors of the Cross, who could not shrink from their engagement. It would have been indecent, disgraceful, ignoble, to throw aside the crosses; so, with true French levity, they laughed and wept at once, owning that they were completely entrapped by the King.

From that time the whole thoughts of Louis were absorbed in the Holy War. He resisted the offers of Pope Innocent to befriend him in a war against England, even in an invasion of England. He made, as he hoped, a lasting peace with his neighbour.

A.D. 1246.

He took no part in the confederacy of the French nobility to resist the exactions of the Pope and of the hierarchy.[b] He laboured earnestly, though ineffectually, to reconcile the Emperor and the Pope.

So far, on the other hand, had his strife with the Emperor absorbed all other religious passions in the Pope, that not only was there no cordial co-operation on the part of Innocent in the Crusade of St. Louis, but exemptions from the Crusades were now notoriously sold, it was believed to defray the expenses of the war against the Emperor. The Crusaders in Italy were urged to join the Pope's forces, with all the privileges and exemptions of a Crusade to the Holy Land.

Louis himself did not embark at the head of a great

---

[b] According to Paris, St. Louis favoured the League. Compare Tillemont, iii. p. 120.

army, like a puissant monarch. The princes, prelates, and nobles were to arrange their own transport. St. Louis passed down the Rhône; he was urged to avenge the death of his father on rebellious Avignon: "I have taken arms to revenge Jesus Christ, not my father." The island of Cyprus was the place of rendezvous. In Cyprus there was a delay of eight months. Want of discipline and a fatal epidemic made great ravages in the army; there seemed a total absence of conduct or command. But for supplies sent by the Emperor Frederick, there had been famine. The grateful Louis made one more effort to mediate between the Pope and the Emperor. The overture was contemptuously rejected.

{Louis embarks on the Crusade.}

At length the armament set sail; its object was the conquest of Egypt, as securing that of the Holy Land. Damietta was abandoned by the Saracens; the Crusaders were masters of that great city.[1] But never were the terror and advantages of a first success so thrown away. Months were wasted; the King was performing the offices of a monk, not of a general. Yet the army of the pious Louis was abandoned to every kind of Oriental luxury.[k] In June they were in Damietta, in November they marched, and shut themselves in a camp in a corner between the hills and the canal of Ashmoun. The flying bands of the enemy, with the Greek fire, harassed the camp. Good fortune and the valour of the soldiery extricated them from this diffi-

{June 7, 1249. (Cyprus.)}
{June 20. (Damietta.)}
{Feb. 8-11.}

---

[1] The instant St. Louis landed and saw the Saracens, he drew his sword and was for charging them at once. The wiser "preudhommes" stopped him. This was St. Louis's notion of military affairs.—Joinville, p. 215.

[k] Not a stone's throw from the King the soldiers "tenoient leurs bardiaux."—Joinville, 217.

culty, only to involve them in more fatal disasters. The King's brother, the Count of Artois, fell in a hasty unsupported advance. The unrivalled valour of the French was wasted in unprofitable victories, like those of Mansourah, or in miserable defeats. The camp was in a state of blockade; pestilence,[m] famine, did the work of the enemy. The King of France was a prisoner to the Sultan of Egypt. Of two thousand three hundred knights and fifteen thousand pilgrims few made their escape. His brothers, Alfonse of Poitou and Charles of Anjou, shared his captivity. His Queen, far advanced in pregnancy, remained with an insufficient force in Damietta. She bore a son prematurely; she called his name "Tristan."

Defeat and captivity. March 21, April 6.

But it was adversity which displayed the great character of St. Louis. He was himself treated at first with courtesy; he was permitted to hear the canonical prayers, after the custom of the Church of Paris, recited by the single priest who had escaped; his breviary, the loss of which he deplored above all losses, was replaced by another. But he had the bitter aggravation of his misery—that, of ten thousand prisoners in Mansourah, all who would not abandon their faith (and some there were guilty of this apostasy) met a cruel death. But to all the courteous approaches of the Sultan, Louis was jealously on his guard, lest he should compromise his dignity as a King or his purity as a Christian: he would not receive the present of a dress from the Unbeliever. To their exorbitant demands and menaces he gave a calm and determined reply. They demanded the surrender of all the fortresses in Syria: these, it was

---

[m] They had no fish all Lent but "bourbettes," which gluttonous fish fed on dead bodies, and produced dreadful maladies.

answered, belonged not to the King of France, but to
Frederick II. as King of Jerusalem. To that of yielding up the castles garrisoned by the Knights of the
Temple and of St. John, the answer was that the
Orders could not surrender them without violating their
vows. The King was threatened with torture—torture
of the most cruel kind—the barnacles, which crushed
the legs. "I am your prisoner," he said, "ye may do
with me as ye will."ᵃ It is said that he defied even
the more degrading menace of carrying him about and
exhibiting him as a spectacle in all the cities of Islam.
At length more reasonable terms were proposed; the
evacuation of Damietta, and a large sum of money—for
the King's ransom one million byzantines; for the
captive Barons five hundred thousand French livres.
Concerning his own ransom Louis made some difficulty;
he acceded at once to that of the Barons. "It becomes
not the King of France to barter about the liberty of
her subjects."ᵇ The Sultan, Turan-Shah, was moved
by the monarch's generosity; with Oriental magnificence, he struck off one-fifth—two hundred thousand
byzantines—from his ransom.

In the new perils which arose on the murder of the
Sultan Turan-Shah before the deliverance of the prisoners, the tranquil dignity of the King of France overawed even the bloody Mamelukes. The
Emirs renewed the treaty; the difficulty was now the
oath. The King demanded, by the advice of Master
Nicolas of Ptolemaïs, that the Mussulmen should swear,
"that if they broke the treaty they should be dishonoured as the Islamite who should go as a pilgrim

Murder of the Sultan Turan-Shah.

ᵃ Joinville, p. 243.
ᵇ "Par ma foy larges est le Frans, quant il ne pas bargignes (marchandes) sur si grant somme de deniers." So said the Saracens. Joinville, 243.

to Mecca bareheaded, as one who should take back a divorced wife, as one who had eaten swine's flesh." A renegade suggested as an equivalent form to be required of the King, that in like case, should he violate the treaty, "he should be dishonoured as a Christian who had denied God and his Holy Mother, and had severed himself from the communion of God, his Apostles, and Saints; or, in mockery of God, had spat on the Holy Cross and trampled it under foot." Louis indignantly repelled the last clause. The Emirs threatened him with death; he declared that he had rather die than live, after having insulted God and his Holy Mother.* His brothers and the other Barons followed the example of his firmness. In vain the Mamelukes seized the Patriarch of Jerusalem, who had come under the Sultan's safe conduct (which they disclaimed) into the camp, a man eighty years old, and tied him to a tent-post with his hands behind his back, till they swelled and almost burst. The Patriarch, in his agony, entreated the King to yield, and offered to take upon himself all the guilt of his oath. The oath was arranged, it is not known how, to mutual satisfaction; but so rigidly scrupulous was Louis, that when it appeared that in the payment of part of the ransom the Christians might have gained an advantage, either fairly or unfairly, of ten thousand byzantines in weight, he peremptorily commanded the full payment.

The release of the King on such favourable terms, at Ransom and release. a price so much below the value of such a captive, astonished both the Christians and the Mussulmen. Damietta could not have resisted many days. Much was attributed to the awe inspired

---

* Joinville, p. 246.

by the majestic demeanour and calm self-command of the King.⁴ Joinville, his faithful seneschal and historian, had persuaded himself that the Emirs, after the murder of Turan-Shah, had determined to offer the crown of Egypt to the King of France; they were only deterred by his stern Christianity, which would never have submitted to the toleration of their creed. The King himself declared to the Seneschal that he should not have declined the offer. Happily it was not made, probably was never contemplated; the death of Louis would soon have vindicated the affront on Islam. But all this, no doubt, heightened the religious romance which spread in Europe around the name of Louis.

Notwithstanding his defeat and humiliation and captivity, the passive courage of Louis was still unbroken; he persisted, contrary to all counsel, in remaining in Palestine. He would not suppose that God would utterly abandon his faithful servants; he would not believe that Christendom would be unmoved by his appeal; he still would fondly expect that the irresolute Henry of England would fulfil his vow, and come to his rescue at the head of his whole realm.ʳ To Henry the summons was earnest and repeated. Louis made the most advantageous overtures; he even, to the indignation and disgust of his own subjects, offered the surrender of Normandy, to which England still laid claim as her King's hereditary dominions.ˢ He still imagined that the Pope would lay aside all his

_{Hopes of Louis.}

---

⁴ The Saracens, according to Joinville, said that if Mohammed had allowed such sufferings to be inflicted on them as St. Louis endured, they should have renounced him.—P. 247.

ʳ Henry took the cross (March 6, 1251), says Tillemont, "soit pour piller plus librement ses sujets, soit pour quelque meilleur dessein." The Pope wrote to Henry early in 1251. Henry swore to go to the Holy Land in three years.—Paris, p. 834.

ˢ Paris, 833, 834.

plans for the humiliation of Frederick, and be compelled, by his own Apostolic character, and the general voice of Christendom, to sacrifice everything to the recovery of the Holy Land; that there would be but one Crusade under his auspices, and that the legitimate one. Louis was deserted by his brothers, whose light conduct had caused him great vexation; while he was in perpetual self-mortification before God for his sins, which he did not doubt had caused his defeat and bondage, they were playing at dice, whiling away the hours with vain amusements. Almost all the Barons followed the Counts of Poitou and Anjou; Louis was left almost alone with Joinville, his faithful Seneschal. Nor was his weary sojourn in Palestine enlivened by any brilliant successes or gallant feats of arms. For these Louis had neither the activity nor the skill. He was performing the pious office of assisting with his own hands to bury the dead warriors. A hasty pilgrimage in sackcloth to Nazareth was almost the only reward; the only advantage of his residence was the fortification of Cæsarea, Ptolemaïs, and Joppa. The negotiations with the Sultan of Aleppo on one side, and the Egyptians on the other, by which he hoped to obtain the country west of the Jordan, came to nothing. He is said to have converted many Saracens;[1] he spent enormous sums in the purchase of Mohammedan or heathen slaves, whom he caused to be baptised.[a]

It was only the death of the Queen-mother Blanche, and the imperious necessity for his presence in his kingdom of France, which forced him at last to leave the hallowed soil. He returned—if with-

---

[1] Tillemont, from MSS., and Duchesne, p. 405.   [a] Ibid.

out fame for arms, or for the conduct of affairs—with the profoundest reverence for his sanctity. Only a few years before, Frederick II. had come back to Europe, leaving Jerusalem in the hands of the Christians; the Christian power in Palestine, but for its own dissensions, formidable both to the Sultan of Egypt and the Sultan of Damascus; he had come back still under the sentence of excommunication, under the reproach with the Papal party of having basely betrayed the interests of the Cross and of God. Louis left Jerusalem unapproachable but with difficulty and danger by the Christian pilgrim, and the kingdom of Jerusalem visibly trembling to its fall; yet an object of devout respect, having made some advance at least, to his future canonisation.

The contrast between Frederick and Louis may be carried on with singular interest, as illustrative of their times. It might have been supposed that Louis would have been the remorseless persecutor of heretics; Frederick, if not the bold asserter of equal toleration, which he allowed to Greeks and Mohammedans, would hardly have been the sovereign to enact and execute persecuting edicts, unprecedented in their cruelty, and to encourage the son to denounce the father.[x] Happily for Louis, his virtue was not tried by this sore temptation; it was not under his government that the spiritual ravagers still wasted Languedoc. After the treaty by which Raymond VII., Count of Toulouse, surrendered his principality, he remained with the barren dignity of sovereign, but without a voice in the fate of a large though concealed part of his subjects. Bishop Fulk of Toulouse, as far as actual power, was half sovereign of the land, and

Further contrast of Frederick and Louis.

Louis escapes being a persecutor.

---

[x] See above, p. 150.

the council of that sovereign, which alone displayed administrative activity, was the Inquisition. Heresy had been extinguished as far as its public services; but the Inquisition of Toulouse determined to root it out from the hearths, from the chambers, from the secret hearts and souls of men. The statutes of the Council of Lateran were too merciful. The Inquisition drew up its code of procedure,[7] a Christian code, of which the base was a system of delation at which the worst of the Pagan emperors might have shuddered as iniquitous; in which the sole act deserving of mercy might seem to be the Judas-like betrayal of the dearest and most familiar friend, of the kinsman, the parent, the child. Though these acts belong neither to Frederick nor to Louis, they must find their place in our history.

The Court sat in profound secresy; no advocate might appear before the tribunal; no witness was confronted with the accused: who were the informers, what the charges, except the vague charge of heresy, no one knew. The suspected heretic was first summoned to declare on oath that he would speak the truth, the whole truth, of all persons whatsoever, living or dead, with himself, or like himself, under suspicion of heresy or Vaudism. If he refused, he was cast into a dungeon—a dungeon the darkest in those dreary ages—the most dismal, the most foul, the most noisome. No falsehood was too false, no craft too crafty, no trick too base, for this calm, systematic moral torture which was to wring further confession against himself, denun-

Form of procedure.

---

[7] The two forms of procedure may be read in Martene and Durand.—Thesaurus Anecdotorum, t. v. Their authenticity is beyond dispute. Nothing that the sternest or most passionate historian has revealed, nothing that the most imaginative romance-writer could have imagined, can surpass the cold systematic treachery and cruelty of these, so called, judicial formularies.

ciation against others. If the rack, the pulleys, the thumbscrew, and the boots, were not yet invented or applied, it was not in mercy. It was the deliberate object to break the spirit. The prisoner was told that there were witnesses, undeniable witnesses, against him; if convicted by such witnesses his death was inevitable. In the meantime his food was to be slowly, gradually diminished, till body and soul were prostrate. He was then to be left in darkness, solitude, silence. Then were to come one or two of the faithful, dexterous men, who were to speak in gentle words of interest and sympathy—"Fear not to confess that you have had dealings with those men, the teachers of heresy, because they seemed to you men of holiness and virtue; wiser than you have been deceived." These dexterous men were to speak of the Bible, of the Gospels, of the Epistles of St. Paul, to talk the very language, the Scriptural language of the heretics. "These foxes," it was said, "can only be unearthed by fox-like cunning." But if all this art failed, or did not perfectly succeed, then came terror and the goading to despair. "Die you must—bethink you of your soul." Upon which if the desperate man said, "If I must die, I will die in the true faith of the Gospel"—he had made his confession: justice claimed its victim.

The Inquisition had three penalties: for those who recanted, penance in the severest form which the Court might enact; for those not absolutely convicted, perpetual imprisonment; for the obstinate or the relapsed, death—death at the stake, death by the secular arm. The Inquisition, with specious hypocrisy, while it prepared and dressed up the victim for the burning, looked on with calm and approving satisfaction, as it had left the sin of lighting the fire to pollute other hands.

Such was the procedure, of which the instructions may now be read in their very words, which Raymond of Toulouse must put in execution in his capital city.

A.D. 1231.

The death of the Bishop Fulk relieved him not; an inflexible Dominican sat on the episcopal seat of Toulouse. The Pope, Gregory IX., issued a bull, in which the Inquisition was placed in the inexorable hands of the Friar Preachers. Two inquisitors were appointed in every city; but the Bishops needed no excitement to their eager zeal, no remonstrance against mistimed mercy to the heretics. At the Council of Narbonne, presided over by the Archbishops of Narbonne, Aix, and Arles, was now issued a decree, that as

A.D. 1233.

there were not prisons vast enough to contain those who, however they had made submission, were still unworthy of the absolution of the Church, and deserved imprisonment for life, further instructions must be awaited from his Holiness the Pope. But the contumacious, who refused to submit to imprisonment, or who broke prison, were to be at once made over to the secular arm. No plea was to be admitted to release from imprisonment; not the duty of the husband to the young wife, of the young wife to her husband; not that of the parents for the care of their children, nor of children for the care of their parents; infirmity, age, dotage, nothing excused, nothing mitigated the sentence. So enormous was the crime of heresy, the infamous, whose witness was refused in all other cases, were admitted against the heretic: on no account was the name of a witness to be betrayed.

But the most oppressed may be overwrought to madness. Witnesses were found murdered; even the awful persons of inquisitors were not secure. An insurrection broke out in the suburbs of

Rebellion.

Narbonne against the Prior of the Dominicans; the Archbishop and the Viscount of Narbonne in their defence suffered a repulse. The insurgents despised the excommunication of the Archbishop, and fought gallantly against the rest of the city, which espoused the cause of the Church. Albi was in tumult, even Toulouse arose. The two great inquisitors, William Arnaud and Peter Cellani, were compelled to leave the city. They marched out at the head of the thirty-eight members of the Inquisition, with the Bishop and the parish priests in solemn procession; they hurled back an excommunication. Count Raymond compelled the re-admission of the clergy, but even Rome was appalled: a Franciscan was sent to allay by his gentleness the popular fury. The proceedings of the Inquisition (this merciful edict was purchased in Rome) were suspended for a time in Toulouse.*

A.D. 1237.

Five years passed. Raymond of Toulouse, under the shelter, as it were, of the wars between Louis IX. and Henry of England, and encouraged by hopes of support from the Spanish kings, aspired at the head of the league among the great vassals of the south to throw off the yoke of Northern France. The downtrodden Albigensians seized their opportunity. They met at Mirepoix, marched on the castle of Avignonet, where William Arnaud, the great inquisitor, held his tribunal. Four Dominicans, two Franciscans, seven Familiars, the whole terrible court, were hewn to pieces. That which had thrown a dreadful grandeur over the murders perpetrated by the inquisitors, gave a majestic endurance to their own. They died like the meekest

Rising. Murder of the Inquisitors.

---

* Martene, Thesaur. Anecdot., I. 992. Vaissette, Hist. de Languedoc, Appendix xxv.

martyrs: they fell on their knees, crossed their hands over their breasts, and, chanting the Te Deum, as wont over their victims, they awaited the mortal blow.[a] They were not long unavenged. Raymond was forced to submit; his act of subjection to Louis IX. stipulated his abandonment of the heretics. Two years after, at another Council at Narbonne, it was enacted that the penitents, who had escaped from prison, should in mercy be permitted to wear yellow crosses on their garments, to appear every Sunday during mass, and undergo public flagellation: the rest were to suffer life-long incarceration. At the same time Mont Segur,[b] the last refuge of the Albigensians, a strong castle on the summit of a ravine in the Pyrenees, to which most of the Perfect with their Bishop had fled, was forced to surrender to the Archbishop of Narbonne, the Bishop of Albi, and the Seneschal of Carcassonne. All the heretics, with their Bishop and the noble lady, Esclarmonde, were burned alive in a vast enclosure of stakes and straw.[c] Of all these atrocities, however, Louis IX. was guiltless; he was not yet, or was hardly, of age, and his whole soul was absorbed in his preparation for his crusade. Even his brother, Charles of Anjou, who by obtaining the hand of the heiress of Provence (to which Raymond of Toulouse aspired) had become lord of that territory, took no active part in these persecutions.

Yet even in the realm of France a frightful holocaust was offered near the city of Rheims. In the presence of the Archbishop and seventeen Bishops, and one hundred thousand people, on Mont Aimé near Vertus, one hundred and eighty-three

*margin:* A.D. 1212.
*margin:* March, 1214.
margin: Persecutions in France. A.D. 1239.

---

[a] Histoire de Languedoc, Preuves, p. 438.   [b] Puy Laurent, c. 46.
[c] Puy Laurent, c. 46.

Manicheans (one Perfect alone) were burned alive with their pastor, who calmly administered absolution to them all. Not one but died without fear. But this execution took place in the territory and under the sanction of Count Thiebault of Champagne, not of the King; of Thiebault (the King of Navarre), whose Troubadour songs were as little respectful to the clergy, or the Papalists, as those of the other Languedocian bards.[d] If even under Louis a monk held his court in Paris, and, unrebuked, inflicted death on many innocent victims, this seems to have been an exceptional case; nor is it quite clear how far it had the concurrence of the King.[e]

Yet for a time suspended, our comparison of Louis IX. and Frederick II. is not exhausted. As legislators there is the most striking analogy between these two, in so many other respects oppugnant sovereigns. The Sicilian laws of Frederick and the "Establishments" of St. Louis agree in the assertion (as far as their times would admit) of the absolute supremacy of the law, the law emanating from the King, and in the abrogation (though Louis is more timid or cautious than Frederick) of the ordeal, the trial by battle, and the still stranger usage of challenging the judges to battle.

The Justiciaries of Frederick belonged to a more advanced jurisprudence than the King himself, Frederick and Louis as seated on his carpet in the forest of Vincennes be given. administering justice.[f] But the introduction under his reign of the civil lawyers, the students and advocates of the Roman jurisprudence, into the courts of France (under Philip the Fair will be seen their strife, even triumph over the canon lawyers), gave a new character

---

[d] Compare H. Martin, Hist. de France. Hallam, I. 29, with his authorities.
[e] Raynald, sub ann., I. p. 29.
[f] See the picturesque description in Joinville, p. 109.

to the ordinances of St. Louis, and of far more lasting influence. The ruin of the house of Swabia, and the desuetude into which, in most respects, fell the constitution of Frederick, prevented Naples from becoming a school of Roman law as famous as that of Paris, and the lawyers of the kingdom of Sicily from rising into a body as powerful as those of France in her parliaments.

Both Kings, however, aimed at the establishment of equal justice. They would bring the haughty feudal nobles and even the churchmen (who lived apart under their own law) under the impartial sovereignty of the law of the land. The punishment of Enguerrand de Couci for a barbarous murder attested the firmness of the King. The proudest baron in France, the highest vassal of the crown, hardly escaped with his life. So, too, may be cited the account of the angry baron, indignant at the judicial equity of the King—" Were I king, I would hang all my barons; after the first step, all is easy." "How, John of Thouret, hang all my barons? I will not hang them; I will correct them if they commit misdeeds."

As to the nobles.

It was the religion, not the want of religion, in St. Louis which made him determine to bring the criminal clergy under the equal laws of the realm. That which Henry II. of England had attempted to do by his royal authority and by the Constitutions of Clarendon, the more pious or prudent Louis chose to effect with the Papal sanction. Even the Pope, Alexander IV., could not close his eyes to the monstrous fact of the crimes of the clergy, secured from adequate punishment by the immunities of their sacred persons.

As to the clergy.

The Pope made a specious concession; the King's judge did not incur excommunication for arresting, subject to the judgement of the ecclesiastical courts, priests notoriously guilty of capital

A.D. 1268.

offences. Alexander threw off too from the Church, and abandoned as scapegoats to the law, all married clergy and all who followed low trades; with them the law might take its course, they had forfeited the privilege of clergy. But neither would Louis be the absolute slave of the intolerance of the hierarchy. The whole prelacy of France (writes Joinville)* met to rebuke the tardy zeal of the King in enforcing the excommunications of the Church. "Sire," said Guy of Auxerre, "Christianity is falling to ruin in your hands." "How so?" said the King, making the sign of the cross. "Sire, men regard not excommunication; they care not if they die excommunicate and without absolution. The Bishops admonish you that you give orders to all the royal officers to compel persons excommunicate to obtain absolution by the forfeiture of their lands and goods." And the holy man (the King) said "that he would willingly do so to all who had done wrong to the Church." "It belongs not to you," said the Bishop, "to judge of such cases." And the King answered, "he would not do otherwise; it were to sin against God and against reason to force those to seek absolution to whom the clergy had done wrong."

The famous Pragmatic Sanction contained only the first principles, yet it did contain the first principles, of limitation as to the power of the Court of Rome to levy money on the churches of the realm, and of elections to benefices. It was, in fact, as the foundation of Gallicanism under specious terms of respect, a more mortal blow to the Papal power than all the tyranny, as it was called, exercised by Frederick II. over the ecclesiastics of the kingdom of Naples. Of this, however, more hereafter.

---

* P. 200.

CHAPTER II.

Pope Alexander IV.

ON the death of Innocent IV., the Cardinal of Ostia, of the famous Papal house of Segni, was elected at Naples: he took the name of Alexander IV. He was a gentle and religious man, not of strong or independent character, open to flattery and to the suggestions of interested and avaricious courtiers.* Innocent IV. had left a difficult and perilous position to his successor. The Pope could not abandon the Papal policy: the see of Rome was too deeply pledged, to retract its arrogant pretensions concerning the kingdom of Naples, or to come to terms with one whom she had denounced as an usurper, and whose strength she did not yet comprehend. But Sinibald could not leave, with his tiara, his own indomitable courage, his indefatigable activity, his power of drawing resources from distant lands. Alexander was forced to be an Innocent IV. in his pretensions; he could but be a feeble Innocent IV. The rapidity with which Manfred after his first successes overran the whole of the two Sicilies, implies, if not a profound and ardent attachment to the house of Swabia, at least an obstinate aversion to the Papal sovereignty. It seemed a general national outburst; and Manfred, by circumstances and by his own sagacious judgement, having separated the

---

* Matt. Paris, sub ann.

cause of the hereditary kings from the odious German tyranny (the Saracen bands were less unpopular than the Germans), as yet appeared only as the loyal guardian of the infant Conradin. He was already almost master of Apulia; he was with difficulty persuaded to send ambassadors, as sovereign princes were wont to do, to congratulate the Pope. During the next year the legate of the Pope was in person at Palermo; the whole island of Sicily had acknowledged Manfred. His triumph was completed by Naples opening her gates; Otranto and Brundusium followed the example of the capital. Manfred ruled in the name of his nephew from Palermo to Messina, from the Faro to the borders of the Papal States. At the first it was evident that the weak army of the Pope, under the Cardinal Octavian, could not make head against this rising of the whole realm. Berthold of Homburg soon deserted the cause of the Pope.[b] Alexander was trammelled with the engagements of his predecessor, who, having broken off his overtures to Charles of Anjou, had acknowledged Edmund of England king of Sicily. The more remote his hopes of success, the more ostentatiously did Henry III. attempt to dazzle the eyes of his subjects by this crown on the head of his second son. Edmund appeared in public as King of

A.D. 1255.
March 12.

England.

---

[b] See the curious letter in Matt. Paris, from which it appears that certain churches and monasteries in England were bound to merchants of Sienna in 2000 marks of new sterling money in favour of Berthold and his brothers. For acts of treason, Berthold and his brothers were declared to have forfeited their claim. But the churches and monasteries were still to discharge the 2000 marks. The Prior and monastery of Durham were assessed at 500 marks; Bath at 400; Thorney at 400; Croyland, 400; Gisburn, 300. Durham and Gisburn refused payment. This is dated Anagni, June 1256. There is also a letter (MS., B. M.) threatening excommunication against the Prior of Winchester and others, if they do not pay 315 marks to certain merchants of Sienna (sub ann. 1255, in init.).

Sicily, affected to wear an Italian dress, and indulged in all the pomp and state of royalty. The King himself, notwithstanding the sullen looks of his Barons, spoke as if determined on this wild expedition. His ambassadors, the Bishops of London and Hereford, the Abbot of Westminster, the Provost of Beverley, accepted the crown. It was agreed that, as Edmund was not of age, his father should swear fealty for him.* Yet England was less liberal than usual of subsidies either to the Pope or to the King for this senseless enterprise. The legate, a Gascon, Rustand, had already received a commission, with the Archbishop of Canterbury and the Bishop of Hereford, to levy a tenth on England, Scotland, and Ireland. The King had an offer of an exemption from his vow of a crusade to the Holy Land, on condition of his appearing at the head of an army to subdue Manfred in Apulia. Rustand himself preached in London and in other places; and made others preach a crusade against Manfred, the enemy of the Pope and of their Lord the King of England, a crusade as meritorious as that to the Lord's sepulchre. The honest English were revolted at hearing that they were to receive the same indulgences for shedding Christian as Saracen blood. Rustand received a rich prebend of York as reward for his services.

Year after year came the same insatiate demands: ambassador after ambassador summoned the King to fulfil his engagements; the Pope condescended to

---

* In Rymer, 1254, are the bulls or terms of grant of the kingdom of Sicily. See in MS., B. M. (vill. 195), letter to the King of England to pay 4500 livres Tournois (libras Turonenses)† for the expenses of W. ternaus (Cardinal of Velletri) "electus de mandato f. m. Innocent. IV. in servitium Ecclesiæ pro stante negotio regni Siciliæ."

† The livre Tournois was about 17 francs.

inform him through what merchants he could transmit his subsidies to Rome. The insolence and the falsehood of Rustand and the other legates, the Archbishop Elect of Toledo and the Bishop of Bologna, increased the exasperation. In the absence of the Primate of England, Rustand ruled supreme in the Church, and excommunicated refractory prelates, whose goods were instantly seized and confiscated to the King. They carefully disguised the successes of Manfred, and spread rumours of the victories of the Papal armies. The King had too much vanity and too much weakness to resist these frauds and violences. The King is said to have bound himself for two hundred thousand pounds sterling, besides fifty thousand levied by the Bishop of Hereford.[d] Even the Cistercian monks could not escape the unusual and acknowledged alienation of the English clergy from the see of Rome. The Pope, or the Nuncio of the Pope, had recourse to violent measures against the second prelate of the realm, Sewal, Archbishop of York. The words of the English historian show the impression on the public mind: "About that time our Lord the Pope laid his hand heavily on the Archbishop of York. He gave orders (by a measure so strong and terrible he would daunt his courage) that Sewal should be ignominiously excommunicated throughout England with the light of torches and tolling of bells. But the said Archbishop, taught by the example of Thomas the Martyr, the example and lessons of the saintly Edmund, once his master, by the faithfulness of the blessed Robert, Bishop of Lincoln, did not despair of consolation from heaven, and patiently supported the tyranny of the Pope; for he would not

Sewal, Archbishop of York. A.D. 1257.

---

[d] Rymer, MS., B. M., sub ann. 1235.

bestow the abundant revenues of the Church on persons unworthy or unknown, from beyond the Alps, and scorned to submit himself, like a woman, to the Pope's will, abandoning his rights. Hence the more he was anathematised by the orders of the Pope, the more was he blessed by the people, though in secret for fear of the Romans."*

But where all this time was the Primate of England, and who was he? On the death of the unworldly and sainted Edmund Rich, the King and the Pope had forced on the too obsequious, afterwards bitterly repentant, monks of Canterbury, a foreigner, almost an Italian. Boniface, Bishop of Bellay, was uncle to the Queen, and brother of that Philip of Savoy, the warlike and mitred bodyguard of Innocent IV., who became Archbishop of Lyons. Boniface was elected in 1241, confirmed by Pope Innocent not before 1244. The handsome, proud prelate found that Edmund, however saintly, had been but an indifferent steward of the secular part of the diocese. Canterbury was loaded with an enormous debt, and Boniface came not to England to preside over an impoverished see. He obtained a grant from the Pope of first-fruits from all the benefices in his province, by which he raised a vast sum. Six years after, the Primate announced, and set forth on a visitation of his province, not as it was said, and as too plainly appeared, for the glory of God, but in quest of ungodly gain. Bishops, chapters, monasteries must submit to this unusual discipline, haughtily and rapaciously enforced by a foreigner.

Boniface, Archbishop of Canterbury.

About Michaelmas, A.D. 1250.

---

* So writes Paris. "Falso pertinaciam illius constantiæ nomine exornat (M. Paris) cum justâ Pontifex pro Sicilia, deposito tyranno, in Edmundum transferendâ, a claro Anglicano pecuniarum subsidia exigeret." Thus wrote Raynaldus in the 17th century.—Sub ann. 1257.

From Feversham and Rochester he extorted large sums. He appeared in London, treated the Bishop (Fulk Basset of the old noble Norman house) and his jurisdiction with contempt. The Dean of St. Paul's (Henry de Cornhill) stood by his Bishop. The Primate appeared with his cuirass gleaming under his pontifical robes. The Dean closed the doors of his cathedral against him. Boniface solemnly excommunicated Henry Dean of St. Paul's and his Chapter in the name of St. Thomas the Martyr of Canterbury. The Sub-Prior of St. Bartholomew's (the Prior was dead) fared still worse. He calmly pleaded the rights of the Bishop; the wrathful Primate rushed on the old man, struck him down with his own hand, tore his splendid vestment, and trampled it under foot. The Bishop of London was involved in the excommunication. The Dean of St. Paul's appealed to the Pope; the excommunication was suspended. But Boniface himself proceeded in great pomp to Rome. The uncle of the Queen of England, the now wealthy Primate of England, could not but obtain favour with Innocent. The Dean of St. Paul's was compelled to submit to the supreme Archiepiscopal authority. On his triumphant return Boniface continued his visitation. The Chapter of Lincoln, headed by the Archdeacon (Bishop Grostête was dead), resisted his demand to dispose of the vacant Prebends of the Church. The Archdeacon bore his own appeal to Rome. After three years he obtained (by what means appears not) what seemed a favourable sentence; but died, worn out, on his way home. 'Boniface trampled on all rights, all privileges. The monks of Canterbury obtained a Papal diploma of exemption, Boniface threw it into the fire, and excommunicated the bearers. The King cared not, for the Pope would not regard the insult.

After the accession of Alexander IV. the Archbishop of Canterbury is in arms, with his brother, the Archbishop of Lyons, besieging Turin, to release the head of his house, the Count of Savoy, whom his subjects had deposed and imprisoned for his intolerable tyranny. The wealth of the Churches of Canterbury and Lyons was showered, but showered in vain, on their bandit army. Turin resisted the secular, more obstinately than London the spiritual arms of the Primate. He returned, not without disgrace, to England. With such a Primate the Pope was not likely to find much vigorous or rightful opposition from the Church of England.'

Pope Alexander IV., while he thus tyrannised in England, was not safe in Rome, or even in Anagni. The stern justice of the Senator Brancaleone had provoked resistance, no doubt not discouraged by the partisans of the Pope. The Nobles urged on an insurrection: Brancaleone was seized and thrown into prison. But his wise precaution had secured thirty hostages of the highest Roman patrician houses at Bologna. His wife fled to that city, and roused Bologna with harangues on the injustice and ingratitude shown to her great citizen. The hostages were kept guarded with stricter vigilance. The Nobles appealed to the Pope, who issued an angry mandate to

The Senator Brancalrone. See p. 322.

' Paris, sub ann. 1241-4, 1250, 1256. See the letter from Pope Alexander, consolatory on the failure before Turin. Godwin de Præsulibus contains a full abstract of the life of Boniface. Compare MS. B. M. vi. p. 347, for the resistance and excommunication (the sentence) of the Dean of St. Paul's: also of Sub-Prior of St. Bartholomew; excommunication of Bishop of London, p. 383. The Archbishop had obtained, under grant of first fruits, "magnam quantitatem pecuniæ," vii. 16. Papal decree against Dean and Chapter of St. Paul's, p. 57. Archbishop Boniface was exempted from visiting his four Welsh dioceses, "propter guerrarum discrimina, penuriam victualium," b. viii.

the Bolognese, which they treated with scorn. The populace of Rome arose and broke the prison of Brancaleone. Brancaleone laid down his senatorship for two years (during which it was filled by a citizen of Brescia, who trod in his footsteps) to resume it with still more inflexible determination. On his reinauguration he summoned all malefactors before his tribunal, not the last the authors of his imprisonment. His sentence was inexorable by prayer or bribe. Men of the highest birth, even relatives of the Pope, were shown on gibbets. Two of the Annibaldi suffered this ignoble doom. He destroyed a hundred and forty castles of those lofty and titled spoilers. The Pope, at Viterbo, was so unadvised as to issue a sentence of excommunication against the Senator and the people of Rome. They were not content with treating this sentence with the bitterest derision. The Senator summoned the whole people to assemble, as one man, in arms; they marched under their banner towards Anagni, the birthplace of the Pope. The inhabitants of Anagni, many of them his kindred, implored Alexander with passionate entreaties to avert their doom. The Pope, to elude the disgrace of seeing his native city razed to the earth, was content to send deputies to Brancaleone, humbly imploring his mercy. The Senator had great difficulty in restraining the people. An alliance grew up between Manfred and Brancaleone. The Senator retained his dignity till his death: his head was then deposited in a coffer, like a precious relique, and placed, with all the pomp of a religious ceremony, by the grateful people, on the top of a marble column. Notwithstanding the prohibition of the Pope, the people raised the uncle of Brancaleone to the Senatorship of Rome.*

A.D. 1256.

* Paris, sub ann. 1258.

Alexander could look for no aid from the Empire. The Papal Emperor, William of Holland, had fallen in an expedition against the Frisians. There was no great German Prince to command the Empire. The Pope, faithful to the legacy of hatred to the house of Swabia, contented himself with prohibiting in the strongest terms the election of the young Conradin. The Germans looked abroad; some of the divided Electors offered the throne again to Richard of Cornwall, others to Alfonso King of Castile. The enormous wealth of Richard of Cornwall, perhaps his feeble character, attracted the ambitious Archbishop of Cologne, who hoped in his name to rule the Empire, and to dispense the wealth of England. Richard was crowned at Aix-la-Chapelle. He had before declined the kingdom of Naples; his avarice had resisted all the attempts of the King his brother and of the Pope to employ his riches in the cause of young Edmund; he retained them to gratify his own vanity.[b]

Death of William of Holland. Jan. 28, 1256.

January, 1257.

March 11. Richard of Cornwall.

For seventeen years the Empire was in fact vacant; better for the Pope such anarchy than a Swabian on the throne.

Rudolph of Hapsburg. A.D. 1273.

France, so long as the treaty existed between the Pope and England for the investiture of Prince Edmund with the throne of Sicily, could be roused by no adequate temptation. The Pope could offer no vigorous resistance, yet would not make a virtue of necessity and acknowledge the house of Swabia. He had now fully discovered the weakness, the impotence of the King of England.[i]

---

[b] Paris says that, independent of the Empire, his revenues would have produced 100 marks a-day for ten years.

[i] "Videns ipsius debilitatem ac im- potentiam quam publice allegabat."— MS., B.M. In a letter, b. viii. p. 40, the Pope recites all the acts of Innocent IV., and the dates.

He had summoned him to execute his contract. Henry truly, but without shame, pleaded his poverty, and demanded a tenth of the ecclesiastical revenues. The excommunication hung over the head of the King for having made a bargain with the Pope which he could not fulfil.

Manfred had won the crown of Sicily in the name of his nephew Conradin; he was but Regent of the realm. Rumours were spread of the death of Conradin; the enemies of Manfred asserted that they were invented and disseminated by his astute ambition; his partisans that he had no concern in their propagation.[a] But Manfred was necessary to the power, to the independence of the Sicilies. The Prelates, Barons, almost the whole realm entreated him to assume the crown. His coronation took place to the universal joy. Hardly was it over when ambassadors arrived from the mother of Conradin, and from her son, imploring Manfred not to usurp the rights which he had defended with so much valour. Manfred received the ambassadors in a great assemblage of his Barons. "He had ascended the throne, which he had himself won by his arms, at the call of his people; their affections could alone maintain that throne. It was neither for the interest of the realm nor of Conradin himself that Naples should be ruled by a woman and an infant: he had no relative but Conradin, for whom he should preserve the crown, and faithfully bequeath it on his death. If Conradin desired to uphold the privileges of an heir-apparent, he should reside at the court of Manfred, and win the love of the people whom he was to govern.

Manfred king. Aug. 11, 1258.

---

[a] Jamsilla. Recordano, c. 147. Le crede lo inrele. Murat. Ann., sub ann. 1258.

Manfred would treat him as a son, and instruct him in the virtues of his glorious ancestors." How far Manfred was sincere, Manfred himself perhaps did not know; how far, if he had himself issue, his virtue would have resisted the fondness of a parent for his own offspring, and that which he might have alleged to himself and to others as an undeniable truth, the interest of the kingdom. What confusion, what bloodshed might have been spared to Naples, to Italy, to Christendom, if the crown of Naples had descended in the line of Manfred; if the German connexion had been broken for ever, the French connexion never formed; if Conradin had remained Duke of Swabia, and Charles of Anjou had not descended the Alps! A wiser Pope, and one less wedded to the hereditary policy and to the antipathies of his spiritual forefathers, might have discerned this, and seen how well it would have coincided with the interests of the see. Manfred acknowledged and fairly treated might have softened into a loyal Guelf; he was now compelled to be the head, a most formidable head, of the Ghibellines. Alexander lived to see Manfred in close alliance with Sienna, the stronghold of the exiled Ghibellines of Florence;[m] to see the fatal battle of Arba, or Monte Aperto, in which the Florentine Guelfs were utterly crushed and forced to abandon their city. Florence was only saved from being razed to the earth at the instigation of the rival cities, Pisa and Sienna, by the patriotic appeal of the great Ghibelline, Farinata di Uberti, a name which lives in Dante's poetry.[n] In all the south of Italy Manfred was supreme: Genoa and Venice were his allies.

Sept. 4, 1260.

---

[m] See throughout Muratori, who quotes impartially Guelfs and Ghibellines.
[n] Inferno, vi. 79, x. 32.

Nor was it the Guelfic or Papal influence, nor even his own unspeakable cruelties; it was his treachery to his friends alone that in the north of Italy caused the fall of the triumphant champion of the Ghibellines, Eccelin da Romano, and with him of his brother Alberic. The character of Eccelin was the object of the profoundest terror and abhorrence. No human suffering, it might seem, could glut his revenge; the enemy who fell into his hands might rejoice in immediate decapitation or hanging. The starvation of whole cities; the imprisonment of men, women, and children in loathsome dungeons touched not his heart, which seemed to have made cruelty a kind of voluptuous excitement.* But what was the social state of this part of Christendom? How had that state been aggravated by the unmitigated dissensions and wars, the feuds of city with city, the intestine feuds within every city! Had the voice of the Father of Christendom, of the Vicegerent of the Prince of Peace ever been earnestly raised in protest or rebuke? Was not the Papal Legate the head of the Guelfic faction, and were the Guelfs on the whole more humane than the Ghibellines? Alexander might have published a crusade against this foe of the human race, and justly might he have offered more splendid promises of pardon and eternal life to him who should rid the world of this monster, than to him who should slay hosts of Moslemin.ᵖ But a fitter, as an abler leader, might have been found for this enterprise than the Archbishop of Ravenna; and

Sept. 27, 1259.

---

* It may be doubted whether Eccelin himself was not gradually trained to this habit of barbarity. Frederick II., though severe and merciless to his foes, would hardly have addressed sportive letters, or given his daughter in marriage to a wild beast, such a wild beast as Eccelin appears in his later days.

ᵖ Compare Alexandri Epist. ad Episcopos.

when the army of the Archbishop got possession of Padua, the ruthless sacking of the town by his mercenary soldiers made the citizens look back with regret to the iron rule of Eccelin. Nor would Papal anathema or Papal crusade have shaken the power of Eccelin.ᵠ With the Marquis Pallavicini and Buoso da Doara, the head of the Cremonese Ghibellines, he had become master of Brescia; but Eccelin never conquered save for himself. The flagrant treachery by which he had determined to rid himself of his colleagues was discovered; the indignant Ghibellines made a league against the common enemy of mankind. Eccelin was defeated, sorely wounded, captured. His end was worthy of his life. On the first night of his imprisonment the bells of a neighbouring chapel rang loudly, perhaps rejoicing at his bondage. He woke up in wrath: "Go, hew down that priest that makes such a din with his bells." "You forget," said his guard, "that you are in prison." He inquired where he was taken. "At Bassano." Like most strong minds of the day, Eccelin, who had faith in nothing else, had faith in divination. His astrologer had foretold that he should die in Bassano. The priests and friars thronged around him, urging, threatening, imploring, that he would confess and repent of his sins. "I repent of nothing, but that I have not wreaked full vengeance on my foes; that I have badly conducted my army, and allowed myself to be duped and betrayed."

<small>Alberic de Romano.</small> He would take neither food nor medicine; but death was slow: he tore the dressings from his wounds, and was found a corpse.ʳ Alberic,

---

ᵠ Rolandini, Monach. Patavin. apud Muratori.

ʳ Throughout see Rolandin, xli. c. 13; Chron. Veron., & B. T., v. viii.; and Muratori, Annali, sub annis 1250, 1260. The B. Museum Chronicle sums up, "nullus in ferocitate et unquam fuit similis."—p. 245.

his brother, once his deadly enemy, was now his ally. Eccelin wanted but one vice, passion for women, which might possibly have given some softness to his heart. No woman was safe from the less sanguinary Alberic. Alberio was besieged during the next year in the castle of San Zeno. All hope of succour was gone; with some remains of generosity he allowed his followers to buy their own free departure by the surrender of himself and his wife, six sons and two daughters. He was at first treated with every kind of mockery; then his six sons slain in his sight, torn in pieces, their limbs thrust in his face. His wife, his beautiful and innocent daughters had their lower garments cut off; in this state of nakedness, in the sight of the whole army, were bound to a stake and burned alive. Alberic's own flesh was torn from his body by pincers; he was then tied to the tail of a horse, and dragged to death.

A.D. 1260.

What wonder that amid such deeds, whatever religion remained, as it ever must remain in the depths of the human heart, either took refuge beyond the pale of the Church, among the Cathari, who never were more numerous in the cities, especially of northern Italy, than in these days: or within the Church showed itself in wild epidemic madness? Against the Cathari the Friars preached in vain; the Inquisition in vain held its courts; and executions for heresy added more horrors to these dire times.

It was at this period too that one of those extravagant outbursts of fanaticism, which constantly occurred during the middle ages, relieved men's minds in some degree from the ordinary horrors and miseries. Who is surprised that mankind felt itself seized by a violent access of repentance, or that repentance disdained the usual form of discipline?

The Flagellants.

The Flagellants seemed to rise almost simultaneously in different parts of Italy. They began in Perugia. The penitential frenzy seized Rome: it spread through every city, Guelf and Ghibelline, crossed the Alps, and invaded Germany and France. Flagellation had long been a holy and meritorious discipline; it was now part of the monastic system; it had obtained a kind of dignity and importance, as the last sign of subjection to the sacerdotal power, the last mark of penitence for sins against the Church.* Sovereign princes, as Raymond of Toulouse; Kings, as Henry of England, had yielded their backs to the scourge. How entirely self-flagellation had become part of sanctity, appears from its being the religious luxury of Louis IX. Peter Damiani had taught it by precept and example.† Dominic, called the Cuirassier, had invented or popularised by his fame the usage of singing psalms to the accompaniment of self-scourging. It had come to have its stated value among works of penance.‡

The present outburst was not the effect of popular preaching, of the eloquence of one or more vehement and ardent men, working on the passions and the fears of a vast auditory. It seemed as if mankind, at least Italian mankind, was struck at once with a sudden paroxysm of remorse for the monstrous guilt of the age, which found vent in this wild but hallowed form of self-torture. All ranks, both sexes, all ages, were possessed with the madness—nobles, wealthy merchants, modest

---

* The "Historia Flagellantium" is a brief but complete history of religious flagellations, first of legal floggings administered by authority, then of the origin and practice of self-flagellation.

† Epistol. ad Clericos Florentin., p. 85.

‡ "Consequitur ergo ut qui viginti psalteria cum disciplinâ decantet, centum annorum penitentiam se persolvisse confidat."—Vit. Dominic Loric., v. 8.

and delicate women, even children of five years old. They stripped themselves naked to the waist, covered their faces that they might not be known, and went two and two in solemn slow procession, with a cross and a banner before them, scourging themselves till the blood tracked their steps, and shrieking out their doleful psalms. They travelled from city to city. Whenever they entered a city, the contagion seized all predisposed minds. This was done by night as by day. Not only were the busy mart and the crowded street disturbed by these processions; in the dead midnight they were seen with their tapers or torches gleaming before them in their awful and shadowy grandeur, with the lashing sound of the scourge and the screaming chant. Thirty-three days and a half, the number of the years of the Lord's sad sojourn in this world of man, was the usual period for the penance of each. In the burning heat of summer, when the wintry roads were deep in snow, they still went on. Thousands, thousands, tens of thousands joined the ranks; till at length the madness wore itself out. Some princes and magistrates, finding that it was not sanctioned by the Roman See or by the authority of any great Saint, began to interpose: that which had been the object of general respect, became almost as rapidly the object of general contempt.[a]

---

[a] "Unde tepescere in brevi cœpit res immoderate concepta."—Herm. Alt. There are two full descriptions of this singular movement: one by an Italian, the Monachus Patavinensis in Muratori, viii. 712; the other by a German, Hermannus Altahensis (Abbot of Nieder Altaisch), in Böhmer, Fontes, II. p. 516. See too D. Museum Chronicle: he adds, "Verumtamen propter hoc multa pacem inter discordantes facto fuerunt, et multa bona acta sunt." His account is curious.—p. 250. See in the Translation of Dr. Hecker's curious book on the Epidemics of the Middle Ages much strange matter on the German Flagellants, and the wild Geissler-Lied, the Hymn of the Flagellants, with an English version, p. 64.

The Flagellant phrensy was a purely religious movement.[f] It had been preceded by about ten years by that of the Pastoureaux (the Shepherds) in Flanders and in France. This rising had something of the fierce resentment of an oppressed and down-trodden peasantry. But it was a democratic insurrection, not against the throne, but against the tyrannous nobles and tyrannous churchmen: it was among those lowest of the low whom the Friar Preachers and the followers of St. Francis had not reached, or had left for higher game. The new Mendicant Orders were denounced as rudely as the luxurious Cluniacs or haughty Cistercians. The Shepherds' first declaration of war was that "the good King Louis was left in bondage to the Mussulmen, through the criminal and traitorous remissness of the indolent and avaricious clergy." They, the peasants of France, had received the direct mission, a mission from the blessed Virgin herself, to rescue him from the hands of the Unbelievers. So sudden, so terrible was the insurrection, that it was as if the fire had burst out at one instant in remote parts of the land. It began in Flanders; at its head was a mysterious personage, who bore the name of the Master of Hungary. He was an aged man with a long beard, pale emaciated face; he spoke Latin, French, and German with the same fluent persuasiveness; he preached without authority of Pope or Prelate; as he preached, he clasped a roll in his hands, which contained his instructions from the blessed Virgin. The Virgin had appeared to him, encircled by hosts of angels, and had given him his celestial commission to

---

[f] Affò, Storia di Parma, lil. p. 256, connects the Flagellants with the believers in the Abbot Joachim. (See forward.)

summon the poor Shepherds to the deliverance of the good King. Terror spread the strangest rumours of this awful personage. He was an apostate Cistercian monk; in his youth he had denied Jesus Christ; he had sucked in the pernicious practices of magic from the empoisoned wells of Toledo (among the Jews and Arabians of that city). He it was that in his youth had led the crusade of children, who had plunged, following his steps, by thousands into the sea; he had made a solemn covenant with the Soldan of Babylon to lead a countless multitude of Christians to certain bondage in the Holy Land, that they and their King being in his power, he might subdue Christendom. Since the days of Mohammed, in the judgement of wise men, no such dangerous scourge of mankind had arisen in the Church of Christ. His title, the Master of Hungary, might lead to the suspicion that he was a Bulgarian Manichee, revenging on the haughty hierarchy the wrongs of his murdered brethren.[s]

The eloquence and mysterious bearing of the Master of Hungary stirred the lowest depths of society. The Shepherds, the peasants left their flocks, their stalls, their fields, their ploughs; in vain friends, parents, wives remonstrated; they took no thought of sustenance. So, drawing men after him, "as the loadstone draws the iron," he marched through Flanders and Picardy. He entered Amiens at the head of thirty thousand men, was received as the Deliverer with festive rejoicings. He passed on to the Isle of France, gathering, as some fell off from weakness or weariness, the whole labouring population in his wake. The villages and fields were desolate behind them. They passed

---

[s] Matt. Paris, sub ann.

through the cities (not one dared to close the gates against them), they moved in battle array, brandishing clubs, pikes, axes, all the wild weapons they could seize. The Provosts, the Mayors bowed in defenceless panic before them. They had at first only the standard of their Master, a Lamb bearing the banner of the Cross, the Lamb the sign of humility, the Cross that of victory.

Soon four hundred banners waved above them; on some were emblazoned the Virgin and the angels appearing to the Master. Before they reached Paris they were one hundred thousand and more. They had been joined by all the outlaws, the robbers, the excommunicate, followers more dangerous, as wielding and accustomed to wield arms, the two-edged axe, the sword, the dagger, and the pike. They had become an army. They seemed worshippers, it was said, of Mary rather than of Christ. Blanche, the Queen-Regent, either in panic or in some wild hope that these fierce hordes might themselves aid in achieving, or compel others to achieve the deliverance of her son, professed to believe their loyal protestations; they were admitted into Paris.

But already they had begun to show their implacable hostility to the Church. They usurped the offices of the clergy, performed marriages, distributed crosses, offered absolution to those who joined their Crusade. They taunted the Friar Preachers and Minorites as vagabonds and hypocrites; the White Monks (the Cistercians) with their covetousness, their vast possessions in lands and flocks; the Black Monks (the Benedictines) with gluttony and pride; the Canons, as worldly, self-indulgent men; Bishops, as hunters and hawkers, as given to all voluptuousness. No one dared to repeat the impious reproaches which they heaped on the Church of Rome.

Hostility to the clergy.

DIVISION OF THE HOST.

All this the people heard with the utmost delight. It was rumoured that the Master miraculously fed the multitudes; bread, meat, and wine, multiplied under his hands. They had entered Paris: the Master was admitted into the presence of the Queen, and was received with honour and with gifts. The Master, emboldened, mounted the pulpit in the church of St. Eustache, with an episcopal mitre on his head, preached and blessed the holy water. Meantime, his followers swarmed in the neighbouring streets, mercilessly slew the priests who endeavoured to oppose their fierce fanaticism: the approaches to the University were closed, lest there should be a general massacre of the scholars.   *In Paris.*

The enormous host divided at Paris into three. One horde went towards Orleans and Bourges, one towards Bordeaux, one to the sea-coast at Marseilles. But though Paris, the seat of all wisdom and of the government, had received them, the southern cities had more courage; or the strange illusion had begun to dissipate of itself. The Shepherds entered Orleans, notwithstanding the resistance of the Bishop and the clergy; the citizens hailed their approach; the people crowded in countless numbers and rapt admiration around the Preacher. The Bishop issued his inhibition to all clerks, ordering them to keep aloof from the profane assembly: the wiser and older obeyed; some of the younger scholars were led by curiosity to hear one who preached unlicensed by Prelate, and who by his preaching had awed Paris and her famous University. The Master was in the pulpit; he was pouring forth his monstrous tenets: a scholar rushed forward, " Wicked heretic! foe to truth; thou liest in thy throat; thou deceivest the innocent with thy false and trea-   *Division of the host. At Orleans.*

z 2

cherous speech." He had hardly uttered these words, when his skull was cloven by one of the Master's followers. The scholars were pursued; the gates of the University broken in; a frightful butchery followed; their books were thrown into the Loire. By another account, the scholars made a gallant resistance. The Bishop, who had been forced to fly, left the city under an interdict, as having entertained these precursors of Antichrist. The complaints of the Bishop reached the ears of Queen Blanche. Her calm wisdom had returned. "I thought," she said, "that these people might recover the Holy Land in simplicity and sanctity; since they are impostors, be they excommunicated, scattered, destroyed."

They entered Bourges: notwithstanding the denunciations of the Archbishop, the city had opened her gates.

In Bourges. Here the first act of the Master of Hungary was to penetrate into the Jews' quarter, to plunder their houses, and burn their books. But in Bourges he was so rash, or so intoxicated with success, as not to content himself with the wonders of his eloquence: after the sermon he promised, or was said to have promised, to work the most amazing miracles. The people, eager for the miracles, were perhaps less wrought upon by the sermon: they waited in breathless expectation, but they waited in vain. At that moment of doubt and disappointment, a man (he is called an executioner) rushed forth, and clove the head of the Master with a two-edged axe; his brains were scattered on the pavement; his soul, as all then believed, went direct to hell. The Royal Bailiff of Bourges was at hand with his men-at-arms; he fell on the panic-stricken followers, cast the body into the common sewer to be torn by hounds. The excommunication was read; the whole host were pursued and massacred like mad dogs.

The second squadron met no better fate; Simon de Montfort closed the gates of Bordeaux against them, and threatened to sally out with his knights and behead them all. Their leader, the favourite companion of the Master of Hungary, was seized, bound hand and foot, and thrown into the Garonne; the scattered followers were seized, hanged; a few found their way home as wretched beggars. Some of these, and part of the third division, reached Marseilles; but the hallucination was over; they were easily dispersed, most perished miserably. So suddenly began, so almost as suddenly ended this religious Jacquerie.*

Marginal notes: Bordeaux. Marseilles.

The pontificates of Innocent IV. and of Alexander IV., besides these great insurrections of one order of society—the very lowest against all above them—beheld the growth of a less tumultuous but more lasting and obstinate civil war within the Church itself. The Mendicant Friars, from the humble and zealous assistants, the active itinerant subsidiary force of the hierarchy, rapidly aspired to be their rivals, their superiors—at least equal sharers, not only in their influence and their power, but also in their wealth and pomp; as far, at least, as in their buildings, their churches, their cloisters. They were no longer only among the poorest, the most ignorant of mankind: they were in the lordly halls of the nobles, in the palaces of kings. St. Louis, as we have heard, held them in such devout reverence, that if he could have

Marginal notes: Civil war in the Church. Progress of the Mendicant Orders.

---

* I have chiefly followed Matt. Paris and William of Naogis, with some few facts from other chronicles. There is a curious letter about them to Adam de Marisco in the Burton Annals, p. 290.

divided his body, he would have given one-half to either saint, Dominic or Francis.

Not only the Popes, the more religious of the hierarchy and of the old monastic orders, had hailed, welcomed, held in honour these new labourers, who took the hard and menial work in the lowly and neglected and despised part of the vineyard. The Popes had the wisdom to discern at once the power of this vast, silent, untraceable agency on the spiritual improvement of Christendom; its power, not only against vice, ignorance, irreligion, but against those who dared, in their independence of thought, to rebel at the doctrines—in the pride of temporal authority to contest the all-embracing supremacy of the See of Rome. We have seen them during the whole war with Frederick II. the demagogues of refractory subjects, the publishers and propagators of the fulminations of the Popes in all lands, the levellers of mankind before the Papal autocracy, the martyrs of the high Papal faith. Those of less worldly views saw them only as employed in their holier work. Conrad of Zahringen, the General of the Cistercian Order, when they established their first house at Paris, vowed brotherhood with the Friar Preachers. When Legate at Cologne, a priest complained that the Preachers interfered in his parish. "How many parishioners have you?" "Nine thousand." The Legate signed himself with the sign of the Cross: "Miserable man! presumest thou to complain, charged with so many souls, that these holy men would relieve you from part of your burthen?"[b] Yet Conrad issued his mandate, that though the Friars might preach

Conrad of Zahringen.

---

[b] Ann. Cistercien. quoted in Hist. Littér. de la France, article "Conrad of Zahringen."

and administer the sacrament of penance, they should refuse it to all who withdrew themselves from the care of their legitimate pastor. Robert Grostête of Lincoln, as has been said, maintained them against his own negligent or luxurious clergy.

But their zeal or their ambition was not yet satisfied. They aspired to the chief seats of learning; they would rule the Universities, now rising to their height of fame and authority. Of all the universities beyond the Alps, Paris was then the most renowned. If Bologna might boast her civil lawyers, Salerno her physicians, Paris might vie with these great schools in their peculiar studies, and in herself concentered the fame of all, especially of the highest—theology. The University of Paris had its inviolable privileges, its own endowments, government, laws, magistrates, jurisdiction; it was a state within a state, a city within a city, a church within a church. It refused to admit within its walls the sergeants of the Mayor of Paris, the apparitors of the Bishop of Paris; it opened its gates sullenly and reluctantly to the King's officers. The Mendicants (the Dominicans and Franciscans) would teach the teachers of the world; they would occupy not only the pulpits in the churches, and spread their doctrines in streets and market-places, they would lay down the laws of philosophy, theology, perhaps of canonical jurisprudence, from the chairs of professors; and they would vindicate their hardy aspirations by equalling, surpassing the most famous of the University. Already the Dominicans might put forward their Albert the Great, the nearest approach to a philosopher; the Franciscans, the Englishman Alexander Hales, the subtlest of the new race of schoolmen. Aquinas and Bonaventura were to come.

The jealous University, instead of receiving these great men as allies with open arms, rejected them as usurpers.^c

But the University was in implacable war with the authorities of Paris; there was a perpetual feud, as in other universities, between the town and the gown. However wild and unruly the youth, the University would maintain her prerogative of sole and exclusive jurisdiction over them. The sober citizens would not endure the riot, and worse than riot, of these profligate boys.^d Their insolent corporate spirit did not respect the Cardinal Legate.^e On one occasion (in 1228), in a fierce fray of many days, two scholars were killed by the city guard. The University haughtily demanded satisfaction; on the refusal closed her gates, suspended her lectures, at first maintained sullen silence, and then, at least a large portion of the scholars shook the dust from their feet, deserted the dark and ungrateful city, and migrated to Rheims, Orleans, Angers, even to Toulouse.^f The Dominicans seized their opportunity; they obtained full license for a chair of theology from the Bishop of Paris and the Chancellor. On the return of

---

^c Tillemont indeed says, "L'Université les reçut même avec joie dans ses écoles, parceque leur vie paroissoit alors édifiante et utile au public, et qu'ils sembloient s'appliquer aux sciences avec autant d'humilité que d'ardeur et de succès. Mais elle éprouva bientôt qu'il est dangereux de donner entrée à des personnes trop puissantes, et de se lier avec ceux qui ont des desseins et des intérêts différens." See the laborious essay on Guillaume de St. Amour, Vie de Louis IX., p. 133 et seqq.

^d The scholars were forbidden to bear arms in 1218. The Official of Paris complains "qu'ils enfonçoient et brisoient les portes des maisons; qu'ils enlevoient les filles et les femmes."—Crevier, i. p. 334.

^e Crevier, p. 335. The dispute was about the University seal.

^f Crevier, 341. The reader who requires more full, learned, and prolix information, will consult Du Boulay, Hist. Univers. Paris. Crevier's is a clear, rapid, and skilful epitome of Du Boulay.

the University to Paris, they found these powerful rivals in possession of a large share in the theologic instruction. Their re-establishment, resisted by the Crown and by the Bishop of Paris (the Crown indignant that the University had presumed to confer degrees at Orleans and at Angers, the Bishop jealous of their exemption from his jurisdiction), was only effected by the authority of Pope Gregory IX. The Pontiff was anxious that Paris, the foundation of all sound learning, should regain her distinction. His mild and conciliatory counsels prevailed: the University resumed her station, and even obtained the valuable privilege that the Rector and Scholars were not liable to any excommunication not directly sanctioned by the Holy See.

Above twenty years of treacherous peace followed. The Mendicants were gaining in power, fame, influence, unpopularity. They encroached more and more on the offices, on the privileges of the clergy; stood more aloof from episcopal jurisdiction; had become, instead of the clergy and the older monasteries, the universal legatees; obscured the University by the renown of their great teachers. The University raised a loud outcry that there were twelve chairs of theology at Paris: of these, five out of the six colleges of the Regulars—the Cistercians, Premonstratensians, Val de Grace, Trinitarians, Franciscans—held each one, the Dominicans two; the Canons of Paris occupied three; there remained but two for the whole Secular Clergy.[e] They issued their edict suppressing one of the Dominicans: the Dominicans laughed them to scorn. The quarrel was aggravated by the refusal of the Dominican and Franciscan Professors to join the

1231-1232. Dispute with the Dominicans.

---

[e] Crevier, p. 590.

rest of the University in demanding justice for the death of a scholar slain in a fray.[h] The University passed a sentence of expulsion against the Dominican Professors. The Dominicans appealed to the Pope. They obtained, it was averred by false representations, a favourable award. Europe rang with the clamorous remonstrances of the University of Paris. They issued an address to the whole Episcopate of Christendom. "Would the Bishops, very many of whom had studied at Paris, allow that famous University, the foundation of the faith, to be shaken?"[i] They pressed their appeal before Pope Innocent IV. Innocent, a great student of the canon law, had always looked on the University of Paris with favour. The Mendicants had done their work; Frederick II. was dead; Innocent master of Italy. The Pope, who had alienated the University by his exactions and arrogance, endeavoured to propitiate them by the sacrifice of his faithful allies the Friars. He promulgated his celebrated bull, subjugating the Mendicant Orders to episcopal authority. The next month Pope Innocent was dead. The Dominicans revenged themselves on the ungrateful Pontiff by assuming the merit of his death, granted to their prayers. "From the Litanies of the Dominicans, good Lord deliver us," became a proverbial saying.[k]

Bull of Pope Innocent.
Nov. 1254.

Alexander IV. was not the protector only, he was the humble slave of the Mendicants.[m] His first act was to annul the bull of his predecessor

Alexander IV.

---

[h] The University obtained justice; two men were hanged for the offence —Crevier, p. 400.

[i] "Si on attaque le fondement (de l'Eglise) qui est l'Ecole de Paris, tout l'édifice est mis en péril."—See Crevier, p. 407.

"Et se ne fust la bonne garde De l'Université, qui garde Le chief de la Chrétienté." *Roman de la Rose,* l. 12118.

[k] Antonini, Sermon. in Chronic. Compare Hist. Lit. de la France, xix. p. 197, article William de St. Amour.

[m] The words of Crevier, p. 411.

without reservation.^o The Mendicants were at once reinstated in all their power. In vain the eloquent William (called St. Amour, from the place of his birth in Franche Comté) maintained the privileges of the University: he returned discomfited, not defeated, to Paris. He was hailed as the acknowledged champion of the University, and devoted himself with dauntless courage and perseverance to the cause.^p He not only asserted the privileges of the University; Paris rung with his denunciations of the Mendicants, of Mendicancy itself. He preached with a popularity rivalling or surpassing the best preachers of the Orders. He accused the Friars as going about into houses, leading astray silly women, laden with sins, usurping everywhere the rule over their consciences and men's property, aspiring to tyrannise over public opinion. "And who were they? No successors of the Apostles; they presumed to act in the Church with no spiritual lineage, with no tradition of authority; from them arose the 'Perils of the days to come.'"

The Dominicans had boasted, according to the popular poet,^q that they ruled supreme in Paris and in Rome: they had lost Paris, but in Rome they ruled without rival. The first, the most famous, it is said, of forty bulls issued by Alexander IV., appeared during the

---

^o He was elected Dec. 12; revoked the bull Dec. 22.

^p To William of St. Amour was attributed the bull of Innocent IV.

"S'il n'avait en sa verité
L'accord de l'Université
Et du peuple communement
Qui oyoient son prêchement."
Roman de la Rose, L. 12113.

^p Opera Gulielm. St. Amour, Præf. p. 23.

^q "Li Jacobin (Dominicales) sont si prodomme,
Qu'il ont Paris et si ont Romme,
Et si sont roi et Apostole
Et de l'avoir ont il grant soume.
Et qui se muert, se il ne's nomme
Pour exécuteurs, s'âme afole,
Et sont apostre par parole.
  *   *   *   *
Lor haine n'est pas frivole,
Je, qui redout ma teste folo
Ne vous di plus mais qu'il sont homme."
Rutebeuf, edit. Jubinal, L 161.

next year.' It commenced with specious adulation of the University, ended with awarding complete victory to the Dominicans. While it seemed to give full power to the University, it absolutely annulled their statute of exclusion against the Dominicans. The Bishops of Orleans and Auxerre were charged with the execution of this bull; they were armed with ample powers of spiritual censure, of excommunicating, or suspending from their office all masters or scholars guilty of contumacy. The University defied or attempted to elude these censures. They obstinately refused to admit the Dominicans to their republic; they determined rather to dissolve the University; many masters and students withdrew, some returned and took up again their attitude of defiance. William de St. Amour was the special object of the hatred of the Mendicants. He was arraigned before the Bishop of Paris, at the suit of Gregory, a chaplain of Paris, as having disseminated a libel defamatory of the Pope. St. Amour appeared; but the courage of the accuser had failed, he was not to be found. St. Amour offered canonical purgation; to swear on the reliques of the Holy Martyrs that he was guiltless of the alleged crime. Four thousand scholars stood forward as his compurgators. The Bishop was forced to dismiss the charge.* In vain the four great Archbishops of France interfered to allay the strife: the pulpits rung with mutual criminations.

William of St. Amour and his zealous partisans arraigned the Mendicants, not merely as usurpers of the rights, offices, emoluments of the clergy, of heredipety

---

* This bull was called "Quasi lignum vitæ." The successive bulls may be read in the Bullarium.

* Crevier, from a letter of the students of the University to the Pope. It was possibly before the arrival of the bull.

and rapacity utterly at variance with their ostentatious poverty, but both orders, indiscriminately, Dominicans as well as Franciscans, as believers in, as preachers and propagators of the *Everlasting Gospel*. This book, which became the manual, I had almost said the Bible of the spiritual Franciscans, must await its full examination till those men—the Fraticelli—come before us in their formidable numbers and no less formidable activity. Suffice it here, that the Everlasting Gospel, the prophetic book ascribed to the Abbot Joachim, or rather the introduction to the Everlasting Gospel, proclaimed the approach, the commencement of the Last Age of the World, that of the Holy Ghost. The Age of the Father—that of the Law—had long since gone by; that of the Son was ebbing on its last sands; and with the Age of the Son, the Church, the hierarchy, its power, wealth, splendour, were to pass away. The Age of the Holy Ghost was at hand, it was in its dawn. The Holy Ghost would renew the world in the poverty, humility, Christian perfection of St. Francis. The Everlasting Gospel superseded and rendered useless the other four. It suited the enemies of the Mendicants to involve both Orders in this odious charge: the Introduction to the Everlasting Gospel was by some attributed to the Dominicans, its character, its spirit, its tone, were unquestionably Franciscan.[t]

---

[t] Matt. Paris (sub ann. 1256), Richar. Cronic. Senens., and the authors of the Roman de la Rose, attribute the Everlasting Gospel to the Dominicans. Such was the tone in Paris. According, however, to the Roman de la Rose, it had another author:

"Ung livre de par le le grant Diable,
Lat l'Evangile pardurable,

Que le Saint Esperit ministre,
Bien est digne d'être brulé.
. . .
Tant surmonte cete Evangile,
Croix que les quatre Evangelistres
Jesu-Christ firent à leurs titres."
—L. 12414, &c.

It appeared, according to the port William de Lorris, in 1250; It was in the hands of every man and woman in the " parvis Nôtre Dame."

These two rival Orders had followed in their development the opposite character of their founders. To the stern, sober, practical views of Dominic had succeeded stern, sober, practical Generals. The mild, mystic, passionate Francis was followed by men all earnest and vehement, but dragged different ways by conflicting passions: the passion for poverty, as the consummation and perfection of all religion; the passion for other ends to which poverty was but the means, and therefore must be followed out with less rigour. The first General, Elias, even in the lifetime of the Saint, tampered with the vow of holy poverty; he was deposed, as we have heard, became no longer the partisan of the Pope, but of Frederick II., was hardly permitted on his deathbed to resume the dress of the Order.[a] It may be presumed that Crescentius, the sixth General, was, from age or temper, less rigorous as to this vital law. He, too, was deposed from his high place, and John of Parma became General of the Order. John of Parma[b] was, it might be said (if St. Francis himself was not the parent of the Spiritualist Franciscans), that parent; he was the extremest of the extreme. His first act was a visitation of all the monasteries of the Order, the enforcement of that indispensable virtue which would brook no infringement whatever. John of Parma was employed by Innocent IV. in Greece, in an endeavour to reconcile the Oriental schism. In 1251 he was again in Rome. In 1256, exactly the very year in which came forth the daring book of William de St. Amour, there were strange murmurs, sullen suppressed murmurs against John

---

[a] Chroniques des Frères Mineurs, c. xlii. p. 27.

[b] The best account which I have read of John of Parma is in the Hist. Littéraire de la France, t. xx. p. 23. But the whole of this development of spiritual Franciscanism will be more fully traced hereafter.

of Parma. He was deposed, and only by the influence of the Cardinal Ottobuoni permitted to dwell in retirement at Rieti. There seems but slight doubt that he was deposed as the author of the Introduction to the Everlasting Gospel.' It needed all the commanding gentleness, the unrivalled learning, the depth of piety, in St. Bonaventura, the new General, to allay the civil feud, and delay for some years the fatal schism among the followers of St. Francis — the revolt of the Spiritualists from the Order.

The war continued to rage in Paris, notwithstanding a short truce brought about by the King and the Bishops. Bull after bull arrived.ˢ Pope Alexander appealed at length to the King; he demanded of the secular power the exile of the obstinate leaders of the Anti-Mendicant party, William de St. Amour, Eudes of Douai, Nicolas Dean of Bar-sur-Aube, and Christian Canon of Beauvais." Before the King (St. Louis), whose awful reverence and passionate attachment to the Mendicant Orders were well known, had determined on his course, William of St. Amour had published his terrible book on the "Perils of the Last Times." This book, written in the name, *The Perils of the Last Times.* perhaps with the aid and concurrence of the theologians of the University, was more dangerous, because it denounced not openly the practices of the Friars, but it

---

ᶠ It was the great object of Wadding and of Staraglia to release the memory of a General of their order from the authorship of an heretical book. It is attributed to him, or to Gerard da Borgo san Domnino, under his auspices, by Nicolas Eymeric. Direct. Inquis. II. v. 24. Bzovius, sub ann. 1250. Bulæus, p. 209. See also Tillemont's impartial summing up, p. 157.
ˢ Tillemont, p. 182.
ᵗ On these men compare Tillemont, p. 144. Thomas Cantepral, among later writers the great enemy of William de St. Amour, admits that he seduced the clergy and people of Rome by his eloquence.

was a relentless, covert, galling exposure of them and of their proceedings. That they were meant as the forerunners of Antichrist, the irrefragable signs of the "perils of the last times," none could doubt. The book was sent by the indignant King himself to Rome. The University had endeavoured in vain to anticipate the more rapid movements of their adversary. They had despatched a mission (the very four men condemned by the Pope) to Rome, bearing the Introduction to the Everlasting Gospel, and demanding the condemnation of that flagrantly heretical book.[b] They had obtained letters of recommendation from all the chapters in the province of Rheims.

Ere they arrived, the all-powerful Dominicans had struck their blow. The "Perils of the Last Times" had been submitted to the examination of four Cardinals, one of them a Dominican—Hugo de St. Cher, who sat as judge in his own cause. It was condemned as unjust, wicked, execrable; it was burned in the presence of the Pope, before the Cathedral at Anagni.

Fate of William de St. Amour. William de St. Amour stood alone in Rome against the Pope Alexander, the Cardinals, and the Dominicans, headed by Hugo de St. Cher.[c] He conducted his defence with consummate courage and no less consummate address. It was impossible to fix upon him the fatal guilt of heresy.[d] His health began to fail; he was prohibited for a time from returning to France, perhaps was not sorry to obey the prohibition. He does not seem even to have been de-

[b] The introduction had been before or was now formally condemned at Rome.
[c] On Hugo de St. Cher, Tillemont, p. 15.
[d] It was condemned "non propter hæresim quam continebat sed quia contra præfatos religiosos seditionem et scandala concitabat."—G. Nangis.

prived of his benefices.[e] His quiet place of exile was his native St. Amour, in Franche Comté, not yet in the dominions of France. He was followed by the respect and fond attachment of the whole University.

But it is singular that William of St. Amour was not only the champion of the learned University, he was the hero of Parisian vulgar poetry. *Popular party.* Notwithstanding that the King, and that King St. Louis, espoused the cause of the Mendicants, the people were on the other side. The popular Preachers, and the popular ministers, who had sprung from the people, spoke the language, expressed at the same time and excited the sympathies and the religious passions of the lowest of the low, had ceased to be popular. They had been even outpreached by William of St. Amour. The Book of the Perils of the Last Times was disseminated in the vulgar tongue. The author of the romance of the Rose,[f] above all, Rutebeuf, in his rude verse addressed to the vulgar of all orders, heaped scorn and hatred on the Mendicants.[g]

---

[e] Tillemont, p. 212.

[f] "Si j'en devoye perdre la vie,
On serre mys contre droiture,
Comme Saint Pol en charure obscure,
Ou mars banny du Royaume,
A tort, comme fut Maistre Guillaume
De St. Amour, que ypocrisie
Fist exiller par grant envie."
Roman de la Rose, l. 12123.

Lorris talks of scorning "papelarderie." Paris writes, "Subsannavit populus, eleemosynas consuetas subtrahens, vocans eos hypocritas, antichristi successores (antecessores?) pseudo-prædicatores."

[g] See especially the two poems, de Maistre Guillaume de St. Amour, pp. 71 and 78, "or est en son pais reclus"—on St. Amour, p. 81.

"On a nul si vaillant homme
Qui por l'apostoille de Romme,
Ne por le roi,
Ne veut deservir son error,
Ains en a souffert le desrur
De perdre honor?"—P. 65.

Compare also "La Bataille des Vices contre les Vertus" (ii. p. 65), "La Discorde de l'Université et les Jacobins," "Les Ordres de Paris," &c. &c., with constant reference to the notes. The curious reader will not content himself with the valuable edition of Rutebeuf by M. Jubinal; he will consult also the excellent article by M. Paullin Paris in the Hist. Lit. de la France, xx p. 710. Rutebeuf reads to me like our Skelton; he has the same flowing rapid doggrel, the same satiric verve,

The war between the University and the Dominicans continued, if in less active, in sullen obstinacy. They were still the rival powers, who would not coalesce, each striving to engross public education. Yet after all the Mendicants won a noble victory, not by the authority of the Pope, nor by the influence of the King, but by outshining the fame of the University through their own unrivalled teachers. On the death of Alexander IV., William of St. Amour returned to Paris; he was received with frantic rapture.[h] His later book,[i] more cautious, yet not less hostile, was received with respect and approbation by Pope Clement IV.[k] Yet who could deny, who presume to question, the transcendant fame, the complete mastery of the Dominicans in theology, and that philosophy which in those days aspired not to be more than the humble handmaid of theology? (Albert the Great might, perhaps, have views of more free and independent science, and so far, of course, became a suspected magician.) Who could compete with their Doctors, Hugo de St. Cher, Albert the Great, Thomas of Aquino? The Franciscans, too, had boasted their Alexander Hales,

---

with not much of poetry, but both are always alive. On the whole of this feud, and its connection with Averroism read the very remarkable pages of M. Ernest Renan, Averroes et l'Averröisme, from page 259. Paris, 1861.

[h] May 1261. "Debacchantibus summâ in lætitiâ omnibus Magistris Parisiensibus."—Du Boulay.

[i] Collectiones Catholicæ.

[k] See on this book, and others, Hist. Lit. de la France, article St. Amour, t. xix. 197. To his earlier works belongs, not only the "De Periculis" (in his works and in Fasciculus of Brown, who translated it, with some sermons), but also a book, De Antichristo, under the pseudonyme of Nicolas de Oresme. The object of this is to show the coming of Antichrist, of which the chief signs are the setting up the Everlasting Gospel against the true Gospels, and the multitudes of false preachers, false prophets, wandering and begging friars.—Ibid. See also account of the writings of Gerard of Abbeville, another powerful antagonist of the Mendicants.

GREAT MENDICANT THEOLOGIANS.

they had now their Bonaventura: Duns Scotus, the rival of Aquinas, was speedily to come.* The University could not refuse to itself the honour of conferring its degrees on Aquinas,[b] and on Bonaventura. And still the rivals in scholastic theology, who divided the world (the barren it might be, and dreary intellectual world, yet in that age the only field for mental greatness), were the descendants of the representatives of the two Orders. The Scotists and the Thomists fought what was thought a glorious fight on the highest metaphysics of the Faith, till the absorbing question, the Immaculate Conception of the Virgin, arose to commit the two Orders in mortal and implacable antagonism.

The hatred of the Mendicants might seem to pass over to the secular clergy. In every part of Europe the hierarchy still opposed with dignity or with passion the encroachments of these fatal rivals. More than twenty years later met a National Council at Paris. Four Archbishops and twenty Bishops took their seats in a hall of the Episcopal Palace. The Masters, Doctors, Bachelors, and Students of the University, were summoned to hear the decrees of the Council. The heads of the other religious orders, not Mendicant, had their writs of convocation. Simon de Beaulieu, Archbishop of Bourges, took the lead. In a grave sermon, he declared that charity to their flocks demanded their interposition; their flocks, for whom

Secular clergy and Mendicants.

---

* Those who esteemed themselves the genuine Franciscans, always sternly protested against the pride of learning, to which their false brethren aspired in the universities. Hear Jacopone da Todi:

"Tal b, qual b, tal b,
Non c' e religione

Mal vedemmo Parigi.
Che n' a desurutto Assisi.
Colla sua lettoria
L' han messo in mala via."

[b] Thomas Aquinas condescended to answer William of St. Amour. See Adversus Impugnantes Religionem.

2 A 2

they were bound to lay down their lives. He inveighed against the Dominicans and the Franciscans, who were sowing discord in every diocese, in every rank, preaching and hearing confessions without license from the Bishop and the curate. Their insolence must be repressed. He appealed to the University to join in an appeal to the Pope to define more rigidly their asserted privileges. William of Macon, Bishop of Amiens, the most learned jurist in France, followed: he explained the bull of Innocent IV., which prohibited the Friars from preaching, hearing confessions, imposing penance without permission of the Bishop or lawful pastor. The whole clergy of France were ready to shed their blood in defence of their rights and duties.*

---

* This is well related in the Hist. Lit. de la France, t. xxi. article Simon de Beaulieu.

CHAPTER III.

Urban IV. Clement IV. Charles of Anjou.

ALEXANDER IV. died an exile from Rome at Viterbo. Either from indolence or irresolution, he had allowed the College of Cardinals to dwindle to the number of eight. These eight were of various nations and orders: two Bishops, Otho a Frenchman, Stephen a Hungarian; two Presbyters, John an English Cistercian, Hugo a Dominican from Savoy; four Deacons, Richard a Roman, and Octavian a Tuscan of noble birth, John another Roman, Ottobuoni a Genoese. There was no prevailing interest, no commanding name. More than three months passed in jealous dispute. The strife was fortuitously ended by the appearance of James Pantaleon, the Patriarch of Jerusalem. He was elevated by sudden acclamation to the Papal throne.

<small>Death of Alexander IV. June 12, 1261.</small>

The Patriarch was the son of a cobbler at Troyes:* and it was a wonderful sight, as it were, a provocation to the first principles of Christianity, to behold in those days of feudal monarchy and feudal aristocracies a man of such base parentage in the highest dignity upon earth. James had risen by regular steps up the ascent of ecclesiastical advancement, a Priest at Laon, a

---

* "Paupercull vetaramentarii calcamenta resarciendis."—S. Antonin. dl, xiv, p. 59—big words to describe a cobbler. According to the Hist. Littér. (article Urban IV., t. xiv. p. 49), there is a tapestry at Troyes, in the Church of St. Urban, representing Pantaleon (the father) in his shop full of boots and shoes, and his mother spinning and watching little James.

Canon at Lyons, Archdeacon of Liège, a Missionary Legate in Livonia, Pomerania, and Prussia,[b] a pilgrim and Patriarch of Jerusalem. Such a man could not so have risen without great abilities or virtues. But if the rank in which he was born was honourable, the place was inauspicious. Had the election not fallen on a Frenchman, Italy might perhaps have escaped the descent of Charles of Anjou, with its immediate crimes and cruelties; and the wars almost of centuries, which had their origin in that fatal event. Any Pope, indeed, must have had great courage to break through the traditional policy of his predecessors (where the whole power rests on tradition, a bold, if not a perilous act). Urban must have recanted the long-cherished hatred and jealousy of the house of Hohenstaufen; he must have clearly foreseen (himself a Frenchman) that the French dominion in Naples would be as fatal as the German to the independence of Italy and of the Church; that Charles of Anjou would soon become as dangerous a neighbour as Manfred.

Urban IV. took up his residence in Viterbo: already might appear his determined policy to renew the close alliance between the Papacy and his native France. The holy character of Louis, who by the death of Frederick and the abeyance of the Empire, by the wars of the Barons against Henry of England, had become the most powerful monarch in Christendom, gave further preponderance to his French inclinations.[c] He filled up the College of Cardinals with fourteen new prelates, at least one half of whom were French.

---

[b] See in Voigt, Geschichte Preussens, ii. p. 591, his wise conduct as a mediator between the Teutonic Order, and Swartobol, Duke of Pomerania, the ally of the heathen Prussians.

[c] See in Raynaldus the verses of Theodoricus Vallicolor, sub ann. 1262, sub fine.

THE CRUSADE FAILS.

The Empire still hung in suspense between the conflicting claims of Richard of Cornwall and Alfonso of Castile: Urban, with dexterous skill, perpetuated the anarchy. By timely protestation, and by nicely balancing the hopes of both parties that his adjudication, earnestly and submissively sought by both, would be in favour of each, he suppressed a growing determination to place the crown on the head of young Conradin. Against this scheme Urban raised his voice with all the energy of his predecessors, and dwelt with the same menacing censure on the hereditary and indelible crimes of the house of Swabia: he threatened excommunication on all who should revive the claims of that impious race. After a grave examination of the pretensions of Richard of Cornwall and Alfonso of Castile, he cited both parties to plead their cause before him, and still drew out, with still baffled expectations of a speedy sentence, the controversy which he had no design to close.

The Empire.

The Latin Empire of Constantinople had fallen: Baldwin II. sought refuge, and only found refuge in the West. The Greek Palæologi were on the throne of the East, and seemed not indisposed to negotiate on the religious question with the Pope. The Holy Land, the former diocese of Pope Urban, was in the most deplorable state: the Sultan of Babylon had risen again in irresistible power; he had overrun the whole country; the Christians were hardly safe in Ptolemais. In vain the Pope appealed to his own countrymen in behalf of his old beloved diocese; the clergy of France withheld their contributions, and whether from some jealousy of their lowly countryman, now so much above them; or since the cause had so utterly failed even under their King, it might seem absolutely despe-

Crusade fails.

rate, the Archbishops of Sens and of Bourges were unmoved by the Papal rebukes or remonstrances, and continued, at least not to encourage the zeal of their clergy.

The affairs of Italy and Naples threatened almost the personal safety of the Pope. Manfred was at the height of his power; he no longer deigned to make advances for reconciliation, which successive Popes seemed to treat with still stronger aversion. Everywhere Ghibellinism was in the ascendant. The Marquis Pallavicini and Buoso da Doara at the head of the Cremonese, maintained more than an equal balance in Lombardy. Pisa and Sienna, rampant after the fall of the Guelfic rule in Florence, received the letters of the Pope with civil contempt. It might appear that Manfred was admitted into the rank of the legitimate Sovereigns of Christendom. In vain the Pope denounced the wickedness, the impiety of a connexion with an excommunicated family, the King of Arragon did not scruple to marry his son to the daughter of Manfred. The marriage of the son of Louis of France to the daughter of Arragon, increased the jealous alarm of the Pope. Even Louis did not permit the Papal remonstrances to interfere with these arrangements.

Manfred.

Miserable, in the meantime, was the state of Italy. Scarcely a city or territory from the confines of Apulia to the Alps was undisturbed by one of those accursed feuds, either of nobles against the people, or of Guelfs against Ghibellines. Nowhere was rest. Now one party, now another must dislodge from their homes, and go into exile. Urban could not remain in Rome. The stronger cities were waging war on the weaker. All the labours of the Holy Inquisition and all the rigour of their penalties, instead of extirpating

State of Italy.

the heresy of the Paterins and various Manichean sects, might seem to promote their increase. In general, it was enough to be Ghibelline, and to oppose the Church, down came the excommunication; all sacred offices ceased. It may be well imagined how deeply all this grieved religious men, the triumph and joy of the heretics.[d]

Only to France could the Pope, even if no Frenchman, have looked for succour, if determined to maintain the unextinguished feud with Manfred. Already the crown of Naples had been offered to Charles of Anjou. Urban IV. first laid it at the feet of Louis himself, either for his brother or one of his sons. But the delicate conscience of Louis revolted from the usurpation of a crown, to which were already three claimants of right. If it was hereditary, it belonged to Conradin; if at the disposal of the Pope, it was already awarded, and had not been surrendered by Edmund of England; and Manfred was on the throne, summoned, it might seem, by the voice of the nation. Manfred's claim, as maintained by an irreligious alliance with the Saracens, and as the possession of a Christian throne by one accused of favouring the Saracens, might easily be dismissed; but there was strong doubt as to the others. The Pope, who perhaps from the first had preferred the more active and enterprising Charles of Anjou, because he could not become King of France, in vain argued and took all the guilt on his own head:[e] "the soul of Louis was as precious to the Pope and the Cardinals as to himself." Louis did not refuse his assent to the

---

[d] See this and much more to the same effect in Muratori, Annal. sub ann. 1263.
[e] Epist. to Albert of Parma, the notary who was empowered to treat as to the conditions of the assumption of the throne of Naples.—Raynald., sub ann. 1262.

acceptance of the crown by his brother. It is said, that he was glad to rid his court, if not his realm, which he was endeavouring to subdue to monastic gravity, of his gayer brother, who was constantly summoning tournaments, was addicted to gaming, and every other knightly diversion.*

Charles of Anjou might seem designated for this service. Valiant, adventurous, with none of that punctilious religiousness which might seem to set itself above ecclesiastical guidance, yet with all outward respect for the doctrine and ceremonial of the Church; with vast resources, holding, in right of his wife, the principality of Provence; he was a leader whom all the knighthood of France, who were eager to find vent for their valour, and to escape the peaceful inactivity or dull control under which they were kept by the scrupulous justice of Louis IX., would follow with headlong zeal. Charles had hardly yet shown that intense selfishness and cruelty which, in the ally, in the king chosen by the Pope for his vassal realm, could not but recoil upon the Pope himself. He had already indeed besieged and taken Marseilles, barbarously executed all the citizens who had defended the liberties of their town, and abrogated all the rights and privileges of that flourishing municipality. His ambitious wife, Beatrice of Provence, jealous of being the sister of three queens, herself no queen, urged her unreluctant husband to this promising enterprise. But the Pope had still much to do; there were disputes between the sisters, especially the Queen of France and the Countess of Provence, on certain rights as co-heiresses of that land. Though the

---

* "Quia sui regni, quam perturbabat Carolus in tornamentis et aleis."
—Ptolom., Luc. c. xiv.

treaty was negotiated, drawn up, perhaps actually signed, it was not yet published. It was thought more safe and decent to obtain a more formal abjuration of his title from Edmund of England.

Bartholomew Pignatelli, Archbishop of Cosenza, a Guelfic prelate of noble blood, received a commission as legate to demand the surrender of the crown of Sicily. He was afterwards to lay the result of his mission before Louis of France, in order to obtain his full consent to the investiture of Charles of Anjou. Henry III., threatened by the insurrection of his barons, might well be supposed wholly unable to assert the pretensions of his son to a foreign crown; yet he complained with some bitterness that the treasures of England, so long poured into the lap of the Pontiff, had met with such return.[g] Urban endeavoured to allay his indignation by espousing his cause against the Earl of Leicester (Simon de Montfort) and the barons of England: he absolutely annulled all their leagues.[h] William, Archdeacon of Paris, the Pope's chaplain, had power to relieve Henry from all his constitutional oaths.[i] As the war became more imminent, more inevitable, both before and after the rejection of the award in favour of the King by the acknowledged arbiter Louis IX., the Pope adhered with imperious fidelity to the King. Ugo Falcodi, Cardinal of St. Sabina, was sent as Legate to command the vassal kingdom to peace: the rebellious subjects were to be ordered to submit to their sovereign, and abandon their audacious pretensions

[margin: England. A.D. 1263.]

---

[g] See despatch to Archbishop of Cosenza, MS., B. M., July 25, 1263, to the King, ibid. v. 1. Instructions at full length, dated Orvieto, Oct. 4.

[h] "Conjurationes omnes cassamus et irritamus. Ad fidelem."—MS., B. M. 23rd Aug. 1263.

[i] MS., B. M., letter to Archdeacon of Paris.

to liberty. The Legate was armed with the amplest power to prohibit the observation of all the statutes, though sworn to by the King, the Queen, and the Prince; to suspend and depose all prelates or ecclesiastics; to deprive all counts, barons, or laymen, who held in fee estates of the Church, and to proceed at his discretion to any spiritual or temporal penalties.* He had power to provide for all who should accompany him to England by canonries or other benefices.™ He had power of ecclesiastical censure against archbishops, bishops, monasteries, exempt or not exempt, and all others.ⁿ He had power to depose all ecclesiastics in rebellion,° and of appointing loyal clerks to their benefices.ᵖ In the case of the rebellion of archbishops or prelates, counts or barons, indulgences were to be granted to all who would serve or raise soldiers for the King, as if they went to the Holy Land: the Friar preachers and Friar minors were to aid the King to the utmost.ʳ After the award of the King of France, which the Pope confirmed,ˢ Urban becomes even more peremp-

---

* "Ad quorum observantiam ipsos decrevimus non tenere, eandem prelatos et clericos per suspensionis sententiam ab officiis, dignitatibus, honoribus et beneficiis: comites vero, barones et laicos predictos per privationem feudorum et omnium bonorum, quæ a quibusdam Ecclesiis predicti regni et aliis detinent et aliàs spiritualiter et temporaliter, prout expedire videria."—MS., B. M., Nov. 23, 1263. See also the next letter.

ᵐ "Non obstante Statuto Ecclesiarum ipsarum de certo clericorum numero, juramento, confirmatione, sive quâcunque firmitate, vallato."—Ibid. v. xi. p. 48.

ⁿ "Communis universitatis et populos locorum quorumlibet."

° Clerks, "indevoti, ingrati, inobedientes."

ᵖ Even at this time peremptory orders were given for provision for Italian ecclesiastics in the English Church. John de Ebulo claimed the deanery of St. Paul's. The chapter resisted. He resigned the deanery, but accepted a canonry; till a canonry should be vacant, a certain pension.—P. 170.

Orvieto, Nov. 27. 1263.
ʳ Ibid., Nov. 27.
ˢ Rymer, l. 776, 778, 780, 784.

tory; he commands the infamous provision, one of those of Oxford, to be erased from the statute book; all those of Oxford are detestable and impious; he marks with special malediction that which prohibited the introduction of apostolic bulls or briefs into the realm, and withheld the rich subsidies from Rome.¹ The Archbishop was to excommunicate all who should not submit to the award. The King's absolute illimitable power is asserted in the strongest terms.² The expulsion of strangers, and the assumption of exclusive authority by native Englishmen, are severely reprobated.³

But the Cardinal Legate dared not to land in the island—even the Archbishop Boniface (of Savoy) would not venture into his province. Ere long the whole realm, the King himself, and Prince Edward are in the power of the Barons. The Legate must content himself with opening his court at Boulogne. There he issued his unobeyed citation to the Barons to appear, pronounced against them the sentence of excommunication, and placed London and the Cinque Ports under an interdict.⁷ Ugo Falcodi, when Pope, cherished a bitter remembrance of these affronting contempts.

Although the negotiations were all this time proceeding in secret with Charles of Anjou, the Pope cited Man-

---

¹ The Pope's letters, at least, were after the award. "Nonnulli maledictionis alumpni, quaedam statuta nepharia in depressionem libertatis ejusdem promulgasse dicuntur, videlicet quod quicunque literas apostolicas aut ipsius archiepiscopi in Angliam deferre praesumpserit, graviter puniatur,"—Orvieto, Feb. 20, 1264.

² "Plenaria potestate in omnibus et per omnia."—Ibid.

³ The King of France "Retractavit et cassavit illud statutum, per quod regnum Angliae debebat per indigenas gubernari, et alienigenae tenebantur ab eodem exire, ad illum minime reversuri."—Ibid.

⁷ "Propter imminentem turbationem." Feb. 15. His citations were to be valid, if issued in France. The Bishop of Lincoln was cited for various acts of contumacy to the Holy See.—June 4, 1264.

fred to appear before him to answer on certain charges, which he published to the world.[a] They comprehended various acts of cruelty, the destruction of the city of Aria by the Saracens, the execution, called murder, of certain nobles, contempt of the ecclesiastical interdict, attachment to Mohammedan rites, the murder of an ambassador of Conradin.[a] Manfred approached the borders; but the Pope insisted that he should be accompanied by only eighty men: Manfred refused to trust himself to a Papal safe-conduct.

Affairs of Naples

But as he was not permitted to approach in peace, Manfred, well informed of the transactions with Charles of Anjou, threatened to approach in war.[b] From Florence, from Pisa, from Sienna, the German and Saracen, as well as the Apulian and Sicilian forces began to draw towards Orvieto. The Pope hastily summoned a Council: and some troops came to his aid from various quarters. But a sudden event seemed to determine the descent of Charles of Anjou upon Italy, and brought at once the protracted negotiations, concerning the terms of his acceptance of the throne of Naples, to a close. The Roman people, having risen against the nobles, and cast many of them out of the city, determined on appointing a senator of not less than royal rank. One party proposed Manfred, another his son-in-law, the King of Arragon, a third Charles of Anjou. The Pope was embarrassed: he was compelled to maintain Charles of Anjou against his competitors: and yet a great sovereign as senator of Rome, and for life (as it was proposed), was the death-blow to the Papal rule in Rome. Charles of Anjou felt his strength; he yielded to the Pope's request to limit

Advance of Manfred.

Charles of Anjou Senator of Rome.

---

[a] Oct. 20, 1264.   [a] Raynaldus, sub ann.   [b] Giammone, xix. 1.

the grant of the senatorship to five years; but he seized the opportunity to lower the terms on which he was to be invested with the realm of Naples. He demanded a diminution of the tribute of ten thousand ounces of gold which Naples was to pay annually to the See of Rome. Such demand was unjust to him who was about to incur vast expense in the cause of Rome; unjust to Naples, which would be burthened with heavy taxation; impolitic, as preventing the new King from treating his subjects with splendid liberality. He required that the descent of the crown should be in the female as well as in the male line: that he should himself judge of the number of soldiers necessary for the expedition. He demanded the abrogation of the stipulation, that if any of his posterity should obtain the Empire, Lombardy or Tuscany, the crown of Naples should pass from them; the enlargement of the provision, that only a limited extent of possession in Lombardy or in Tuscany should be tenable with the Neapolitan crown.

Charles was so necessary to Urban, the weight of Urban's influence was so powerful in Rome, that the treaty was at length signed. Charles sent a representative to Rome to accept the Senatorship.[*]

Manfred now kept no measures with the hostile Pope. His Saracen troops on one side, his German on the other, broke into the Roman territories. But a crusading army of Guelfs of some force had arisen around the Pope; and some failures and disasters checked the career of Manfred. Pandolf, Count of Anguillara, recovered Sutri from the Saracens. Peter de Vico, a powerful noble, had revolted from the Pope, and having

---

[*] Charles agreed to surrender the senatorship when master of Naples. How far did he intend to observe this condition?—See Sismondi, p. 141.

secret intelligence in Rome, hoped to betray the city into the power of Manfred: he was repelled by the Romans. Percival d'Oria, who had captured many of the Guelfic castles, was accidentally drowned in the river Negra during a battle near Rieti: his death was bruited about as a miracle. Yet was not the Pope safe; Orvieto began to waver: he set forth to Perugia; he died on the road.

Oct. 3 or 10, 1264.
Death of Urban IV. Oct. 2, 1264.

Christendom at this peculiar crisis awaited with trembling anxiety the determination of the conclave: but this suspense of nearly five months did not arise altogether out of the dissensions in that body. Urban IV. had secured the predominance of the French interest; the election had been long made before it was published. It had fallen on Ugo Falcodi, that Papal Legate, who, on the northern shore of France, was issuing Urban's sentence of excommunication against the Barons of England, while that Pope was no longer living. Ugo Falcodi was born at St. Gilles upon the Rhône: he had been married before he took orders, and had two daughters. He was profoundly learned in the law; from the Archdiaconate of Narbonne he had been brought to Italy, and created Cardinal of S. Sabina. Of his policy there could be no doubt; Manfred has but a new and more vigorous enemy; Charles of Anjou a more devoted friend. The Cardinal of S. Sabina passed secretly over the Alps, suddenly appeared at Perugia, accepted the tiara, assumed the name of Clement IV., and then took up his residence at Viterbo.

Clement IV. Feb. 5, 1265.

Yet Manfred could hardly have dreaded a foe so active, so implacable, so unscrupulous, or Charles hoped for an ally so zealous, so obsequious, above all, so prodigal. Letters were despatched through Christendom, to England, to France, urging immediate succour to the Holy See, imperilled by the Saracen Manfred, and trusting for her relief only to the devout Charles. Everywhere the tenths were levied, notwithstanding the murmurs of Bishops and clergy; tenths still under the pretext of aid for Constantinople and Jerusalem. It was rebellion to refuse to pay; the Pope was even lavish of the Papal treasures; he pledged the ecclesiastical estates; usurious interest accumulated on the principal. A loan of 100,000 livres was raised on the security of the possessions of the Church in Rome (in vain many of the Cardinals protested), even on the churches from whence the Cardinals took their titles: St. Peter's, the Lateran, the Hospitals, and the convent of St. George were alone excepted. The Legates, the Prelates, the Mendicants were ordered to preach the Crusade with unwearied activity. They had new powers of absolution; they might admit as soldiers of Christ incendiaries, those excommunicated for refusing to pay tenths, sacrilegious persons, astrologers, those who had struck a clerk, or sold merchandise to Mohammedans, ecclesiastics under interdict, or under suspension, married clerks; those who, in violation of the canons, had practised law or physic. All attempts were made to maintain the Papal interests in Rome, and to excite revolt in the kingdom of Naples.[4]

Charles of Anjou had now declared himself Senator of Rome, and invested with the crown of Naples. He had been long collecting his forces for the conquest. But Italy might seem to refuse access to the stranger. The Ghibellines were in the ascendant in Lombardy. The Marquis Pallavicini and Buoso da Doara, with the Cremonese, watched the passes of the Alps. The fleets

---

[4] Martene. Compare Cherrier, iv. 79.

of Pisa and of Manfred swept the sea with eighty galleys; the mouth of the Tiber was stopped by a great dam of timber and stone. But courage and fortune favoured Charles: he boldly set sail from Marseilles with hardly more than twenty galleys and one thousand men-at-arms. A violent storm scattered the fleet of Pisa and Naples: he entered the Tiber, broke through all obstacles, and appeared at Rome at Pentecost, the time appointed for his inauguration as Senator. He chose for his abode the Pope's Lateran palace. That was an usurpation which the Pope could not endure: he sent a strong remonstrance against the presumption of the Senator of Rome, who had dared without permission to occupy the abode of the Pope: he was commanded to quit the palace and seek some more fitting residence. Yet even at this time Clement IV. insisted on dictating the terms on which Charles was to hold the kingdom of Naples, its reversion to the Papacy in default of heirs of his line, its absolute incompatibility with the Empire, the tribute of eight thousand crowns of gold, the homage and the white horse in token of fealty. Manfred attempted to provoke Charles to battle before the arrival of his main army; he advanced with a large force, many of them Saracens, to the neighbourhood of Rome. The prudence of the Pope restrained the impatience of Charles.*

Charles at Rome.

It was not till the end of the summer that the main army of Charles came down the pass of Mont Cenis into friendly Piedmont. It was splendidly provided, and boasted some of the noblest knights of France and Flanders. The Pope had absolved all those who had taken the cross for the Holy Land: equal hopes of

---

* Raynaldus, sub ann. 1265.

Heaven were attached to this new Crusade against Manfred, whom it was the policy to represent as more than half a Saracen. The Legate, Cardinal of S. Cecilia, had exacted a tenth from the French clergy. Robert of Bethune took the command; Guy of Beauvais, Bishop of Auxerre, was among the most distinguished warriors; there were Vendôsmes, Montmorencies, Mirepoixs, De Montforts, Sullys, De Beaumonts. The Ghibellines made a great show of resistance: the Carroccios of Pavia, Cremona, and Piacenza moved out as to a great battle. But the French army passed on, threatened Brescia; Milan and the Marquis of Montferrat ventured not to take their part openly, but supplied them with provisions. But through the treachery of the Ghibellines, bought, according to some writers of the time, by French gold, or intimidated by the great French force (which the Chronicles, perhaps faithfully recording the rumours of the day, represented as sixty thousand, forty thousand, thirty thousand strong) the allies of Manfred[1] finally stood aloof in sullen passiveness. The French reached the Po. They advanced still without serious encounter, and joined their master in Rome. Charles, though it was the depth of winter, allowed no long repose. He advanced to Ceperano, with the Legate, the Cardinal St. Angelo, preaching the Crusade on the way. Manfred prepared himself for a gallant resistance; but he had neither calculated on the treachery of some of his own subjects, nor on the impetuous valour of the French. The passage of the Garigliano was betrayed by the Count of Caserta. San Germano, in

Advance of the army.

In Rome.

In Naples.

---

[1] The annals of Modena give 5000 horse, 15,000 foot, 10,000 bowmen.— See the Chronicles in Muratori.

which he had secured a strong force and ample stores, was taken by assault. Manfred's courage was unshaken; he concentrated his army near Benevento, but he sent messengers to Charles to propose negotiations. "Tell the Sultan of Nocera that I will have neither peace nor treaty with him; I will send him to Hell, or he shall send me to Paradise!" Such was the reply of Charles of Anjou. The French army defiled into the plain before Benevento. Manfred is accused of rashness for venturing on a decisive battle. The French army were in want of money and of provisions; a protracted war might have worn them out. Manfred's nephew, Conrad of Antioch, was in the Abruzzi, Count Frederick in Calabria, and the Count of Ventimiglia in Sicily; but Manfred perhaps knew that nothing less than splendid success could hold in awe the wavering fidelity of his subjects. He drew up his army in three divisions. On the French side appeared, beside the three, a fourth. "Who are these?" inquired Manfred. "The Guelfs of Florence and the exiles from other cities." "Where are the Ghibellines, for whom I have done and hazarded so much?" The Germans and the Saracens fought with desperate valour. Manfred commanded the third army of the Barons of Apulia to move to the charge. Some, among them the great Chamberlain, hesitated, turned, fled.[a] Manfred plunged in his desperation into the midst of the fray, and fell unknown by an unknown hand. The body was found after three days and recognised by a boor, who threw it across an ass, and went shouting along, "Who will buy King Manfred?" He was struck down by one

Battle of Benevento, Feb. 6, 1266.

Death of Manfred.

---

[a] Dante brands the treason of the Apulians: this was the field
"ove fu bugiardo
Ciascun Pugliese."—*Inferno*, xxviii. 16.

of Manfred's Barons; the body was taken to King
Charles.ᵇ Charles summoned the Barons who were
prisoners, and demanded if it was indeed the body of
Manfred. Galvano Lancia looked on it, hid his face in
his hands, and burst into tears. The generous French
urged that it should receive honourable burial. "It
might be," said Charles, "were he not under excommunication." The body was hastily interred by the
bridge of Benevento: the warriors, French and Apulian,
cast each a stone, and a huge mound appeared,ⁱ like
those under which repose the heroes of ancient times.
But the Papal jealousy would not allow the Hohenstaufen to repose within the territory of the Church.
The Archbishop of Cosenza, by the command
of the Pope, ordered him to be torn up from Feb. 26.
his rude sepulchre. He was again buried in unconse-
crated ground, on the borders of the kingdom of Naples,
near the river Verde.ᵏ

So perished the noble Manfred, a poet like his father,
all accomplished as his father,ᵐ a man of consummate
courage and great ability. Naples could hardly have
had a more promising founder for a native dynasty.
But Naples was too near Rome; and the house of
Hohenstaufen had not yet fulfilled its destiny.

The first act of the triumphant army of the Cross,
under the Pope's ally, was the sacking of the Papal
city of Benevento, a general massacre of both sexes,

ᵇ Compare the letter of Charles announcing the victory of the Pope, before the body was found. Ricordano Malespini.

ⁱ — "L' ossa del corpo mio sarieno ancora
In co del ponte, presso a Benevento,
Sotto la guardia della grave mora;
Or le bagna la pioggia, e muove 'l
vento."

"Di fuor dal regno, quasi lungo 'l Verde
Ove le trasmutò a lume spento."
Dante, *Purgat*. III, 128.

ᵐ "Lo Re spesso la notte andava per Barletta, cantando Strambuotti e canzoni, che iva pigliando il fresco, e con esso ivano dei Musici Siciliani ch' erano gran Romanzatori."—Matteo Spinelli.

of all ages, violation of women, even of women dedicated to God: the churches did not escape the common profanation. Charles was King of Naples: the Capital yielded, Capua surrendered the vast treasures accumulated by Manfred. The King's officers were weighing these treasures. "What need of scales?" said Ugo di Balzo, a Provençal knight: he kicked the whole into three portions: "This is for my Lord the King, this for the Queen, this for your Knights." The whole of Apulia, Calabria, Sicily submitted to the Sovereign invested by the Pope.[o] But they soon began to appreciate the change, to which they had looked as a great deliverance, as the dawn of a golden age of peace and plenty. The French soldiers spread wanton devastation wherever they went, neither respecting property, nor the rights of men nor the honour of women. Naples was at first disposed to admire the magnificence of Charles and his Barons; but those who had reproved the luxuriousness of Frederick's or the ruder splendour of Manfred's court, found that of the Provençal King at least not more favourable to the higher morals.[o] Instead of being relieved from their heavy taxation, they were the prey of still more merciless exaction. King Charles seized the books and registers of the royal revenues in the hands of Gazzolino de Marra. Every royal privilege, subsidy, collection, or

Sack of Beneventa

Tyranny of the French.

---

[o] Clement writes to Cardinal Ottobuoni, Legate in England; "Carissimus in Christo filius E. (C.) Rex Siciliæ illustris tenet totum regnum, illius hominis pestilentis cadaver putidum, uxorem et liberos optinens et thesaurum."—MS., B. M., May 1266. The March, Florence, Pistoia, Sienna, Pisa, had returned to their allegiance. Messengers were come from Uberto Pallavicini and the Cremonese. There were hopes of Genoa.

[o] Muratori writes thus:—"Per altor la venuta de' Franzesi quella fu, che cominciò ad introdurre il lusso, e qualche cosa di peggio e fece mutar i costumi degl' Italiani."—Sub ann.

tax was enforced with more rigorous severity. New justiciaries, officers of customs, notaries, and revenue collectors sprung up in hosts, draining without restraint the impoverished people. The realm began too late to deplore its own versatility, to look back on the days of good King Manfred. Thus are these feelings expressed by a Guelfic historian: "O King Manfred, little did we know thee when alive! Now that thou art dead, we deplore thee in vain! Thou appearedst as a ravening wolf among the flocks of this kingdom; now fallen by our fickleness and inconstancy under the present government, after which we groaned, we find that thou wert a lamb. Now we know by bitter comparison how mild was thy rule. We thought it hard that part of our substance must be yielded into thy hands, now we find that all our substance and even our persons are the prey of the stranger."[p]

Clement IV. could not close his ears to these sad complaints. He had forced himself to remonstrate on the sack of Benevento; but throughout Italy the Guelfs rose again to power, Florence was in their hands, Pisa made supplication to the Pope to be released from excommunication. In Milan there was a Provençal governor, whose cruelties even surpassed Italian cruelties. Charles was manifestly aspiring to be supreme in Italy.[q]

The Pope.

But the Pope did not neglect more remote offences. The Cardinal of S. Sabina had not forgotten the contemptuous refusal of the Barons of England to accept his mediation.[r] Henry III. was too useful, too

England.

---

[p] Saba Malespina, iii. 16.
[q] See all the historians.
[r] Letter to the Queen, complaining of the insolence of the Barons, who had not permitted him to land in England when Legate.—MS., B. M., v. xii. p. 3.

profitable a vassal of the Roman See to be abandoned to his unruly subjects. Immediately on his accession the Pope had sent the Cardinal of S. Hadrian (Ottobuoni) as Legate, with the same ample powers with which himself had been invested. An interdict was laid upon the island if it refused to admit the Legate. If the Legate should not be permitted to land, he was to transmit inhibitions to the clergy, having equal force, inhibitions to allow no matrimonial rites to the rebels, or to communicate with them in any way whatever. He had the same authority to thrust his followers into dignities or benefices from which the rebellious clergy or those connected with the rebels were to be ejected. All sons of rebel Barons or Nobles, all nephews of rebel Churchmen were to be deprived of their parsonages or benefices, and declared incapable of holding them. No promotions were to be made to bishoprics or archbishoprics without express consent of the Holy See. It was admitted that many bishops were on the side of the Barons; no favour was to be shown to those of London, Worcester, Lincoln, or Ely; they were on no account to be released from excommunication. Tenths were to be levied for the Holy War. The Legate was to preach or cause to be preached a Crusade in England and even in Germany against the insurgent Barons.

---

* The bulls addressed to Ottobuoni are transcripts of those before addressed to the Cardinal S. Sabina, in the usual form, mutatis mutandis.—MS., B. M. They fill several pages.

* Ibid., dated Perugia, June 1, 1265, p. 119. Since he had excommunicated "nonnullos barones et fautores eorum, et inhabitatores Quinque Portuum," if any of them had obtained letters of absolution, "in aegritudine verâ aut simulatâ," unless they abandoned the party of Leicester they were to be as heathens and publicans.

* Ibid., same date.

* Ibid., same date.

* Ibid., some months later, Oct. 1265.

* Ibid., July 1. The Cistercians, Carthusians, Templars, Hospitallers, Teutonic Knights, Sisters of S. Clare, were alone exempt.

Louis of France was urged to take arms in defence of the common cause of monarchy against those rebels who were accused of a design to throw off altogether the kingly sway. Nothing less than a general league of Princes could put down those sons of wrath and of treason, the Barons of England.[a]

The Pope, as Cardinal Legate, had excommunicated Simon de Montfort, Roger Earl of Norfolk, Hugo the Chief Justiciary, the City of London, and the Cinque Ports; he had summoned four of the English Prelates before him at Boulogne, and ordered them to publish the excommunication in England. The excommunication had been taken from the unreluctant hands of the Bishops. The excommunicated had appealed to the Pope; the appeal was ratified in a convocation of the clergy. But the excommunication was solemnly confirmed at Perugia. "Nothing could be done unless that turbulent man of sin (Leicester) and all his race were plucked up out of the realm."[b] The new Cardinal Legate was urged to hasten to England to consummate his work.

Ere he had ceased to be Cardinal Legate, the Pope (Ugo Falcodi) had heard at Boulogne the fatal tidings of the battle of Lewes, the captivity of the King and of Prince Edward. Then after his accession had come the news of the escape of Prince Edward, and the revolt of the Earl of Gloucester from the Barons. The Pope wrote in triumph to the Prince,[c] urging him to make every effort to release his father from slavery; the excommunication was at once removed from the Earl of

---

[a] Ibid., Perugia, May 6, 1265, p. 75, &c.
[b] Epist. ad Card. S. Hadrian. "Nisi dictus vir pestilens cum totâ suâ progenie de regno Angliæ avellatur."—
July 19, 1265. At this time Manfred was advancing on Rome.
[c] To Prince Edward. The letter enters into some details.

Gloucester.[4] The tidings of the battle of Evesham, of the death of Simon Earl of Leicester, filled him with melancholy and joy.[e] Yet extraordinary as it may seem, Simon de Montfort, excommunicated by the Pope, to the Pope the Man of Sin, was the Saint and Martyr of popular love and worship;[f] he was equalled with Becket.[g] Poetry, Latin, English, French, celebrated, sanctified, canonised him. His miracles, in their number, wonderfulness, and in their attestations might have moved the jealousy of S. Francis or of Becket himself.[h] Prayers were addressed to him;[i] prayer was offered through his intercession.[k]

Victory of the King. The King's victory seemed complete, the Barons crushed, the liberties of England buried in the grave of Simon de Montfort. The Cardinal Legate crossed to England with the Queen. The Queen Eleanor was not the least odious of the foreigners who ruled the feeble mind of the King: to her influence had been attributed the unjust, ill-considered award *The Legate Oct. 29, 1265.* of Louis of France. The Legate assumed a kind of dictatorial authority.[m] In the church of Westminster, the splendid foundation of Henry III. (under whose shadow I wrote these lines), he appeared in his

---

[d] Ibid., p. 191.

[e] " Læta nobis et tristia enarrastis."—Clement IV., Epist. L 89.

[f] Rishanger says that all ranks heard of his death with the most profound sorrow, " præcipue religiosi, qui partibus illis favebant."—Chronic. p. 48. Compare also Lords' Report on Dignity of a Peer. In the Parliament summoned after the battle of Lewes were 23 Barons, 122 Ecclesiastics.—pp. 145-6.

[g] See in Wright's Political Songs that on the battle of Lewes. After his death we read in another :—

" Mors par sa mort, la cueste Monfort
Conquist la victoire,
Comme li Martyr de Canterbyr
Finist sa vie " (p. 129);

and the long Latin poem, p. 71.

[h] See the " Miracula," published by Mr. Halliwell at the end of Rishanger, Camden Society, 1840.

[i] " Salve Simon Monteforti,
Totius flos militiæ,
Duras pœnas passus mortis,
Protector gentis Angliæ."

[k] " Ora pro nobis, Beate Simon, ut digni simus promissionibus Christi."—Ibid. p. 109.

[m] See the Papal Bulls, gratulatory

full scarlet pontifical robes, recited the act of excommunication passed on Simon de Montfort and all his adherents, abrogated all the oaths sworn by the King, declared null and void all the constitutions and provisions of the realm." At Northampton he held a council, and by name confirmed the excommunication of the Prelates who had made common cause with the Barons, Winchester, Worcester, London, Chichester.° The Pope, while he made large grants of the tenths, and triumphed in the King's triumph, in more Christian spirit enjoined him to use his victory with mercy and moderation.º If any mercy was shown to the persons (and this is doubtful, for all the bravest and most formidable had perished in the field), there was none to their estates. The obsequious Parliament passed a sweeping sentence of confiscation on the lands of all who had joined or favoured De Montfort. The Legate was not less severe against the obnoxious clergy.' There was a wide and general ejection of all who had been or were suspected of having been on the proscribed side. The Pope is again busy in reaping for his own colleagues and followers some grains of the golden harvest. Demands are made, at first modest for prebends, for pensions in favour of Roman ecclesiastics.º He is compelled by the poverty of the Car-

---

to the King and Prince, and admonitory to the Barons to return to the King's allegiance.—Rymer, I. 817, 819.

ª Wilkes, 72.   º Rishanger, p. 47.

ᵇ Rymer, loc. cit.

ᶜ "Qui non solum et post terras et possessiones occisorum in bello et captivorum necessaria etiam bona tam spiritualia quam temporalia religiosorum violavere, nulli parcentes ordini, dignitati, vel ecclesiasticæ libertati . . .

infinitam pecuniam ab eis immisericorditer extorserunt, abbates et quascunque domos religiosas tantæ suppeditationi mancipando quod vix non nunquam poterunt respirare."—Rishanger, p. 48.

ᵍ MS. B. M., p. 202. Assignment of 260 marks on England to the Bishop of Ostia and Velletri, "propter egestatem." One or two benefices to be obtained in England to make up dinals to become more pressing, more exorbitant in his exactions.

During the next year there is a formidable reaction; a wide and profound dissatisfaction had spread through the realm. The discontented are defending themselves with desperate resolution in the isle of Ely. Rome is alarmed by the gloomy news from England: the Pope is trembling for the lives of the King, the Queen, and the Prince; he is trembling for the irrecoverable loss of that noble fief of the See of Rome.* The affrighted Cardinal is disposed to abandon his hopeless mission. The Pope reproves him for his cowardice, but leaves it to his discretion whether he will remain or not in the contumacious and ungrateful island.

Reaction. A.D. 1264.

The King's cause again prospers: at Christmas the King and the Legate are seen dining together in public at Westminster. The indignant people remark that the seat of honour, the first service of all the dishes are reserved to the Legate; the King sits lower, and partakes of the best fare, but after the Legate. At St. Edmondsbury the ecclesiastics resisted the demand not only of the tenths, but of thirty thousand marks more,

---

this sum. "In eundem modum pro domino veterrano (Velletri) cxxxvi. marks." He intends to write, on account of the general poverty of the Cardinals, not only "pro duobus, pro pluribus, licet non in tanta summa sed minore."—Perugia, Oct. 26, 1265, p. 117. "Importabilis fratrum persuasio, quae fonte liberalitatis ipsius qui ad Romanam Ecclesiam de mundi diversis partibus fluere consuevit, pæne, vel quasi penitus arefacto, crescit, nec cessat crescere."—P. 223.

* "Nihil aliud esset penitus, nisi totum everti negotium, Regem, Reginam et liberos tradi morti, et Ecclesiæ Romanæ feodum tam nobile sine spe qualibet recuperationis amitti."—MS., B. M., p. 235.

† Ibid., May 16, 1266.

" "Legato in sedili regis collocato, singulisque ferculis eorum eo primitus appositis, et postremo coram rege, unde murmurabant multi in aulâ regis."—Rishanger, p. 59.

claimed by the Pope as arrears of the King's debt for the subjugation of Naples.[x]

About a year and a half after, at the close of the Pontificate of Clement IV., the Cardinal Legate holds a Council of the Church of England and Ireland in the cathedral of St. Paul. The famous constitutions of Ottobuoni, the completion and confirmation of those of Cardinal Otho, are passed, which were held for some time as the canon law of England.[y] Of these constitutions some must be noticed, as giving a view of the religion of the times. I. The absolute exemption of the property of the Church from all taxation by the state, the obedience of the laity to the clergy, were asserted in the fullest and most naked simplicity.[z] II. One was directed against the clergy bearing arms. Some of the clergy are described (awful wickedness!) as little better than robber chieftains.[a] It was forgotten that but a few years before the Archbishop of Canterbury had been in arms with the Archbishop of Lyons before Turin; that French Bishops were in the army of Charles of Anjou, the army blessed, sanctified by the Pope! III. Pluralities were generally condemned:[b] pluralities without Papal dispensations

Margin notes: Council to St. Paul's. Constitutions of Ottobuoni.

---

[x] Rishanger, p. 61.

[y] April 21, 1268. Wilkins' Concilia. It has been suggested to me that the author of these constitutions may have been no less than Benedetto Gaetani, afterwards Boniface VIII. He was the companion and counsellor of Ottobuoni in England.

[z] "Nec alicui liceat censum ponere super ecclesiam Dei. Admoneantur Reges et principes et omnes qui in potestate sunt, ut cum magnâ humilitate archepiscopis omnibusque aliis episcopis obediant."

[a] "In his ergo tam horrendis sceleribus clericos debacchantes"—they had been described as joining bands of robbers—"prosequimur excommunicationis, deprivatione."—Art. viii.

[b] John Mansel is described (Rishanger, p. 12) as "multarum in Angliâ rector ecclesiarum et possessor reddituum quorum non erat numerus, ita quod ditior clericus eo non in orbe videretur." Mr. Halliwell quotes the Chron. Mailros, as giving him 700 livings, bringing in 18,000 marks. I cannot find the passage.

altogether proscribed.° IV. There was a strong canon against the married clergy: not merely were many clergy married,⁴ but the usage existed to a great extent of the transmission of benefices from father to son, and these benefices were not seldom defended by violence and force of arms.°

We return to Italy, with a glance at Spain, and the earlier years of Clement's Pontificate. The triumphs of James, the King of Arragon, over the Saracens of Spain, and the capture of Murcia, called forth the triumphant gratulations of the Pope. But James of Arragon was not to be indulged in weaknesses unbecoming a Christian warrior. The Pope summoned him to break the chains in which he was fettered by a

[margin note: James of Arragon]

° Henry de Wingham is a good example of what might be and was done by Papal dispensations (MS., B. M., ix. p. 314). Wingham has licence to hold the deanery of St. Martin's-le-Grand, the chancellorship of Exeter, a prebend of Salisbury, so *universos alios personatus, etiam alia beneficia* (dated Anagni, July 23, 1259). A month after De Wingham (of whom Paris speaks as a disinterested man, *sub ann.* 1257) is bishop elect of London; he petitions to hold all these benefices with London for five years. He was also Lord Chancellor. The nephew of this poor man, holding only two livings, has Papal licence to hold two more.—P. 411, Anagni, Aug. 28, 1259.

⁴ "Nisi clerici et maxime qui in sacris ordinibus constituti, qui in domibus suis detinent publicè concubinas."—Art. viii.

° The MSS., B. M., are full of notices of married clergy in England. Letter to the Archbishop of York (xi. 124).

Sons succeeded to their fathers' benefices, "quidam in ecclesiis, in quibus patres ministrarint eorum, se immediatè patribus ejus substituti, tanquam jure hereditario possidere sanctuarium Dei." The same in diocese of Lincoln, p. 132; Worcester, p. 136; Carlisle, p. 177. Complaints to Bishop of Salisbury of priests who have "focariæ." To Bishop of Coventry, of their holding these benefices "violenter et armatâ manu," Dec. 21, 1235. So also to Bishop of Norwich, June 12, 1240; Winchester, p. 5 and 35, 1245. The Synod of Exeter (Wilkins, Concilia, c. xviii. p. 142) complains of clerks on their deathbeds providing for their concubines and children out of the ecclesiastical revenues, "præsumptione tam damnatâ in extremis laborantes, et de infernis minimè cogitantes in suis ultimis voluntatibus . . . . bona ecclesiæ concubinis relinquere non formidant." These wills were declared illegal.

beautiful mistress, and to return to his lawful wife: he urged him to imitate the holy example of Louis of France. King James pleaded that his wife was a leper, and demanded the dissolution of the marriage. "Thinkest thou," rejoined the Pope, "that if all the Queens of the earth were lepers, we would allow Kings to join in adulterous commerce with other women? Better that all the royal houses should wither root and branch." He put the obedience of the King of Arragon to another test: he ordered him inexorably to expel all Mussulmen from his dominions, to depose all the Jews from the high places which they held in this as in many of the Spanish kingdoms.[f]

In less than two years after the conquest of Naples, the insupportable tyranny of the French under Charles of Anjou, and the resentment of the Ghibellines throughout Italy, had wrought up a spirit of wide-spread revolt. The young Conradin could alone deliver Sicily from the foreign yoke, check the revengeful superiority of the Guelfs, and restore the now lamented house of Hohenstaufen. Many secret messages were sent from Tuscany and Lombardy. Galvano and Frederick di Lancia, and the two chiefs of the house of Capece, whose lives had been excepted from the general proscription of Manfred's partisans, found their way to Germany. They called on Conradin to assert his hereditary rights; to appear as a deliverer from foreign oppression. The youth, not yet sixteen, listened with too eager avidity. At the head of four thousand German troops he crossed the Alps, and held his court at Verona.

Naples. Conradin. A.D. 1267.

End of 1267.

Pope Clement heard the intelligence with dismay.

---

[f] Clement Epist. Raynaldus, sub ann.

He instantly cited the presumptuous boy, who had dared to claim a kingdom granted away by the See of Rome, to answer before his liege lord at Viterbo. There, in the Cathedral of Viterbo, in May, and on the festival of St. Peter and St. Paul, he proclaimed his excommunication. He wrote to Florence to warn the Republic of "the young serpent which had sprung up from the blood of the old." He wrote to Ottocar, King of Bohemia, to make a diversion by attacking the Swabian possessions of Conradin. He declared Conradin deposed from the kingdom of Jerusalem. At the same time he wrote to Charles of Anjou, in terms which showed his own consciousness that the danger was in the tyranny and in the hatred of Charles rather than in the strength or popularity of Conradin. He entreated him "to moderate the horrible exactions enforced under the royal seal;[a] to listen to the petitions of his people; to put some check on the wasteful extravagance of his court; to keep a balance of his receipts and expenditure; to place on the seat of justice men of incorruptible integrity, with ample salaries, so as to be superior to bribery; not to permit unnecessary appeals to the King; to avoid all vexatious inquisitions; not to usurp the guardianship of orphans; to punish all attempts to corrupt magistrates; not to follow the baleful example of his predecessor in encroaching on the rights of the Church."[b] Yet this King, who needed these sage admonitions as to the administration of his kingdom, was raised at this very juncture by the Pope to the extraordinary office now vacant—an office the commanding title of which was

A.D. 1268.

---

[a] "Sigillo tuo legem impera, ut tollatur infamia de horrendis exactionibus eo nomine factis," et seqq. Clem. Ep.

[b] See the letter of Pope Clement in Martene, and in Raynaldus, sub ann.

ill-suited to the man and to the times—that of Peacemaker,¹ or Conservator of the Peace throughout Tuscany and all the provinces subject to the Roman empire; in other words, to keep down the Ghibellines, and by force of arms to compel them to lay down their arms.ᵏ King Alfonso of Castile heard with jealousy of this new title, which sounded as though Charles of Anjou was usurping the prerogative of the Empire, if not intending to supplant both himself and his competitor, Richard of Cornwall. The Pope was compelled at once to soothe and to alarm the Spaniard; to allay his fears as to any designs of Charles upon the Empire, not without some significant hint that the coronation by the Archbishop of Cologne was indispensable for a just title to the Empire; and the Archbishop of Cologne had crowned Richard. Alfonso was awed into silence, if not satisfied.ᵐ

But, not at the instigation, nor with any encouragement from the King of Castile, two of his brothers had become the most dangerous adversaries of the Pope. Henry and Frederick of Castile had been driven from their native land,ⁿ had taken to a wild adventurous life,

---

¹ "Paciarium non partiarium."
ᵏ There is a curious letter from the Pope to the Cardinal S. Hadrian. MS., B. M. When he had created Charles paciarius, "opponentibus Senensibus, Pisanis et pluribus Ghibellinis." The Romans, under the Senator, Henry of Castile, were in league with the Ghibellines. Henry had taken some cities, and seized in Rome the brothers Napoleon and Matthee Orsini, Angelo Malebranca, John Savelli, Peter Stefaneschi, Richard Annibalrechi, some of whom he had sent by night prisoners to Monticelli. "We would, as far as possible, war with the Romans: Conradin is in Verona with all Lombardy, except Pavia, and the march of Treviso. Sicily is in full revolt under Frederick of Castile." "God's will be done," concludes the devout Pope.—Viterbo, Nov. 23, 1267.

ᵐ Clement, Epist.
ⁿ They seem to have been at the head of a constitutional opposition against their brother Alfonso, who aspired to rule without the Cortes.

and found hospitality at the court of the King of Tunis. It was said that they had adopted at least Mohammedan manners, attended Mohammedan rites, and more than half embraced the Mohammedan creed.* They returned to Europe. Frederick landed in Sicily, where some short time after he raised the standard of Conradin. Henry went on to Italy; he was received by his cousin, Charles of Anjou, who bestowed on him sixty thousand crowns. Henry had hopes, fostered by the Papal Court, if not by the Pope, of obtaining the investiture of Sardinia, which the Pope would fain wrest from the rule of Ghibelline Pisa. But Charles of Anjou grew jealous of Henry of Castile; he too had pretensions on Sardinia; it was withdrawn from the grasp of Henry; and the Castilian was brooding in dissatisfaction and disappointment, when the opportunity of revenge arose. The people of Rome were looking abroad for a Senator. Charles had surrendered or forfeited his office when he became King of Naples. A short lived rule of two concurrent Senators had increased the immitigable feud. Angelo Capucio was a noble Roman, still attached to the fallen fortunes of Manfred. By his influence, notwithstanding the repugnance of the rest of the nobles, and strong opposition from some of the Cardinals, Henry of Castile was chosen Senator of Rome. He commenced his rule with some of those acts of stern equity which ever overawed and captivated the Roman people. Clement too late began to suspend his design of investing Charles of Anjou with the throne of Sardinia, to which

<small>Henry of Castile.</small>

---

* Mariana describes Henry as "In rebus bellicis potens et strenuus, et nimium callidus, sed sceleratissimus et in fidei catholicæ cultu non diligens prosecutor." For private reasons for the hatred of Henry and Charles, see Hispan. Illustrat. ii. p. 647; Amari; Vespro Siciliano, ciii. p. 30.

Henry might again aspire. But the hatred of Charles was deep in Henry's heart; he openly displayed the banner of Conradin. Galvano Lancia, the kinsman and most active partisan of Manfred, hastened to Rome; and the Pope heard with indignation that the Swabian standard was waving from the hallowed Lateran, where Lancia had taken up his quarters, and was parading his forces before it.[p] The censures of the Pontiff addressed to the authorities of Rome made no impression. The Senator summoned the people to the Capitol; his armed bands were in readiness; he seized two of the Orsini, and sent them prisoners to the strong castle of Monticelli, near Tivoli; two of the Savelli were cast into the dungeons under the Capitol, many others into different prisons; Henry of Castile took possession of St. Peter's and of the Papal palaces.[q]

Rome for Conradin.

The few German troops with which Conradin had crossed the Alps fell off for want of pay:[r] but the Ghibelline interest, the nobler feelings, awakened in favour of the gallant boy thus cruelly deprived of his inheritance, and the growing hatred of the French, soon gathered an army around him. He set out from faithful Verona; he was received in Pavia, in Pisa, in Sienna, as the champion of Ghibellinism; as the lawful King of Sicily.[s] In Apulia,

Movements of Conradin. A.D. 1268.

---

[p] "Ac loca, specialiter Lateranl ad quæ ingredienda viri etiam justi vix digni sunt habiti, pompis lascivientibus circuire, ac ibidem hospitium accipere non expavit."—Lib. Pontif. quoted in Raynald. 1267.

[q] See note above from MS., D. M.

[r] It is curious to observe (in Böhmer's Register), of the few acts of Conradin in Italy, how large a part are on the pawning (Verpfändung) of estates or rights for sums of money.— p. 287.

[s] In Pavia, March 22; in Pisa, April 4; in Sienna, July 7; in Rome, July 7 or August 11. In Rome he is said to have had 5000 German knights, Henry of Castile 800 Spaniards.

the Saracens of Lucera were in arms; in Sicily, Frederick of Castile, with the Saracens and some of Manfred's partisans, who had taken refuge in Africa and now returned. The island was in full revolt; the Lieutenant of Charles was defeated; except Messina, Palermo, and Syracuse, Sicily was in the power of Conradin. Already, in his agony of apprehension, the Pope, finding that Charles was still in Tuscany, pressing his advantages in favour of the Guelfs of Florence, hastily summoned him to return to Naples. "Why do we write to thee as King, while thou seemest utterly to disregard thy kingdom? It is without a head, exposed to the Saracens and to the traitorous Christians; already exhausted by your robberies, it is now plundered by others. The locust eats what the cankerworm has left. Spoilers will not be wanting, so long as its defender is away. If you love the kingdom, think not that the Church will incur the toil and cost of conquering it anew; you may return to your Countship, and, content with the vain name of king, await the issue of the contest. Perhaps, in reliance on your merits, you expect a miracle to be wrought in your favour; that God will act in your behalf, while you thus follow your own counsels, and despise those of others. I had resolved not to write to thee on this affair: my venerable brother, Rudolph, Bishop of Alba, has prevailed on me to send you these few last words."[1]

Charles obeyed, and returned in all haste to Naples; he formed the siege of Lucera, the stronghold of his most dangerous foes, the Saracens. Conradin advanced towards Rome; he marched under the walls of Viterbo, intending perhaps to insult or intimi-

Conradin advances to Rome.

---

[1] Clement, Epist. apud Raynald. A.D. 1269 p. 233.

date the Pope, who had a strong garrison in the city.
The affrighted Cardinals thronged around the Pope,
who was at prayer. "Fear not," he said; "they will
be scattered like smoke." He even ascended the walls,
beneath which Conradin and his young and faithful
friend Frederick of Austria were prancing on their
stately coursers. "Behold the victims for the sacrifice."[a]

The dark vaticinations of the Pope, though sadly
verified by the event (perhaps but the echo of the
event), if bruited abroad in Rome, had no more effect
than the ecclesiastical thunders which at every onward
step Clement had hurled with reiterated solemnity at
the head of Conradin. Notwithstanding these excommunications, the Romans welcomed with the loudest
acclamations Conradin, called by the Pope "the accursed branch of an accursed stem, the manifest enemy
of the Church:" "Rome had calmly seen that son of
malediction, Galvano Lancia, who had so long walked
the broad road to perdition, from whose approach they
should have shrunk with scorn, displaying the banner
of Conradin from the Lateran." It was an event as
yet unheard, which disturbed the soul of the Pontiff,
that although occasional discords, and even the scandal
of wars, had taken place between the Pope and his
City, now their fidelity should revolt to the persecutor
of the Church; that Rome should incur the guilt of
matricide.[x] Yet not the less did the Senator and
Rome welcome the young Swabian. Henry the Senator
marched at the head of the Roman forces in Conradin's
army, having first plundered the churches and monasteries. The Pope heard with deeper resentment that

[a] Raynald. c. xiii. Ficher.   [x] Apud Raynald, A.D. 1269.

the Lateran, the churches of St. Paul, St. Basil on the Aventine, Santa Sabina, and other convents, had been obliged to surrender their treasures, which were expended upon the army of the excommunicate.[y]

But the destiny which hovered over the house of Hohenstaufen had not yet exhausted its vials of wrath. At the battle of Tagliacozzo, the French for once condescended to depend not on their impetuous valour alone, but on prudence, military skill, and a reserve held by the aged Alard de St. Valery, a French knight, just returned from that school of war, Palestine. St. Valery's eight hundred men retrieved the lost battle. Conradin, Frederick of Austria, Henry of Castile, were in the hands of the remorseless conqueror. Conradin had almost bribed John Frangipani, Lord of Astura, to lend him a bark to escape. The Frangipani sold him for large estates in the princedom of Benevento.[z]

Battle of Tagliacozzo.

Christendom heard with horror that the royal brother of St. Louis, that the champion of the Church, after a mock trial, by the sentence of one judge, Robert da Lavena—after an unanswerable pleading by Guido de Suzaria, a famous jurist—had condemned the last heir of the Swabian house—a rival king, who had fought gallantly for his hereditary throne—to be executed as a felon and a rebel on a public scaffold. So little did Conradin dread his fate, that when his doom was announced, he was playing at

Execution of Conradin.

---

[y] Apud Raynald. A.D. 1269.

[z] "En 1256, quatre ans après les Vêpres Siciliennes, un amiral de Jacques d'Arragon emporta Astora, qu'il réduisit en cendres. Les biens des Frangipani furent ravagés; Jacob, le fils de Jean, périt dans le combat. Sa postérité s'éteignit, et, de cette branche, dont le blason était taché du sang royal, il ne reste qu'un souvenir de déshonneur." Astura was near the spot where Cicero was killed.—Cherrier, iv. p. 212.

chess with Frederick of Austria. "Slave," said Conradin to Robert of Bari, who read the fatal sentence, "do you dare to condemn as a criminal the son and heir of kings? Knows not your master that he is my equal, not my judge?" He added, "I am a mortal, and must die; yet ask the kings of the earth if a prince be criminal for seeking to win back the heritage of his ancestors. But if there be no pardon for me, spare, at least, my faithful companions; or if they must die, strike me first, that I may not behold their death."[a] They died devoutly, nobly. Every circumstance aggravated the abhorrence: it was said—perhaps it was the invention of that abhorrence—that Robert of Flanders, the brother of Charles, struck dead the judge who had presumed to read the iniquitous sentence.[b] When Conradin knelt, with uplifted hands, awaiting the blow of the executioner, he uttered these last words—"O my mother! how deep will be thy sorrow at the news of this day!"[c] Even the followers of Charles could hardly restrain their pity and indignation. With Conradin died his young and valiant friend, Frederick of Austria, the two Lancias, two of the noble house of Donaticcio of Pisa. The inexorable Charles would not permit them to be buried in consecrated ground.

The Pope himself was accused as having counselled this atrocious act. One of those sentences, which from its pregnant brevity cleaves to the remembrance, lived

---

[a] Bartholomeo di Neocastro apud Muratori, p. 1027.

[b] There is evidence, it appears, that this judge, or prothonotary, was alive some years after.

[c] "Ad cœlum jungebat palmas, mortemque inevitabilem patienter expectans, suum Domino spiritum commendabat: nec divertebat caput, sed exhibebat se quasi victimam et cruoris traces ictus in patientiâ expectabat."—Malespina apud Muratori, viii. 851.

long in the memory of the Ghibellines: "The life of Conradin is the death of Charles, the death of Conradin the life of Charles." But to have given such advice, Clement must have belied his own nature, his own previous conduct, as well as his religion. Throughout he had been convinced of the impolicy, and was doubtless moved with inward remorse at the cruelties of Charles of Anjou. Clement had tried to mitigate the tyranny of the King. Even the colder assent, at least the evasive refusal to interfere on the side of mercy—"It becomes not the Pope to counsel the death of any one," is hardly in the character of Clement IV.[d] There is another, somewhat legendary, story. Ambrose of Sienna, afterwards a Saint, presented himself on the first news of the capture of Conradin before the Pope; he dwelt on the parable of the prodigal son, received with mercy into his father's house. "Ambrose," said the Pope, "I would have mercy, not sacrifice." He turned to the Cardinals, "It is not the monk that speaks, it is the Spirit of the Most High."[e]

But if he was responsible only for not putting forth the full Papal authority to command an act of wisdom as of compassion, Clement himself was soon called to answer before a higher tribunal. On the 29th October the head of Conradin fell on the scaffold; on the 29th November died Pope Clement IV. It is his praise that he did not exalt his kindred—that he left in obscurity the husbands of his daughters.[f] But the wonder be-

---

[d] Compare the fair and honest Tillemont, Vie de Saint Louis, vi. 129. Poor Conradin had said in one of his proclamations of Clement's hostility, "Clemens cujus nomen ab effectu non modicè distat."—B. Mussum Chronicon, p. 273.

[e] Vit. S. Ambrosii Senen. apud Bollandistas, c. iii.

[f] "Nec invenitur exaltâsse parentes,

trayed by this praise shows at once how Christendom had already been offended; it was prophetic of the stronger offence which nepotism would hereafter entail upon the Papal See.

---

totus Deo dicatus."— Ptolem. Luc. xxxviii. Tillemont has collected the passages (and they are many) to the praise of Clement IV. Tillemont is not perhaps less inclined to admire him because he was a Frenchman.—Vie de St. Louis, iv. p. 350 et seq.

CHAPTER IV.

Gregory X. and his Successors.

AFTER the death of Clement IV. there was a vacancy of more than two years in the Pontificate. The cause of this dissension among the fifteen Cardinals[a] nowhere transpires: it may have been personal jealousy, where there was no prelate of acknowledged superiority to demand the general suffrage. The French Cardinals may have been ambitious, under the dominant influence of the victorious Charles of Anjou, to continue the line of French Pontiffs: the Italians, both from their Italian patriotism and their jealousy of the power of Charles, may have stubbornly resisted such promotion. During this vacancy, Charles of Anjou was revenging himself with his characteristic barbarity on his rebellious kingdom, compressing with an iron hand the hatred of his subjects, which was slowly and sullenly brooding into desperation. He was thus unknowingly preparing his own fall by the terrible reaction of the Sicilian Vespers. He was becoming in influence, manifestly aspiring to be, through the triumphant Guelfic factions, the real master of the whole of Italy.

At this period was promulgated an Edict, before briefly alluded to,[b] apparently unobserved, but which,

---

[a] Ciacconius gives 17—5 or 6 French, 4 Romans.—p. 178.

[b] See back, page 319. Ordonnances des Rois, i. 97, March, 1268. Sis- mondi, viii. p. 104. I cannot see the force of the objection to the authenticity of the Ordinance, to which Mr. Hallam seems to give some weight.

nevertheless, in the hands of the great lawyers, who were now establishing in the minds of men, especially in France, a rival authority to that of the clergy, became a great Charter of Independence to the Gallican Church. The Pragmatic Sanction, limiting the interference of the court of Rome in the elections of the clergy, and directly denying its right of ecclesiastical taxation, being issued by the most religious of Kings, by a King a canonised Saint, seemed so incongruous and embarrassing, that desperate attempts have been made to question its authenticity: Louis IX. might seem, in his servile time, himself servilely religious, to be suddenly taking the lofty tone of Charlemagne. But it was this high religiousness of Louis which suggested, and which enabled him to promulgate this charter of liberty: as he intended none, so he might disguise even to himself the latent, rather than avowed hostility to the power of Rome. Among the dearest objects to the heart of Louis was the reformation of the clergy; that reformation not aiming at the depression, but tending to the immeasurable exaltation of their power, by grounding it on their piety and holiness. It is to this end that he asserts the absolute power of jurisdiction in the clergy, the rights of patrons, the right of free elections in the cathedrals and other

Pragmatic Sanction.

---

that St. Louis had not any previous difference with the See of Rome. The right of patronage seems to have been a standing cause of quarrel throughout Christendom, as we have seen in England. See, too, in Tillemont, iv. p. 408-412—the king (Louis) asserting his rights of patronage to the prebends of Rheims and the archdeaconry of Sens against the Pope. Tillemont does not doubt its authenticity, and refers to these disputes as a possible cause. See also the strange account of John of Canterbury, who paid 10,000 livres Tournois for confirmation in the Archbishopric of Rheims. John had expended it for the honour of his Holiness and the Roman court. The Pope blushed at this great expense for his honour. — p. 410. Clement, Epist. p. 308.

churches. The Edict was issued in the name of "Louis by the grace of God, King of the French. To ensure the tranquil and wholesome state of the Church in our realm; to increase the worship of God, in order to promote the salvation of the souls of the faithful in Christ; to obtain for ourselves the grace and succour of Almighty God, to whose dominion and protection our realm has been ever subject, as we trust it will ever be, we enact and ordain by this edict, maturely considered and of perpetual observance :—

"I. That the prelates, patrons, and ordinary collators to benefices in the churches of our realm, have full enjoyment of their rights, and that the jurisdiction of each be wholly preserved.

"II. That the cathedral and other churches of our realm have full freedom of election in every point and particular.

"III. We will and ordain that the pestilential crime of simony, which undermines the Church, be for ever banished from our realm.

"IV. We will and ordain in like manner that promotions, collations, provisions and dispositions of the prelacies, the dignities, the benefices, of what sort soever, and of the ecclesiastical offices of our realm, be according to the disposition, ordinance, and determination of the common law, the sacred Councils of the Church of God, and the ancient institutions of the Holy Fathers.

"V. We will that no one may raise or collect in any manner exactions or assessments of money, which have been imposed by the court of Rome, by which our realm has been miserably impoverished, or which hereafter shall be imposed, unless the cause be reasonable, pious, most urgent, of inevitable necessity, and recognised by our express and spontaneous consent, and by that of the Church of our realm.

"VI. By these presents we renew, approve, and confirm the liberties, franchises, immunities, prerogatives, rights, privileges, granted by the Kings our predecessors of pious memory, and by ourselves to all churches, monasteries, holy places, religious men and ecclesiastics in our realm."

This Edict appeared either during the last year of Clement IV., when the Pope absolutely depended on the protection of Charles of Anjou against the reviving Ghibellinism under Conradin, and he might be reduced to take refuge under the tutelage of Louis; or during the vacancy in the Pontificate. In either case it would have been dangerous, injurious, it would have been resented by the common voice of Christendom, if the acts of Louis had been arraigned, or even protested against, as impious aggressions on the rights of Rome. The Edict itself was profoundly religious, even submissive in its tone; at all events, the assertion of the supremacy, of the ultimate right of judgement in the temporal power, was very different coming from Louis of France than from Frederick II., or any of his race. Louis was almost Pope in the public mind; his piety, his munificence, his devotion to the Crusade, in which he was again about to embark, his profound deference in general to the clergy and to the Pope himself, which had almost already arrayed him in worshipped sanctity, either allayed the jealousy of the Roman See, or made it imprudent to betray such jealousy. Hence it was that neither at the time of its publication, nor subsequently, did it provoke any counter protestation; it had already taken its place among the Ordinances of the realm, before its latent powers were discovered, denounced, condemned. Then, seized on by the Parliaments, defended, interpreted, extended by the legists, strengthened by the memorable decree of the *Appeal against abuses*, it became the barrier against which the encroachments of the ecclesiastical power were destined to break; nor was it swept away till a stronger barrier had arisen in the unlimited power of the French crown.

During this vacancy in the Pontificate, St. Louis closed his holy life in the most ignoble, and not the least disastrous of the crusades, into Africa. It was the last, except the one desperate (in some degree brilliant) struggle, which was even now about to take place under our Prince Edward, for the narrow remnant of the Holy Land. Again the beauty of the passive virtues of Louis, his death, with all the submissive quietness of a martyr, blinded mankind to his utter incompetency to conduct a great army, and to the waste of noble blood; the Saint in life assumed in the estimation of mankind the crown of martyrdom.[e] Nothing was wanting but his canonisation; and canonisation could add no reverence to the name of St. Louis.

Year after year had passed, and still the stubborn fifteen Cardinals persisted in their feud; still Christendom was without a Pontiff; and might discover (at least the dangerous question might arise) the fatal secret that a supreme Pontiff was not necessary to Christendom. They withstood the bitter mockery of one of their brethren, the Bishop of Porto, that it were well to remove the roof of their chamber, that the Holy Ghost might descend upon them. The Franciscans seem to have been astonished that the

---

[e] Joinville. Tillemont has collected all the striking circumstances of the death of St. Louis.—Vol. v. p. 169.

virtues and learning of the pride of their order, S. Bonaventura, did not command the general homage. They fabled, at least the annalist of the Church declares it a fable, that Bonaventura would not condescend to the proffered dignity.[a] At length the Cardinals determined to delegate to six of their members the full power of the conclave.

The wisdom or felicity of their choice might, if ever, justify the belief in a superior overruling counsel. It fell upon one, towards whom it is difficult to conceive how their thoughts were directed, a man neither Cardinal nor Prelate, of no higher rank than Archdeacon of Liège, and dispossessed of his Archdeaconry by the unjust jealousy of his bishop; upon one now absent in the Holy Land on a pilgrimage. Gregory X., such was the name he assumed, was of a noble house, the Visconti of Piacenza, but having early left his country, was not committed to either of the great Italian factions: he was unembarrassed with family ties; he was an Italian, but not a Roman, not therefore an object of jealousy and hatred to rival houses among that fierce baronage. He had been a canon of Lyons, but was by no means implicated with French interests. One great religious passion possessed his soul. The Holy Land, with its afflictions and disasters, its ineffaceable sanctity, had sunk into the depth of his affections; the interests of that land were his highest duties. It was to this end that Gregory X. devoted himself with all the energy of a commanding mind, or rather to a preparatory object, perhaps greater, at all events indispensable to that end. It was in order to organise a Crusade, more powerful than any former Crusade, that he aspired

*margin:* Gregory X.

---

[a] Raynald. sub ann.

to pacify, that he succeeded for a time in pacifying, Western Christendom. This greatest of pontifical acts, but this alone, Gregory X. was permitted to achieve.

The reception of this comparatively obscure ecclesiastic, thus suddenly raised to the chair of St. Peter, might encourage his most holy hopes. He landed at Brundusium, was escorted by King Charles to Capua, and from thence, passing by Rome, to Viterbo, where the Cardinals met him with reverential unanimity. He was crowned at Rome with an elaborate ceremonial, published by himself as the future code, according to which the Roman Pontiffs were to be elected, inaugurated, invested: the most minute particulars of dress were arranged, and the whole course of processional service.* Gregory X. took up his residence at Orvieto.

<small>Inauguration. Jan. 31, 1272.</small>

<small>March 27, 1272.</small>

Gregory had hardly ascended the Pontifical throne, when he determined to hold a great Œcumenic Council. That it might be a Council worthy of the title, he summoned it for two years later. The pacification of Christendom was the immediate, the reconquest of the Holy Land the remote, object of this great diet of Christendom. The place of the Council was debated with grave prudence. Within the Alps it was more convenient, perhaps it was more dignified, for the Pope to receive the vassal hierarchy; but beyond the Alps alone was there hope of re-awakening the slumbering enthusiasm for the sepulchre of the Saviour.

<small>Determines on a Council.</small>

---

* The Jews were to offer, as a regular part of the ceremony, their congratulations, and to present the book of the Old Testament. The Pope was seated on the Sedes Stercoraria, emblematic of the verse in the Psalm "de stercore erigit pauperem." This is noticed on account of misapprehensions sometimes prevalent on this singular usage. See on the Sedes Stercoraria, Mabillon, Iter Italicum, p. 57.

Lyons was the chosen city. Gregory in the mean time laboured assiduously at the great work which was to be consummated in the Council—the pacification of Christendom. Three measures were necessary: I. The extinction of the wars and feuds in Italy. II. The restoration of the Empire, in the person of a great German Prince. III. The acknowledgment of the Greek Emperor of Constantinople, and the admission of that Emperor into the league of Christian princes; with the reunion of the Greek and Latin Churches.

Gregory began his work of pacification in Lombardy: he did not at once withdraw himself from the head of the Guelfic confederacy; he still asserted the power of Charles of Anjou as Vicar of the Empire; he even confirmed the excommunication against the Ghibelline cities, Pisa, Pavia, Verona, and the Duke of Tyrol: nor did he take up the cause of Otho Visconti, the exiled Ghibelline Archbishop of Milan, against the Della Torres, who held that city.[*] But he began gradually to feel his strength. He negotiated peace between Genoa and Venice, rivals for the mastery of the sea; between Venice and Bologna, rivals for the command of the navigation of the Po. Pisa was reconciled to the Church; the archiepiscopal dignity restored to the city. In Florence, on his way to the Council, Gregory attempted to awe into peace the Guelfs and Ghibellines. The Guelfs heard this strange doctrine applied to their enemies, "They are Ghibellines, it is true, but they are citizens, men, Christians."[#] He made the two factions, both at Florence and Sienna, swear to a treaty of peace, and to the re-admission of

A.D. 1272.

---

* Annal. Mediolanen. Muratori, Ann., sub ann. 1272.
# S. Antonin. ii. tit. 20, c. 2.

the exiles on both sides, in his own presence and in that of Charles of Anjou, and Baldwin of Constantinople. But the hatred of Guelf and Ghibelline was too deeply rooted; Charles of Anjou openly approving the treaty, secretly contrived a rupture; the Ghibellines were menaced with assassination: the Pope paused on his journey to cast back an excommunication on forsworn and disobedient Florence. Nor would Genoa enter into terms of reconciliation with Charles of Anjou. Yet on the whole there was at least a surface of quiet; though under the smouldering ashes lay everywhere the fires, nursing their strength, and ready to burst out again in new fury.

Richard, Earl of Cornwall, died, having squandered his enormous wealth for the barren honour of bearing the imperial title of King of the Romans for fourteen years, and of displaying in London the splendour and majesty of his imperial pomp.[h] Notwithstanding the claim of Alfonso of Castile, who had exercised no other right than sending a few troops into Lombardy, the Pope commanded a new election. Perhaps he already anticipated the choice of Rodolph of Hapsburg, the founder of the great house of Austria. The Pope confirmed the choice; he tried all means of soothing the pride; he used the gentlest, most courteous persuasions, but he paid no regard to the remonstrances of the King of Castile. Rodolph of Hapsburg, whose great activity and abilities had been already displayed in the internal affairs of Germany, who had commanded the suffrages of all the

April 2, 1772.

Sept. 29, 1273.

---

[h] The Germans soon saw, according to Paris, the contempt in which England held Richard of Cornwall; and withdrew, ashamed of their Emperor. He passed as much time in England as in Germany.—Matt. Paris, pp. 953-4.

electors, except the hostile Ottocar, King of Bohemia,[1] was the sovereign whose accession any Pope, especially Gregory X., might hail with satisfaction. He seemed designated as the chief who might unite Christendom in the Holy War.[k] He had none of the fatal hereditary claims to possessions in Italy, or to the throne of Naples. In the north of Italy he might curb the insatiate ambition, the restless encroachments of Charles of Anjou: the Pope exacted his promise from Rodolph that he would not assail Charles in his kingdom of Sicily or in Tuscany. Gregory X. aspired to include within the pale of the great Christian confederacy, to embark in the common crusade, even a more useful ally, the Greek Emperor of Constantinople. A Greek was again Emperor of the East; Michael Palæologus ruled in Constantinople; Baldwin II., the last of the Latin emperors, was an exile in Europe. Instead of espousing his cause, or encouraging the ambition of Charles of Anjou, who had married his daughter to the heir of Baldwin, and aspired to the dominion of the East in the name of his son-in-law, Gregory embraced the wiser and bolder policy of acknowledging the title of the Greek. Palæologus consented to pay the great price of this acknowledgment,

A.D. 1272.

---

[1] The electors were Wernher of Eppstein, Archbishop of Mentz; Henry of Fustingen, Archbishop of Treves; Engelbert of Falkenstein, Archbishop of Cologne; Louis, Palatine of the Rhine and Duke of Bavaria; John, Duke of Saxony; John, Margrave of Brandenburg. According to some authorities, Ottocar, King of Bohemia, declined the crown. The reader will find a fair popular account of the elevation of Rodolph of Hapsburg in Coxe's House of Austria.

[k] Rodolph was besieging the Bishop of Basle when he received the intelligence of his election. The city at once surrendered to the King of the Romans. The Bishop was furious. "Sit firm," he cried, "O Lord God, or Rodolph will occupy thy throne." "Sede fortiter, Domine Deus, vel locum Rudolfus occupabit tuum."—Albert. Argentin. p. 100.

no less than submission to the Papal supremacy, and the union of the Greek with the Latin Church.ᵃ Palæologus had no great reason for profound attachment to the Greek clergy. The Patriarch Arsenius, with boldness unusual in the Eastern hierarchy, had solemnly excommunicated the Emperor for his crime in cruelly blinding the young John Lascaris, in whose name he held the empire. Arsenius had been banished on a charge of treason; a new patriarch sat on the throne, but a powerful faction of the clergy were still Arsenites. On his death, they compelled the burial of the banished prelate in the sanctuary of Santa Sophia; absolution in his name alone reconciled the Emperor to God. Palæologus, though the ruling Patriarch was more submissive, might not be disinclined to admit larger authority in a more remote power, held by a Pope in Italy rather than a Patriarch in Constantinople. By every act, by bribery, intimidation, by skilfully softening off the points of difference, and urging the undoubted blessings of union, he wrung a slow consent from the leading clergy of the East: they were gradually taught to consider that the procession of the Holy Ghost, from the Father and the Son, was not a doctrine of such repulsive heterodoxy, and to admit a kind of vague supremacy in the Pope, which the Emperor assured them would not endanger their independence, as dear to him as to themselves.ᵇ Ambassadors arrived at

---

ᵃ Pachymer, II. 15; III. 1, 2; v. 10; p. 369, &c. Nicephorus Gregoras, III. 1; iv. 1. Gibbon, edit. Milman, xi. 313, *et seq.*

ᵇ Pachymer complains, not without bitterness, that the Latins called the Greeks, in their contempt, "white Hagarenes." προΐστατο γὰρ τὸ σαδ- θαλον, καὶ τὸ λευκοὺς Ἀγαρηνοὺς εἶναι Γραικοὺς παρ' ἐκείνοις μεῖζον ὄρετο.—Lib. v. p. 367, edit. Bonn. The Greek clergy were secretly determined to maintain their independence, to acknowledge no primacy, and not to subject themselves to the judgment of traitors and low men. I presume they thought

Rome with splendid offerings for the altar of St. Peter, and with the treaty of union and of submission to the Roman see, signed by the Emperor, his son, thirty-five archbishops and metropolitans, with their suffragan synods. The Council of Lyons witnessed with joy this reunion—a reunion unhappily but of few years—of the Church of Basil, the Gregories, and Chrysostom, with that of Leo and Gregory the Great.

Nothing could contrast more strongly than the first and second Councils of Lyons. The first was summoned by Innocent IV., attended by hardly one hundred and fifty prelates, to represent the whole clergy of Christendom; its aim to perpetuate a desperate war, and to commit the Empire and the Papacy in implacable hostility; its authority disclaimed by the larger part of Christendom, cordially and fully accepted by scarcely one of the great kingdoms. At the second Council of Lyons, Gregory X. took his seat at the head of five hundred bishops, seventy abbots, and at least a thousand dignified ecclesiastics. Every kingdom of the West acknowledged its œcumenic power. The King of Arragon was present; the Latin patriarchs of Constantinople and of Antioch, fourteen cardinals, ambassadors from Germany, France, England, Sicily, the Master of the Templars, with many knights of St. John. Of the two great theologic luminaries of the age, the Dominican Thomas Aquinas and the Franciscan Bonaventura, Thomas died on his way to the Council:* Bonaventura was present, preached

Council of Lyons.

May 7, 1274.

---

all Italians like the Genoese of Pera, merchants, ἀλλὰ μένων καὶ αὐτὸς ἐν τῇ πόλει τὴν ἐκκλησίαν ἡγούμενοι, καθὼς καὶ ἄρχειν εἶχε, καὶ μὴ παρὰ καιρὸν εὐδοκεῖν ἀρίστοις—

καὶ βαρβάρων.—p. 368. Strange collision of Greek and Roman pride! The sovereign did not like the φόρτος who were very busy.

* Dante has given perpetuity to the

during its sittings, but died before its dissolution. The Council of Lyons aspired to establish peace throughout Christendom; the recognition of an Emperor, elected with the full approval, under the closest bonds of union with the Pope; the re-admission of the Eastern Empire, and of the Greek Church, within the pale of Western Christendom. Such was the function of this great assembly, perhaps the first and last Council which was undisturbed by dispute, and uttered no sentence of interdict or excommunication. The declared objects for which the Council was summoned were succour to the Holy Land, the reconciliation of the Greek Church, the reformation of manners. The session opened with great solemnity. The Pope himself officiated in the religious ceremonial, assisted by his cardinals. For the first object, the succour to the Holy Land, a tenth of all ecclesiastical revenues was voted for six years. The Council, as it awaited the arrival of the Greek ambassadors, occupied itself on regulations concerning the discipline and morals of the clergy. On the 24th June arrived the ambassadors. After the edict of the Emperor of Byzantium, sealed with a golden seal, had been exhibited and read, the act for the union of the two Churches was solemnly passed; the Pope himself intoned the *Te Deum* with tears of joy; the Latin clergy chanted the creed in Latin; the Greek, those of the embassy, assisted by the Calabrese bishops, chanted it in Greek. As they came to the words, "who proceedeth

---

charge against Charles of Anjou of having poisoned St. Thomas; adduced also by Villani, ix. 218 :—

"Carlo venne in Italia, e per ammenda Villana fè di Corradino, e poi Ripiime al ciel Tommaso per ammenda."
Purgat. xx. 67.

Compare commentary of Benvenuto da Imola (apud Muratori). The Guelf Villani assigns as a motive the fear that St. Thomas (a Neapolitan), the oracle of Christendom, would expose the cruelty and wickedness of Charles. It is probably an invention of the profound Neapolitan hatred.

from the Father and the Son," they repeated it, with more emphatic solemnity, three times. The representative of the Eastern Emperor acknowledged in ample terms (such were his secret instructions) the supremacy of St. Peter's successor.

Gregory X. did not permit this Council to be dissolved until he had secured the Papacy from the scandals which had preceded his own election; but to the stern law with which he endeavoured to bind the cardinals, he found strong opposition. It was only by his personal authority with each single prelate, that he extorted their irrevocable signature and seal to the statute which was to regulate the proceedings of the conclave on the death of a Pope. The statute retained to the cardinals the proud prerogative of sole election; but it ordained that only ten days after the death of the Pope they were to be shut up, without waiting for absent members of the college, in a single chamber in the deceased Pope's palace, where they were to live in common; all access was to be strictly prohibited, as well as writing or message: each was to have but one domestic; their meals were to be received through a window too narrow to admit a man. Any communication with them was inhibited under the menace of interdict. If they agreed not in three days, their repast was to be limited, for five days, to a single dish; after that to only bread and wine; so they were to be starved into unanimity. If the Pope died out of Rome, in that city where he died was to be this imprisonment of the conclave, under the municipal magistrates, who were sworn to allow the liberty permitted by statute, but no more. All offenders against this decree, of whatever rank, were at once excommunicate, infamous, and could rise to no dignity or public office;

any fief or estate they might hold of the Church of Rome, or any other Church, was forfeit. All former pacts, conventions, or agreements, were declared null and void; if under oath, the oath was abrogated, annulled. In every city in Christendom public prayers were to be offered up to God to infuse concord, speedy and wise decision, into the hearts of that venerable conclave.* So closed the second Council of Lyons. One act of severity alone, the degradation of Gregory's old enemy, the Bishop of Liège, appears in the annals of this Council. The Christian world was, on the other hand, highly edified by the appearance and solemn baptism of certain Tartars.

Gregory X., after an interview with the King of Castile at Beaucaire, whom he strove to reconcile to the loss of the Empire, and an interview with the Emperor Rodolph at Lausanne, repassed the Alps. He was received with deserved honours; only into excommunicated Florence — excommunicated, no one could deny, with perfect Christian justice—the peaceful prelate refused to enter. The world was anxiously awaiting the issue of these sage and holy counsels. The pontificate of peace, peace only to be broken by the discomfiture of the infidels in the East, was expanding, it was to be hoped, into many happy and glorious years. Suddenly Gregory sickened on his road to Arezzo; he died, and with him broke up the whole confederation of Christendom. The world again, from the conclave to the remotest limits not of Europe alone, but of Christianity, became one vast feud. With Gregory X. expired the Crusades; Christianity lost this principle of union, the Pope this

---

* Mansi et Labbe, sub ann.

principle of command, this title to the exaction of tribute from the vassal world. From this time he began to sink into an Italian prince, or into the servant of one of the great monarchies of Europe. The last convulsive effort of the Popedom for the dominion of the world, under Boniface VIII., ended in the disastrous death of that Pope; the captivity of the Papacy at Avignon.

After the death of Gregory X., in hardly more than three years three successive Popes rose and passed like shadows over the throne of St. Peter, and a fourth commenced his short reign. The popular superstition and the popular hatred, which, unallayed by the short-lived dignity, holiness, and wisdom of Gregory X., lay so deep in the public mind, beheld in these deaths which followed each other in such darkening rapidity, either the judicial hand of God or the crime of man. The Popes were no sooner proclaimed than dead, either, it was believed, smitten for men's sins or their own, or cut off by poison.[q] *Innocent V. 1276.*
The first of these, Peter of Tarantaise (Innocent V.), was elected in January, took up his residence in Rome, and died in June. Ottobuoni Fieschi, the nephew of Innocent IV., answered his kindred, who crowded around him with congratulations on his election, "Would that ye came to a cardinal in good health, not to a dying Pope." He just lived to take the name of Hadrian V., to release his native Genoa from interdict, and to suspend with his dying breath the constitution of Gregory X. concerning the Conclave. He was not crowned, consecrated, or even ordained priest. Hadrian V. died at Viterbo.

Hadrian V. Elected July 9, died Aug. 16.

---

[q] "Papæ quatuor mortui, duo divino judicio, et duo veneno exhausti."—Chronic. Foro Livien. Muratori, S. I. xiii.

The immediate choice of the cardinals now fell on Pedro Juliani, a Portuguese, the Cardinal Bishop of Tusculum. Though the cardinals had already obtained from the dying Hadrian the suspension of the severely restrictive edict of Gregory X. concerning the Conclave, the edict was popular abroad. There were many, and among them prelates who declared that, excepting under that statute, and in conformity with its regulations, the cardinals had no right to the sole election of the Pope.ʳ There was a great uproar in Viterbo, instigated by these prelates. The Archbishop of Corinth, with some other ecclesiastics who were sent forth to read the suspension of the edict by Hadrian V., confirmed by John XXI., the new Pope, was maltreated; yet, even if the ceremonial was not rigidly observed, there had been the utmost speed in the election of John XXI. The Pope was a man of letters, and even of science; he had published some mathematical treatises which excited the astonishment and therefore the suspicion of his age. He was a churchman of easy access, conversed freely with humbler men, if men of letters, and was therefore accused of lowering the dignity of the Pontificate. He was perhaps hasty and unguarded in his language, but he had a more inexpiable fault. He had no love for monks or friars: it was supposed that he meditated some severe coercive edicts on these brotherhoods. Hence his death (he was crushed by the falling of the roof in a noble chamber which he had built in the palace of Viterbo) was foreshown by

[John XXI.]

---

* "In tantam prorupere temeritatis insaniam, ut in dubium auctoritatem et jurisdictionem collegii ejusdem Ecclesiæ revocarent, et de illis in derogationem ipsarum disputantes quilibet, enervare immo et evacuare pro viribus alterentur insanibus argumentis."—Rescript. Joann. XXI., apud Raynald. 1276.

gloomy prodigies, and held either to be a divine judgement, or a direct act of the Evil One. John XXI. was contemplating with too great pride the work of his own hands, and burst out into laughter; at that instant the avenging roof came down on his head. Two visions revealed to different holy men the Evil One hewing down the supports, and so overwhelming the reprobate Pontiff. He was said by others to have been, at the moment of his death, in the act of writing a book full of the most deadly heresies, or practising the arts of magic.*

May 16 (?) 20 / 1277.

For six weeks, the Cardinals, released from the coercive statute, met in conclave without coming to any conclusion. At length the election fell on John Gaetano, of the noble Roman house, the Orsini, a man of remarkable beauty of person and demeanour. His name, "the Accomplished," implied that in him met all the graces of the handsomest clerks in the world; but he was a man likewise of irreproachable morals, of vast ambition, and of great ability. This age of short-lived Popes was the age of magnificent designs as short-lived as their authors. The nobler, more comprehensive, more disinterested scheme of Gregory X. had sunk into nothing at his death; that of Nicolas III. had deeper root, but came not to maturity during his reign, or in his line. An Italian, a Roman, was again upon the throne of St. Peter. The Orsini at first took up his residence at Rome. He built a splendid palace, the Vatican, near St. Peter's, with gardens around, and fortified with a strong wall.† He repaired, enlarged, and strengthened the Lateran Palace.

Nov. 26, 1277. Nicolas III. il Composto.

---

* Ptolem. Luc. xxvi. Nangis, however, says that he died "perceptis omnibus sacramentis ecclesiasticis."—
Sub ann. 1277. Siffred. in Chronic.
† Bunsen und Platner, Roms Beschreibung, ii. p. 231.

Unlike his rash predecessor, he was a friend to the great monastic orders: he knew how completely the preachers and other mendicants still, notwithstanding the hatred of the clergy, now they had taken possession of the high places of theology, ruled the public mind. To Thomas Aquinas and S. Bonaventura the world looked up as to its guiding lights; nor had they lost their power over the popular passions.

Nicolas III. did not in any degree relax the Papal superintendence over Christendom to its extreme limits: he is interfering in the affairs of Poland and Hungary, mediating in the wars between France and Spain, watching over the crumbling wreck of the Christian possessions in the Holy Land. In the East he not merely held the justly alarmed Emperor, Michael Palæologus, to his plighted fidelity and allegiance, but insisted on the more ample recognition of the Papal supremacy.ᵃ He demanded that a solemn oath of subordination should be taken by the Patriarch and the clergy. To the prudent request of the Emperor, that the obnoxious words which asserted the procession of the Holy Ghost from the Son, should not be forced at once into the creed, he returned a haughty reply that no indulgence could be granted, though some toleration might be conceded for a time on the other points in which the Greek differed from the Roman ritual. He even required that the Greek Church should humbly seek absolution for the sin of their long schism. A strong faction broke out in the Empire, in Constantinople, in the Court, in the family of the

---

ᵃ Raynald. sub ann. 1279, 80. Pachymer (vi. 10, p. 461) calls the Pope υψβασος. The Jesuit Possin, Chronol. in Pachymerum, conjectures Ορρσιρος, the Orsini—perhaps a blunder of the Greeks. The whole long intrigue may be traced through two or three books of Pachymer.

CHAP. IV.   GREEKS RETURN TO INDEPENDENCE.   413

Emperor. They branded the Pope, the Patriarch, the Emperor, as heretics. Palæologus became that most odious of persecutors, a persecutor without the excuse of religious bigotry; confiscation, scourging, mutilation, punished the refractory assertors of the independence of the Greek Church. The Pope's Legates were gratified by the sight of four princes of the blood confined in a loathsome prison. But discontent led to insurrection. The Prince of Trebisond, who had always retained the title of Emperor, espoused the cause of Greek orthodoxy. His generals betrayed the unhappy Palæologus: his family, especially his nieces, intrigued against him. He hesitated; for his hesitation he was excommunicated at Rome by Martin IV., the slave of his enemy Charles of Anjou. On his death the Greeks with one consent threw off the yoke; the churches were purified from the infection of the Latin rites; the creed resumed its old form; Andronicus, the son of Palæologus, refused burial to his schismatic father.[x]

Return of the Greek Church to independence.

But Italy was the scene of the great achievements, it was to be that of the still greater designs, of Nicolas III. The Emperor Rodolph was not yet so firmly seated on his throne (he was involved in a perilous war with Ottocar of Bohemia) as to disdain the aid of the Roman Pontiff. He could not but look to the resumption at least of some imperial rights in Lombardy; if the Pope should maintain the cause of Charles of Anjou, Italy was entirely lost. From the magnificence, the policy, or the fears of Rodolph, the Pope extorted the absolute cession to the Roman See, not only of Romagna, but of the exarchate of

---

[x] Raynald. 1279. ii.

Ravenna. The Chancellor of the Emperor had exacted an oath of allegiance from the cities of Bologna, Imola, Faenza, Forlì, Cesena, Ravenna, Rimini, Urbino, and some other towns. Rodolph disclaimed the acts of his Chancellor, recognised the donation of the Emperor Louis, and made a new donation, in his own name, of the whole territory from Radicofani to Ceperano, the march of Ancona, the duchy of Spoleto, the county of Bertinoro, the lands of the Countess Matilda, the exarchate of Ravenna, the Pentapolis, Ferrara, Commachio, Montefeltro, and Massa Trabaria, absolutely; and with all his full rights to the See of St. Peter. The Pope obtained a confirmatory acknowledgment of his sovereignty, as well as over Sardinia, Corsica, and Sicily, from the great electors of the Empire.[y] This document is signed by the Archbishop of Saltzburg, and other prelates, by the Chancellor of the Empire, by Albert the eldest, and Hartman the second son of the Emperor, by many of the nobles with their own hand, by some with that of their notaries.[z] This cession Nicolas determined should not be, as it had heretofore been, an idle form in the officers of the Empire; and the Legates of the Pope presented themselves at the gates of the greater cities, demanding the acknowledgment of the Papal sovereignty. The independent principalities, the republics which had grown up in these territories, made no resistance; they were released from their oath to the Emperor, and took the oath to the Pope; even Bologna submitted on certain terms. The Pope was actual ruling sovereign of the whole of

May 29, 1278.

Feb. 14, 1279.

---

[y] Raynald. p. 473.

[z] Boehmer observes of this document that the two sons of the Emperor could write: the Burgrave of Nuremburg and the Archbishop of Saltzburg ! could not.—Regesta, p. 98.

the dominions to which the Papal See had advanced its pretensions.[a] The extent of this sovereignty was still vague and undefined: the princes maintained their principalities, the republics their municipal institutions and self-government. They admitted no rulers appointed by the Pope; his power of levying taxes was certainly not unrestricted, nor the popular rule absolutely abrogated. Thus strong in the manifest favour of the Emperor Rodolph, Nicolas III. made a great merit to Charles of Anjou that he had stipulated that the Emperor should abstain from all warlike operations against Charles. The ambitious Frenchman overawed, quietly allowed himself to be despoiled first *Sept. 16 in the following year.* of his vicariate of Tuscany, and then of his senatorship of Rome. Charles humbly entreated that he might not suffer the indignity of surrendering that office, which, on the expulsion of Henry *Schemes of Charles of Anjou.* of Castile, had been regranted to him for ten years by Pope Clement IV., before the expiration of that term, now almost elapsed. Nicolas condescended to grant his humble petition; but on the abdication of Charles he passed a rigorous edict that the senatorship from that time should never be held by emperor, king, prince, marquis, duke, count, or baron, or any man of great rank or power, or even by their brother, son, or grandson; no one could hold it for above a year; no one without special licence of the Apostolic See.[b] This hostility to Charles may have been the deliberate policy of the Pope: it was said that the Pope had demanded the niece of Charles in marriage for his nephew; Charles contemptuously answered, the Pope

---

[a] "Ma quello, che i cherici prendono, tardi sanno rendere."—Villani, vii. 53.
[b] Nicolai III., Regesta. Raynald. sub ann.

was no hereditary prince, and that notwithstanding the red shoes he wore, he must not presume to mix his blood with that of kings." There can be no doubt that Charles had used his influence in the conclave to oppose the elevation of the Roman Orsini.

Charles retired to his dominions to brood over revenge, to meditate a league against the Eastern Empire which was to compensate for his losses in the West. The Popes had taken the reconciled Greeks, the submissive Palæologus (the fear of Charles had been a chief motive for the religious tractableness of the Greeks⁴), under their protection. Gregory X. had refused to sanction or to consecrate the banner which Charles was prepared to unfold in the name of the Latin Philip; Charles had been seen to gnaw his ivory sceptre in wrath, in the antechamber of the Pope, at this desertion of what he asserted to be the cause of legitimate right and orthodox belief.° Charles was now negotiating with the Latins of the Eastern Empire and the republic of Venice to take arms and replace the son of Baldwin on the throne of Constantinople. Even in Sicily Charles of Anjou was not absolutely secure: the Pope was understood to entertain secret relations with the enemies of the French rule.

But Nicolas III. had ulterior schemes, which seem to foreshow and anticipate the magnificent designs of later nepotism. Already, under pretence of heresy, he had confiscated the castles of some of the nobles of Romagna, that particularly of Suriano, and invested his nephews with them. The castle of St. Angelo, separated from the Church, was

Nepotism of Nicolas III.

° Ricordano Malespina, 204. Villani, vii. 53.
ᵈ This appears throughout the Byzantine accounts.
ᵉ Pachymer, v. 26, p. 410.

granted to his nephew Orso. His kinsmen were by various means elected the Podestàs of many cities. Three of his brethren, four more of his kindred, had been advanced to the Cardinalate. Bertoldo Orsini, his brother, was created Count of Romagna. His favourite nephew, by his sister's side, Latino Malebranca (a Brancaleone), the Cardinal Bishop of Ostia, a powerful preacher, had great success in allaying the feuds in many of the cities,[f] even in Bologna, wearied by the long strife of the Lambertazzi and the Gieromei; wherever the Cardinal established peace, the Count of Romagna assumed authority. Himself he had declared perpetual Senator of Roma. His nephew Orso was his vicar in this great office. But these were but the first steps to the throne which Nicolas III. aspired to raise for the house of Orsini. It was believed that he had laid before the Emperor Rodolph a plan by which the Empire was to become hereditary in his house, the kingdom of Vienna was to be in Charles Martel, grandson of Charles of Anjou, the son-in-law of the Emperor. Italy was to be divided into the two kingdoms of Insubria and Tuscany, besides that of Sicily; and on these thrones were to be placed two of the house of Orsini.[g]

A sudden fit of apoplexy at his castle of Soriano cut short all these splendid designs.[h] From this favourite residence he had dated his Bulls, a practice which had given great offence. The Pope

Aug. 22, 1280.
Death of Nicolas III.

---

[f] Villani, li. c. 55. Villani calls Bertoldo Orsini nepote of Nicolas III.

[g] Muratori, Annal. sub ann. 1280, with authorities.

[h] Nicolas is in Dante's hell for his unmeasured nepotism:—

"Sappi ch' io fui vestito del gran manto;
E veramente fui figliool del Orsa.
Cupido sì per avanzar l' Orsatti,
Che sù l' avere, e qui mi misi in borsa."
Inferno, xix. 64.

"Però ti sta; chè tu se' ben punito,
E guarda ben la mal tolta moneta,
Ch' esser ti fece contra Carlo ardito."—97.

was, as it were, merging himself in the stately Italian sovereign.

Charles of Anjou heard with the utmost joy the unexpected tidings of the death of his enemy Nicolas III. He instantly took measures to secure himself against the calamity of a second hostile Pope, to wrest the Pontificate from the aspiring family of the Orsini, and form an independent Italian interest.[1] The family of the Annibaldeschi rivalled that of the Orsini in wealth and power. There was a rising in Rome; the divided people had recourse to the vain step for the preservation of peace, the creation of two Senators, one out of each of the rival houses. This, as might have been expected, increased the confusion; Rome became a scene of strife, murder, anarchy. But Viterbo, where the conclave of Cardinals was assembled, was even of more importance, an Annibaldeschi was Lord of that city.[2] The people of Viterbo were won, by force or bribery, to the party of Charles. The constitution of Gregory X. was utterly forgotten; the conclave prolonged its sittings. The Pope had crowded the college with Orsinis and their dependants. The Viterbans surrounded the chamber; they accused the Orsini Cardinals as disturbing or arresting the freedom of election, dragged forth two of them, and cast them into prison. With them they seized and incarcerated Malebranca the Cardinal Bishop of Ostia: the rest were kept on the statutable bread and wine; the French Cardinals, it was said, were furtively provided with better viands. Yet the strife endured for nearly six months before the stubborn conclave would yield to the election of the Cardinal of Santa

Marginal notes: The conclave at Viterbo. Feb. 22, 1281. Latino Malebranca.

---

[1] Villani, vii. c. 57.   [2] Muratori, sub ann. 1281.

Cecilia, a Frenchman, the slave and passive instrument of Charles of Anjou.

Martin IV. was born at Mont Pencé in Brie; he had been Canon of Tours. He put on at first the show of maintaining the lofty character of the Churchman. He excommunicated the Viterbans for their sacrilegious maltreatment of the Cardinals; Rinaldo Annibaldeschi, the Lord of Viterbo, was compelled to ask pardon on his knees of the Cardinal Rosso, and forgiven only at the intervention of the Pope.^m Martin IV. retired to Orvieto.

But the Frenchman soon began to predominate over the Pontiff; he sunk into the vassal of Charles of Anjou. The great policy of his predecessor, to assuage the feuds of Guelf and Ghibelline, was an Italian policy; it was altogether abandoned. The Ghibellines in every city were menaced or smitten with excommunication; the Lambertazzi were driven from Bologna. Forli was placed under interdict for harbouring the exiles; the goods of the citizens were confiscated for the benefit of the Pope. Bertoldo Orsini was deposed from the Countship of Romagna: the office was bestowed on John of Appia, with instructions everywhere to coerce or to chastise the refractory Ghibellines.ⁿ The Pope himself was elected Senator of Rome, in defiance of the decree of Nicolas III.; Charles of Anjou was his vicegerent. Nor did excommunication confine itself to Italy; Charles was now in a state to carry on his league for the subjugation of the Eastern Empire, in conjunction with the exiled Latin Sovereign and the Venetian republic. Palæologus, who had sur-

---

^m Ptolem. Luc. xxiv. 2.
ⁿ "Che votò l' erario delle munichae per fulminar tutti i Ghibellini, e chiunque era nemico o poco amico del medesimo Rè Carlo." So writes the calm Muratori, p. 185.

rendered the liberties of the Greek Church to the supremacy of Rome, who, at the command of the Pope, had persecuted, had provoked his subjects, his kindred to rebellion, had raised up a rival Greek Patriarch to contest Constantinople, who had been denounced as worse than a heretic, as an apostate, was now, because something was yet thought wanting to his base compliance, or rather because he maintained his throne in defiance of Charles of Anjou, solemnly excommunicated by Martin IV.° The last hope of union between the Churches was thus cut away by the Pope's suicidal hand; Palæologus died repudiated as a renegade by his own Church, under the interdict of the Church of Rome. His son Andronicus, as has been said, dissolved the inauspicious alliance; and the Churches were again for above two centuries in implacable oppugnancy.

Charles of Anjou, with the Pope as his obsequious minister, might seem reinstated in more than his former plenitude of power; he resided with the Pope at Orvieto, as it were to dictate his counsels. Though Martin did not yet venture to dispossess the Emperor Rodolph of the Vicariate of Tuscany, Charles might have been justified in the noblest hopes of his ambition in Italy, but he was looking with more wide-grasping predilection to the East. Under the pretext of a Crusade to the Holy Land, he was aspiring to add Constantinople to his realm.

° This passionate and partial excommunication shocked his own age. From the date of this act, writes Ptolemy of Lucca, all went wrong with Charles and the Church. See back, 413.

CHAPTER V.

Sicilian Vespers.

BUT a mine had long been working under his throne, which in the next year burst with all the suddenness and terror of one of his kingdom's volcanoes. While he contemplated the sovereignty of the East, Sicily was lost to his house. Around one man has gathered all the glory of this signal revolution; John of Procida has been handed down as almost the sole author of the expulsion of the French, and the translation of the crown of Sicily to the house of Arragon: Peter of Arragon, the Emperor Palæologus, Nicolas III., the revolted Barons of Sicily were but instruments wielded by his strong will, brought into close alliance through negotiations conducted by him alone; excited, sustained, guided by his ubiquitous presence. Even the Vespers of Palermo were attributed to his secret instigation. John of Procida perhaps achieved not all which is ascribed to him alone; in the vast system of secret agency he was not the sole mover; much which was traced to his suggestion arose out of natural passions, resentment, revenge, ambition, interest, patriotism, love of power and glory in those who conspired to this memorable work. A fatal revelation, but too trustworthy, shows John of Procida in his early career (he had been already physician to Frederick II. and to Conrad, and confidential counsellor of Manfred) as basely abandoning the cause of the fallen Manfred, crouching at the feet of the Pope at Viterbo, protesting that he had only bowed beneath the storm of Manfred's tyranny; he was commended to the mercy of Charles of Anjou by the Pope, as his beloved son, as the future faithful servant of King Charles. How far he was admitted to favour appears not, but three years after he is involved in a charge of high treason, and flies from Naples. But however base instead of noble, revenge disappointed treachery and ambition are hardly less strong and obstinate motives to action than generous indignation at tyranny, and holy love of country.[a]

In all the conspiracy, a conspiracy of thoughts, feelings, passions, if not of compacts and treaties, the most fatal to Charles was the insupportable, unexampled, acknowledged tyranny of the French dominion.[b] Sicily had groaned and bled under the cruel despotism of the Emperor Henry; the German rudeness aggravated the harshness of his rule. Frederick II., as also his son, had been severe, though just; if his fiscal regulations were oppressive, they were repaid by the brilliancy of his court, by his wise laws, by noble foundations, by the national pride in beholding Naples and Sicily the most civilised kingdom in the world. Charles and his French and Provençal nobles, with the haughtiness and cruelty of foreign rulers, indulged without restraint those outrages which gall to madness. Charles from the first treated the realm as a conquered land; after the insurrection in

Tyranny of the French.

---

[a] See the document among the Pièces justificatives in Cherrier, iv. 324, from a copy in the Royal Library at Paris. Compare Amari's preface and document first edit. iv., Florence, 1851;

St. Priest, Histoire de la Conquête de Naples, Paris, 1847.

[b] "Sub tyrannica turbine tempestatis."

favour of Conradin, as a revolted kingdom. The insurgents, or reputed insurgents, were hunted down, torn from their families: happy if only put to a violent death!° To the exactions of Charles there were no limits. The great fiefs seized, confiscated on the slightest suspicion of disaffection, were granted to French nobles; the foreign soldiers lived at free quarters; they were executioners commissioned to punish a rebellious race. To all complaints of cruelty, outrage, extortion, Charles replied with a haughty scoff, as though it were fit treatment for the impious rebels against himself and the Pope. The laws, severe enough before, were aggravated by still more sanguinary enactments, and by their execution with refined mercilessness. But there were worse cruelties than these; those women only were safe who, being heiresses, were compelled to marry French nobles; of these there was a regular register; of all others the honour was at the mercy of those who in this respect knew no mercy: there was no redress, no pity; it might seem as if Sicilian women were thought honoured by being defiled by French and Provençal brutality.⁴ Over this tyranny, which himself had inflicted on this beautiful land, Clement IV. had groaned in bitter remorse. Charles in his impartial rapacity spared not the property of the Church; if in his cruelty he respected the sacred persons of ecclesiastics, he taxed even the Templars and Knights of St. John. The Pope had sent remonstrances, embassies, to warn, to threaten, but in

---

° Amari, c. iii., for a full account of these horrors, with his authorities.

⁴ See these enactments, quoted in Amari. On the forced marriages, p. 61. His fourth chapter we read with a revulsive shudder, and would fain disbelieve; but the industry of Amari has been too searching, his facts and documents are too strong even for charitable palliation.

vain.* He had entreated the intervention of the holy Louis. Gregory X. menaced that for the tyrannies of the same kind which Charles exercised in Tuscany the wrath of God would fall on such a tyrant. "I know not," answered Charles, "what that word tyrant means; this I know, that so far I have been protected by God; I doubt not that he will still protect me." The Archbishop of Capua denounced him at the Council of Lyons; he laughed to scorn the complaints of the Prelates, the Legates of the Council, the letters of the Pope to Philip of France. In Sicily all the abuses of the government were felt in their extreme weight. Naples was the residence of the court, and derived some glory or advantage from its splendour; Palermo sank to a provincial town, Sicily to a province. The Parliament had fallen into desuetude; it was an iron reign of force without justice, without law, without humanity, without mercy, without regard to morality, without consideration of any one of the rights, or of the interests or the welfare of mankind.

The race of Sicily's old kings was not utterly extinct. House of Arragon. In Constance, the daughter of Manfred, the wife of Peter of Arragon, lingered the last drops of Swabian blood: it was said that on the scaffold Conradin had cast down his glove, to be borne to the King of Arragon, as the heir of his rights, the avenger of his death. To the court of the King of Arragon had fled those Sicilians of the Swabian party who had the good fortune to become exiles—among these three of great name, Roger Loria, Conrad Lancia, John of Procida. John of Procida was an exile soon after the

---

* See two letters especially, in Raynaldus, 1267; also in Martene and Durand, Thes. Nov. Anecd. II. 530, 537, &c.

failure and death of Conradin. His hatred to the French is said to have been deepened by the worst outrage, perpetrated on his wife and his daughter. Existing grants to his wife Landolfina intimate that she was under the protection of some powerful influence, not improbably of a French paramour.[f] John of Procida was born at Salerno; though a noble, he was profoundly skilled, as in other learning, in the science of his native city, that of medicine. He rose in the favour of Peter of Arragon, became his bosom counsellor, was endowed with lands, the lands of Luxen, Beneazano, and Palma, in the kingdom of Valencia; he was a Valencian noble.[g]

Peter of Arragon, with his court and his confidential council, thus occupied by Sicilian exiles, who were constantly urging upon him the odious tyranny of Charles the usurper, and the discontent, disaffection, despair of the Sicilians; with his Queen not likely to forget her own hereditary claims, or the wrongs of her noble father Manfred and his ancient house; lord but of his own narrow kingdom hardly won from the Moors, and held, as it were, in a joint sovereignty with his Nobles, was not likely to avert his eyes from the prospect of a greater monarchy, which expanded before him. He had made treaties of peace with the rival Kings his neighbours, a treaty for five years with the King of Granada, a league with Castile; and over King Sancho of Castile he held the menace of letting loose the two young princes, nearer to the throne than Sancho, and resident at the court of Arragon.[h] He kept up friendly relations with Philip of France, the husband

Peter of Arragon.

---

[f] Amari, note, p. 82. [g] See Amari's note, p. 83.
[h] Montaner, c. 40, 45; in Buchon, Collection des Memoires, D'Esclot, c. 76.

of his sister; he even made advances to Charles of Anjou; there was a proposal of marriage between his son and the daughter of Charles. Peter was embarked in suspicious negotiations with the Saracens in Tunis.[1] At the same time he was making great preparations for war; in his arsenals in Valencia, Tortosa, and Barcelona was gathering a powerful fleet; his subjects granted subsidies; provisions, stores, arms, accoutrements of war were accumulated as for some momentous design. How far John of Procida instigated these designs, or only encouraged the profound ambition of the King for dominion, of the Queen for revenge for her injured house, none can know: nor how far Procida acted from his own intense patriotism or revenge, or but as an instrument in the hand of others.

There can be no doubt that there was a secret understanding, that there was direct communication between the enemies of Charles, the Emperor of the East, Pope Nicolas III., the King of Arragon, perhaps the Sicilian nobles, Alaimo da Lentini and his colleagues: Procida may have been, no doubt was, one of the chief of those agents;[k] if not actually commissioned, tacitly recognised. He was once, if not twice, at the court of Constantinople. There he needed not to rouse the fears and jealousy of Palæologus; the designs of Charles against the Eastern Empire were, if not avowed, but half disguised. Charles was the open ally of Philip, the Latin claimant of the Empire. Palæolo-

John of Procida.

---

[1] Amari, p. 86, with his notes.

[k] Amari is inclined to treat as romance this primary organization of the whole confederacy by John of Procida; his ubiquitous agency; his disguises; especially his frequent intercourse with the Sicilian nobles. But there seems a great difficulty as to the growth of this romance, and this elevation of Procida into the sole hero of the war and the great deliverer, after his apostasy from the cause of Arragon, and after he had incurred the hatred of the Arragonese party.

gus might well enter into correspondence, or admit to a
secret interview, the bosom counsellor of King Peter of
Arragon. To Procida Palæologus may have entrusted
his secret offers of large sums of money for the Pope,
the hundred thousand byzantines, not to detach him
from the interests of Charles of Anjou, against whom he
had already taken hostile measures, but to enable him
to defy the power of the Angevine.* Procida, according
to the common account—an account contradicted only
by the silence of other writers—left Constantinople, pretending to be driven away by the Emperor; he disguised
himself as a Mendicant Friar, reached Malta, landed
in Sicily, had frequent interviews with the disaffected
nobles, Walter of Caltagirone, Palmerio Abbate, Alaimo
da Lentini. From them he obtained an invitation to
Peter of Arragon to advance his claims to the inheritance of his wife. In the friar's garb he made his way to
Nicolas III. in Soriano, revealed himself to the Holy
Father, explained the extent, the success of his negotiations; laid the treasures of Palæologus at his feet.
Nicolas consented to recognise the claims of Peter of
Arragon, and by letters of the most profound secrecy
promised him the investiture of the realm. Procida
appeared at Barcelona with these animating tidings to
rekindle the somewhat slumbering ambition of the
King. The warlike preparations were urged with
greater activity. Procida set forth on a second mission:
he landed at Pisa; at Viterbo he saw the Pope; at
Trapani conferred with the Sicilian nobles; passed to
Negropont undiscovered, reached Constantinople. He
was welcomed by the Emperor; negotiations were com-

---

* " E guarda ben la mal tolta moneta,
  Ch' esser ti fece contra Carlo ardito."
  Dante, *Inf.* xix. 97.

Amari's new interpretation of this verse is to me quite unsatisfactory.

menced for an alliance by marriage between the courts of Arragon and Constantinople. Accardo, a Lombard knight, was secretly despatched by the Emperor to the court of Peter with thirty thousand ounces of gold. Procida embarked on board a ship of Pisa, Accardo was concealed in the ship. At Malta they met the Sicilian conspirators, with the news of the death of Nicolas III. The Sicilians would have abandoned the hopeless enterprise; Procida reinvigorated them by the introduction of Accardo, and the sight of the Byzantine gold. All Procida's eloquence, all his ability, it is said, but very improbably, was needed to dissuade the King of Arragon from the abandonment of the hopeless enterprise. Again the plan was fully organised; the manner, the time of the insurrection arranged.[a]

It is certain that the warlike preparations of the King of Arragon had not escaped the jealous observation of Charles of Anjou; he could not but know the claims, the wrongs, of the Queen of Peter of Arragon and the stern, reserved, ambitious character of Peter; perhaps he had obtained some clue to the great league which was secretly forming against him. The vague rumours industriously propagated of designs against the Saracens of Africa by Peter of Arragon, however at other times they might have justified vast and secret armaments, could not blind the Augevine's keen apprehensions. Charles had himself demanded explanations. Among the first acts of Martin IV. was to require, through Philip of France, and from Peter himself directly, the scope and object of these menacing preparations: if they were against the infidels, he offered his sanction,

---

[a] The sons of Manfred were living, but in prison, from whence they never came forth.

his prayers, his contributions. Peter baffled his inquiries with his dexterous but inflexible reply. He implored the prayers of the Pope on his design; "but if he thought his right hand knew his secret, he would cut it off, lest it should betray it to his left."

Charles, on his part, had been making great preparations; he had a large fleet in the ports of Sicily and Naples; a powerful land force was assembled for embarkation. He had increased the burthens of the kingdom to provide this army, compelled the Sicilian nobles to furnish vessels; and he was as little disposed to disclose his own secret objects as the King of Arragon. The ostensible object was the deliverance of the Holy Land; the immediate one the subjugation of the Greek Empire. These forces were still in the garrisons and towns of Sicily. Forty-two castles had been built, either in the strongest positions, or to command the great cities, and were held by French feudatories. They were provided with arms, and could summon at an instant's notice all their French sub-feudatories, or the Sicilians on whom they could depend for aid. Heribert of Orleans, the King's Lieutenant, was in Messina; in Palermo, John di San Remi, the Justiciary of the Val di Mazzaro.

At this juncture the crisis was precipitated by one of those events which no sagacity could have foreseen,* which all the ubiquitous activity ascribed to John of Procida could not have devised—an outburst of popular fury excited by one of those acts of insulting tyranny which goad an oppressed people to

Sicilian Vespers.

---

* Amari, c. v. p. 89. "Le trame coi Ghibellini e con alcuni Baroni di Napoli o di Sicilia, non si possono ormai revocare in dubbio. Falso è che la pratica, sì strettamente condotta, fosse a punto riuscita a produrre lo scoppio del Vespro." I fully subscribe to this latter clause.

madness. The insurrection of Palermo received the darkly famous name of the "Sicilian Vespers."

The Sicilians still crowded to their religious festivals with all the gaiety and light-heartedness of a southern people. Even their churches, where they assembled for the worship of that God whose representative on earth had handed them over to their ruthless tyrant, where alone they found consolation under the grinding tyranny, were not secure against the all-present agents of that tyranny. The officers of the revenue watched the doors of the churches: as all who had not paid their taxes went in or came forth, even from within the sanctuary itself they dragged off their miserable victims, whom they branded with the name of heretics—"Pay, ye Paterins, pay!"

It was at a festival on Easter Tuesday that a multitude of the inhabitants of Palermo and the neighbourhood had thronged to a church, about half a mile out of the town, dedicated to the Holy Ghost. The religious service was over, the merriment begun; tables were spread, the amusements of all sorts, games, dances under the trees, were going gaily on; when the harmony was suddenly interrupted, and the joyousness chilled by the appearance of a body of French soldiery, under the pretext of keeping the peace. The French mingled familiarly with the people, paid court, not in the most respectful manner, to the women; the young men made sullen remonstrances, and told them to go their way. The Frenchmen began to draw together. "These rebellious Paterins must have arms, or they would not venture on such insolence." They began to search some of them for arms. The two parties were already glaring at each other in angry hostility. At that moment the beautiful daughter of Roger Mas-

March 31.

trangelo, a maiden of exquisite loveliness and modesty, with her bridegroom, approached the church. A Frenchman named Drouet, either in wantonness or insult, came up to her, and under the pretence of searching for arms, thrust his hand into her bosom. The girl fainted in her bridegroom's arms. He uttered in his agony the fatal cry, "Death to the French!" A youth rushed forward, stabbed Drouet to the heart with his own sword, was himself struck down. The cry, the shriek, ran through the crowd, "Death to the French!" Many Sicilians fell, but of two hundred on the spot, not one Frenchman escaped. The cry spread to the city: Mastrangelo took the lead; every house was stormed, every hole and corner searched; their dress, their speech, their persons, their manners denounced the French. The palace was forced; the Justiciary, being luckily wounded in the face, and rolled in the dust, and so undetected, mounted a horse, and fled with two followers. Two thousand French were slain. They denied them decent burial, heaped them together in a great pit. The horrors of the scene were indescribable: the insurgents broke into the convents, the churches. The friars, especial objects of hatred, were massacred; they slew the French monks, the French priests. Neither old age, nor sex, nor infancy, was spared; it is a charge more than once repeated in the Papal acts, that they ripped up Sicilian women who were pregnant by Frenchmen, in order to exterminate the hated brood. A government was hastily formed; Roger Mastrangelo, Arrigo Barresi, Niccoloso d'Ortoleva (knights), with Niccolo de Ebdemonia were summoned by acclamation to be Captains of the people. They then proclaimed the "Good estate and liberty," unfolded the banner of the city, an eagle on a field of gold; the keys of the Church were still quartered upon it.

The Justiciary was pursued to Vicari, thirty miles distant; the people rose at the cry of "Death to the French!"* The garrison at first refused to capitulate, and to be sent safe to Provence; it was now too late, the Justiciary was shot down by a random arrow, every Frenchman massacred. Sicily was everywhere in arms; Corleone first followed the example of Palermo. Everywhere the French were hunted down and murdered. One man alone was spared. William Porcelet, Governor of Calatafimi, who had ruled with justice and humanity, was, by common consent, sent safe on board ship by the Palermitans, and returned to Provence. In Messina was the strength of the French force, under the Viceroy, Heribert of Orleans. Messina rose. Heribert was compelled to submit to terms; he swore to transport himself and all his soldiers to Aigues Mortes, in Provence. He broke his oath, and landed in Calabria; the Messinese revenged his perjury on every Frenchman who was left behind. In one month, that of April, Sicily was free; the French had disappeared.

Such was the revolution which bears in history the appalling name of the Sicilian Vespers, sudden, popular, reckless, sanguinary, so as to appear the unpremeditated explosion of a people goaded to phrensy by intolerable oppression; yet general, simultaneous, orderly, so as to imply, if not some previous organisation, some slow and secret preparation of the public mind. John of Procida, the barons in league with John of Procida, appear not during the first outburst; the fleets of Peter of Arragon are yet within their harbours. The towns take

---

* Muoian le Francese! In this account I am quite with Amari against Mon. de St. Priest, who cannot forget to be a Frenchman.—See Amari's authorities, p. 103, and Appendix.

the lead: they assert their own independence, and form a league for mutual defence. Acts are dated as under the rule of the Church and the Republic. The Church is everywhere respected; it might seem as if the Sicilians supposed Nicolas III. still on the Pontifical throne, or that they would not believe that the Pope was so servile an adherent of the Angevine. They were soon disabused. When Charles first heard of the revolt, of the total loss of Sicily, and the massacre of at least two thousand Frenchmen, he lifted his eyes to Heaven in devout prayer: "O Lord God, if it hath pleased thee to visit me with adverse fortune, grant at least that it may come with gentle steps."[q] As though he had satisfied his religion by this one stern act of humility, no sooner had he reached Naples than he burst into the most furious paroxysms of wrath. Now he sat silent, glaring fiercely around him, gnawing the top of his sceptre; then broke forth into the most horrible vows of vengeance: "if he could live a thousand years, he would go on razing the cities, burning the lands, torturing the rebellious slaves. He would leave Sicily a blasted, barren, uninhabited rock, as a warning to the present age, an example to the future." Pope Martin, less violent in his demeanour, was hardly less so in his public acts. The Palermitans sent an embassy declaring their humble submission to the Papal See. The messengers were monks. They addressed the Pope—"O Lamb of God, that takest away the sins of the world, have mercy upon us!" Martin compared them to the Jews, who smote the Saviour, and cried "Hail, King of the Jews."[r] His Bull of excommunication describes in the blackest terms the horrors

---

[q] Villani, vii. 71.   [r] Ibid, 62.

of the massacre.[a] A crusade was proclaimed against the Sicilians: all ecclesiastics, archbishops, bishops, abbots, who favoured the insurgents, were at once deprived and deposed; all laymen stripped of their fiefs or estates. The people of Palermo sternly replied, that "they had unfolded the banner of St. Peter, in hopes, under that protection, to obtain their liberties; they must now unfold the banner of another Peter, the King of Arragon."[b]

Charles made the most vigorous preparations for war. The age and state of the public mind are singularly illustrated by the following story: a Mendicant Friar, Bartolomeo Piazza, appeared in his camp, a man of blameless morals and some learning; he disdained the disguise of a spy. He was led before the King. "How darest thou," Charles abruptly accosted him, "come from that land of traitors?" "Neither am I a traitor, nor come I from a land of traitors. I come, urged by religion and conscience, to warn my holy brethren that they follow not your unjust arms. You have abandoned the people committed by God to your charge to be torn by wolves and hounds; you have hardened your heart against complaints and supplications; they have avenged their wrongs, they will defend, they will die for, their holiest rights. Think of Pharaoh!" Either awe, or the notion that Bartolomeo would bear back a true account of his overwhelming forces, induced the King to endure this affront; the Friar returned to Messina.[c]

The Mendicant Friar.

Before Messina appeared Charles with all his army, burning for revenge. At first he obtained some suc-

---

[a] Saba Malaspina. The Bull in Raynald. sub ann. 1282.
[b] Compare Amari, Documento 1.;
a long oration, assuredly made after the time.
[c] Bartolom. de Neocastro, cap. 32, 34.

ceases; but the popular leader, Manfrone, was deposed, the Noble Alaimo da Lentini placed at the head of the garrison. The resistance became obstinate. The women were most active, as perhaps most exposed to the vengeance of the French. Their delicate hands bore stones, ammunition; they tended the sick and wounded.[x] The Legate of the Pope, the Cardinal Gerard, accompanied the King; he was armed with the amplest powers. He demanded, or was invited to enter the city. He was received with general jubilation, and escorted to the Cathedral; Alaimo da Lentini laid at his feet the keys of the city and his own staff of command. They entreated him to accept the dominion of the city in the name of the Church, to appoint a governor: "to the Church they would willingly pay their tribute, but away with the French! in the name of God let them be driven from the lands of the Church!" Gerard replied, if not in the fierce and criminatory tone ascribed to him by one historian as to insolent rebels, yet with a haughty condescension.[y] "Heinous as were their sins, they were not beyond the mercy of their mother the Church; he would reconcile the Messinese to their King; subjects must not speak of terms to their sovereign. Let them trust the magnanimity, the clemency of Charles; the savage murderers alone would meet with condign punishment. Let Messina lay herself in the lap of the Church; in her name to be restored to King Charles." "To Charles! Never!" shouted Alaimo; he seized his staff from the hand of the astonished Prelate. "To the French, never! so

---

[x] "Deh com' egli è gran pietate,
Delle donne de Messina.
Vaggendole scapigliate,
Portando pretia e calcina.
Iddio gli dia briga e travaglia,
A chi Messina vuol guastar."
—Popular song, quoted by Villani, vii. 77.

[y] Neocastro, Villani, Malaspina, &c.

long as we have blood to shed and swords to wield." The whole people took up the cry; Gerard made one more effort: thirty citizens were appointed to treat with the Legate; but all was in vain. They knew too well the mercy of Charles. "O, candid counsel of the Church to lay our necks down before the headsman! We are sold to the French; we must ransom ourselves by arms. We offer to the Pope the sovereignty of the land: Martin declines it. Instead of being the mild and gentle Vicar of Christ, he is but the tool of the French. Go and tell the Angevine tyrant that lions and foxes shall never more enter into Messina."

In the mean time, the fleets of Peter of Arragon were upon the seas; still disguising his aim, as if he designed to make war only on the Saracens of Africa, he landed his forces on the coast of Tunis. He appeared as the ally of the Prince of Constantina. He disembarked in the Port of Collo: he had some vigorous engagements with the Saracens.[1] He despatched ambassadors to Rome to implore the blessing of the Pope on his Crusade against the infidels, the protection of the Church for his dominions in Spain, the presence of a Legate, the right to levy the tenths for a war against the infidels. This specious embassage was received with specious civility by the Pope at Monte Fiascone.

*Peter of Arragon.
June 1.
June 28.*

The Parliament had met at Palermo; it had been determined to offer the throne of Sicily to Peter. He received the ambassadors of the Sicilians with grave solemnity; as offering to him unexpected, unsolicited honours. The Holy War was at an end; Peter and his fleet in the port of Trapani. At

King of Sicily.

---

[1] Zurita.

Palermo he was saluted by acclamation King of Sicily. The relief of Messina was the first aim of the new King. He ordered a general levy of all who could bear arms: men crowded to his banner. To Charles he sent an embassy of the noble Catalonians, Pietro Queralto, Ruy Ximenes de Luna, William Aymeric, Justiciary of Barcelona. He demanded safeconduct by two Carmelite Friars. In two days Charles declared that he would give them audience; two days—during which he hoped to find himself master of Messina. But his terrific assault by sea and land was repelled; instead of receiving the ambassadors of the King of Arragon as a haughty conqueror, he received them weary with toil, boiling with rage and baffled pride. He was seated on his bed, which was covered with rich silk drapery. He threw disdainfully aside on his pillow the letter of the King of Arragon: he awaited the address of the ambassador Queralto. Queralto's words were doubtless those of the letter, they ran thus: "The illustrious Peter, King, by the grace of God, of Arragon and Sicily, commands you, Charles, Count of Provence and King of Jerusalem, to depart from his kingdom; to give him free passage into his city of Messina, which you are besieging by sea and land; he is astonished at your presumption in impeding the passage of the King through his own dominions."* The ambassadors no doubt asserted the hereditary claim of the King of Arragon. Charles, with the gesture constantly ascribed to him, bit his sceptre in his wrath; his reply had his usual pride, but, by one account, something of dejection. He told the ambassadors to survey his vast forces; he expressed

Aug. 30.

Sept. 11.

Ambassadors to Charles.

---

* See, in Amari, the variations in the copies of this letter, p. 166, note.

utter astonishment that the King of Arragon should
presume to interfere between him and his rebellious
subjects; he held Naples and Sicily as a grant from
the Pope; but he intimated that he might withdraw his
weary troops to refresh them in Calabria: it would
only, however, be to return and wreak his vengeance
on Sicily; the Catalonian dominions of the King of
Arragon would not be safe from his resentment.

From this period the mind of Charles, never strong,
Conduct of Charles. but so insolent and tyrannical in prosperity,
sank into a strange prostration, in which fits
of an absurd chivalry alternated with utter abjectness.
He would neither press vigorously, nor abandon the
siege of Messina. Now he wreaked his vengeance on
all the lands in his possession, burned churches and
monasteries; now offered advantageous terms to the
Sicilians; now endeavoured openly to bribe Aluimo da
Lentini, who cast back his offers with public scorn. At
length, threatened by the fleets of Arragon, he withdrew to his continental dominions.

The climax of this strange state of mind was his
challenge to the King of Arragon, to determine their
quarrel by single combat. In vain the Pope denounced
the impiety, and remonstrated against the wild impolicy
of this feudal usage, now falling into desuetude. The
King of Arragon leaped at the proposition, which he
could so easily elude; and which left him full time to
consolidate undisturbed his new kingdom, to invade
Calabria, to cover the sea with his fleets. This defiance
to mortal combat, this wager of battle, was an appeal,
according to the wild justice of the age, to the God of
Battles, who, it was an established popular belief, would
declare himself on the righteous side. Charles of Anjou
had the opportunity of publicly arraigning before Chris-

tendom his hated rival of disloyal treachery, of secret
leaguing with his revolted subjects, of falsehood in his
protestations of friendship. The King of Arragon stood
forth on the broad ground of asserting his hereditary
right, of appearing as the deliverer of a people most
barbarously oppressed, as summoned to the crown by
the barons and people of Sicily. He was almost
admitted as possessing an equal claim with him who
had received the Papal investiture. The grave and
serious manner in which the time, the place, the manner
of holding those lists were discussed might seem to
portend a tragic close; this great ordeal would be commended to still greater honour and acceptance by the
strife of two monarchs for one of the noblest kingdoms
of the earth, the kingdom of Naples. Italy itself offered
no fair or secure field. The King of England, Edward I.,
was the one powerful and impartial monarch, who might
preside as umpire; his Gascon territories, a neutral
ground, on which might be waged this momentous combat. All proceeded with the most serious and solemn
dignity, as if there could be no doubt that the challenge
so given, so accepted, would come to direct and inevitable issue. Bordeaux was chosen as the scene of the
kingly tournament. The lists were prepared at great
cost and with great splendour. Each King proceeded
to enrol the hundred knights who were to have the
honour of joining in this glorious conflict with their
monarch. The noblest and bravest chivalry of France
offered themselves to Charles of Anjou; his nephew,
Philip the Hardy, offered to enter the lists with him.
On the side of Peter of Arragon were the most valiant
Spanish knights, men accustomed to joust with the Moor,
to meet the champions of the Crescent from Cordova or
Granada. A Moorish Prince presented himself; if God

gave the victory to Peter, not only would the Moor share the triumph, but submit to baptism in the name of the Christian's God. The Pope was overborne; the Church had pronounced its condemnation on judicial combats. Martin had condemned this on general grounds[b] and on the special objection, that it was setting on the issue of arms that which had already been solemnly adjudged by the supreme Pontiff; it was to call in question the Pope's right of granting the kingdom of Naples. He commanded Charles to desist from the humiliating comparison of himself and his heaven-sanctioned claims, with those of a presumptuous adventurer, of one already under the censure, under the excommunication of the Roman See; he offered to absolve the King from all his oaths: yet even on this point the Pope was compelled to yield his reluctant consent to the imperious will of his master.

The Pope endeavours in vain to prohibit the battle.

The wrath of the Pope on the first intelligence of the insurrection, still more at the invasion of the realm by Peter of Arragon, had been hardly less violent than that of Charles of Anjou. At Orvieto he proclaimed more than the excommunication, the degradation of Peter. He denounced again the crime of the Palermitans in the massacre of the French; the impious rebellion of the realm of Sicily; he boasted the mild attempts of the Church, especially through Cardinal Gerard in Messina, to reconcile them to their lawful Sovereign. "Since Peter, King of Arragon, under the false colour of an expedition to Africa, has invaded the island of Sicily—the peculiar territory of

His censure on the King of Arragon. March 21, 1283.

---

[b] Martin writes to King Edward of England that he had power "impediendi tam detestanda tam nociva."—MS., D. M., vol. xiv. Orvieto, April 15, 1284.

the Roman Church—with horse and foot; has set up the claim of his wife, the daughter of the accursed Manfred, to the throne; has usurped the name of King of Sicily;[c] has openly countenanced the Messinese as he before secretly instigated the Palermitans to rebel against their Sovereign: he has incurred the severest penalties, of usurpation, sedition, and violence. His crime is aggravated by the relation of the crown of Arragon to the See of Rome. That crown was granted by the Pope; his grandfather, Peter of Arragon, received it from the Pope, and swore fealty in his own name and in that of his successors to the successor of St. Peter." The King was now not only in rebellion; he had practised an impious fraud on his holy Father; he had implored the aid of the Pope, his blessing on his army, as though designed against the African barbarians. For these reasons not only was Peter adjudged a lawless usurper of the realm of Sicily, but deposed from his kingdom of Arragon; his subjects were discharged from all their oaths of fealty. His kingdom was to be seized and occupied by any Catholic Sovereign, who should be duly commissioned to that end by the Pope. The Cardinal of St. Cecilia was sent into France to offer the forfeited throne of Arragon to any one of the King's sons who would undertake the conquest: the only provision was the exclusion of the heir to the French throne: the two kingdoms could not be united under the same Sovereign. The subjugated realm was to be held of Pope Martin and his successors in the Apostolic

---

[c] The Pope seems here to charge Peter of Arragon with being the prime mover of the rebellion. "Sicque non solum Panormitanos eosdem, quos alias pluries ad haec solicitasse per nuncios dicebatur, in inchoatæ contra præfatum regem seditionis et rebellionis contumaciâ obfirmavit," &c. &c.—Raynald. 1283, xix.

See. The forfeiture comprehended the whole dominions of Peter, the kingdom of Arragon, the kingdom of Valencia, Catalonia, and Barcelona.

The wager of battle between the Kings, which maintained its solemn dignity up almost to the appointed time, ended in a pitiful comedy, in which Charles of Anjou had the ignominy of practising base and disloyal designs against his adversary; Peter, that of eluding the contest by craft, justifiable only as his mistrust of his adversary was well or ill grounded, but much too cunning for a frank and generous knight. He had embarked with his knights for the South of France; he was cast back by tempests on the shores of Spain. He set off with some of his armed companions, crossed the Pyrenees undiscovered, appeared before the gates of Bordeaux, and summoned the English Seneschal. To him he proclaimed himself to be the King of Arragon, demanded to see the lists, rode down them in slow state, obtained an attestation that he had made his appearance within the covenanted time, and affixed his solemn protest against the palpable premeditated treachery of his rival, which made it unsafe for him to remain longer at Bordeaux. Charles, on his part, was furious that Peter had thus broken through the spider's web of his policy. He was in Bordeaux, when Peter appeared under the walls, and had challenged him in vain. Charles presented himself in full armour on the appointed day, summoned Peter to appear, proclaimed him a recreant and a dastardly craven, unworthy of the name of knight.

Wager of battle.

Peter at Bordeaux.

May 31.

Pope Martin's enmity was as indefatigable as the ambition of Peter of Arragon. He strained his utmost power to break off a marriage proposed between Alfonso, the elder son of Peter, with Eleanora, the daughter of Edward of England. He expostulated with Edward on the degradation of allying his illustrious house with that of an excommunicated prince; he inhibited the marriage as within the fourth degree of consanguinity. By enormous charges on the Papal treasury he bought off the Venetians from a treaty, which would have placed their fleet on the enemy's side.[d] He borrowed still larger sums on the security of the Papal revenues, above 28,393 ounces of gold: the tenths decreed by the Council of Lyons were awarded to this new Crusade. The annual payment of 8000 ounces of gold for the kingdom of Naples was postponed, on account of the inability of the Prince of Salerno to discharge the debt. Thrice in the following year, on Holy Thursday, on Ascension Day, on the Dedication of St. Peter's church, the excommunication was promulgated at Orvieto, in Rome, in every city in Italy which would admit this display of Papal authority. The Cardinal Gerard, of S. Sabina, was commissioned to preach everywhere the Crusade: he might offer unlimited indulgences to all who would take up arms against Peter and the Sicilian rebels. The kingdom of Arragon, with the county of Barcelona and the kingdom of Valencia were solemnly adjudged to Charles of Valois, the son of the King of France. Great forces were prepared in France to invade these Spanish realms of Peter. But in the mean time, Martin himself might tremble in his dominions. Guido of Montefeltro was in arms, hardly kept in check by John of Epps, the Papal General. At Rome were threatening commo-

A.D. 1283.

---

[d] Five thousand ounces of gold, which were likewise to hire and man twenty galleys for the fleet of Charles.

tions: the Pope endeavoured to maintain his influence by the purchase of corn in great quantities in Apulia during a famine, its free or cheap distribution, and by other concessions. But the King of Arragon was not without his secret allies within the city.

Worse than this, Charles of Anjou returned to Italy; he was met by the disastrous tidings of the utter destruction of his fleet by Roger Loria, and the capture of his son Charles, Prince of Salerno. This precious hostage was in the power of his enemies; on him they might wreak their vengeance for the death of the young Conradin. Charles put on a haughty equanimity: "I had rather have heard of his death than of his captivity." He overwrought this proud endurance. He assembled the nobles; he enjoined them to rejoice with him that he had lost a priest, who had only impeded the vigour and success of his arms.* He entered Naples, and declared it mercy that he impaled only one out of a hundred and fifty, who were suspected or accused of tampering with the victorious Arragonese.

But his arms were to be arrested by a mightier power. One fatal year was to witness the death of all the great personages engaged in this conflict; it was to be bequeathed to a new generation of combatants. In the midst of his preparations for a more determined invasion of Sicily, Charles, exhausted by disappointment and sorrow, died at Foggia: the Papal writers aver he made a most Christian end. Philip of France, after a doubtful campaign in Catalonia, for the conquest of the Spanish dominions of Peter of Arragon, in behalf of his brother, Charles of Valois, died at Perpignan: Peter of Arragon about a month

Feb. 7, 1285.
Oct. 5.
Nov. 11.

* Ptolem. Luc. xiv. 9. Compare throughout Raynaldus, and Muratori, Annal. sub annis, with their authorities.

later at Villa Franca di l'enades. Alfonso, the elder son, quietly succeeded to his father's Arragonese crown; the infant James, according to his father's will, to that of Sicily. On the 29th of March before had died at Orvieto Pope Martin IV., who had emptied the whole armoury of excommunication against the enemies of Charles of Anjou.ᶠ Such was the issue of all the interdicts, the anathemas, the crusades, and all the blood shed to determine the possession of the throne of Sicily.

There was now no commanding interest to contest the Pontificate. The Emperor Rodolph did not busy himself much in Italian politics. A Roman Prelate, John Boccamuzza, Archbishop of Monreale, Cardinal Bishop of Tusculum, resided as Legate in Germany; he presided over a Council at Wurtzburg, in the presence of the Emperor Rodolph. A chronicler of the times compares him with the Dragon in the Revelations, dragging his venomous tail (a host of corrupt Bishops) through Germany, which he contaminated with his simoniac perversity, amassing riches from all quarters, selling privileges, which he instantly revoked to sell them again, bartering with utter shamelessness the patrimony of the Crucified: he was insulted by the lofty German Prelates; he retired muttering vengeance.ᵍ In Italy the Angevine cause was paralysed by the death of Charles, and the imprisonment of his son. The house of Arragon had no footing in the conclave. Under such circumstances the great families of Rome had usually some Prelate of sufficient weight and character, if parties among themselves were not too equally balanced, to advance to the highest eminence in the Church.

ᶠ Muratori, sub ann. 1285.
ᵍ Gothofridus Mon. apud Boehmer, Fontes, U. 111. Labbe, Concil. sub ann. 1286.

An Orsini had but now occupied the Papal throne, then a Savelli, and then a Pope of humble birth, enslaved by a nepotism of favour, not of blood, to the family of Colonna, followed in rapid succession. The Savelli, Honorius IV., was a man of great ability, a martyr to the gout. Almost his only important acts were the publication of two Edicts, matured under his predecessor Martin, which if issued and carried out under the Angevine reign in Naples and Sicily, might perhaps have averted the revolt. One was designed to propitiate the clergy of the realm: it asserted in the highest terms their independence, immunities, freedom of election, and other privileges. The second re-enacted the laws, and professed to renew the policy of William the Good, the most popular monarch who had ever reigned in Sicily.[b] But they came too late. Sicily first under James, the second son of Peter of Arragon, afterwards, on the accession of James to the throne of Arragon, under Frederick, defied the Papal authority, and remained an independent kingdom. The captive Charles, now King of Naples, had framed a treaty for his own deliverance; he bought it at the price of his kingdom of Sicily and the city of Reggio. Although the Pope annulled the treaty which granted away the dominion of the Apostolic See, it was held to be of force by the contracting parties. This was the last act of Honorius IV.[1]

The Conclave met; for months, the hot summer months, they sate in strife: six of them died. The Cardinal Bishop of Præneste, by keeping a constant fire in his chamber, corrected the bad air, and maintained his vigour; the rest fled in fear. In February they met

---

[b] Raynald. sub ann. Sept. 17.   [1] He died April 3, 1287.

again: their choice fell on the Cardinal of Præneste, the General of the Franciscan Order, the _{Feb. 22, 1288.} first of that Order who had ascended the _{Nicolas IV.} Papal throne. The Bishop of Præneste, born, it is said, of lowly race, at Ascoli, owed his elevation to the Cardinalate to the Orsini, Nicolas III. In gratitude to his patron he took the name of Nicolas IV. His first promotion of Cardinals, though it seemed impartially distributed among the great local and religious interests, betrayed his inclinations. There was one Dominican, Matthew Acquasparta, the General of the Order; an Orsini, Napoleon; one of the house of Colonna, Peter; there was one already of that house in the Conclave, Jacobo Colonna. On the Colonnas were heaped all the wealth and honours; under their safeguard the Pope, who at first took up his residence at Rieti, ventured to occupy the Papal palace at Rome.

The liberation of Charles the Lame, the King of Naples, from his long captivity, was the great affair of Christendom. The mediation of Edward of England, allied with the houses of Arragon and of Anjou, and now the most powerful monarch in Europe, was employed to arrange the terms of some treaty which should restore him to freedom. The King of Arragon would not surrender his captive, still in prison in Catalonia, but at the price of the recognition of the Arragonese title to the kingdom of Sicily; Charles, weary of bondage, had already at Oleron acceded to this basis of the treaty.

By the treaty of Oleron,[k] Charles was to pay fifty thousand marks of silver. He pledged himself _{July 15, 1287.} to arrange a peace in a manner satisfactory to the Kings of Arragon and of Sicily: in the mean time

---

[k] The treaty and documents in Rymer, 1286-7.

there was to be a truce between the two realms, including Sicily. Charles was to obtain the ratification of the Pope, and the cession of Charles of Valois, who still claimed, as awarded by the Pope, the crown of Arragon; or at the close of that period he was to return into captivity. He was to surrender his three sons, and sixty Provençal Nobles and Barons, as hostages: the Seneschals of the fortresses in Provence were to take an oath that if the King did not terminate the peace or return into bondage, they were to surrender those fortresses to the King of Arragon. This treaty had been annulled first during the vacancy by the College of Cardinals, again at Rieti by Nicolas IV. The King of England was urged to find some other means of releasing the royal captive. King Alfonso was forbidden to aid the cause of his brother James of Sicily; in that cause Alfonso himself had grown cool. A new treaty was framed at Campo Franco; it was written by a Papal notary. Charles was to pay at once twenty thousand marks (England lent ten thousand); he was to give security for the rest. He was to pledge his word to the other conditions of the compact.* In this treaty there was a vague silence concerning the kingdom of Sicily: within one year Charles was bound to procure peace between France and Arragon: for this he left his three sons as hostages; and solemnly swore that if this peace was not ratified, he would return to his prison. He obtained his freedom.

Oct. 20, 1288.

Liberation of Charles the Lame. Nov. 1288.

Nicolas IV. on his accession had not dared to take up his residence at Rome; Charles appeared before him at

---

* Rymer, p. 368 et seq. The whole progress of the negotiation is well and accurately traced by Amari, in a note to c. 13, p. 321.

Rieti. He was crowned, if not in direct violation of the words, of the whole spirit of the treaty, King of Naples and Sicily; for the whole of the dominions claimed by the house of Anjou he did homage and swore fealty to the Pope.* The Pope boldly and without scruple annulled the treaty written by his own notary, signed, executed without any protest on his part, by which Charles the Lame had obtained his freedom. This decree of Nicolas was the most monstrous exercise of the absolving power which had ever been advanced in the face of Christendom: it struck at the root of all chivalrous honour, at the faith of all treaties. It declared, in fact, that no treaty was to be maintained with any one engaged in what the Holy See might pronounce an unjust war, that is a war contrary to her interests—a war such as that now waged between James of Arragon, as King of Sicily, and the crusading army of the son of Charles the Lame. The war of the house of Arragon against the house of Anjou being originally unjust, no compact was binding. The kingdom of Naples, including Sicily, having been granted by the Holy See as a fief, the title of Charles was indefeasible; himself had no power of surrendering it to another. It declared that all obligations entered into by a prince in captivity were null and void, even though oaths had been interchanged and hostages given for their performance. Charles had no right to pledge the Roman See and the King of France, and the King of Arragon (Charles of Valois had assumed that title) to such terms. If Charles had sworn that should those Kings not accede to the treaty, he would return into captivity, the Pope replied that the imprisonment having been from the first unjust, Charles

---

* May 29 (Muratori), June 19 (Amari), 1289.

was not bound to return to it: his services being imperiously demanded as a vassal and special athlete for the defence of the Church, he was bound to fulfil that higher duty.* On these grounds Pope Nicolas IV. declared the King and his heirs altogether released from all obligations and all oaths. He went further; he prohibited Charles the Lame from observing the conditions of the treaty, and surrendering his eldest son, according to the covenant, as one of the hostages. Nor was the Pope content with thus entirely abrogating the treaty; he anathematised King Alfonso for exacting, contrary to the commands of the Church, such hard terms; he ordered him, under pain of the highest ecclesiastical censure, to release Charles from all the conditions of the treaty; he even threatened the King of England with interdict, if, as guarantee of the treaty, he should enforce its forfeitures. But Charles the Lame himself would not be content with the Papal absolution: he satisfied his chivalrous honour with a more miserable subterfuge. He suddenly appeared near the castle of Panicas, on the borders of Arragon, proclaimed that he was come in conformity to his oath to surrender himself into captivity. But as no one was there on the part of the King of Arragon to receive him, he averred that he had kept his faith, and even demanded the restoration of the hostages and of the money left in pawn.

The war continued: James, not content with the occupation of Sicily, invaded Apulia; before Gaeta he suffered an ignominious failure. Charles, weakly, to the disgust of the Count of Artois and his other French followers who returned to France,

Spring, 1289.

---

* "Nominatæ Ecclesiæ incommoda' athleta ab illius per hoc defensionem submulta proveniant, dum ipse ejusdem trahitur."—Bulla Nicolai IV. Com-ecclesiæ vassallos præcipuus, et specialis pars Raynaldus, sub ann.

agreed to a truce of two years. The death of his brother Alfonso made James King of Arragon: he left his younger brother Frederick his Viceroy in Sicily. Frederick became afterwards the founder of the line of Arragonese Kings of the island.

Nicolas IV. closed his short Pontificate in disaster, shame, and unpopularity. He had in some respects held a lofty tone; he had declared the kingdom of Hungary a fief of the Holy See; and rebuked the Emperor Rodolph for causing his son, Albert, without the Pope's permission, to be chosen King of the Romans.[p] But the total loss of the last Christian possessions in the East, the surrender of Berytus, Tripoli, even at last Acre,[q] to the irresistible Sultan: the fatal and ignominious close of the Crusades, so great a source of Papal power and Papal influence, the disgrace which was supposed to have fallen on all Christendom, but with special weight upon its Head, bowed Nicolas down in shame and sorrow. The war between Edward of England and Philip of France, in which his mediation, his menace, were loftily rejected or courteously declined, destroyed all hopes of a new Crusade; that cry would no longer pacify ambitious and hostile Kings.

Nicolas had become enslaved to the Colonnas. No doubt under their powerful protection he had continued to reside in Rome.[r] They were associated in his munificence to the Churches. On the vault of S. Maria Maggiore, repaired at their common

---

[p] Raynald. sub ann.
[q] Read the siege of Acre (Ptolemais) in Michaud, iv. 458 et seq. Wilken, vii. p. 735 et seq. Acre fell, May 18, 1291. Michaud quotes the emphatic sentence of a Mussulman writer on this, it seems, final close of the Crusades:—"Les choses, s'il plait à Dieu, resteront ainsi jusqu'au dernier jugement."—P. 487.
[r] Franciscus Pipin., S. R. I., t. ix.

cost, appeared painted together the Pope and the Cardinal James Colonna. John Colonna was appointed Marquis of Ancona, Stephen Colonna Count of Romagna: this high office had been wrested from the Monaldeschi. Cesena, Rimini after some resistance, Imola, Forlì were in his power. In attempting to seize Ravenna he was himself surprised and taken prisoner by the sons of Guido di Polenta. But they were afterwards overawed by the vigorous measures of the Pontiff, urged by the Colonnas. Ildobrandino da Romagna, Bishop of Arezzo, was invested with the title of Count of Romagna; the subject cities leagued under his influence;* the sons of Polenta were compelled to pay three thousand florins of gold for their daring attack on the Pope's Court.† The Romans seemed to enter into the favouritism of the Pope. James Colonna was created Senator; he was dragged, as in the guise of an Emperor, through the city, and saluted with the name of Cæsar; he gratified the Romans by marching at their head to the attack of Viterbo and other cities over which Rome, whenever occasion offered, aspired to extend her sovereignty.‡

There were acts in these terrible wars that raged in almost every part of Italy which might have grieved the heart of a wise and humane Pontiff more than the loss of the Holy Land. The mercy of Christendom might seem at a lower ebb than its valour. The Bishop of Arezzo, an Ubaldini, was killed in a battle against the

---

* Muratori, sub annis 1290, 1291.
† Rubeus, Chronic. Ravennat., Chronic. Parm., Chronic. Forliviens. S. R. I. xiii.
‡ The play upon the name of Colonna, which Petrarch afterwards enshrined in his noble verse, had long occurred to the Saturnalian wit of Rome. In the frontispiece of a book, entitled "The Beginning of Evils," the Pope Nicolas IV. was represented as a column crowned by his own mitred head, and supported by two other columns.—Muratori.

Florentines; the Florentines slung an ass, with a mitre fastened on his head, into his beleaguered city.ˣ The Marquis of Montferrat, the most powerful prince in northern Italy, was taken prisoner by the Alexandrians, shut up in an iron cage, in which he languished for nearly two years and died.ʸ Dante has impressed indelibly on the heart of man the imprisonment and death of the Pisan Ugolino (a man, it is true, of profound ambition and treachery) with that of his guiltless sons.

A.D. 1290.

Nicolas is said to have died in sorrow and humiliation; he died accused by the Guelfs of unpapal Ghibellinism,ᵃ perhaps because he was more sparing of his anathemas against the Ghibellines, and had consented, hardly indeed, but had consented to the peace between France and Arragon, Naples and Sicily: still more on account of his favour to the Colonnas, Ghibelline by descent and by tradition, and hereafter to become more obstinately, furiously, and fatally Ghibelline in their implacable feud with Boniface VIII.ᵇ

April 4, 1292

ˣ 1289. Villani, vii. c. 130. Muratori, sub ann.

ʸ Annal. Mediolanens. S. R. T. t. xvi.

ᵇ Rodolph of Hapsburg, the Emperor, died July 15, 1291.

ᵃ "Ma molto favoreggiò i Ghibellini." So writes the Guelf Villani, vii. c. 150.

CHAPTER VI.

Cœlestine V.

Conclave. NICOLAS IV. died on the 4th of April, 1292. Only twelve Cardinals formed the Conclave. The constitution of Gregory X. had been long suspended, and had fallen altogether into disuse. Six of these Cardinals were Romans, of these two Orsinis and two Colonnas; four Italians; two French.[a] Each of the twelve might aspire to the supreme dignity. The Romans prevailed in numbers, but were among themselves more implacably hostile: on the one side stood the Orsinis, on the other the Colonnas.[b] Three

---

[a] The list in Ciacconius:—

Romans.

1. Latino Malabranca, a Franciscan, Cardinal of Ostia, the nephew of, and created by, Nicolas III.
2. John Buccamazza, Cardinal of Tusculum (once Legate in Germany), created by Martin IV.
3. Jacobo Colonna, Cardinal of S. Maria in Viâ Latâ, created by Nicolas III.
4. Peter Colonna, Cardinal of S. Eustachio, created by Nicolas IV.
5. Napoleon Orsini, Cardinal of S. Hadrian, created by Nicolas IV.
6. Matteo Rosso (Rubeus), Cardinal of S. Maria in Portico, created by Urban IV.

Italians.

7. Gerard Bianchi of Parma, Cardinal Sabinus, created by Honorius IV.
8. Matthew Acquasparta, Cardinal of Porto, created by Nicolas IV.
9. Peter Peregrosso, a Milanese, Cardinal of S. Mark, created by Nicolas IV.
10. Benedetto Gaetani of Anagni, Cardinal of S. Silvester (afterwards Boniface VIII.), created by Martin IV. He was dangerously ill, retired to his native Anagni, and recovered.

Frenchmen.

11. Hugh de Billiom, Cardinal of S. Sabina, created by Nicolas III.
12. Jean Cholet, Cardinal of S. Cecilia, died of fever in Rome, Aug. 2, 1292.

[b] The proceedings of each member of the Conclave, during this interval,

times they met, in the palace of Nicolas IV., near S. Maria Maggiore, in that of Honorius IV. on the Aventine, and in S. Maria sopra Minerva.[c] The heats of June, and a dangerous fever (of which, one, the Frenchman, Jean Cholet, died), drove them out of Rome; and Rome became such a scene of disorder, feud, and murder (the election of the Senator being left to the popular suffrage), that they dared not reassemble within the walls. Two rival Senators, an Orsini and a Colonna, were at the head of the two factions.[d] Above a year had elapsed, when the Conclave agreed to meet again at Perugia. The contest lasted eight months more. At one time the two Colonnas and John of Tusculum had nearly persuaded Hugh of Auvergne and Peter the Milanese to join them in electing a Roman, one of the Colonnas. The plan was discovered and thwarted by the Orsini, Matteo Rosso. The Guelfic Orsini were devoted to the interests of Charles, the King of Naples; they laboured to advance a prelate in the Angevine interest. The Colonnas, Ghibelline because the Orsini were Guelf, were more for themselves than for Ghibellinism. Charles of Naples came to Perugia, by his personal presence to overawe the refractory members of the Conclave. The intrepid Benedict Gaetani, the future

Oct. 16, 1292. St. Luke's day.

In Perugia.

---

are described in the preface to the poem of the Cardinal St. George.—Muratori, v. p. 616. The Cardinal describes himself as being "veluti præsens, videns, ministrans, palpans, et audiens, notusque Pontifici, quis Pontificibus carus."—P. 614.

[c] The Cardinal of St. George highly disapproved of the building of new palaces, by Honorius IV. on the Aventine, by Nicolas IV. near S. Maria Maggiore. It implied the desertion of the Lateran and the Vatican:—

"ære utile mundo
Exemplum, nam quisque suos (eo) ducet in
  suam
Ædes, et reputia Petri delubra relinquet,
Ac Lateranæuore aulas, regalia dona,
Despiciet, sanctaos proprios habitare palatos.'—P. 621.

[d] One of the Senators was Peter the son of Stephen, father of the author; the other, Otho de San Eustasio.—See Cardinal St. George.

Boniface VIII., haughtily rebuked him for presuming to interfere with the office of the Holy Spirit. No one of the Cardinals would yield the post to his adversary, and expose himself to the vengeance of a successful rival; yet all seemed resolute to confine the nomination to their own body.

Suddenly a solitary monk was summoned from his cell, in the remote Abruzzi, to ascend the Pontifical throne. The Cardinal of Ostia, Latino Malebranca, had admired the severe and ascetic virtues of Peter Morrone, a man of humble birth, but already, from his extraordinary austerities, held by the people as a man of the highest sanctity. He had retired from desert to desert, and still multitudes had tracked him out in vast swarms, some to wonder at, some to join his devout seclusion. He seemed to rival if not to outdo the famous anchorites of old. His dress was haircloth, with an iron cuirass; his food bread and water, with a few herbs on Sunday.

<small>Latino Malebranca.</small>

Peter Morrone has left an account of his own youth. The brothers of his Order, who took his name, the Cœlestinians, vouched for its authenticity. His mother was devoutly ambitious that one of her eleven children should be dedicated to God. Many of them died, but Peter fulfilled her most ardent desires. His infancy was marked with miracles. In his youth he had learned to read the Psalter; he then knew not the person of the Blessed Virgin, or of St. John. One day they descended bodily from a picture of the Crucifixion, stood before him, and sweetly chanted portions of the Psalter. At the age of twenty he went into the desert: visions of Angels were ever round him, sometimes showering roses over him. God showed him a great stone, under which he dug a hole, in which he

<small>Peter Morrone.</small>

could neither stand upright, nor stretch his limbs, and there he dwelt in all the luxury of self-torture among lizards, serpents, and toads. A bell in the heavens constantly sounded to summon him to prayers. He was offered a cock; he accepted the ill-omened gift; for his want of faith the bell was thenceforth silent. He was more sorely tried; beautiful women came and lay down by his side.* He was encircled by a crowd of followers, whom he had already formed into a kind of Order or Brotherhood; they were rude, illiterate peasants from the neighbouring mountains.†

Either designedly or accidentally the Cardinal Malebranca spoke of the wonderful virtues of the hermit, Peter Morrone; the weary Conclave listened with interest. A few days after the Cardinal declared that a vision had been vouchsafed to a Holy Man, that if before All-Saints' Day they had not elected a Pope, the wrath of God would fall on them with some signal chastisement. "This, I presume," spake Benedetto Gaetani, "is one of the visions of your Peter Morrone." In truth it was; Malebranca had received a letter purporting to be in his hand. The Conclave was in that perplexed and exhausted state, when men seize desperately on any strange counsel to extricate themselves from their difficulty. To some it might seem a voice from heaven. Others might shelter their own disappointment under the consolation that their rivals were equally disappointed: all might think it wise to

<small>Election of Cœlestine V.</small>

<small>* One vision is too coarse almost to allude to; but how are we to judge of the times or the men without their coarseness? The question was whether he should offer mass "post pollutionem nocturnam." The vision which sets his mind at rest is that of "stercorandi" on the steps of a palace, that of the Holy Trinity. One of these awful persons is represented as pointing the moral of this foul imagination.

† "Non nulla salis ad rusticos turba Montibus altisonis."—Card. St. George.</small>

elect a Pope without personal enmity to any one. It might be a winning hazard for each party, each interest, each Cardinal; the Hermit was open to be ruled, as ruled he would be, by any one. Mulebranca saw the impression he had made; he pressed it in an eloquent speech. Peter Morrone was declared supreme Pontiff by unanimous acclamation.*

The fatal sentence was hardly uttered when the brief unanimity ceased. Some of the cardinals began to repent or to be ashamed of their precipitate decree. No one of them (this they were hereafter to rue) would undertake the office of bearing the tidings of his elevation to the Pope. The deputation consisted of the Archbishop of Lyons, two Bishops, and two notaries of the Court.

The place of Morrone's retreat was a cave in a wild mountain above the pleasant valley of Sulmona. The ambassadors of the Conclave having achieved their journey from Perugia, with difficulty found guides to conduct them to the solitude. As they toiled up the rugged ascent, they were overtaken by the Cardinal Peter Colonna, who had followed them without commission from the rest, no doubt to watch their proceedings, and to take advantage of any opportunity to advance his own interests. The cave, in which the saint could neither sit upright nor stretch himself out, had a grated window with iron bars, through which he uttered his oracular responses to the wondering people. None even of the brethren of the order might penetrate into the dark sanctuary of his austerities. The ambassadors of the Conclave found an old man with

His retreat.

---

* The Cardinal St. George describes the order and manner in which the Cardinals gave their accession to this vote.—P. 617.

a long shaggy beard, sunken eyes overhung with heavy brows, and lids swollen with perpetual weeping, pale hollow cheeks, and limbs meagre with fasting: they fell on their knees before him, and he before them. The future Cardinal-Poet was among the number: his barren Muse can hardly be suspected of invention.[h]

So Peter Morrone the Hermit saw before him, in submissive attitudes, the three prelates, attended by the official notaries, who announced his election to the Papacy. He thought it was a dream: and for once assuredly there was a profound and religious reluctance to accept the highest dignity in the world. He protested with tears his utter inability to cope with the affairs, to administer the sacred trust, to become the successor of the Apostle.[i] The news spread abroad; the neighbouring people came hurrying by thousands, delighted that they were to have a saint, and their own saint, for a Pope. The Hermit in vain tried to escape; he was brought back with respectful force, guarded with reverential vigilance. Nor was it the common people only who were thus moved. King Charles himself may not have been superior to the access of religious wonder, for to him especially (if indeed there was no design in the whole affair) this sudden unanimity among the ambitious Cardinals might pass for a miracle, more miraculous than many which were acknowledged by the common belief. The King of Naples, accompanied by his son, now in right of his wife entitled King of

---

[h] Cardinal St. George, apud Muratori.

[i] The Cardinal St. George, however, asserts that Celestine hardly affected reluctance; and the Cardinal says that he was among a great multitude of all ranks, who clambered up the mountain, "cursu concertadere monstrum Gliscrtham vates, montis vulusque readans," to catch a glimpse of the Pope.

Hungary, hastened to do honour to his holy subject, to persuade the Hermit, who perhaps would be dazzled by royal flatteries into a useful ally, to accept the proffered dignity. The Hermit-Pope was conducted from his lowly cave to the monastery of Santo Spirito, at the foot of the mountain. He still refused to be invested in the pontifical robes. At length arrived the Cardinal Malebranca: his age, dignity, character, and his language, urging the awful responsibility which Peter Morrone would incur by resisting the manifest will of God, and by keeping the Popedom longer vacant (for all which he would be called to give account on the day of judgement), prevailed over the awe-struck saint. Not the least earnest in pressing him to assume at once the throne were his rude but not so unambitious hermit brethren: they too looked for advancement; they followed him in crowds wherever he went, to Aquila and to Naples. Over his shaggy sackcloth at length the Hermit put on the gorgeous attire of the Pontiff; yet he would not go to Perugia to receive the homage of the Conclave. Age and the heat of the season (he had been accustomed to breathe the mountain air) would not permit him to undertake the long unwonted journey. He entered the city of Aquila riding on an ass, with a King on each side of him to hold his bridle. Some of the indignant clergy murmured at this humiliation of the Papal majesty (the successor of St. Peter was wont to ride on a stately palfrey), but they suppressed their discontent.

Peter Morrone Pope.

If there had been more splendid, never was there so popular an election. Two hundred thousand spectators (of whom the historian, Ptolemy of Lucca, was one[k])

---

[k] "Quibus ipse interfui."—Ptolem. Luc.

crowded the streets. In the evening the Pope was compelled again and again to come to the window to bestow his benediction; and if hierarchical pride had been offended at the lowliness of his pomp, it but excited greater admiration in the commonalty: they thought of Him who entered Jerusalem "riding on an ass's colt." Miracles confirmed their wonder: a boy, lame from the womb, was placed on the ass on which the Pope had ridden; he was restored to the full use of his limbs. *Inauguration.*

But already the Cardinals might gravely reflect on their strange election. The Pope still obstinately refused to go to Perugia, or even to Rome, though they suggested that he might be conveyed in a litter. The Cardinals declared that they were not to be summoned to the kingdom of Naples. Two only, Hugh of Auvergne and Napoleon Orsini, condescended to go to Aquila. Malebranca probably had begun to droop under the illness which ere long carried him off. But the way in which the Pope began to use his vast powers still more appalled and offended them. He bestowed the offices in his court and about his person on rude and unknown Abruzzese; and to the great disgust of the clergy, appointed a layman his secretary. High at once in his favour rose the French Prelate, Hugh Ascalon de Billiom, Archbishop of Benevento under Nicolas IV., Cardinal of S. Sabina. He had been the first to follow Malebranca in the acclamation of the Pope Morrone. On the death of Malebranca he was raised to the Bishopric of Ostia and Velletri, and became Dean of the College of Cardinals. Large pensions, charged on great abbeys in France, gilded his elevation. The Frenchman seemed destined to rule with undivided sway over the feeble Cœlestine: *The Cardinals repent.* *Hugh of Ascalon.*

the Italians looked with undisguised jealousy and aversion on the foreign prelate.ᵐ

The Cardinal, Napoleon Orsini, assisted at the inauguration, gave to the Pope the scarlet mantle, the mitre set with gold and jewels; he announced to the people that Peter had taken the name of Cœlestine V. The foot of the lowly hermit was kissed by kings, cardinals, bishops, nobles. He was set on high to be adored by the people.ⁿ The numbers of the clergy caused singular astonishment; but the Cardinals, though reluctant, would not allow the coronation to proceed without them; they came singly and in unwilling haste.º Last of all came Benedetto Gaetani:

Coronation. he had deeply offended Charles of Naples by his haughty rebuke at Perugia. Yet still, though all assisted at the ceremony, the place of honour was given to the French Cardinal: he anointed the new Pope, but the Pontiff was crowned by Matteo Rosso, after Malebranca's death, probably the elder of the Cardinals present.ᵖ

A few months showed that meekness, humility, *Cœlestine V.* holiness, unworldliness might make a saint; *in Naples.* they were not the virtues suited to a Pope. To Naples he had been led, as it were, in submissive triumph by King Charles; he took up his residence in the royal palace, an unsuspecting prisoner, mocked

---

ᵐ Compare on Hugh Ascalon de Billiom, Hist. Littér. de la France, xx. 73.

ⁿ "Quod stupori erat videre, quia magis venishant ad suam obtinendam benedictionem, quam pro præbendæ acquisitione."—Ptolem. Luc.

º "Domini Jacobus de Colonna, et Dominus Rubeus, et Dominus Hugo de Ascalon"—(he must have been there before)—"Aquilam veniunt, factique sunt domini Curiæ, quod alii Cardinales videntes Aquilam properant."— Ptolem. Luc. Annal. p. 1298.

"Hæc postquam videre Rubri, seu morte Latini
Fracti animos, coierunt ad tanta pericula
euntes."—Cardin. N. George, p 635.

ᵖ He was created by Urban IV.

CHAP. VI.   CONDUCT OF CŒLESTINE V.   463

with the most ostentatious veneration. So totally did
the harmless Cœlestine surrender himself to his royal
protector, that he stubbornly refused to leave Naples.
His utter incapacity for business soon appeared; he
lavished offices, dignities, bishoprics, with profuse hand;
he granted and revoked grants, bestowed benefices,
vacant or about to be vacant.[q] He was duped by the
officers of his court, and gave the same benefice over
and over again; but still the greater share fell to his
brethren from the Abruzzi. His officers issued orders
of all kinds in his name. He shrunk from
publicity, and even from the ceremonial duties   *His conduct.*
of his office; he could speak only a few words of bad
Latin. One day, when he ought to have sat on the
pontifical tribunal, he was sought in vain; he had
taken refuge in the church, and was with difficulty
persuaded to resume his state. His weakness made
him as prodigal of his power as of his gifts.[r]
At the dictation of King Charles he created   *Sept. 1294.*
at once thirteen new Cardinals, thus outnumbering the
present conclave.[s] Of these, seven were French; the

---

[q] "Dabat enim dignitates, prælationes, officia et beneficia, in quibus non sequebatur curiæ consuetudinem, sed potius quorundam suggestionem, et suam rudem simplicitatem."—Jacob. a Vorag. apud Muratori S. R. T. iii. p. 54. "Multa fecit de plenitudine potestatis sed plura de plenitudine simplicitatis," ibid. The favouritism of the French Cardinal of S. Sabina, by this author's account, was generally odious.

"O quam multipliere indocta potentia fortunæ Edidit, indulgens, damans, factumque recremt,
Atque vacaturus concedens atque vacansem."—Card. S. Georg.

—See also Ptolem. Luc. lxxiv. c. 29.

[r] There was a small monkish tyranny about the good Cœlestine. He compelled the monks of the ancient and famous abbey of Monte Casino to wear the dress of his own order. The Cardinal-Poet is pathetic on this:—

"Syderei colla, Montisque Casini
Occupatit, heu! monachos habitum assumere fratrum
Devotum sub lege Petri (Morrona) non nollus ab inde,
Dum parere urgat, monachus tanc exalat,
O quam
Decipieris!"

[s] See the list in Ciacconius. One, a Beneventan, Cardinal of S. Vitale, died the next year.

rest Italians; of the latter, three Neapolitans, not one Roman. In order to place the Conclave more completely in the power of Charles, who intended to keep him till his death in his own dominions, he re-enacted the Conclave law of Gregory X.

<small>Wishes to abdicate.</small>

<small>Benedetto Gaetani.</small>

The weary man became anxious to lay down his heavy burthen. Some of the Cardinals urged upon him that he retained the Papacy at the peril of his soul. Gaetani's powerful mind (once at Naples, he resumed the ascendancy of his commanding abilities) had doubtless great influence in his determination. He was soon supposed to rule the Court and the Pope himself, to be Cœlestine's bosom counsellor.* It was reported, and the trick was attributed to Gaetani his ambitious successor, that through a hole skilfully contrived in the wall of his chamber, a terrible voice was repeatedly heard at the dead of night, announcing itself as that of a messenger of God. It commanded the trembling Pontiff to renounce the blandishments of the world, and devote himself to God's service. Rumour spread abroad that Cœlestine was about to abdicate. The King secretly, the monks of his brotherhood openly, worked upon the lower order of Naples, and instigated them to a holy insurrection. Naples was in an uproar at this rumoured degradation of the Pope. A long and solemn procession of all the clergy, of whom Ptolemy of Lucca was one, passed through the city to the palace. A Bishop, a kind of prolocutor, addressed him with a voice like a trumpet, urging him to abandon his fatal design. The speech was heard by Ptolemy of Lucca. Another

---

[1] "Gaetani—eo quod Regem Carolum Perusii multum exasperasset, qui statim suis ministeriis et artibus factus est Dominus Curiæ et amicus Regis."—Ptolem. Luc. p. 1299.

Bishop from the walls announced that the Pope had no such intention. The Bishop below immediately broke out into a triumphant *Te Deum*, which was taken up by a thousand voices. The procession passed away."

But Advent was drawing on. Cœlestine would not pass that holy season in pomp and secular business. He had contrived a cell within the royal palace, from whence he could not see the sky. He had determined to seclude himself in all his wonted solitude and undisturbed austerities, like a bird, says the Cardinal-Poet, which hides its head from the fowler, and thinks that it is unseen." He had actually signed a commission to three Cardinals to administer during his seclusion the affairs of the Popedom: it wanted but the seal to be a Papal Bull. But this perhaps more dangerous step of putting the Papacy in commission was averted.

Long and inconclusive debates took place on the legality of a Papal abdication. Could any human power release him who was the representative of Christ on earth from his obligations? Could the successor of St. Peter, of his own free will, sink back into the ordinary race of men? Holy Orders were indelible: how much more indelible must be the consecration to this office, the fount and source of all Apostolic ordination? Cœlestine himself, from irresolution doubtless rather than artful dissimulation, had lulled his supporters, even the King himself, into security.' On a sudden, on the day of S. Lucia, the Conclave was summoned to receive the abdication

---

" Ptolem. Luc. apud Muratori.
" P. 638.
' " Dissimulans, seu vera loquens, allisque vacare sollicitas, quo ad illa domus secreta, Patresque

Credidervint, hunc nolle quidem dimittere primum.
Cumque forot generalis fides, capiscaque pararent,
Rex etiam, miri cæpisse oblivis facti, immemorem varioinque l'etrum, &c."
Card. St. George.

of the Pope. The trembling Cœlestine alleged as the cause of his abdication, his age, his rude manners and ruder speech, his incapacity, his inexperience. He confessed humbly his manifold errors, and entreated the Conclave to bestow upon the world of Christendom a pastor not liable to such infirmities. The Conclave is said to have been moved to tears, yet no one (all no doubt prepared) refused to accept the abdication. But the Pope was urged first, while his authority was yet full and above appeal, to issue a Constitution declaring that the Pope might at any time lay down his dignity, and that the Cardinals were at liberty to receive that voluntary demission of the Popedom. No sooner was this done than Cœlestine retired;

Abdication. he stripped off at once the cumbrous magnificence of his Papal robes and his two-horned mitre; he put on the coarse and rugged habit of his brotherhood. As soon as he could, the discrowned Pope withdrew to his old mountain hermitage.

The abdication of Cœlestine V. was an event unprecedented in the annals of the Church, and jarred harshly against some of the first principles of the Papal authority. It was a confession of common humanity, of weakness below the ordinary standard of men, in him whom the Conclave, with more than usual certitude, as guided by the special interposition of the Holy Ghost, had raised to the spiritual throne of the world. The Conclave had been, as it seemed, either under an illusion as to this declared manifestation of the Holy Spirit, or had been permitted to deceive itself. Nor was there less incongruity in a Pope, whose office invested him in something at least approaching to infallibility, acknowledging before the world his utter incapacity, his undeniable fallibility. That idea, formed out of many conflicting conceptions, yet forcibly harmonised by long traditionary reverence, of unerring wisdom, oracular truth, authority which it was sinful to question or limit, was strangely disturbed and confused, not as before by too overweening ambition, or even awful yet still unacknowledged crime, but by avowed weakness, bordering on imbecility. His profound piety hardly reconciled the confusion. A saint, after all, made but a bad Pope.

It was viewed, in his own time, in a different light by different minds. The monkish writers held it up as the most noble example of monastic, of Christian perfection. Admirable as was his election, his abdication was even more to be admired. It was an example of humility stupendous to all, imitable by few.[a] The divine approval was said to be shown by a miracle which followed directly on his resignation;[b] but the scorn of man has been expressed by the undying verse of Dante, who condemned him who was guilty of the baseness of the "great refusal" to that circle of hell where are those disdained alike by mercy and justice, on whom the poet will not condescend to look.[b] This sentence, so accordant with the stirring and passionate soul of the great Florentine, has been feebly counteracted, if counteracted, by the praise of Petrarch in his declamation on the beauty of a solitary life, for which the lyrist professed a somewhat hollow and poetic admiration.[c] Assuredly there was no magnanimity contemptuous of the Papal

How thought of in his own time.

Dante.

Petrarch.

---

[a] "Præbuit humilitatis exemplum, stupendum cunctis, imitabile paucis."—Jordan. M.S., quoted by Raynaldus.

[b] Bernard, in Chron. Roman. Pontif.

[b] "Che fece per viltà il gran rifiuto." *Inferno,* iii. 64.

I cannot for an instant doubt the allusion to Cœlestine; perhaps it was embittered by Dante's hatred of Boniface VIII.

[c] "Petrarch de Vità solitarià," a rhetorical exercise.

greatness in the abdication of Cœlestine: it was the weariness, the conscious inefficiency, the regret of a man suddenly wrenched away from all his habits, pursuits, and avocations, and unnaturally compelled or tempted to assume an uncongenial dignity. It was the cry of passionate feebleness to be released from an insupportable burthen. Compassion is the highest emotion of sympathy which it would have desired or could deserve.

But coeval with Dante there was another, a ruder poet, who must be heard, that we may fully comprehend the times. Jacopone da Todi, the Franciscan, had been among those who hailed with mingled exultation and fear the advancement of the holy Cœlestine.[d] "What wilt thou do, Peter Morrone, now that thou art on thy trial?" "If the world be deceived in thee, malediction! Thy fame has soared on high; it has spread through the world. If thou failest, there will be confusion to the good. As the arrow on its mark, the world is fixed on thee. If thou holdest not the balance right, there is no appeal but to God." "The Court of Rome is a furnace which tries the fine gold." "If thou takest delight in thine office (there is no malady so infectious), accursed is that life

---

[d] "Che farai, Pier da Morrone?
Se' venuto al paragone.

Se 'l mondo è di te ingannato,
Seguirà m. lediti... ne
La tua fama alto è salita,
E 'n molta parte n' è gita;
Se ti torni a la finita,
A i boni sarai confusione.
Como segno a saetta
Tutto 'l mondo a tè si afflitta;
Se tra llen bilanza ritta,
A Dio ne va appellatione.

Questa corte è una fucina,
Ch' l' buon auro si ci affina

Se l' officio ti diletta,
Nulla malsania più infetta;

Bene è vita maledetta,
Perder Dio per tal bucone.

Che' l' hai posto giogo in coglia,
De temer tua damnatione.

L' ordine Cardinalato,
Presto ha in homo stato;
Chi suo partito sio
D' arrivear ha intentione.

Guardati da baratiere,
Ch' ei acc biazzo fan videre;
Se non ti sai ben schermire,
Canterai mala canzone."—*Satir.* xv.

There are other passages which betray the pride in the elevation of Pier Morrone.

which for such a morsel loses God." "Thou hast put the yoke on thy neck, must we not fear thy damnation?" "The order of Cardinals has sunk to the lowest level: their sole aim is to enrich their kindred." "Guard thyself from the traffickers who make black white. If thou dost not guard thyself well, sad will be the burthen of thy song." Yet in these mistrustful warnings of the poet there is the manifest pride and hope of a devoted partisan that a new era has begun, that Peter Morrone is destined to regenerate the Papacy. The abdication, no doubt, was the last event to which these hermit followers of Peter Morrone looked forward. Bitter must have been their disappointment when he himself thus frustrated their pious expectations, their passionate vaticinations; yet they adhered to him in his self-chosen lowliness; they were still his stedfast admirers; they denied his right to abdicate, no doubt they disseminated the rumours of the arts employed to frighten him from the throne. Their hatred of Boniface, who supplanted him, was as deep and obstinate as their love of Cœlestine. This poet will appear as at least cognisant of the formidable conspiracy which threatened the power of Boniface VIII. Nor was the poet alone: his was but the voice which expressed, in its coarse but vigorous strains, the sense of a vast and to a certain extent organised party, in every rank, in every order, but especially among the low, and the lowest of the low.

END OF VOL. VI.

www.ingramcontent.com/pod-product-compliance
Lightning Source LLC
Chambersburg PA
CBHW051240300426
44114CB00011B/819